Fundamentals of
Human
Communication

Dan West
Ohio University

Kendall Hunt
publishing company

Kendall Hunt
publishing company

www.kendallhunt.com
Send all inquiries to:
4050 Westmark Drive
Dubuque, IA 52004-1840

Copyright © 2015 by Dan West

ISBN 978-1-4652-4596-0

Printed in the United States of America

Contents

Introduction: Why Study Communication?

LEARNING OBJECTIVES

After reading this chapter, you should understand the following concepts:

- Communication is a complex, multidisciplinary process in which participants create meaning by using symbols and behavior to send and receive messages with a social and cultural context.
- The freedoms of speech, of the press, of association, of assembly, and of petition constitute the freedom of expression represent—the right to communicate.
- The rapid growth of technology enhances our abilities to communicate, but also complicates the issues of communication.
- Several themes are woven into this text, each involving values that are represented in your rights and responsibilities to communicate.
- This book is designed to help the reader formulate strategies and learn the skills necessary to accomplish communication goals, with the understanding that expertise is not acquired over a semester but is honed with time and practice.

INTRODUCTION

Have you ever experienced a communication gap? Try this. Which of the following statements can you interpret or translate?

- Hey, don't bogart the brewski. Everythingi copasetic. It's gnarly.[1]
- What It Is, What It Is? The Man came around today, can you dig it? Yeah, that's sick.[2]
- The dinks next door just barf me out. They are such hosers.[3]
- The straight edge is a buzz kill. Let's dip. Don't go there! Back in the day we were tight![4]

When you first signed up for this course, you might have thought that communication is too simple. It's too "obvious" to study, and it's just silly to

KEYWORDS

communication
freedom of expression
culture

Why would you have to study communication when you do it every day?
© digitalskillet, 2008, Shutterstock.

have a whole course about it! You probably told others that you communicate all the time, and you feel pretty proud of your abilities. Perhaps those phrases have given you second thoughts. But they're just words, right? Can't you just speak more clearly and resolve any confusion those phrases might have created? Do you really need a whole course just about word choice? Is that what this course is?

You might think that studying communication is a waste of time because it's nothing more than common sense. Because you have been communicating all your life and seem to be reasonably good at it, you figure there *can't* be much to it, right? You should be spending your academic time more profitably, considering topics that *should* be studied. We should be studying how to fly an airplane or how to practice medicine, because those things are complex and people don't just intuitively learn how to navigate through heavy clouds or how to successfully remove a spleen. However, there is no need to study communication— we do that every day!

Because communicating is so familiar to everyone, it is often taken for granted and, as a result, it is ignored. The only time we really ever pay attention to or notice the communication process is when something goes wrong or if some rule is violated. Instead of waiting around for a communication disaster to strike, the purpose of this course is to challenge you to call your participation in the communication process into question and raise it to the level of conscious awareness. At this level you can examine it, take it apart, put it back together, and use that new awareness to improve your own abilities as a communicator.

Think for a minute *how* and *how often* you communicate. Not only do you carry on conversations with others, work successfully in groups with them, participate in interviews, make presentations, and tell entertaining stories, but you also have to have a pretty good facility with various electronic communication tools that provide you with efficient means of reaching out to others. In their book *Connecting to the Net.Generation: What Higher Education Professionals Need to Know about Today's College Students,* Reynol Junco and Jeanna Mastrodicasa revealed the following information gathered in a survey of 7,705 college students in the United States:[5]

- 97 percent own a computer.
- 94 percent own a cell phone.
- 76 percent use instant messaging.
- 15 percent of IM users are logged on 24 hours a day/7 days a week.
- 34 percent use Web sites as their primary source of news.
- 28 percent own a blog, and 44 percent read blogs.
- 49 percent download music using peer-to-peer file sharing.
- 75 percent of students have a Facebook account.
- 60 percent own some type of expensive portable music and/or video device such as an iPod.

Do these figures surprise you? Do you think these media have an effect on how you communicate and what you expect from others? Add in the work groups, commuting partners, friends and family members that you talk with daily. All of these influence how you develop relationships with others, your awareness of things going on near and far, the ways that you view time, what you think is important, and a thousand other perceptions. Your beliefs, attitudes, and values are all affected by the amount, type, and success of your communication efforts. For example, if you use many of those media, you probably expect responses more quickly than someone from a previous generation. You might think that finding information is better done on a computer than by personal interviews or even reading a book or a print newspaper. Your means of telling others about yourself have expanded, leaving both privacy and personal safety at risk. You can create images of yourself that reflect what you'd like to be, rather than what you are. Your language evolves with blinding speed, with new words being coined daily and shared immediately. You live in a communication-saturated world, where symbols evolve, media change, and people adapt.

How does the media you use affect your communication with others?
© Konstantin Sutyagin, 2008, Shutterstock.

Are you starting to believe that communication is much more complex than you first realized? Theorists and researchers have studied it for hundreds of years, attempting to discover what constitutes effective communication, involving different sources, messages, audiences, contexts, and purposes. Other studies have investigated the use of technology ranging from Sumerian writing and its impact on later Egyptian hieroglyphics, through the impact of print and photography, to electronic means ranging from the telegraph to the computer, PDAs, cell phones, and emerging new technologies. These studies have been undertaken by researchers in diverse fields such as art, anthropology, history, philosophy, computer science, linguistics, sociology, psychology, English, and a relatively new field called **communication.**

Today, the study of communication spans multidisciplinary interests and has developed interlocking and independent theoretical approaches. This text will introduce you to the basics of the theories and practice of some of those approaches to communication in different contexts. Ranging from the situational contexts of intrapersonal, interpersonal, and small group communication, to interviewing and finally public speaking, you'll traverse the discipline. Although you will find that these different contexts allow you to examine the communication process more clearly, the categorization is not perfect, because you'll find overlap among the strategies suggested in different contexts.

Depending on the situation, different communication strategies are most effective.
© Dmitriy Shironosov, 2008, Shutterstock.

Maybe you're starting to be convinced that this text might teach you some necessary skills, but you'll be exposed to more than skill competency. Communication involves considering cultural values and issues, along with developing shared meaning with others.

WHAT IS THE IMPACT OF COMMUNICATION STUDY BEYOND SKILLS?

Communication is important and central to nearly all that we do. Think about it. We make our laws through a process of debate and voting in legislatures. Our legal system depends on people to make a good case; to present and

Why is competent communication important to almost anything we do?
© Laurence Gough, 2008, Shutterstock.

interpret evidence in a compelling way to allow important decisions to be made. Our political system requires citizens to make decisions concerning candidates for office, laws to adopt, and where to spend tax money. Religion, culture, science, and education all involve a series of beliefs passed along to each new generation by the people who hold those beliefs. It's all done through communication. Fundamental to our American culture is the right to use our ability to communicate. Let's consider the freedoms and responsibilities inherent in that right in an attempt to discover the complexity of communication.

The freedoms of speech, of the press, of association, of assembly, and of petition: this set of guarantees, protected by the First Amendment, constitutes the concept of **freedom of expression.** They represent the right to communicate. Without this freedom, other fundamental rights, like the right to vote and to participate in our own governance, would lack force. Members of a democratic society have both the right and responsibility to participate in governance. At the very least, you should be an informed voter. But being an informed voter requires doing research and interpreting and critically analyzing information and values related to candidates and issues. This activity often means that you have to sift through and weigh heaps of campaign slogans, sound bytes, and promises to get to the "meat" of the matter.

The essence of being a citizen in a democratic society goes beyond the privilege of voting, however. From childhood, you may have been taught the core values of being an individual, of tolerating the differences and diversity of others, or of having the right to speak and think as you want. You learn to express your mind, to speak out against decisions you disagree with, to praise people who do a good job, to associate with whomever you want, and to criticize both individuals and government. This freedom of expression is the essence of a democracy. Let's consider a few examples that demonstrate the nation's commitment to freedom of expression and how it has been tested.

When the country music group the Dixie Chicks' lead singer Natalie Maines said at a London concert on March 10, 2003, that she was "ashamed the president of the United States is from Texas," the backlash started. Country music stations across the country pulled Dixie Chicks' songs from their playlists, others called for boycotts of their concerts, and some organizations sponsored bonfires in which the group's CDs were destroyed.[6] In response, on his Web site, Bruce Springsteen defended the group's right to say what they believe. He asserted that they are American artists who were using their right to free speech, and that anyone who thought it was right to punish them for speaking out is un-American.[7]

Is burning the American flag an issue of the freedom of expression? In 1989, the Supreme Court ruled in the case of *Texas v. Johnson* that the First Amendment rights of citizens to engage in free speech, even if that speech is "offensive," outweigh the government's interest in protecting the American flag as a symbol of American unity. The action of flag burning, as repugnant as it may be to many citizens, was defined by the Supreme Court and Texas Court of Criminal Appeals as an example of "symbolic speech."[8] For the majority opinion, Justice Brennan wrote: "If there is a bedrock principle underlying the First Amendment, it is that the Government may not prohibit the expression of an idea simply because society finds the idea itself offensive or disagreeable. Punishing desecration of the flag dilutes the very freedom that makes this emblem so revered, and worth revering."[9]

What about protest marches and sit-ins? What about protesting the actions of the courts? Are these activities representative of freedom of expression? In 1963, the Southern Christian Leadership Coalition mounted a campaign that focused on direct action, committed to ending segregation in Birmingham, Alabama. The campaign began with a series of mass meetings, including one featuring civil rights leader Martin Luther King Jr., who spoke about the philosophy of nonviolence and appealed to the volunteers to practice its methods. The actions included lunch counter sit-ins, marches on City Hall, a boycott of downtown merchants, sit-ins at the library, and a voter registration march. When the city government obtained a court injunction directing an end to all protests, King and the SCLC disobeyed the court order, and on April 12, King was arrested in Birmingham. He was kept in solitary confinement and was allowed only minimal contact. It was at this time that King penned his famous Letter from the Birmingham Jail.[10]

The rapid growth of technology enhances our abilities to communicate and adds additional cautions to what we say and how we say it. It has multiplied the channels by which we can create relationships, gather information, conduct business, and make decisions. The 2005 Pew Foundation's Major Moments Survey showed increases in the number of Americans who report that the Internet played a crucial or important role in various aspects of their lives.[11] Consider the growth of blogs, "web logs," which allow anyone with a computer to post thoughts, opinions, histories, anecdotes, and political ideas to a worldwide platform, unhindered by time and distance. Blogger and public relations writer Jeneane Sessum of Atlanta is the founder of Blog Sisters, a group blog with more than 100 female members from around the world. The group discusses everything from gender and international politics to family life and career quandaries, without fear of being censored. Sessum says, "Blogs make it really easy to express yourself. It's an amazing tool to help you figure out who you are, what you care about and to connect with other human beings. Plus, it's a place for me to exercise my voice. I've been so busy writing for clients that I've never kept up with my personal writing. Blogging has really helped me refine my voice."[13]

How has technology changed the way we communicate with others?
© Kurhan, 2008, Shutterstock.

Does the existence of blogs raise questions about freedom of expression? Some critics assert that bloggers have transformed the Internet into a virtual soapbox, resulting in an impact on the public dialogue with questions about social responsibility and the law. Bradley Smith, chairman of the Federal Elections Commission (FEC), has suggested that there is a need to regulate political speech in blogs, saying that bloggers could soon invite federal punishment if they improperly link to a campaign's Web site.[14]

Broadcast media have a responsibility to check sources when providing news coverage. On September 20, 2004, CBS news anchor Dan Rather apologized for a "mistake in judgment" in relying on apparently bogus documents for a *60 Minutes* report about President George W. Bush's time in the Texas Air National Guard. In his on-air statement, Rather said,

Martin Luther King Jr.'s Letter from Birmingham Jail

Sometimes a law is just on its face and unjust in its application. For instance, I have been arrested on a charge of parading without a permit. Now, there is nothing wrong in having an ordinance which requires a permit for a parade. But such an ordinance becomes unjust when it is used to maintain segregation and to deny citizens the First Amendment privilege of peaceful assembly and protest.

I hope you are able to embrace the distinction I am trying to point out. In no sense do I advocate evading or defying the law, as would the rabid segregationist. That would lead to anarchy. One who breaks an unjust law must do so openly, lovingly, and with a willingness to accept the penalty. I submit that an individual who breaks a law that conscience tells him is unjust and who willingly accepts the penalty of imprisonment in order to arouse the conscience of the community over its injustice, is in reality expressing the highest respect for law.[12]

Reprinted by arrangement with The Heirs to the Estate of Martin Luther King, Jr., c/o Writers House as agent for the proprietor New York, NY. Copyright © 1963 Martin Luther King, Jr. © renewed 1991 Coretta Scott King.

Now, after extensive additional interviews, I no longer have the confidence in these documents that would allow us to continue vouching for them journalistically. I find we have been misled on the key question of how our source for the documents came into possession of these papers. That, combined with some of the questions that have been raised in public and in the press, leads me to a point where—if I knew then what I know now—I would not have gone ahead with the story as it was aired, and I certainly would not have used the documents in question. But we did use the documents. We made a mistake in judgment, and for that I am sorry.

Rather's admission of a mistake resulted in great damage to the CBS news division's credibility. Boston *Phoenix* media writer Dan Kennedy said, "They were way too late in acknowledging there may be problems with this. The short-term damage is just horrendous. You have a large percentage of the public believing—falsely, I would argue—that the media are suffused with liberal bias, and this just plays right into that."[15]

There are many examples of the impact of communication rights and responsibilities that span the entire history of the United States. Freedom of expression is codified in law, and it is part of who we are as Americans. The core values represented in the right to express your thoughts and to communicate freely with others are central to our society. These values are vital to the attainment and advancement of knowledge and the search for the truth. These are only a few examples of instances where the privilege and attendant responsibility of freedom of expression have impacted your life. In this text, we will "bring it home" by your participation in discussions about the freedom of expression in your daily life in personal and public arenas.

Now it's time to ask: How does this concept of communication responsibilities impact what you'll learn in this course?

WHAT ARE THE THEMES OF THIS TEXT?

Several themes are woven into the fabric of the course material in the print volume and the companion Web site. These illustrate the key assumptions and topics that you'll discover. Each also involves values that are represented in your rights and responsibilities to communicate.

Themes

- *Transactional perspective:* The assumption that participants cooperate to create meaning is clearly described and explained in the theory chapter and is reflected in the explanations for all communication contexts treated in the book. Public speaking, group decision making, interviewing, and interpersonal communication are all transactional processes. Messages are sent and received by all participants simultaneously in a cooperative effort to create and share meaning.
- *Critical thinking:* Participants in communication should be able to formulate and argue their own opinions and propositions and not merely accept as true what is taken from the media or heard from other people.
- *Participants:* Understanding communication assumes an understanding of the people who participate in communication. We assume that the meaning participants give to messages is influenced by a myriad of factors: the self-concept of the participant, the intentions or goals of the participant, the totality of experience of the participant, and the other participants.
- *Context:* Communication is influenced by the various physical, symbolic, and social contexts in which it occurs.
- *Culture:* Communication is influenced by the culture in which it occurs and by the cultural perspectives of the participants. Think of **culture** as a *community of meaning;* we all belong to multiple cultures and we come into contact with other cultures on a professional and social basis every day.
- *Technology:* We live in a world in which communication between and among people is more and more often mediated by some form of technology. From the responsibilities of sound research and investigation, to the use of instantaneous communication technology used to facilitate regional and global collaboration, to the effective use of presentational materials, you will be asked to consider the development and use of technology to enhance your message.

SUMMARY

You're now ready to begin your study of unique features of the communication discipline, along with its attendant values and responsibilities. You will bring your established abilities into the mix, but you will also begin to take into account aspects of communicating that you never considered before. *Communication is serious, complex, and important!* By the end of this book, we want you to believe this is true. Perhaps more importantly, though, we want to challenge you to become a full and influential participant communicating in personal, business, and civic affairs.

Before you can accept this challenge and begin your exploration of the strategies communication requires, you need to consider the scope of communication via a definition. *Communication is a process in which participants create meaning by using symbols and behavior to send and receive messages within a social and cultural context.* This book is devoted to helping you understand and apply this definition so you will be able to formulate strategies and learn the skills necessary for accomplishing all of your communication goals. You are not likely to become an expert communicator by the time you complete this course, but you should have a good start. You'll be exposed to a series of questions in every chapter that will lead to some beliefs, attitudes, and values, along with skills. Like any expertise that you learn, your competence improves with time, practice, and use. The goal of this text is to assist you in developing strategies and practicing skills in a variety of communication contexts.

ENDNOTES

1. Samples of 1960s slang, defined at 1960s slang, http://www.cougartown.com/slang.html (accessed Sept. 23, 2007).

2. 1970s slang, http://www.inthe70s.com/generated/terms.shtml (accessed Sept. 23, 2007).

3. 1980s slang, http://www.i80s.com/80s_slang/slang1.htm (accessed Sept. 23, 2007).

4. http://www.inthe90s.com/generated/terms.shtml (accessed Sept. 23, 2007).

5. Junco, Reynol and Jeanna Mastrodicasa, *Connecting to the Net.Generation: What Higher Education Professionals Need to Know About Today's College Students.* (Washington, DC: National Association of Student Personnel Administrators, 2007).

6. CNN.Com/Entertainment. Dixie Chicks pulled from air after bashing Bush. March 14, 2003 (accessed June 14, 2007).

7. BBC News (bbc.co.uk) Springsteen backs under-fire Dixies. April 28, 2003 (accessed June 14, 2007).

8. *Texas vs. Johnson,* 491 U.S. 397. (June 21, 1989).

9. PBS.Org PBS Online. United States v. Eichman. Issue: Burning the American Flag. (Undated) (accessed June 18, 2007).

10. Stanford University. King Encyclopedia. "Birmingham Campaign." (accessed June 18, 2007).

11. Horrigan, John and Lee Rainie. "The Internet's Growing Role in Life's Major Moments." (April 19, 2006.) Pew Internet & American Life Project, http://www.pewinternet.org/PPF/r/181/report_display.asp (accessed June 20, 2007).

12. MLK Online. "Letter from Birmingham Jail, April 16, 1963." (accessed March 30, 2008).

13. Trimbath, Karen. "Women Go Blogging and Find Freedom of Speech." Women's eNews. August 2, 2004 http://www.womensenews.org/article.cfm/dyn/aid/1934 (accessed June 22, 2007).

14. "Are Blogs Protected under the First Amendment?" http://www.legalzoom.com/articles/article_content/ article14006.html (accessed June 22, 2007).

15. Kurtz, Howard. "Rather Admits 'Mistake in Judgment.'" (September 21, 2004) http://washingtonpost.com/ wp-dyn/articles/A35531-2004Sep20_2.html (accessed June 22, 2007).

2

What Is Communication?

LEARNING OBJECTIVES

After reading this chapter, you should understand the following concepts:

- The goal of communication is to build theory used to guide communicators in the formulation of strategies to achieve communication goals.
- There are many definitions of communication, but they share common characteristics: Communication is a process, messages are sent and received, participants interact in social contexts, and meaning is created and shared through symbols and behavior.
- The action model was the necessary first step in the evolution of communication models, but it has a weakness in that it lacks interaction.
- The interaction model includes the important aspect of feedback.
- The transactional model recognizes that communication is a process, it is irreversible, it means shared responsibility, and it occurs in context and culture.

INTRODUCTION

"Oh, that's just a theory. It doesn't mean anything!"

Have you heard this before? There is a common misconception that a **theory** is the same thing as a "guess." A theory is a "shot from the hip," or it's a "Monday morning quarterback's" explanation of why his team won or lost on Sunday. Sometimes you hear people express doubt about "relativity" or "evolution" because they are "only theories," and not fact. Not true! A theory is not idle speculation unsupported by evidence that is spontaneously created or made up.

Theories are not guesses! Littlejohn states, "Any attempt to explain or represent an experience is a theory; an idea of how something happens."[1] Kerlinger says that a theory is "a set of interrelated constructs (concepts), definitions, and propositions that present a systematic view of phenomena by specifying relations among variables, with the purpose of explaining and predicting the phenomena."[2]

KEYWORDS

theory
empirical
Aristotle
Claude Shannon
Warren Weaver
source
message
code
encoded
transmitted
channel
receiver
decodes
destination
noise
action model
interaction model
Wilbur Schramm
David Berlo
feedback
transactional model
process
participant
carrier
environmental noise
psychological noise
physical context
social context
culture

From *Communication: Principles of Tradition and Change* by Samuel P. Wallace, Kimberely N. Rosenfeld, David L. Bodary and Beth M. Waggenspack. Copyright © 2009 by Kendall Hunt Publishing Company. Reprinted by permission.

WHAT IS THE NATURE OF COMMUNICATION THEORY?

Our definition is that a theory is *an attempt to describe, predict, and / or explain an experience or phenomenon.* The purpose of generating a theory is the attempt to understand something:

- Theory is a collection of statements or conceptual assumptions.
- It specifies the relationships among concepts or variables and provides a basis for predicting behavior of a phenomenon.
- It explains a phenomenon.

Here's an illustration from the distant past:

Og the cave dweller comes out of his cave in the morning and sees the sun shining in the east. When Og visits the village well later in the day, he and his friends are able to *describe* what happened: "When I came out of my cave, I saw the bright light in the sky!" They can all try to agree on the description, and they will all know what happened.

Over the next several months, Og and his pals emerge from their caves every morning, and every morning they see the sun in the eastern sky. They also notice that the sun has moved to the western sky when they return to their caves in the evening. After several conversations at the village well, they discover or

Og the cave dweller systematically observes the environment.
© 2008, JupiterImages Corporation.

recognize that a *pattern* seems to exist in the behavior of the sun. In the morning, the bright light is over there. But in the evening, the bright light is on the other side. They set up an observational plan to see if their pattern holds up. In the mornings, when Og comes from his cave (which faces south), he looks to his left and he *expects* to see the sun. There it is! Eureka! The observations support the hypothesis (or informed assumption) that the sun will rise in the east! Og and his associates can now *predict* the behavior of the sun!

Og is attempting to build a theory. He is able to describe and predict, but he still comes up short because he does not understand *why* the sun behaves as it does. Og still has much uncertainty about the sun's behavior, and that makes him and all the rest of us humans uncomfortable. So we continue to study it. Now, please "fast forward" from this point several thousand years when, after gathering lots and lots of information, we were finally able to *explain* why the sun appears to rise in the east and set in the west.

Og and his buddies made some observations of phenomena and were able to describe it, then they noticed patterns in the phenomena and were able to predict its behavior. They might have even tried to explain the activity they observed, but they did not have enough knowledge to make a good explanation. The explanation came much later and is beyond the scope of this book. But you can go look it up!

What they *did* do was create a partial theory, and that theory was based on empirical observation. Not bad for cave dwellers! **Empirical** means that knowledge claims are based on observations of reality (i.e., the real world) and are not merely subjective speculation based on the observer's perspective. The

Observation ⟶ Pattern Recognition ⟶ Theory ⟶ Hypotheses ⟶ Observation

conclusions are based on *observed* evidence, which helps the observer remain more objective.[3] The cycle of study is repeated over and over: Observation is made, which leads to recognizing a pattern; attempts to predict and explain are made, which become basic theories; the theories help the observer create new hypotheses (predictions) about the behavior of the phenomenon; observation is made and the information analyzed in search of patterns; and those recognized patterns add to the basic theory.[4] As this cycle repeats itself, the body of theory becomes larger and more sophisticated, and the field of study matures.

The goal of any field of study, including communication, is to *build theory*. The body of communication theory is subsequently used to guide communicators in the formulation of strategies for achieving communication goals and to help communicators understand what skills are necessary for carrying out the strategies.

The purpose of this chapter is to help you understand the basic theory supporting human communication behavior. The skills and strategies necessary to accomplish your communication goals are derived from this theory. This chapter includes the following:

- A definition of communication
- An evolution of conceptions of communication
- A transactional model of communication
- A discussion of essential terms

HOW IS COMMUNICATION DEFINED?

Defining communication is not quite as easy as it sounds because almost all people, even scholars, think they know what it is. We all communicate every day, so we all have an opinion. The problem is that nearly nobody agrees! Clevenger says that the term *communication* is one of the most "overworked terms in the English language."[5]

To try to make sense of the literally hundreds of different definitions, we will examine some significant attempts to define communication, and then we will draw out the commonalities in the attempt to build our own point of view. Here are some influential examples:

- An individual transmits stimuli to modify the behavior of other individuals.[6]
- Social interaction occurs through symbols and message systems.[7]
- A source transmits a message to receiver(s) with conscious intent to affect the latter's behavior.[8]
- "Senders and receivers of messages interact in given social contexts."[9]
- "Shared meaning through symbolic processes" is created.[10]
- There is mutual creation of shared meaning through the simultaneous interpretation and response to verbal and nonverbal behaviors in a specific context."[11]
- "Communication occurs when one person sends and receives messages that are distorted by noise, occur within a context, have some effect, and provide some opportunity for feedback."[12]

The perspective of this book is that *communication is a process in which participants create meaning by using symbols and behavior to send and receive messages within a social and cultural context.* This perspective will be expanded and explained in the remainder of this chapter.

HOW HAVE THE CONCEPTIONS OF COMMUNICATION EVOLVED?

Now that we have a working definition of communication, let's examine where it came from. This section looks at classic models of communication spanning about 2,500 years. The goal of this section is to illustrate the evolution of the communication perspective taken by this book; to show you how we arrived at the point of view that influences every strategy and skill that we teach. We believe that if you understand why we teach it, you will be more motivated to learn and to use this point of view to plan and execute your own communication strategies!

WHAT ARE THE MODELS OF COMMUNICATION?

You have seen and used a map many times. If you are looking for a particular street in your town, you pick up a map to find where the street is and to learn how to get there from where you are. A map is not your town, however, but a *representation* of your town. It's a picture or drawing that helps you understand the way your town is arranged. A *model* is the very same thing. But instead of representing a physical space, like a town, the model represents a process, or the way something happens.

The models discussed here represent three views of communication that have enjoyed popularity over the years. Those three views are action (or linear), interaction, and transaction. These models help illustrate and explain the current view of communication, the transactional perspective. Each will be discussed in the following pages.

The Action Model

As a map represents a place, a model represents a process.
© Stephen VanHorn, 2008, Shutterstock.

Although many perspectives of communication contributed to what we are calling the action model, Aristotle and the Shannon and Weaver models had the most impact.

We'll start with **Aristotle,** a philosopher, scientist, and teacher who lived in ancient Greece. Educated by Plato and the son of a physician, he was trained as a biologist.[13] He was skilled at observing and describing, and at categorizing his observations.[14] Aristotle found himself interested in nearly all things that occupied the attention of the citizens of Athens, including the study of speaking.

Ancient Athens was a democracy, and all citizens had the right and opportunity to influence public affairs and public policy. The more articulate citizens were able to affect events by persuading or influencing other citizens and law makers in public meetings. Because individual citizens had a voice, teachers of public speaking and persuasion were always in demand.

Aristotle's *Rhetoric* is a published collection of his teachings,[15] and it has been suggested that it is the "most important single work on persuasion ever written."[16] The focus of the *Rhetoric* is primarily on the speaker and the message. Some, but little, attention is paid to the audience. The philosophy is that a well-crafted message delivered by a credible speaker will have the desired effect with the audience. If Aristotle had a model of persuasion, the simple version would probably look something like this:

Aristotle used his observation skills to study communication in ancient Greece.
© 2008 JupiterImages Corporation.

WELL-CRAFTED MESSAGE + CREDIBLE SOURCE = DESIRED EFFECT

Aristotle's contribution to communication would not have been this model. His contributions came in the form of instructions for how to use logic and emotions (*logos* and *pathos*) to craft a message, and how to establish and build credibility as a speaker or source of a message (*ethos*).

For the second time in this chapter, please fast forward in time, but this time only about two thousand years. Stop when you get to the 1940s, and we'll take a look at **Claude Shannon** and **Warren Weaver.** Claude Shannon was a mathematician who worked at Bell Labs, and he was interested in ways to make more efficient use of telephone lines for the transmission of voices. He was not concerned about human communication, but he was very focused on electronic communication. Shannon teamed with Warren Weaver, a scientist and mathematician, to publish the *Mathematical Theory of Communication*. Shannon's focus was on the engineering aspects of the theory, while Weaver was more interested in the human and other implications. Communication scholars found this model to be very useful in helping them to explain *human* communication.[17]

The Shannon–Weaver model is consistent with Aristotle's point of view, and it extends it to include a transmitter, a channel, and a receiver. It also introduces the concept of *noise* to the explanation. The process is illustrated in Figure 2.1. The **source** (a person) initiates a **message** that is turned into a **code** (language), and the **encoded** message is sent (**transmitted**) through a **channel** (sound waves created by the voice, or some mediated signal). The **receiver decodes** the signal (turning it again into a message), which is sent to the **destination** (the other person). **Noise** is anything that can interfere with the signal. See Figure 2.1.

This model helps to understand human communication, but it has a significant shortcoming: it doesn't adequately capture the reality or the complexity of the process. It assumes that the participants in the process take on discrete speaker or listener roles, and that while one person speaks, the other person quietly listens with no response, until the speaker is finished. Then the roles are reversed. Then the roles are reversed again, and again and again, until the conversation is complete. *Human communication is arguably not that linear!* It is equivalent to placing a message in a bottle, throwing it into the sea, and waiting for it to reach the proper destination. The person (receiver) removes the message from the bottle, reads the message, writes a new message, places it back in the

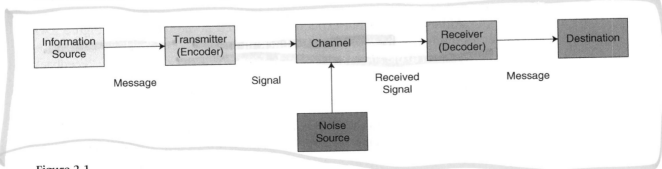

Figure 2.1
The Shannon–Weaver Mathematical Model

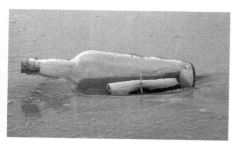

A message in a bottle lacks the interaction we have in everyday conversations.
© R. Gino Santa Maria, 2008, Shutterstock.

bottle, and throws it back into the sea. The model works, but it doesn't represent the way that we communicate in everyday conversations. It lacks *interaction!*

As you consider the two models just discussed, you can see that they are primarily concerned with the source of the message and the content of the message itself. The focus is on the source and how he or she constructs and delivers the message. So a source that creates well-designed messages has done everything possible to ensure effective communication. Say the right thing and you will be successful! If something goes wrong, or if the source is not clearly understood by the potential receiver, the **action model** states that the fault is with the source. However, when everything goes well and the message is clearly understood, it is because the source crafted and sent a good-quality message. See Figure 2.2 for a depiction of the action model. The action model was the necessary first step in the evolution of the contemporary communication model.

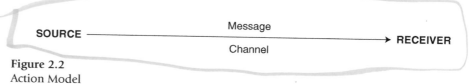

Figure 2.2
Action Model

The Interaction Model

The **interaction model** remains linear, like the action model, but it begins to view the source and receiver as a team in the communication process.

Wilbur Schramm introduced a model of communication that includes a notion of *interaction.*[18] The Schramm model does not consider the context or environment in which the communication takes place, and it does not explicitly treat codes (language) or noise. Although it is still very linear, it describes the dual roles played by the participants instead of viewing one as a source (speaker) and the other as a receiver (listener), and it makes a strong case for *interaction* among the participants. The flow of information can be seen as more ongoing or continuous, rather than a linear, back-and-forth type of flow. The conception of communication is emerging as a *process.* See Figure 2.3.

David Berlo, in *The Process of Communication,* began to discuss process and the complexity of communication.[19] This model fully includes the receiver, and it places importance on the *relationship* between the source and receiver. It also illustrates that the source and receiver are not just reacting to the environment or each other, but that each possesses individual differences based on knowledge and attitudes, and that each operates within a cultural and social system that influences meaning. Because we all have different knowledge and attitudes, we interpret or give meaning to messages in different ways. This makes human communication very complex!

Although it was not explicitly mentioned in the model (see Figure 2.4), Berlo discussed the notion of **feedback** in his book. Feedback is information that is routed to the source, or fed back, from the receiver. Berlo said, "Feedback provides the source with information concerning his success in accomplishing his objective. In doing this, it exerts control over future messages which the source encodes."[20]

Berlo completed the loop left unfinished by the Shannon–Weaver model. The source encodes a message, sent through a channel to a receiver, who decodes it and assigns meaning. The receiver then sends a message back to the source (feedback) indicating, among other things, that the message was understood.

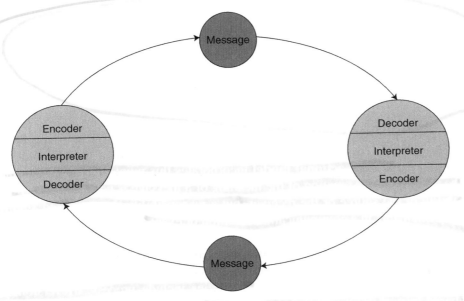

Figure 2.3
Schramm's Model of Communication

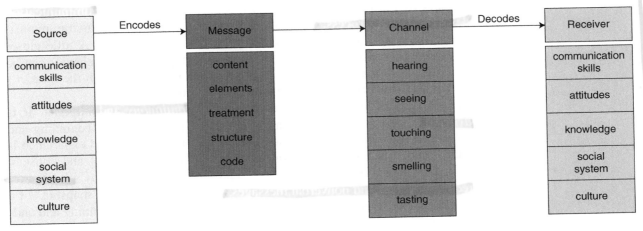

Figure 2.4
Berlo's Model of Communication

Even though this is still a linear model, we are getting closer to a model that begins to capture the nature of human communication. But it's not quite there yet!

These two models, and models like them, can be *summarized* in what we call the *interaction model* (see Figure 2.5). A source sends a message through a noise-filled channel to a receiver. The receiver responds to the source through feedback, which is a message sent by the receiver to the source through a noise-filled channel. The core of the interaction model is that the source is the originator and that the receiver creates feedback to that message. Like the action model, the interaction model implies that the process is linear; that is, communicators take turns being first a source then a receiver, and so on. The interaction model was the second step in the evolution of the contemporary communication model.

The Transactional Model

More contemporary conceptions view communication as an ongoing process in which all participants send and receive messages simultaneously.

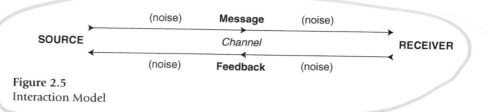

Figure 2.5
Interaction Model

All participants are both speakers *and* listeners.[21] "A person is giving feedback, talking, responding, acting, and reacting through a communication event."[22] The **transactional model** incorporates this point of view along with the notion that the creation of the meaning of a message is not the sole responsibility of the source or the receiver, but a responsibility that is shared among all participants in a communication situation or event.

Properties of Transactional Communication.   To get a clear view of the transactional model of communication, it is necessary to understand the important properties of communication. Properties include process, irreversibility, shared responsibility, context, and culture. These five properties are discussed in this section.

Communication Is a Process.   Any conceptualizations of communication describe it as a **process.** The notion of process is not unique to communication; it comes to us from the literature of *theoretical physics*. A little closer to home, the notion of process and its relationship to human behavior can be found in *general systems theory*.[23] Although we use this term all the time, it's important to understand what the term *process* implies.

Process implies that communication is *continuous* and ongoing. It is *dynamic:* It never stops. Barnlund[24] says that a process has no beginning and no end. It constantly changes and evolves, new information and experience is added, and it becomes even more complex.[25] There is ongoing and constant mutual influence of the participants.[26] Participants are *constantly* sending and receiving verbal and nonverbal messages. You can try to take a "snapshot" of a single episode, and you can observe the date and time of its beginning and ending, but you can't say that this is where the communication began and ended. Heisenberg stated that to observe a process requires bringing it to a halt.[27] This gives us a fuzzy look at what is really happening, because stopping a process alters the process. So we have to do the best we can to observe, understand, and participate in communication events.

Consider, for example, a father asking his son to practice his saxophone. The father says, "Pete, please go to your room and practice your saxophone for 20 minutes." Pete (clearly annoyed) responds, "Come on, Dad! I'm right in the middle of this video game. Can't I do it later?" The father immediately gets angry and sends Pete to his room "to think about what he has done," followed by 20 minutes of saxophone practice.

The episode seems to be over, but we wonder why the young man was so annoyed at being asked to practice and why the father got angry so quickly. Could it be that this was only *one* installment in a series of episodes in which the father tries to get Pete to practice? Or could it be that Pete was having some difficulty with the saxophone that made him not want to practice? Or is there something else going on that we can't see in only this one episode? Will this episode affect future episodes?

The answer to the last question is yes! Communication is influenced by events that come before it, and it influences events that follow it.

Communication Is Irreversible.   Messages are sent and received, and all participants give meaning to those messages as they happen. Once the behavior has occurred, it becomes part of history and can't be reversed. Have you ever said something that you wish you could take back? It doesn't matter if you meant it or not; once it's out there, you have to deal with it.

As mentioned in a previous section, the prior experience or history of the participants influences the meaning created in the current interaction. Even if you try to take something back or pretend it didn't happen, it still has influence in the current and future interactions. Occasionally, in a court case, an attorney or a witness will say something that the judge decides is inappropriate to the case, and he or she will instruct the jury to "disregard" the statement. Do you think the members of the jury are able to remove the statement from their memories? Have you ever heard that as a member of a jury? What did you do?

A friend of ours was asked the question that no married person wants to hear. While clothes shopping, the spouse asked, "Do these pants make me look fat?" Instead of pretending not to hear the question or saying an emphatic no, our friend said, "The pants are very nice, honey. It's your backside that makes you look fat!" For almost a whole minute, it seemed pretty funny. Multiple attempts to take back the comment failed. That communication episode affected the meaning of nearly every conversation they had for several months. *Communication is irreversible.* And you thought this book would have no practical advice!

Communication Means Shared Responsibility.   Poor communication is not the fault of *one* participant in a conversation. If communication breaks down, you can't blame it on the "other guy." It is the fault of *all* the participants. The transactional perspective implies that it is the responsibility of all participants to cooperate to create a shared meaning. Even if a few of the participants are deficient in some communication skills, it is the responsibility of each person to adapt to the situation and ensure that everyone understands. Even the less capable have responsibilities: If they do not understand, they have the responsibility to ask the other participants to help them understand. *All participants cooperate to create meaning.*

Communication Occurs in a Context.   The participants in the communication event affect or influence each other, and they are also affected and influenced by the context or environment in which the communication event occurs.

Communication Occurs within Cultures.   Much like context, the participants are affected or influenced by the culture of which they are members and by the culture in which the communication event takes place.

How does your culture affect communication?
© 2008 JupiterImages Corporation.

> "You are the master of the unspoken word. Once the word is spoken, you are its slave."
> –Anonymous

Specifics of the Transaction Model.   The evolution of communication theory through the action and interaction models has brought us to the current perspective, the transaction model. This book is based on the transaction model, and all of the communication strategies we suggest are based on the model and its properties.

Wallace and others view the transactional perspective as *the joint creation of shared meaning through the simultaneous perception of verbal and nonverbal behaviors within a specific context.*[28] Although you are speaking or sending messages, you constantly receive and give meaning to information from the environment and from other participants. Similarly, while you are listening

How do you prepare for a meeting with a new business associate?
© Kiselev Andrey Valerevich, 2008, Shutterstock.

to another participant, you are sending nonverbal messages through eye contact, facial expressions, posture, and body movements. So we don't really take turns being the source and receiver as illustrated by the action and interaction models. Instead, we are constantly sending *and* receiving messages!

For example, a husband asks a wife if she minds if he plays golf on a Saturday afternoon. All the time he is asking the question, he is constantly scanning for every nonverbal clue to find out how she really feels. It might be her posture, or the way she looks at (or away from) him, or a particular facial expression, or some combination of everything that provides her response long before she speaks. Lots of information is being exchanged in this situation, which helps this couple create and share meaning.

Think about the first time you met your girlfriend's or boyfriend's parents. Think about your first date with somebody you were really interested in. Or consider meeting a potential client for a business deal. Doing business is important to both participants, so you both are very careful to gather all the available information to reduce uncertainty, become more comfortable, and formulate and confirm strategies for accomplishing communication goals. You use the information to create and share meaning!

In the transaction model, *participants create shared meaning* by simultaneously sending and receiving verbal and nonverbal messages within a specific

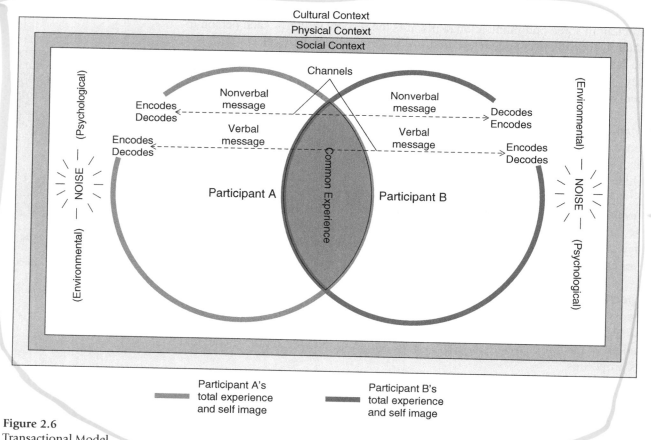

Figure 2.6
Transactional Model

context. Please see Figure 2.6 for a depiction of the model. The transaction model is reflected and applied in every chapter of this book.

WHAT DO THE TERMS MEAN?

We know that you're tired of all the theory talk, but we have to define some terms so that we are all on the same page. All of these terms have been used in this chapter, but some have been used in different ways in the various models. This section will establish the way each term will be used throughout the book.

Communicators/Participants

Although the action and interaction models use the terms *source* and *receiver* or *speaker* and *listener,* we will simply use the term **participant.** Because there is no exchange of speaker and listener roles, and because all persons in communication events are simultaneously sending and receiving verbal and nonverbal messages, the terms used in earlier models are no longer descriptive.

The message contains the content of the thought we wish to share with other participants.

Encoding/Decoding

Communication is symbolic. That is, we use symbols to convey our thoughts to each other in the effort to create meaning. When we have a thought or idea that we want to share with others, we must first translate that thought into a set of symbols, or a language, that the other participants will be able to understand. This process of converting our thoughts to symbols is called encoding.

In turn, when we listen to or receive symbols/language, we have to translate that language into thoughts. That is, we give "meaning" to the symbols. This process is called decoding. Symbols are used to represent objects or ideas.

Channel

The means by which a message is conducted or transmitted is the channel. Berlo says that a channel (or medium) is a **carrier** of messages.[29] As such, a channel can be sound waves that travel from a participant's mouth to another participant's ear. It can also be a form of sound amplification to reach a crowd of people in a large room. A channel can also be a radio or television signal, or a book or a newspaper that carries messages to millions of people. More recently, the Internet is a very popular channel for carrying messages to individuals or large groups of people.

Noise

Noise is anything that interferes with or distorts the transmission of the signal. **Environmental noise** is interference with the signal as it moves from the source to the destination. This could take the form of sounds in the room that prevent the receiver from hearing the message; it could be static on a telephone line, or even a dropped call on a cellular phone. **Psychological noise** takes place inside the sender or receiver, such as misunderstanding or failing to remember what was heard.

How does an event's context affect communication?
© 2008 JupiterImages Corporation.

Context

Context can be viewed as physical or social. The **physical context** is made up of the space surrounding the communication event, or the place in which the communication event occurs. The context could be a classroom, a meeting room at work, a church, a physician's office, your house, your favorite "night spot," or about any other place you can imagine. The place in which the event takes place influences communication behaviors and the meanings attributed to them. How would your behavior change if you moved from your favorite night spot to a classroom? Would you behave the same way?

The **social context** considers the nature of the event taking place in a physical context. The social expectations tied to particular events influence meaning attributed to communication. Even though you were still in a classroom, you would behave differently during an exam than during a group work session. You would behave differently in church during a funeral than celebrating a festive holiday, and you would certainly behave differently while playing bingo in the church basement!

Culture

The **culture** in which the communication occurs and the native cultures of the participants can influence meaning. People belong to a variety of nations, traditions, groups, and organizations, each of which has its own point of view, values, and norms.[30] A culture is made up of the collective beliefs or principles on which a community or part of a community of people is based. These beliefs are often passed from generation to generation and provide a perspective through which the community makes sense of its experiences. The culture, then, provides a very powerful context or backdrop for communication events and has a profound influence on the meaning that participants create and share.

SUMMARY

That's enough of the theory, at least for the moment. Let's get to the application! Keep in mind, however, that a solid understanding of the basics of the transactional model will provide a lot of help to you as you attempt to plan strategies and practice your skills to help you achieve your communication goals.

ENDNOTES

1. S. Littlejohn, *Theories of Human Communication* (Belmont, CA: Wadsworth, 1999), 2.
2. F. Kerlinger, *Foundations of Behavioral Research* (New York: Holt, Rinehart, and Winston, 1973), 9.
3. M. Polanyi, *Personal Knowledge* (Chicago: University of Chicago Press, 1958).
4. W. Wallace, *The Logic of Science in Sociology* (Chicago: Aldine, 1971).
5. T. Clevenger, "Can One Not Communicate? A Conflict of Models," *Communication Studies* 42 (1991), 351.
6. C. Hovland, I. Janis, and H. Kelley, *Communication and Persuasion* (New Haven, CT: Yale University Press, 1953).
7. G. Gerbner, "On Defining Communication: Still Another View," *Journal of Communication* 16 (1966), 99–103.

8. G. Miller, "On Defining Communication: Another Stab," *Journal of Communication* 16 (1966), 92.

9. K. Sereno and C. D. Mortensen, *Foundations of Communication Theory* (New York: Harper & Row, 1970), 5.

10. J. Makay, *Public Speaking: Theory into Practice* (Dubuque, IA: Kendall/Hunt, 2000), 9.

11. L. Hugenberg, S. Wallace, and D. Yoder, *Creating Competent Communication* (Dubuque, IA: Kendall/Hunt, 2003), 4.

12. J. DeVito, *Human Communication: The Basic Course* (Boston, Allyn & Bacon, 2006), 2.

13. J. Golden, G. Berquist, W. Coleman, and J. Sproule, *The Rhetoric of Western Thought, 8th ed.* (Dubuque, IA: Kendall/Hunt, 2003).

14. D. Stanton, and G. Berquist, "Aristotle's Rhetoric: Empiricism or Conjecture?" *Southern Speech Communication Journal* 41 (1975), 69–81.

15. L. Cooper, *The Rhetoric of Aristotle* (New York: Appleton-Century-Crofts, 1932).

16. Golden et al., 65.

17. C. Shannon, and W. Weaver, *The Mathematical Theory of Communication* (Urbana: University of Illinois Press, 1949). Also W. Weaver, "The Mathematics of Communication," in C. D. Mortensen (ed.), *Basic Readings in Communication Theory* (New York: Harper & Row, 1979).

18. W. Schramm, "How Communication Works," in W. Schramm, (ed.), *The Process and Effects of Communication* (Urbana: University of Illinois Press, 1954).

19. D. Berlo, *The Process of Communication* (New York: Holt, Rinehart, and Winston, 1960).

20. Ibid pp. 111–112.

21. Barnlund, D. (1970). "A Transactional Model of Communication," in *Foundations of Communication Theory*, Sereno, K. and Mortensen, C. D. (eds.). New York: Harper & Row, 1970. Also P. Watzlawick, *How Real Is Real? Confusion, Disinformation, Communication: An Anecdotal Introduction to Communications Theory* (New York: Vintage, 1977).

22. M. Burgoon and M. Ruffner, *Human Communication.* (New York: Holt, Rinehart, & Winston, 1978), 9.

23. E. Lazlo, *The Systems View of the World: A Holistic Vision for Our Time* (New York: Hampton Press, 1996). Also L. von Bertalanffy, *General System Theory: Foundations, Development, Applications* (New York: Braziller, 1976).

24. Barnlund.

25. F. Dance, "Toward a Theory of Human Communication," In F. Dance (ed.), *Human Communication Theory: Original Essays* (New York: Holt, 1967).

26. K. Miller, *Communication Theories: Perspectives, Processes, and Contexts* (New York: McGraw-Hill, 2005).

27. W. Heisenberg, *The Physical Principles of Quantum Theory* (Chicago: University of Chicago Press, 1930).

28. S. Wallace, D. Yoder, L. Hugenberg, and C. Horvath, *Creating Competent Communication*, 5th ed. (Dubuque, IA: Kendall/Hunt, 2006).

29. Berlo.

30. Yoder, Hugenberg, and Wallace. *Creating Competent Communication.* (Dubuque, IA: Kendall/Hunt, 1993).

REFERENCES

T. Newcomb, "An Approach to the Study of Communicative Acts," *Psychological review* 60 (1953), 393–404.

P. Watzlawick, J. Beavin, and D. Jackson, *Pragmatics of Human Communication* (New York: Norton, 1967).

The Field of Communication

IN THIS CHAPTER

Why. . .

- Communication is one of the oldest yet newest disciplines.
- Early Greeks saw communication theory and practice as critical.
- The popularity of communication is a mixed blessing.
- Communication is an activity, a social science, a liberal art, and a profession.

Early Communication Study

- Rhetoric and Speech
- Journalism

The 1900s–1930s: Development of Speech and Journalism

The 1940s and 1950s: Interdisciplinary Growth

The 1960s: Integration

The 1970s and Early 1980s: Growth and Specialization

- The Popularity of Communication

The Late 1980s and 1990s: The Information Age

- Information As a Commodity
- Converging Media

The Twenty-First Century: Communication Study Today

- Ancient and Newly Emergent
- Discipline and Interdisciplinary Link
- Personal and Professional Applicability

- Old and New Technology
- Problem and Solution
- Practical Skill and Fundamental Life Process

Implications and Applications

Summary

EARLY COMMUNICATION STUDY

It is difficult to determine precisely when and how communication first came to be regarded as a significant factor in human life. According to historians, considerable concern about communication and its role in human affairs was expressed prior to the fifth century B.C., in classical Babylonian and Egyptian writings and in Homer's *Iliad*.[1] An essay written about 3000 B.C. offers advice on how to speak effectively, while *The Precepts,* composed in Egypt about 2675 B.C., provides guidance on effective communication.

One of the most familiar historic statements on the importance of communication appears in the Bible. In the opening passage of the Old Testament the spoken word is described as the incredibly powerful force through which God created the world—God said, "Let there be light; and there was light." This statement carries considerable rhetorical power for people who belong to various religious communities.

As with other disciplines that have sought to explain human behavior, the beginning of systematic theory development in communication can be traced to the Greeks. Their initial interest sprang from the practical concerns of day-to-day life. Greece had a democratic form of government, and virtually all facets of business, government, law, and education were carried on orally. Greek citizens also had to be their own lawyers. Accused and accuser alike presented their cases before a jury of several hundred persons who would have had to be convinced of the rightness of a position. Lawsuits were common in Athens, and, as a result, public speaking in legal contexts became a preoccupation.

Rhetoric and Speech

What might be considered as the first theory of communication was developed in Greece by Corax and later refined by his student Tisias. The theory dealt with courtroom speaking, which was considered the craft of persuasion. Tisias became convinced that persuasion could be taught as an art and provided encouragement for instructors of what was called *rhetoric.* Corax and Tisias developed the concept of message organization, suggesting that a message should have three parts corresponding to today's concepts of introduction, body, and conclusion.

The sophists were a group of itinerant teachers in Athens in the fifth century B.C. who set up small schools and charged their pupils for tutoring. Protagoras of Abdara taught concepts that are embodied in the modern idea of debate. He taught that a good speaker should be able to argue both sides of a proposition. In addition, he encouraged students to write short messages that did not refer to a particular occasion to be used whenever they were called upon to speak in public.

Gorgias of Leontini was a contemporary of Protagoras and was one of the first to advocate the use of emotional appeals in persuasive speeches. Gorgias was especially concerned about style and the use of appropriate figures of speech.

Isocrates, another famous Greek Sophist, wrote speeches for others to deliver and was very influential in his time. He is known for his belief that an orator should be trained in the liberal arts and should be a good person.

The writings of two other scholars—Cicero (106–43 B.C.) and Quintilian (A.D. 35–95)—also contributed to the broadening theory of communication. Like Plato and Aristotle, Cicero developed rhetorical theories and saw communication as both an academic and practical matter. His view of communication was so comprehensive that it included all of what is now considered the domain of the social sciences. He believed a successful speaker was a knowledgable person. Quintilian is remembered primarily as an educator and synthesizer, bringing together in his writing the previous five hundred years' thinking about communication.[2] His practical guidelines demonstrate how a good communicator should be educated.

The view that communication was critical to virtually all aspects of human life was widely held during the Classical period.[3] However, the comprehensive perspective that characterized communication during this era was largely reversed in the Medieval and Renaissance periods. With the decline of the oral tradition and democracy, much of the interest in communication also waned, and the study of rhetoric was dispersed among several different fields. By the end of the fourteenth century, most of the communication theory that had originally been developed in rhetoric was now being studied in religion.

Eventually, the work of Augustine led to a rediscovery of classical Greek theory. His writings applied communication to the interpretation of the Bible and other religious writings, and to the art of preaching. In so doing, Augustine united the practical and theoretical aspects of communication study.

Early in the seventeenth century, Sir Francis Bacon included both speech-making and writing that was designed for more practical purposes in his theories. He proposed an ethical basis for communication and argued that the function of true rhetoric was the furtherance of good. His ideas had a major influence on later writers.

During the eighteenth and nineteenth centuries, emphasis in communication study was placed on written argument and literature. There was also great interest in speaking style, articulation, and gesture, leading to the formation of the National Association of Elocutionists in 1892. The elocutionists were a powerful force at this time who produced a very stylized mode of delivery that included vocal manipulation and physical gestures.

George Campbell, a contemporary of the elocutionists, wrote on the philosophical aspects of rhetoric. He maintained that rhetoric had four purposes: to enlighten, to please the imagination, to move the passions, or to influence the will.

Another eighteenth-century writer, Hugh Blair, proposed theories that could be applied either to writing or to speaking. His book, *Lectures on Rhetoric and Belles Lettres,* was very influential at the time.

By the end of the nineteenth century, most colleges and universities were organized into departments, and rhetoric and speech were often taught within departments of English.

Journalism

The other field that contributed significantly to the heritage of communication study is *journalism.* Like rhetoric and speech, journalism also dates back several thousand years. The practice of journalism began some 3,700 years ago in Egypt, when a record of the events of the time was transcribed on the tomb of an Egyptian king. Years later, Julius Caesar had an official record of the news of the day posted in a public place, and copies of it were made and sold.[4]

Early newspapers were a mixture of newsletters, ballads, proclamations, political tracts, and pamphlets describing various events. Like speech and rhetoric, they were forms of public communication. The mid-1600s saw the emergence of the newspaper in its modern form; and the first paper published in the United States, *Publick Occurrences Both For-reign and Domestick,* appeared in 1690 in Boston.

THE 1900S–1930S: DEVELOPMENT OF SPEECH AND JOURNALISM

In the early twentieth century, speech emerged as a discipline in its own right. In 1909, the Eastern States Speech Association—now the Eastern Communication Association—was formed, and in 1910, held its first annual conference. The National Association of Academic Teachers of Public Speaking, which became the Speech Association of America and the Speech Communication Association—now, the National Communication Association—was formed in 1914.[5] In 1915, the *Quarterly Journal of Public Speaking* was first published, followed soon after by the *Quarterly Journal of Speech. Communication Monographs* began publication in 1934. Unlike previous publications which emphasized speech practices, the new journal stressed research. Most of the studies published in the early volumes dealt with speech phonetics and phonology, physiology and pathology.[6] By 1935, the speech association had 1700 members, and speech was well established as a field.

Although the practice of journalism dates back many years, formalized study in the area did not progress rapidly until the early 1900s. In 1905, the University of Wisconsin offered what were perhaps the first courses in journalism, at a time when there were few, if any, books on the topic. By 1910, there were half a dozen volumes available, and between 1910 and 1920, some twenty-five works on journalism and newspaper work were compiled, signaling a pattern of continued growth.[7]

The advent of radio in the 1920s and television in the early 1940s resulted in the wider application of journalistic concepts. These new media gave impetus to the development of a broadened view of the nature of journalism.

Interest in communication was not limited to speech and journalism. In philosophy, scholars wrote about the nature of communication and its role in human life. Anthropologists, psychologists, and sociologists focused on communication and its role in individual and social process; and writers in the area of language also contributed to the advancement of communication study.

THE 1940S AND 1950S: INTERDISCIPLINARY GROWTH

In the 1940s and early 1950s, the scope of the field of communication broadened substantially. A number of scholars from the various behavioral and social science disciplines began to develop theories of communication which extended beyond the boundaries of their own fields. In anthropology, for example, research concerned with body positioning and gestures in particular cultures laid the groundwork for more general studies of nonverbal communication. In psychology, interest focused on persuasion, social influence, and, specifically, attitudes—how they form, how they change, their impact on behavior, and the role of communication in these dynamics. Researchers were especially concerned with issues of persuasion, including how propaganda persuaded individuals, how public opinion was created, and how the developing media contributed to persuasive efforts.[8] Kurt Lewin and his colleagues conducted a major research program on group dynamics. Carl Hovland and Paul Lazarsfeld conducted early research on mass communication.

Sociologists and political scientists studied the nature of mass media in various political and social activities, such as voting behavior, and other facets of life. In zoology, communication among animals began to receive considerable attention among researchers. During these same years, scholars in linguistics, general semantics, and semiotics, fields that focused on the nature of language and its role in human activity, also contributed to the advancement of communication study.

Studies in rhetoric and speech in the late 1940s and 1950s broadened to include oral interpretation, voice and diction, debate, theater, physiology of speech, and speech pathology. In journalism and mass media studies, growth and development were even more dramatic, spurred on in no small way by the popularity of television and efforts to understand its impact. In a number of classic works in the 1950s, the focus on specific media—newspapers, magazines, radio, and television—began to be replaced by a more general concern with the nature and effects of *mass media* and *mass communication.*

By the end of the 1950s a number of writings had appeared that paved the way for the development of more integrated views of communication. It was during these years that the National Society for the Study of Communication (now the International Communication Association) was established with the stated goal of bringing greater unity to the study of communication by exploring the relationships among speech, language, and media.[9] These developments set the stage for the rapid growth of communication as an independent discipline.

THE 1960S: INTEGRATION

In the 1960s, scholars synthesized thinking from rhetoric and speech, journalism and mass media, and the other social science disciplines. Among the noteworthy contributions to this integration were landmark books such as *The Process of Communication* (1960), *The Effects of Mass Communication* (1960), *On Human Communication* (1961), *Diffusion of Innovations* (1962), *The Science of Human Communication* (1963), *Understanding Media* (1964), and *Theories of Mass Communication* (1966).

The generalized views of communication reflected in these volumes were applied beginning in the middle of the decade. The term *communication* was linked to *speech* and *rhetoric* in basic books on the field during these years. In 1966, *Speech Communication: A Behavioral Approach* appeared, and two years later, *An Introduction to Rhetorical Communication* was published. In the mid-1960s, major volumes also linked *communication* with *culture* and *persuasion.* Additionally, the first books with *interpersonal communication* in their titles were published during this decade.

Communication was of interest in many disciplines during the 1960s. Sociologists focused on group dynamics, social relations, and the social origins of knowledge. Political scientists wrote about the role of communication in governments, governance, public opinion, propaganda, and political image building, providing the foundation for the development of the area of political communication that was to blossom a decade later.[10]

In administrative studies, writings on organizations, management, leadership, and information networks provided the basis for the growth of *organizational communication,* an area of study that also emerged in the 1970s. Writings in anthropology and linguistics, together with those in communication, set the stage for the emergence of intercultural communication as an area of study. Advances by zoologists during the 1960s encouraged the study of animal communication.

THE 1970S AND EARLY 1980S: GROWTH AND SPECIALIZATION

The expansion and specialization that began in the late 1960s reached new heights in the 1970s. *Interpersonal communication* became an increasingly popular area, as did the study of nonverbal interaction. Information science, information theory, and information and communication systems were other topics of increasing interest. During these same years, *group, organizational, political, international,* and *intercultural communication* emerged as distinct areas of study.

Rhetoric, public speaking, debate, theater, speech pathology, journalism, mass media, photography, advertising, and public relations continued to grow and prosper alongside communication, speech communication, and mass communication. New areas such as instructional, therapeutic, and developmental communication also became attractive to researchers and practitioners. Feminist scholars in communication also began to contribute to many of these areas.

Increased interest in communication study during the 1970s was also evident in periodicals and scholarly journals. Increased research activity led to a remarkable increase in the publication of books and periodicals. The first publications with the term *communication* in their titles were published in the mid-1930s, and during the 1950s four more appeared. Eight new periodicals appeared during the 1960s, and the 1970s brought the arrival of seventeen new publications bearing *communication* in their titles. A number of new academic journals were introduced, and several other journals of speech and journalism added the word *communication* to their titles to reflect a broadened focus. By the end of the decade, *Ulrich's International Periodical Dictionary* listed one hundred and thirty-seven publications on communication.

The expansion and diversification of communication study was reflected in college and university curricula. A number of new departments of communication were formed throughout the 1970s, and some programs in speech changed their names to speech communication or communication. The same was true in some journalism departments, where the shift was from journalism to mass communication, communication, or communications.

The Popularity of Communication

Interest in communication was apparent in the popular, as well as the academic, realm. In 1975, the *Harper Dictionary of Contemporary Usage* listed communication as a "vogue word—a word . . . that suddenly or inexplicably crops up . . . in speeches of bureaucrats, comments of columnists . . . and in radio and television broadcasts." This notoriety focused attention on the importance and relevance of communication and brought individuals with various perspectives and backgrounds to the field. However, it also resulted in such widespread use that the meaning of communication became somewhat less precise.

Discipline, Activity, and Profession.   One factor that contributed to the ambiguity of the term during this period of increasing popularity was the use of a single term to refer to a field of study, a set of activities, and a profession. People study communication, people communicate (or more accurately, engage in communication), and people earn their livelihood creating communication products and services. This potential source of confusion does not occur in most other disciplines. For example, scholars study psychology and English, but they do not "psychologize" or "Englishicate." They study English literature and write. Or they study psychology and engage in therapy or counseling. In these fields, as in most others, different terms are used to differentiate the discipline from the phenomenon itself and from its professional practice. With communication, one word refers to the discipline, the activity, and the profession.

In an attempt to clarify the distinction, some writers suggested the terms *communication science* or *communication studies* to refer to the discipline, and *communicologist* and *communication scientist* or *communication researcher* to refer to those within it. The phrase *communication professional* was sometimes used to refer to individuals who earned their livelihoods engaged in communication activities. These terms were not widely adopted, leaving a source of confusion that continues to the present day.

Communication and Communications.   Another factor adding to the confusion was the use of *communication* and *communications*. Traditionally, *communications* has been used to refer to media or to specific messages being transmitted through these media. *Communication* has historically been used to refer to the activity of sending and receiving messages (through media or face-to-face) and to the discipline as a whole. With the increasing interest in communication technology, the term communications began to be used interchangeably with communication in popular—and sometimes academic—contexts, blurring what had originally been a useful technical distinction.

THE LATE 1980S AND 1990S: THE INFORMATION AGE

The *Information Age* is a popular term used to refer to the period beginning in the late 1990s, and in many senses continuing to the present time. This has been a period in which communication and information technology came to play an increasingly important role in our society. So pervasive are the impacts of these new media and the communication and information services they have created, that it is difficult to find an aspect of our personal and professional lives that has not in some way been affected.

Information As a Commodity

During the 1980s and 1990s, there was an increasing interest in information communicated via messages as an economic good or commodity—something that can be bought and sold—and in the technologies by which this commodity is created, distributed, stored, retrieved, and used. In the United States communication and information companies have emerged as some of our largest businesses. Communication and information became central in the telecommunication, publishing, Internet, and computer industries, as well as in banking, insurance, leisure and travel, and research. People in these fields spent an increasing amount of their time packaging information into products and services that could be sold in domestic and foreign markets. In the United States, Japan, Sweden, England, and a number of other countries at least half of the society's labor force was engaged in communication and information-related work.

Converging Media

New and converging media were a fundamental feature of the landscape of the period. Certainly the most obvious change during this period was the growth of the Internet, and other information storage, transmission, and retrieval systems using computers.

During these years, media were brought together to form hybrid technologies that permitted communication sources and receivers to carry out functions that were once difficult, time-consuming, or even impossible. In earlier periods, specific technologies had more or less specific uses. Television was a medium for viewing mass-produced and -distributed programs which reached the set via the airwaves. During the Information Age, television became not only a medium for the mass distribution of standardized programs but also a device for use with the Internet, DVDs, personal photos, interactive video games, cable systems, and a display for print as well as visual computer output. The telephone underwent a similar transformation. Designed for one-to-one conversation, telephones and telephone lines were used not only in this way but also in conjunction with computers and facsimile machines for the transmission of text and graphics as well as voice. Typewriters, once used exclusively for print correspondence and report preparation, were combined with the telephone and television screen to form new, hybrid telecommunication systems.

Thus, the infamous "Information Age" brought new labels, new and hybrid media, extended concepts of communication and information, changing economic realities, and new jobs for an increasing number of communication and information workers. During these years our perspective broadened to include newer media and the nature and function of communication technology in general. The Information Age greatly heightened attention to the pervasive role of technology in our lives and its impact on human behavior.

THE TWENTY-FIRST CENTURY: COMMUNICATION STUDY TODAY

This chapter has traced the development of the discipline from its early beginnings, through periods marked by interdisciplinary development, through its emergence and growth as a discipline in its own right through the end of the twentieth century. From this overview, one can draw a number of conclusions about the present period that are helpful in understanding communication study as it exists today.

Ancient and Newly Emergent

The core of modern communication study has its origins in the work of the early Greek philosophers. The 1900s, however, brought a number of changes to the discipline, including a new name. Within the last fifty years, the scope of the field has broadened, its structure has changed, and every facet of it has grown substantially. In this respect, communication can be viewed as a newly emergent field, the newest of the disciplines concerned with the study of human behavior.

Discipline and Interdisciplinary Link

As has been the case for at least the past half century, communication in the present period is a strong discipline in its own right. At the same time, interest in communication extends well beyond the boundaries of the communication field.

This duality attests to the central role of communication in human affairs. And, at a time when the boundaries between these and other fields are becoming less rigid, communication serves as an important intellectual link among scholars of various persuasions and points of view.

In communication studies, we approach issues such as these from the perspective of the creation, transmission, interpretation, and use of information by individuals in relationships, groups, organizations, cultures, and societies. The value of integrating our efforts with the works of scholars in other disciplines has become increasingly apparent. Potential connections exist with a number of areas, including

- *Cognitive psychology and neuroscience*. Focus on perception, thinking, interpretation, memory, and use of information
- *Cultural and critical studies*. Focus on the historical, social, political, and cultural influences on message creation, transmission, interpretation, impact, and use
- *Economics*. Focus on the production and consumption of information as an economic resource
- *Computer science and electrical engineering*. Focus on the storage, retrieval, manipulation, and transmission of information
- *Information science*. Focus on information classification, management, and storage
- *Journalism*. Focus on information sources, content, public communication, and mass media
- *Literature*. Focus on the creation and reader interpretations of textual material
- *Marketing*. Focus on user needs and preferences in relation to adoption and use of messages, products, and services
- *Philosophy*. Focus on ethical dimensions of the communication process involving both individuals and the mass media

Personal and Professional Applicability

The importance attached to communication in contemporary life can also be seen in the extent to which the phenomenon is regarded as essential to our personal as well as our occupational roles. The shelves of libraries and book stores are filled with writings emphasizing the importance of communication to the establishment and maintenance of meaningful interpersonal and family relationships. And, but a few rows away, are an equal number of writings describing the importance of communication to successful professional and organizational functioning. Such writings talk about the importance of communication for individual leaders, team collaboration, organizational effectiveness, and marketplace competitiveness, among other topics.

Old and New Technology

Speaking and listening are as basic to communication and human behavior in the twenty-first century as they were at the time of the ancient Greeks. And yet, in the present period, we benefit from any number of technologically enhanced forms of communication, which give permanence and portability to the messages of face-to-face communication. Beyond taken-for-granted media such as newspapers, radio, television, and magazines are a broad array of new technologies that find their way to the market every year. Whether one thinks of customized news and information Web applications, Internet innovations, cell phones, MP3 software and players, wireless local networks, global positioning systems, high definition LCD television screens/monitors, sophisticated video games, or the many other emerging tools, toys, and technologies, the possibilities for new forms of communication are quite remarkable. And yet as we shall discuss in greater detail later, for all the new forms of communication, many if not most of the basic communication challenges and functions remain. Inquiring minds might legitimately ask if all the new communication forms that fill our pockets, briefcases, homes, and offices have improved the quality of our lives. Are we better informed than we were fifty years ago? Are we better entertained? Is world understanding improving? Are our personal and family relationships better, more meaningful? These are good questions, we think, and are precisely the kind of questions that should increasingly be addressed by those interested in communication study in the 2000s and beyond.

Problem and Solution

Few topics are as pervasive in the popular culture as communication. We have become so accustomed to hearing and reading commentaries on the challenges we face in crossing social, demographic, political, gender, cultural, lifestyle, religious, or occupational boundaries that it is easy to overlook the central role communication is perceived to play in these matters. In such conversations, communication—or, more precisely, the lack thereof—is seen as the fundamental *problem*. And yet, as John Peters has pointed out, communication is also seen as the essential *solution*.[11] Paradoxically, communication is seen as both a chasm and a bridge.[12] The significance afforded to the phenomenon in our time is quite remarkable, and a factor that contributes to the vitality and importance of communication study and communication practice.

Practical Skill and Fundamental Life Process

Another interesting contrast regarding communication study today is its breadth. In many communication courses, the primary emphasis on communication continues to be as a skill, and more specifically on the set of techniques associated with creating and disseminating messages, orally or in written form, in face-to-face or technologically mediated settings. There are other courses, however—more often the type that would make use of a book such as this—that approach communication theoretically, viewing it as a fundamental life process, one that is basic to our physical, personal, social, political, and cultural existence. The fact the communication study encompasses such a broad range of interests is a source of some confusion, and frequently requires definitional clarification in discussions. At the same time, as in previous periods, this breadth also creates what is a useful tension for the field—a tension between the search for practical technique and the quest for theoretical understanding. Each makes a useful and complementary contribution to the field in its effort to advance human knowledge and capability.

IMPLICATIONS AND APPLICATIONS

- Communication has long been regarded as important to the practice and understanding of human affairs.
- In the past several decades, communication study has become an increasingly popular academic subject.
- Communication study offers students the richness and diversity of the liberal arts tradition, blended with the applied focus of a professional field.
- Communication study today continues to be the center of a very strong discipline in its own right, and also the basis for linkages between scholars and practitioners from many other fields in which communication is important.
- Paradoxically, communication is both the basis for many of the problems of human affairs and also the potential solution.

SUMMARY

Communication has a rich and lengthy history, which can be traced back to Babylonian and Egyptian writings prior to the fifth century B.C. The initial contributions to communication study came from scholars in what was termed *rhetoric*. They viewed communication as the practical art of persuasion. Aristotle and Plato, who were particularly significant to early communication study, saw rhetoric and the practice of public speaking not only as an art but also as a legitimate area of study.

Along with rhetoric and speech, journalism also contributed to the heritage of communication study. As with rhetoric, journalism initially was concerned primarily with practical rather than theoretical matters. By the beginning of the twentieth century, rhetoric and speech were clearly established as disciplines in their own right; and journalism began to take shape as a field as well.

During the early twentieth century, interest in communication continued in rhetoric and speech, and the advent of radio and later television led to the wider application of journalistic concepts and the development of more theories of the overall process. The 1940s and 1950s were years of interdisciplinary growth, as scholars from various disciplines advanced theories of communication that extended beyond the boundaries of their own fields.

The 1960s were a period of integration. A good deal was done to synthesize the writings of rhetoric and speech, journalism and mass media, as well as other disciplines. A number of landmark books appeared within the field.

During this most recent period of history, additional models of the communication process were advanced, extending the work of earlier scholars.

The 1970s and early 1980s were a time of unprecedented growth within the field. It was also a period in which much specialization occurred, giving rise to progress in our understanding of interpersonal, group, organizational, political, international, and intercultural communication.

Continuing growth and interdisciplinary advancement have distinguished the communication field in the late 1980s and 1990s, and developments of the Information Age have been important influences. Converging media, along with economic and marketplace developments, have underscored the pervasive impact of communication and communication media on our lives.

At the opening of the twenty-first century, the discipline of communication and the phenomena it studies are center stage in human affairs. The subject is at once ancient and newly emergent, a discipline in its own right and an interdisciplinary crossroad for scholars from a wide variety of fields. Communication is as relevant to personal as it is professional affairs, and the role of new and old technology continues to be a focus of the times and the discipline. As John Peters has noted, communication study is concerned with both the major problem and most hopeful solution of contemporary life, and the focus of the field of communication is at once on some of the most practical of skills and on the most fundamental of life processes.

The overview of the history of communication reveals a number of changes during the 2,500-year heritage of the field—changes both in the theory of the communication process and in the discipline in which it is studied.

We have seen that the communication field is both ancient as well as a product of the twentieth century, interdisciplinary in heritage, the home of scholars and professionals, a discipline which benefits from the approaches of both the humanities and behavioral sciences, and an area in which media are of continuing concern.

ENDNOTES

1. For a detailed summary of the early history of speech and rhetorical communication study overviewed here, see Nancy L. Harper, *Human Communication Theory: History of a Paradigm* (Rochelle Park, NJ: Hayden, 1979), pp. 16–68, and James C. McCroskey, *An Introduction to Rhetorical Communication* (Englewood Cliffs, NJ: Prentice-Hall, 1986), pp. 261–272.

2. Harper, 1979, pp. 27–30.

3. For a comprehensive and thoughtful discussion of the history of communication study, see John D. Peters, *Speaking Into Air: A History of the Idea of Communication* (Chicago: University of Chicago Press, 1999).

4. J. F. Frank, *The Beginnings of the English Newspaper 1620–1660* (Cambridge, MA: Harvard University Press, 1961), p. 2.

5. See H. Cohen, *The History of Speech Communication: The Emergence of a Discipline, 1914–1945* (Annandale, VA: National Communication Association, 1994).

6. E. G. Bormann, *Theory and Research in the Communicative Arts* (New York: Holt, 1965), pp. 16–17. See also Penny Demo, "Celebrating Our 75th Anniversary and Our Early Publications," in *Spectra*, May, 1989, p. 4.

7. Grant M. Hyde, "Foreword," in *Survey of Journalism.* Ed. by G. F. Mott (New York: Barnes & Noble, 1937), p. viii.

8. Jesse G. Delia, "Communication Research: A History," in *Handbook of Communication Science.* Ed. by C. R. Berger and S. H. Chaffee (Newbury Park, CA: Sage, 1987), pp. 25–30.

9. Carl H. Weaver, "A History of the International Communication Association," in *Communication Yearbook 1.* Ed. by Brent D. Ruben (New Brunswick, NJ: Transaction-International Communication Associatiion, 1977), pp. 607–609

10. Wilbur Schramm, *The Beginnings of Communication Study in America: A Personal Memoir* (Thousand Oaks, CA: Sage, 1997).

11. Peters, 1999, p. 5.

12. Peters, 1999, p. 5.

Communication in Action

Activity #1

Introducing Yourself

This activity is a way for you to introduce yourself to me. Since we do not meet in person, use this opportunity to help me get to know you a little better.

1. Please use the Assignment Submission Form as your cover page.

2. Open a word processing document and insert a picture of yourself into this document. (HINT: Use the "Insert" command on Microsoft Word.)

3. In the space below the photo, please take a few minutes to tell me about yourself. You can say whatever you would like but some basic biographical information would be helpful. You may want to tell me about your major or your family or your career plans. MINIMUM 1000 words. USE word count to check this—I will!

   BEFORE YOU WRITE ANYTHING—READ THIS: Here is the deal. When I give this assignment, most people start by writing about where they are from and who is in their family and the activities that they have done. And there is nothing wrong with that. That is a good place to START!!! The reason I ask for a MINIMUM of 1000 words is because I want you to pick 2–3 stories about your life and go into a little more detail about them. It's like on the first day of class, when you met your COMS buddies, you told them some stuff about you. As you get to know them better, you will tell them longer and longer stories. That's what I want you to do here. I LOVE teaching this class but I don't like not getting to talk with each of you. This exercise allows you to go a little more in depth about yourself and your experiences. I posted my CIA 1 on our Blackboard site, so you could find out a little more about me. HAVE FUN!

Information Reception

IN THIS CHAPTER

Why . . .

- The reception of information is at least as complex and important as message sending.
- You can listen to two conversations at once at a party.
- A receiver's needs have a major impact on communication outcomes.
- The absence of a message can itself be a powerful message.
- Grocery stores often place the most popular items farthest from the door.

Selection

Interpretation

Retention—Memory

- Short-Term and Long-Term Memory
- Semantic and Episodic Memory

Receiver Influences

- Needs
- Attitudes, Beliefs, and Values
- Goals
- Capability
- Use
- Communication Style
- Experience and Habit

Message (Information) Influences

- Origin
- Mode

- Physical Characteristics
- Organization
- Novelty

Source Influences

- Proximity
- Physical and Social Attraction and Similarity
- Credibility and Authoritativeness
- Motivation and Intent
- Delivery
- Status, Power, and Authority

Technological and Environmental Influences

- Technology
- The Environment

An Active and Complex Process

Implications and Applications

Summary

Information reception involves attending to and transforming environmental messages into a form that can be used to guide behavior. This process is an active one, consisting of three elements—*information selection, interpretation,* and *retention.* We will discuss each of these in detail in the pages ahead, beginning with an illustration.

Ed awoke this morning at 7:30 to a grey sky and light rain. He noticed the weather almost immediately, because it was a Saturday and he had looked forward all week to a chance to get outside. He chatted with his wife, Jane, about a variety of topics while he dressed and ate breakfast. He began to ponder his options as to how to spend the day, given that he was stuck inside. Ed left the breakfast table and walked down the hallway.

He glanced in the study and saw the piles of pages strewn about his desk. "I should work on the report due next month," he thought to himself. "My annual review will depend on how well that's received."

He continued into the family room where he noticed his children, Robert and Ann, sitting in front of the television set. He reflected to himself on how fast time goes by, and decided that he really ought to spend more time with the kids. "Maybe a computer game or some sort of craft project that we could work on together . . ." He exchanged a few brief words with his children, and it seemed that Elmo was of more interest to the kids than he was, so he turned his attention to a stack of newspapers and magazines lying across the room on a table. As he looked at the pile of reading material, he thought about how he had spent only a few minutes with the mail, newspapers, and magazines all week. "I really should go through them today," he thought. "No . . . the report has got to come first!"

He made his way back to the study, turned on the radio, and searched for a station that played the kind of music he liked as "background." Ed situated himself at the desk and began to shuffle through the materials before him. He came across a book he had been using as a primary source in his report, picked it up, and began rereading sections of the text and leafing through the illustrations.

The FM station kept fading in and out, and the occasional interruptions for news were annoying him. He walked over to a nearby CD rack, and picked several jazz instrumentals, which he thought would be enjoyable, but not distracting.

As he walked back to the desk, Ed happened to glance out the window. Incredible! The grey skies had cleared, the rain had stopped, and the sun was shining brightly. Ed heard the distant whine of a neighbor's lawn mower and glanced almost instinctively at his own lawn. "My yard really does need to be mowed . . . And the car is dirty," he thought to himself. "I could do both jobs tomorrow, if the weather holds."

He turned the FM on again and scanned for a local station and the weather report. "Clearing this afternoon, highs in the low 80's."

"I'll wash the car today, so it will be clean for the weekend, and put off mowing the lawn until tomorrow," he decided. "This grass might still be a bit wet now, anyway . . . But what if the weather report is wrong? *If* it's wrong? It's always wrong. If I put off mowing until tomorrow, and it rains, I might not be able to mow until next weekend; and by then the grass will be so long it would take most of two days to mow."

"How ridiculous this is!" he concluded. "The lawn is ruling my life. It's amazing how one's priorities evolve by default. Back to the report!"

The foregoing vignette reveals a good deal about Ed's communication habits, values, orientations, and, at the same time, helps to illustrate how communication works. For analytic purposes, let's briefly reconstruct the scenario, paying particular attention to the cues Ed attended to, the meanings he attached to them, and the manner in which these meanings guided his behavior.

There are a number of things Ed might think about upon waking on a given day. On this particular day, he was primarily concerned with the day of the week and the weather—*Saturday* and *rain*. That he chose to be interested in these particular things and not others had largely to do with the meanings each had for him. Saturday was a special day, one he had looked forward to all week. Grey clouds and rain meant it would be impossible for him to pursue some of the activities he had hoped and planned for. Together, *Saturday* and *rain* signified plans ruined, nothing more, nothing less.

Despite this reality, Ed moved through the sequence necessary to the activities he had come to think of as essential to the start of each day: taking a shower, shaving, selecting clothes, dressing, making his way to the kitchen, sitting down at the table, talking to his wife Jane, eating breakfast, and so forth.

As he chatted with Jane, new messages were introduced into his environment. These provided an opportunity for him to overcome the "plans ruined" aura, which to that point had been the dominant theme in his information processing.

In talking to his wife—and himself—Ed determined that there was little to be gained by stewing over one set of plans ruined. There were, after all, a number of plans one might have that *Saturday* + *rain* would not ruin. As he began to attach new meaning to the situation, his attention was directed toward information sources and possible interpretations he was unaware of only minutes earlier.

Because Ed was ready to consider options as to how to spend the day, the stack of printed pages from his report was singled out from other potential sources of information in the environment. At some level of awareness, those pages meant a variety of things to him at that point, including *job unfinished, frustration, guilt,* and *challenge.* None of these meanings were compelling enough, however, to lead him to undertake work on the report at that instant.

In the family room, his children almost instantly became prominent communication sources. They triggered a variety of meanings—*affection, enjoyment, responsibility, concern.* As with the significance of the report, these meanings were central to his self-concept and sense of what matters, and as a result they commanded his interest and receptivity.

In passing, he also attended momentarily to the television show they were watching. He recognized at some slightly-less-than-conscious level that the messages generated by the cartoon were performing very different functions for Robert and Ann than for him. In some sense, Ed was competing with Elmo for his children's attention.

The presence of the week's mail, magazines, and newspapers became additional sources of communication. In the context of his own life they signified *knowledgeability, credibility, enjoyment,* and *responsibility.* Ed was also aware of a need to be familiar with the "news" in order to be current in discussions with his friends and colleagues.

Though these meanings were also important to his definition of himself, they were not, at that instant, as critical as the meanings related to the report. Ed "decided"—again, in a less-than-wholly-aware manner—to reject these and other options in favor of returning to work on the report.

The communication process continued as he selected a particular information source—FM radio—and a specific frequency on the dial with a message set he had learned to associate with that station. His unstated objective in so doing was to control the background cues in the immediate environment.

In looking through the materials on his desk, his eyes fell upon a book that had been significant earlier in his work. It became a primary object of attention for several minutes, as he recalled its contents and his reaction to them. Noise resulting from the fading of the radio station became another unavoidable information source, and he acted to replace the messages from FM with others from CDs, which he assumed would better meet his needs.

On glancing out the window, the clearing skies and sun were especially meaningful cues. They signified "original plans O.K.; no need to pursue the present options, unless you want to" As his attention shifted to the environment outside, Ed noted the whine of a lawn mower, which triggered a variety of meanings, each of which required attention and resolution—the lawn, the car, and so on.

In examining the alternative meanings called up from memory, he inadvertently began a self-reflexive thought process. As he reflected on his own information processing, this time quite consciously, he decided to execute more control over himself and his surroundings and pursue what he had determined to be the most "logical" alternatives for use of his time.

In returning his attention to work on the report, Ed, in effect, decided to attach less value to messages related to the physical environment external to his study—the lawn, cars, and so on. He chose instead to focus on information sources that were pertinent to his report. The act of selecting the option he did also had the effect of reaffirming his priorities.

Many interesting facets of communication are illustrated in even a commonplace situation such as the one just described. As simple and automatic as such events may seem, they involve an array of factors operating in the very active processes of information selection, interpretation, and retention.

SELECTION

At any instant in time we are surrounded in our environment by persons, objects, and circumstances that are sources of messages vying for our attention and interest. In the foregoing sequence, Ed's FM receiver, CD player, wife

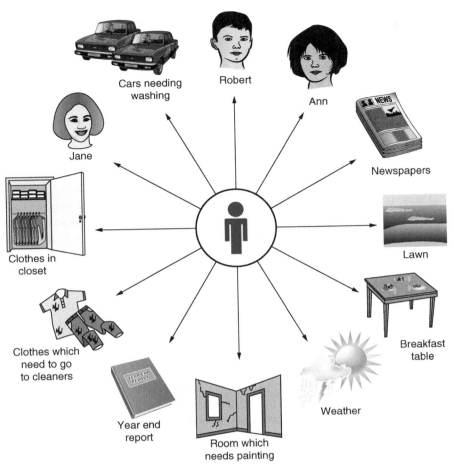

Figure 4.1
At any one point in time we are surrounded by a large number of people, events, objects, and circumstances that are communication sources competing for our attention.

and children, the pages of his report, the outdoors, the lawnmower, and the weather were each potential communication sources that were competing for his attention, as illustrated in Figure 4.1.

Predictably, in such circumstances we select certain information sources to attend to and disregard others. Even in a simple situation we make a number of elaborate decisions, and we are unaware of many of them. Ed "decided" to give attention to the weather, the day of the week, his children, and the report rather than to other information sources in his environment—such as a room that needed painting, clothes that were to be taken to the cleaners, an unopened package on the table, the expressions on his children's faces when they exchanged words, and so on.

This selection process operates similarly in all situations. Consider a circumstance where we pause in a hallway to chat with an acquaintance. First, the very act of noticing the other person involves selection of particular communication sources. Triggered by the constellation of factors associated with the appearance of the other person, and perhaps some verbal cue—"Hi"—we begin focusing ourselves on the other person and on things that we believe will be necessary to the interchange that will follow. In so doing, we ignore other potential cues—the temperature, the color of the carpeting, the appearance of other persons who may pass by, the noise of a nearby copy machine, or the thunderstorm outside—through a complex selectivity process that has occupied the attention of many scholars over the years.[1]

The classic illustration of *selective attention* is provided by large parties and similar social gatherings. During such events, one finds that it is not at all difficult to carry on a series of perfectly intelligible discussions without being overly distracted by other conversations. It is even possible to tune in to an exchange between several other persons a good distance away, without shifting one's position and while appearing to be deeply engrossed in conversation with a person close at hand. In that same setting, we are able to tune out the entire external environment, periodically, in order to concentrate on our own feelings, decide what we ought to be doing, or think about how we are being perceived by others. It is also possible to attend to the gathering as a whole, paying attention to the level, pitch, rhythm, number of interactions, and level of activity, as a basis for making some general assessments of the gathering as a whole—whether it is sedate or wild, winding up or down, and so on.[2]

Given these examples, it may seem as though selection operates much like a filter, letting in some sounds, images, or smells, while screening out others.[3] However, the process is often more complex than this way of thinking implies. For instance, we know that even when we have "tuned in" to a particular communication source and "tuned out" others, the selected-out messages may, nonetheless, be taken note of. This is the case, for instance, when a honking horn interrupts our attention in a discussion with a colleague while crossing the street, or when the sound of one's own or a friend's name is heard "through" the otherwise unintelligible din of a party.[4] Additionally, there is evidence to suggest that it is possible to take note of and attach meaning to messages even when one is unaware of doing so.[5] And some studies suggest that under hypnosis we may be able to remember information that we were not fully aware of selecting for attention in the first place.[6]

An understanding of the complexity of the attention process has led to the adoption of a "modified filter model" as a way of thinking about selection.[7] It is thought that we assign priorities to competing information sources and allocate attention among them, while monitoring other messages and perhaps even attending to still other sources that are unknown even to the individuals involved.

INTERPRETATION

Interpretation occurs when we assign meaning or significance to a cue or message in the environment—whether to regard it as important or trivial, serious or humorous, new or old, contradictory or consistent, amusing or alarming.

Figure 4.2
Interpretation—The
Construction of Meaning
© Juriah Mosin, 2014. Shutterstock, Inc.

Depending on the way we select and interpret messages, very different consequences result. For example, in Figure 4.2, if we are drawn first to the large white portion, we see three columns. Attention to subtleties of the image in black, however, reveals two women conversing.

Even our reaction to a simple, "Hi, how are you?" will depend, among other things, on whether the person is male or female (and the significance we attach to each), whether we regard the individual as attractive or unattractive, whether the person is a family member or a stranger, how the person is dressed, where the event takes place, and how we interpret the other person's motives.

RETENTION—MEMORY

From the preceding discussion, it should be apparent that memory plays an indispensable role in the interpretative process. We are able to store and actively use an incredible amount of information, and we can locate and use it with an efficiency and ease of operation that is astounding.[8]

We have little difficulty accessing the information we need in order to go about our daily routine—to locate the bathroom, closet, and kitchen; to select appropriate clothing and to dress; to start and operate an automobile; or to find the way to the bus or train. In a split second, and with a high degree of accuracy, we can answer questions like "Who was the first president of the United States?" or "What is the name for the sound frequently heard following lightning?" These certainly seem like "simple" questions. But think how long it would take to answer these questions in a book, library, or electronic database using a table of contents, index, or other search technique. Or a quick electronic search may turn up incorrect information.

As Morton Hunt notes:

> Although every act of thinking involves the use of images, sounds, symbols, meanings, and connections between things, all stored in memory, the organization of memory is so efficient that most of the time we are unaware of having to exert any effort to locate and use these materials. Consider the ranges of kinds of information you keep in, and can easily summon forth from, your own memory: the face of your closest friend . . . the words and melody of the national anthem . . . the spelling of almost every word you can think of . . . the name of every object you can see from where you are sitting . . . the way your room looked when you were eight . . . the set of skills you need to drive a car in heavy traffic . . . and enough more to fill many shelves full of books. . . .[9]

These are examples of *recall*—active, deliberate retrieval of information from memory, a capability that may well be unique to humans. We share with other animals the capacity to use information for *recognition*—recognizing objects, places, circumstances, and people when in their presence.[10]

Much effort has been directed to understanding the complex processes by which memory operates, particularly in the area concerned with identifying stages of information processing.[11]

Short-Term and Long-Term Memory

Information enters the system through one or several communication modes. In selecting and attending to particular messages, we begin to attach meaning to those symbols following rules we have learned and frequently used.[12] A good deal of sensory information can be processed within the system at any one time. If, for example, you looked through the newspaper to determine what movie was playing at a particular theater, not only that information but also information relative to other items in the paper, such as other movies and other theaters, would also be processed at some level of awareness. The information other than that being sought would be lost and would decay very rapidly—probably within a second or so.[13]

Information that is to be further used becomes a part of what is called *short-term memory* and is available for a relatively restricted period of time—perhaps fifteen seconds.[14] Our short-term memory capacity is limited under normal circumstances to a few pieces of information only—a phone number, an e-mail address, or a string of several letters or words. Most of us have had the experience of looking up a number or an address, only to forget it by the time we walked across the room to get the phone or computer. This forgetting illustrates how rapidly information is lost from short-term memory. Through recitation or rehearsal, however, we can extend the time available to use information. Thus, if we repeat a phone number to ourselves several times as we walk across the room, the likelihood of remembering it for the needed time period greatly increases.

Some of the information is further processed and elaborated to become a part of our *long-term memory*. Generally, the longer time information is available to us in short-term memory, the greater the chance it will become a part of our long-term memory. Therefore, a phone number looked up, rehearsed, and dialed several times over the period of an hour because of a busy signal, is far more likely to be remembered than a number successfully reached on the first try. Phone numbers that are dialed often become a part of an individual's long-term memory naturally, or actively, through memorization. Of course, if we use autoredial or store the number in a cell phone, we don't get the chance to learn it through practice.

Recall and recognition exemplify the two general classes of human memory: (1) relatively slow retrievals that require conscious processing, and (2) relatively fast retrievals that require no conscious processing. Some of the other characteristics of these two retrieval processes include:[15]

Slow Retrievals	Fast Retrievals
Nonautomatic	Automatic
Conscious	Unconscious
Controlled	Uncontrolled
Indirect access	Direct access
Voluntary	Involuntary

Semantic and Episodic Memory

Our general knowledge of the people, places, and things in the world is called *semantic memory*. *Episodic memories* relate to recollections and retrieval of information regarding personal happenings, particular objects, people, and events experienced by an individual at a specific time and place.[16] *Autobiographical memories*—memories of oneself—are considered to be episodic.[17] While this distinction is a useful one, scholars also point out that the two types of memory are related: Semantic knowledge is derived from episodic memory, and episodic memories are organized and categorized based on semantic categories.[18]

In the summary of his book, *Memory in the Real World,* Gillian Cohen provides the following list of characteristics of memory:

- Memory is an overloaded system—there is more to be remembered than can possibly be managed by the brain.
- Memory must be selective—decisions must be made as to what to remember and what to ignore.
- Memory must be dynamic—adjustments must be made to changes in the world around us.
- Memory must link past, present, and future—memory provides for continuity of meaning across time.
- Memory must be able to construct hypothetical representations—imagination, creativity, and consideration of possibilities are necessary characteristics of memory.
- Memory must store both general and specific information—generalized and specialized knowledge are both required in human activity.
- Memory must store information implicitly—information must be easily and automatically stored and organized for retrieval. Often this is done in terms of categories, time periods, and level of generality/specificity.
- Memory processes must be complex—elaborate information sorting and organizing processes are necessary to integrate new information with past experience.
- Memory retrieval strategies are critical—retrieving information becomes more critical and difficult as memories proliferate.
- Memory retrieval must utilize spontaneous and deliberate retrieval—memories must be able to be retrieved spontaneously as well as deliberately.[19]

As useful as the foregoing view of information processing is, it is important to be aware of the limitations of what has been termed the sequential-stage model. Researchers remind us that information processing is an extremely complex operation. It is often difficult to distinguish between its various stages. The distinction between selection, interpretation, and episodic and semantic memory can be fuzzy. Further, a sequential-stage model could imply that the individual plays a passive role in information processing. Clearly this is not the case; complex interactions between the individual and environment are fundamental to the ongoing dynamics of information reception.

RECEIVER INFLUENCES

For each of us, a complex set of influences works together to influence our decisions as to which messages we will attend to and how we will interpret and retain the information that results. Many of these have to do with the nature of the *receiver.*

As children we adapt to a world in which we are highly dependent upon parents and other adults for the satisfaction of our needs, wants, and desires. That dependence carries with it a particular set of information-reception tendencies for most of us, in which our parents, relatives, and, gradually, peer relations are highly significant.

Needs

Among the most crucial factors that play a role in reception are what are commonly termed *needs.* Scholars generally agree that our most basic needs, like those of other animals, have to do with our physiological well-being—food, shelter, physical well-being, and sex.[20] Basic needs can be potent forces in directing our behavior. When needs are not met, our efforts to satisfy them are important guiding forces in information reception and processing. To the individual who hasn't eaten for several days, for example, few message sources are likely to be as noteworthy, or *salient,* as those relating to food. A knowledge that unsatisfied needs often increase the salience attached to particular messages has led nutritionists to suggest that a good way to save money and diet is to shop for groceries after eating, rather than before.

The same pattern occurs with regard to our health. A headache or upset stomach, which is readily dismissed by persons who believe themselves to be well, may become the focus of great attention and concern for persons who believe they may be ill.

Other needs or motives, including social contact, reality exploration and comprehension, socialization, diversion, entertainment, and play, have to do with our spiritual, psychological, social, and communicative well-being.[21] Perhaps the most basic of these needs has to do with maintaining and developing our identity and self-concept.[22] All of us want to be seen positively, as worthy, desirable, competent, and respectable. There are, of course, differences between us as to the particular qualities for which we wish others to value us. Some of us aspire to be seen as creative, intelligent, professionally competent, and an occupational success. Being seen as religious, honest, honorable, or empathetic may be more important to others. Some of us would prefer to be admired for our leadership capacity; others wish to be respected for their loyalty as followers, and so on.

Personal, social, and communicative needs play an important role in selection, interpretation, and retention. Their role has been highlighted by scholars who focus on the "uses and gratifications" of mass media.[23] This work helps substantiate the view that there can be a direct relationship between particular unsatisfied, or ungratified, needs and resulting patterns of exposure to mass media programs and other message sources.

Attitudes, Beliefs, and Values

The attitudes, preferences, and predispositions one has about particular topics, persons, or situations also play a critical role in information-receiving activities and outcomes. For instance, people will generally attend to and be favorably disposed toward messages, sources, and interpretations that support their present views before they consider nonsupportive messages, sources, or conclusions.[24] The person who supports candidate X for a particular elective office is likely to pay far more attention to articles and political ads and sources of new information about that candidate than he or she will to items about candidate Y or Z. And such a person is also likely to spend time talking politics with others who share his or her view.

Values is a term used to refer to basic principles that we live by—our sense of what we ought and ought not do in our relations with the environment and one another. As with attitudes and beliefs, values influence selection, interpretation, and retention. Individuals who are opposed to abortion, for instance, are likely to take notice of and have strong reactions to those who advocate a "prochoice" position.

There are instances where messages that are likely to be interpreted as inconsistent and nonsupportive of our attitudes, beliefs, or values can lead to *more,* rather than *less,* attention and interest. We may devote attention and effort to converting individuals who espouse beliefs or values that differ from our own. Following a similar logic, we sometimes spend more time reflecting upon people and events that trouble us than on those that reassure and comfort us, perhaps because we have come to take the latter for granted.

Goals

Most of us are at best only partially aware of our needs, attitudes, beliefs, and values. In contrast, we consciously set our *goals.*

When an individual decides to pursue a particular plan, career, personal relationship, or personal challenge, that goal serves to direct his or her attention toward certain information sources and away from others, as suggested in Figure 4.3.

If a woman has the goal of driving from Princeton, New Jersey, to JFK Airport in New York City to catch a specific flight, this objective plays a major role in guiding information selection, interpretation, and retention. On the way to the airport, she must process messages concerning the location, direction, and rate of speed of her car and other vehicles in the vicinity. She must also attend to, interpret, and remember the road markings and signs that provide pertinent information and those that indicate the way to the airport. The gauges, instruments, and other controls of the car must also be monitored. Additionally, the driver must take account of weather conditions, time remaining before arrival at the final destination, location of the long-term parking area, the proper terminal, the flight number, the seat assignment, and so on. Until the goal is achieved and the individual is comfortably seated aboard the airplane, a substantial amount of the person's information-receiving effort is influenced by the commitment to the self-determined goal of catching a plane.

When an individual sets the goal of achieving certain competence in an area such as athletics, this objective shapes not only the messages to which the individual attends but also the interpretations of them that he or she makes. First, the goal increases the likelihood that the individual will expose himself or herself to communication sources and situations that pertain to athletics in general and his or her sport in particular. Secondly, the goal may well increase the individual's contact with other people interested in a similar activity, and this will have an additional influence on information reception. The demands of physical fitness may also play an important role in determining how information about food, drinking, smoking, health, and drugs will be attended to, interpreted, and remembered.

Figure 4.3
At any point in time, one's goals have a direct and profound effect on information selection, interpretation, and retention.
© spirit of america, 2014.
Shutterstock, Inc.

In a similar manner, a decision to pursue a particular career—to become a medical doctor, for instance—directs one's attention toward certain messages and away from others. The aspiring doctor is influenced by his or her goal toward knowledge based in physiology, anatomy, and chemistry and away from information pertinent to students of engineering, business administration, and journalism. Acquiring appropriate interpretations for these information sources is a priority until the goal is achieved or revised. A change of goals often also implies a change in information processing.

Capability

Our level of intelligence, previous experience with a particular topic area, and facility with language have an important impact on the kinds of messages we attend to and the manner in which we interpret and retain them. The probability of a person who speaks only English spending much time listening to Spanish radio broadcasts, watching French television programming, or reading Russian publications is naturally very low, simply because he or she lacks the capability of meaningfully processing the information. By the same token, it is unlikely that an individual who has no quantitative or research background will read articles in technical or scholarly journals. While the individual may possess the intellectual potential, his or her lack of familiarity with research and with the technical language used in the publications affects potential interest and comprehension, not to mention retention.

Use

We attend to and devote effort to understand and remember messages we think we will need or be able to use. The learning of language offers an excellent example. It is a virtual certainty that children will learn to speak the language of those around them. For the most part, this learning occurs irrespective of whether there are efforts at formal instruction. We attend to, learn to interpret, and retain messages about how to use spoken language because it is essential to our participation in most human activities.

In school we attend to and retain a large quantity of information on a variety of topics that may have no immediate personal relevance. Were it not for the opportunities and requirements to "rehearse" and "use" this retained knowledge to demonstrate course mastery on exams and quizzes, much less information would be remembered.

The same principle operates in many other domains. To the individual who is thinking about purchasing a new automobile, statistics such as safety ratings, estimated miles per gallon, and price suddenly become much more salient and far easier to remember than they were prior to the decision to shop for a new car.

Communication Style

Communication style can influence information reception in two ways: first, depending on our habits and preferences, we may be drawn to or may actively avoid the opportunity to deal with other people. People who are shy or apprehensive about engaging in verbal communication in a group setting, for example, may avoid such circumstances whenever possible.[25] Such an individual might prefer to watch a television show on health or consult an Internet site for information on a particular illness, rather than ask a doctor for information. Even when a person with this style of communication makes an effort to take part in interpersonal situations, he or she may be uncomfortable. This discomfort may well affect the way he or she attends to, interprets, and retains information.

A less direct influence of our communication style on information reception has to do with the manner in which we present ourselves to others. The way we "come across" to those with whom we interact can have a substantial impact on the way they react to us, and this will influence both the quality and quantity of information they make available. People who are highly talkative, for instance, often have less verbal information available to them than they otherwise might, because the people with whom they converse are often limited in their interest and in the time available to speak. Various aspects of our interpersonal style—our greetings, tone, word choice, level of openness, dress, and appearance—also have an impact on the messages other people make available to us, and this, in turn, has a direct bearing on our selection, interpretation, and retention.

Experience and Habit

Many of our information reception tendencies develop as a result of our experiences. These "communication habits" are no doubt the major guiding influence in how we select, interpret, or retain messages at any moment in time. Whether one thinks of reading a daily newspaper, watching a particular television show, exchanging pleasantries with an acquaintance on the way to work, checking our e-mail or cell phones throughout the day, or arguing with a friend or family member, our previous experiences, and the communication patterns we have developed as a result of these experiences, have a definite influence on our message reception. See Figure 4.4.

MESSAGE (INFORMATION) INFLUENCES

In addition to factors associated with *receivers,* characteristics of the information, or *message,* also have a major impact on selection, interpretation, and retention. Five particularly important considerations are origin, mode, physical character, organization, and novelty.

Figure 4.4
Glance at the items in the illustration to the left for five to ten seconds, close the book, and list the items that you can remember on a sheet of paper. When you compare the resulting list with the picture, it is obvious that many items were forgotten and others were perhaps never noticed in the first place. Further study of those things noticed and remembered, and those not, can underscore aspects of the information reception process, the impact of memory on selection and retention of new information, and the complexity of information processing. Generally speaking, in any situation what we notice and remember directly reflects our past experiences. Sometimes an item is taken note of precisely because we cannot relate to and identify it. In any case, those things noticed and remembered and those forgotten in any situation generally say as much or more about us—our past experiences, interests, priorities, hobbies, and so on—as they do about the actual information sources present in the environment.
© tovovan, 2014. Shutterstock, Inc.

Origin

Some of the messages we attend to have their origins in our physical environment. When we select an item on which to sit, identify a landmark as a guide to navigation, pick out an apartment in which to live, decide whether the temperature in our room is too high, or develop a theory of why apples fall from trees, we do so using information based on the objects, events, relationships, or phenomena in the physical environment.

We also make use of information we create ourselves through *intrapersonal* communication. When we listen to and think about what we have said to someone else, try to recall our knowledge about a particular topic, talk to ourselves, or look at ourselves in a mirror before leaving for an important engagement, we are dealing with information of which we ourselves are the source. We also use messages we ourselves create to assess our own internal feelings. Our sense of illness, fear, happiness, frustration, confusion, excitement, pain, and anxiety result from information that originates in our own physiological functioning.

Certainly the great majority of information of significance to us in our environment arises either directly or indirectly from the activities of other persons—through *interpersonal communication.* Often these messages originate in face-to-face interaction with others. Other interpersonal messages are the product of the activities of people separated from us in either time or space or both, transported to us by means of various communication media. A favorite television program, the evening news, an e-mail, or a text message from a friend, a best-selling novel, the morning paper, a cherished painting, or the latest CD by a favorite group can satisfy some of the same needs as face-to-face encounters, though the originator and receiver of the information are separated from one another physically.

In many circumstances we are limited as to which of these message sources we can use. If, for example, we wish to find out the temperature in Tokyo last night, we have little choice but to rely on messages provided by other people through technology. If we want to know how we feel about some situation facing us tomorrow, we rely on information we create ourselves. If we need to determine the exact temperature of our bath water, that information can be best derived by placing a thermometer in water.

There are many other instances in which we can choose among these sources. We can seek an answer to the question, "Is it hot in here?" using any of these sources: We can make a determination based on our personal "feelings"; we can ask the opinion of one or several other people; or we can use a nearby thermometer. A similar situation occurs when we undertake a project such as figuring out how to set up a new computer. We may choose to tackle the chore ourselves making use of the manufacturer's instructions. We could seek the assistance of a friend, or we may "dig right in" without consulting the instructions, relying on our own resources and prior experience with similar projects. Or, we can use a combination of these information sources.

The availability or lack of availability of various message sources has an obvious and direct impact upon the way in which we attend to, interpret, and retain information. Individuals may vary in terms of their preferences for particular types of sources; however, when there is a choice many of us rely on "self-created" messages first. That is, if we think we already have the information necessary in a particular circumstance, we may go no further. When we feel we lack the internal resources to make sense of or handle a particular situation on our own, we turn to other sources. For instance, when we enter an electronics store to shop for particular items, we will probably go directly to the shelves where we expect to find them. If, however, the store is an unfamiliar one, or the items are not where we expected, we are likely to look around for signs to help us navigate or to ask a clerk for assistance.

Mode

Information reception varies depending upon whether visual, tactile, auditory, gustatory, or olfactory modes are involved. In any number of situations, a touch or reassuring embrace will be taken note of and interpreted in quite a different way than spoken words of encouragement. In such an instance, actions may speak louder than words. Likewise the smell of decaying garbage may be a much more poignant message than a newspaper story about the consequences of a garbage strike or a description of the odor from a friend who witnessed the accumulating trash. In other circumstances, however, words may be extremely important, such as in a brainstorming session, a term paper, a letter to a friend, a legal brief, or a debate.

Physical Characteristics

Physical characteristics such as size, color, brightness, and intensity can also be important to information processing. In general, symbols, actions, objects, or events that are large or prominent attract more attention than those which are not. A bright light is more salient than a dim light; large type is more noticeable than small type.

Actions and circumstances that have major consequences for large numbers of people—a fire, natural disaster, or international conflict for instance— are more likely to be taken note of than less important events of less widespread impact. These events appear on the front page of the newspaper or as lead stories on the evening news. The extent of their impact is a major factor in the information-reception processes of reporters and editors, who recognize that readers and viewers are also likely to attend to and be interested in these events.

Other things being equal, messages that have vivid color, brightness, or intensity are more apt to be noticed and taken account of than those lacking these characteristics. A four-color advertisement, a brightly colored dress or jacket, or a high intensity light are likely to be attended to before objects lacking these attributes. The intensity of potential visual or verbal messages can also be an important consideration in message reception.

Organization

A good deal of research in the area of persuasion has been directed toward determining the way in which the ordering of ideas or opinions affects reception. Research suggests that when we are presented with a series of items, we devote greatest attention to the items listed first. As a result, this information has the greatest likelihood of becoming a part of our long-term memory.[26] When asked to recall items from a list after it has been completed, individuals do best with those things presented near the beginning (primacy) and those near the end (recency). The items at the end are thought to be recalled because they are still a part of one's short-term memory, while those at the beginning are remembered because the information can be retrieved from long-term memory.[27]

The significance of organization on information reception is evident in a variety of settings. Within a picture or a report the arrangement of elements can

Figure 4.5
People, objects, events, or patterns that are unique or novel often grab our attention far more than the usual, commonplace, or predictable. Barbara Cartland reports, for example, that during the two years after the Mona Lisa was stolen from the Louvre in Paris in 1911, more people came to stare at the place in the museum where the famous painting had hung than had come to see the actual painting during the 12 previous years.

Niagara Falls provides another interesting case in point. One of the first things that strikes most visitors to the falls is the pervasive sound created by the pounding of the falls to the river below. To residents of the area, however, the noise goes generally unnoticed. Ironically, it was the sudden absence of the thundering falls during a hard freeze in the winter of 1936 and previously in 1909 that reportedly awoke the residents.

Source: Barbara Cartland, *Barbara Cartland's Book of Useless Information.*
© Songquan Deng, 2014. Shutterstock, Inc.

have a substantial impact on the overall impression created. The ordering of material within a database is also an important factor in whether and how that material will be used. Even the arrangement of foods at a grocery store often has an impact on the communication process. How many times do we pick up grocery items we hadn't intended to because we noticed them while on our way to the place in the store where bread or milk were shelved?

Novelty

Information that is novel, unfamiliar, or unusual stands out, "grabbing our attention" if only for the moment. While we may generally devote very little attention to the color of automobiles, a bright pink or yellow car is likely to "catch the eye" of even the most preoccupied motorist.

The same principle applies in other areas such as dress, language, appearance, or greetings, to which we may devote little conscious attention unless these message sources dramatically violate what we have come to expect. An unfamiliar foreign language, unusual dress, or a normally tidy room in disarray often become very salient to us. Other examples are provided in Figures 4.5 and 4.6. Though we are typically only somewhat aware when we engage in a

Figure 4.6
Unusual objects, events, individuals, or actions often command attention and interest.
© Havoc, 2014. Shutterstock, Inc., © Jeffrey J. Coleman, 2014. Shutterstock, Inc.

ritualistic handshake greeting, we certainly do take note when the other person squeezes our hand too firmly, too loosely, or continues to shake long after the conventional number of pumps.

SOURCE INFLUENCES

Some of our most interesting and complex information-reception decisions involve interpersonal sources. Why do we listen to and believe some people more than others? Why are we more influenced by some people than others? Our decisions depend on a number of factors including: *proximity, attractiveness, similarity, credibility, authoritativeness, motivation, intent, delivery, status, power,* and *authority.*

Proximity

Our distance from a source can have a major influence on the likelihood of our attending to particular messages. We are more likely to be exposed to sources that are close at hand than to those that are farther away.[28] The closer we are, the less time, effort, and money that must be expended to engage in communication.

For example, if we walk into a library to find a reference and must pass by the librarian, we may decide to ask his or her advice simply because of proximity. For this same reason, we are far more likely to attend to the actions and reactions of a next-door neighbor or colleague at work than to those of persons who live a block away or work in the next building.

The significance of distance as a factor in communication is highlighted by considering the function of technology. By means of television, radio, newspapers, magazines, books, cell phones, and the Internet, information from thousands of miles away becomes available without leaving the comfort of one's home. It is, in fact, the ease of access to television, e-mail, online services, phones, and other technology that has helped to make these technologies and the information they transport such a central part of our lives.

Physical and Social Attraction and Similarity

The way in which we engage in interpersonal communication often has a great deal to do with how attractive we believe a particular message source to be. Particularly when we first meet an individual, we react largely to his or her general appearance. If, based on first impressions, we are attracted to the person, it is likely that we will pay increased attention to, remember, and attach special significance to his or her words. In this way, attraction plays a significant, though often subtle, role in influencing the nature of communication.

Though we tend to think of attractiveness primarily in physical terms, we often find people appealing for other reasons as well. An individual who appears to be friendly, warm, empathetic, and concerned, and who expresses interest in or respect for us, may be quite attractive to us as a social companion. Like physical attractiveness, *social attractiveness* also can be an important influence in information reception.

Similarity is another factor of significance in communication. The more like a source we are, or believe ourselves to be, the more likely we are to pay special attention to that person and what he or she says.[29] Sometimes similarities that interest us in others are basic characteristics such as gender, level of education, age, religion, ethnic background, hobbies, or language capacity. In other instances, we are drawn to people because they share our needs, attitudes, goals, or values.

The influence of similarity on reception is vividly illustrated by the great impact of our peer group, beginning in our early school years. Our peers play a significant role in shaping our reactions to clothing, movies, music, school, books, various occupations, and also to our parents, friends, and acquaintances. Preferences for persons with similar cultural, religious, racial, occupational, political, and educational backgrounds continue to influence communication throughout our lifetimes.

Credibility and Authoritativeness

We are likely to attend to and retain information from sources we believe to be experienced and/or knowledgeable.[30] Certain people—or groups—may be viewed as credible and authoritative, regardless of the topic. Information provided by medical doctors, clergy, or professors, for example, may be regarded as more noteworthy than messages from people with other vocations, even on topics that are outside the professional's areas of expertise. Similarly, many of us afford actors, television personalities, politicians, and other people who are in the public eye particular attention and credibility. Thus, the actor speaking on politics or the medical doctor lecturing on religion may be given more than the usual level of attention by receivers.

In some instances, the attention and credibility accorded a particular person depends upon the topic in question. Other things being equal, we are more likely to attend to and retain information on international affairs presented by a network news commentator than to messages on the same topic offered by our next-door neighbor. When the topic is insurance, however, we may well attach more weight to the views of a neighbor who has twenty-five years' experience working in that field than to reports provided on television.

Motivation and Intent

The manner in which we react to a particular interpersonal message source also depends on the way we explain his or her actions to ourselves.[31] Depending on what motives we attribute to an individual, our response may vary substantially. If we assume a person intends to inform or help us, we are likely to react in quite a different way than if we believe the intention is to persuade or deceive us.

Delivery

The manner in which a source delivers a message can be an important influence in information reception. Among the factors that come into play in delivery of spoken messages are volume, rate of speaking, pitch, pronunciation, and the use of pauses. Other visual factors, such as gestures, facial expressions, and eye contact may be significant.

Status, Power, and Authority

The presence or lack of *status*—position or rank—can also be important in determining how likely it is that an information source or message will be selected and acted on. The *power* or *authority* of a source—the extent to which the source is capable of dispensing rewards or punishment for selecting, remembering, and interpreting messages in a particular way—is also influential in communication.

Generally speaking, parents, teachers, employers, supervisors, or others who have status, power, or authority relative to us have a better than average chance of obtaining our attention to their messages. The significance we attach to their role directs our attention to their words and actions in an effort to be aware of their opinions or to seek their favor. To the extent that we can be rewarded or punished through grades, money, favors, or praise for interpreting their messages in particular ways, we may be especially attentive.

TECHNOLOGICAL AND ENVIRONMENTAL INFLUENCES

Beyond the *receiver, information,* and *source, technology* and the *environment* also have a substantial impact on communication.

Technology

The technology, or channel, through which messages reach us can be a significant factor in information reception. Differences, such as whether messages are presented via print or electronically, film or videotape, radio broadcast or the spoken words of a friend, can have a direct, and in some cases obvious, influence. Simply in terms of availability, some technologies provide a greater likelihood of exposure to information than others. More people watch television than participate in chat rooms, and the size of both of these is much larger than the group that reads scholarly journals.

Of the various mass media, television has traditionally received the most attention among scholars. This interest is not surprising given the central role of television in the lives of most Americans. Even as early as the 1950s, families viewed television on the average of four and one-half hours a day. That number jumped to over five hours in the 1960s, over six hours in the 1970s, nearly seven hours in the 1980s.[32] Current figures indicate that White households view an average of 7.2 hours of television each day and African American households 10.7 hours per day.[33]

In terms of exposure to messages alone, television is clearly a major force in the lives of most Americans. As noted in the classic summary of a National Institute of Mental Health report, *Television and Behavior,* television is an influential source of information processing.

> The simplest representations (on television) are literal visual and auditory pictures of something in the real world, for example, a car moving along a highway. To process this information, children probably depend on the same perceptual and cognitive skills they use in processing information in the real world. . . . At the next level are the forms and conventions that do not have real-world counterparts. Some of them are analogs of real-world experiences. . . . For example, a "zoom in," in which the object in front of the camera seems to get larger and more focused, is similar to moving closer to something in real life. But some effects, for example, slow motion, do not appear in the real world, and children—and others who are unfamiliar with television—must learn what they mean.
>
> Once they are learned, these media conventions can be used by people in their own thinking. For example, children may learn to analyze a complex stimulus into its smaller parts by watching the camera zoom in and out. The forms can take on meaning, sometimes as a result of associations seen on television.[34]

RESEARCH PROFILE

Mobile Communicating • James Katz

Have you ever seen two people having dinner in a restaurant talking to other people on their cell phones? Professor Katz's research on mobile communication explores the implications of the public use of new communication technologies.

• • •

We often do not realize how dramatically ordinary technologies like the telephone can affect our lives. Yet they give us powers of communication that would seem superhuman to those who lived in earlier eras. Just think for a moment about the way mobile phones make a difference in people's lives. This question is the focus of my research.

The mobile phone has improved the lives of many people. But one communication process, known as the "actor–observer" paradox, leads to some uncomfortable moments when people use mobile phones around their friends. The person who wishes to use the mobile phone (the actor) may do so despite being with someone else because she or he feels that the call is important. That is

the caller feels that she or he has a good and necessary reason to make or take the call, and does so with the expectation that others should understand and accept this necessity. On the other hand, the people around the user (the observer) will view the situation differently. Observers may feel that the mobile phone user is being selfish and self-indulgent, and is failing to respect the moral conventions of polite society.

The public use of mobile phones is likely to remain a source of normative conflict since the sources of irritation are not merely conventional. Instead, they seem to go to the core of human cognitive processes. The result could be that as mobile phone users pursue their private pleasures of conversation there will be a reduction in the *civility* and *personal engagement* in public. The enjoyment of being in public space, or having an evening with friends, could be diminished to the detriment of all. By using research, we can understand just how big a problem this is and what might be done about it. Think about these issues the next time you answer your phone!

The report also indicates that the rapid movement and visual and audio contrasts presented by television are particularly salient to very young viewers, who often become "passive consumers of audio-visual thrills."[35] Much of what can be said of television in this connection can be applied also to other technologies that use screens to display information.

Twenty years ago, e-mail, Web pages, chat rooms, online vendors and auctions, and the many other services now afforded by the Internet were unheard of. In 1997, 18.6 percent of U.S. homes had computers with active Internet connections. By 2003, that number had grown to 54.6 percent. With this remarkable growth has come a significant new communication medium—one that is capable of providing personalized and specialized information to meet user needs.

The Environment

Context.   The manner in which a particular person or event is reacted to depends on whether we are at home or on vacation, at work or at school or engaged in a leisure activity. It will depend also on whether the messages are received in an office, a church, a bedroom, a classroom, or an auditorium. It is not difficult to think of examples of how the same message would be interpreted very differently depending on the context in which it was encountered. See Figure 4.7.

The presence of others often has a very direct bearing on how we select as well as interpret and retain information. How we want to be seen, how we think other people see us, what we believe others expect from us, and what we think they think about the situation we are in are among the considerations that shape the way we react in social situations.

Figure 4.7
The context or setting in which potential information sources are encountered can be an important factor influencing whether and how messages are selected, interpreted, and remembered.
© bloomua, 2014.
Shutterstock, Inc.

If we are in the company of colleagues or friends, we may pay particular attention to the people, events, and circumstances they attend to. In our effort to decide how well we liked a particular movie, lecture, painting, or person, the reactions of other persons are often of major significance to our own judgments. Sometimes, we conform our own information processing to that of others for appearances only; in many other instances the influence is more subtle and far-reaching.

Repetition.   We are likely to take into account and remember messages that are repeated often. Advertising slogans and jingles, lyrics of popular songs, multiplication tables, and birth dates of family members stand out in our minds, in part because they have been repeated so often. Repetition also contributes to our learning our native language, our parents' and friends' opinions, the slang and jargon of our associates, and the accent of our geographic region.

Consistency and Competition.   When a person has been exposed over a long period of time to one religious orientation, one political philosophy, or one set of values, there is a likelihood that the individual will come to select and accept messages consistent with that position. *Brainwashing* is the extreme example of this sort of communication phenomenon. In such circumstances, the individual is bombarded with messages that advocate a particular position, and information supporting alternative points of view is systematically eliminated from the environment. When coupled with the promise of reward (or absence of punishment) and consistency, the lack of competitive messages becomes a powerful shaping force influencing the probability of message selection and the manner of interpretation and retention.

In considerably less extreme forms, the educational process makes use of these same principles. Math, language, reading, and spelling are taught not only through repetition but also through consistency. The arrangement of classroom furniture and the use of examinations, lectures, books, and homework assignments are among the strategies typically used to minimize the influence of competing messages.

AN ACTIVE AND COMPLEX PROCESS

Selection, interpretation, and reception are basic to message reception, and reception is fundamental to communicating. These activities are influenced by any number of the factors discussed in this chapter, making information processing one of the most active and complex facets of human communication.

Morton Hunt makes this point eloquently in discussing the opening sentence of Gibbon's *Decline and Fall of the Roman Empire:*

> "In the second century of the Christian era, the Empire of Rome comprehended the fairest part of the earth, and the most civilized portion of mankind."
>
> A reader who finds this sentence perfectly intelligible does so not because Gibbon was a lucid stylist but because he or she knows when the Christian era began, understands the concept of "empire," is familiar enough with history to recognize the huge sociocultural phenomenon known as "Rome," has enough information about world geography so that the phrase "the fairest part of the earth" produces a number of images in the mind, and, finally, can muster a whole congeries of ideas about the kinds of civilization that then existed. What skill, to elicit that profusion of associations with those few well-chosen cues—but what a performance by the reader! One hardly knows which to admire more. . . .[36]

Without doing any injustice to Hunt's intent, we could extend the point to apply equally to the impressive accomplishments of a listener in a personal, group, technologically mediated, or public setting, or to the observer of visual images in an art gallery, a baseball game, or a television program.

IMPLICATIONS AND APPLICATIONS

- Reception is a fundamental aspect of our communication behavior—an aspect to which we often pay little attention.
- Listening and observing are our primary means for gathering information about the people, events, problems, and opportunities in our environment.
- Listening and observing involve selection. While we attend to and attach importance to some people, circumstances, and objects, we inevitably ignore others.
- Our selections, interpretations, and memories of messages are subjective and are influenced by what we, personally, bring to the situation, as well as by available information, sources, technology, and environmental influences.
- Our personal characteristics, previous experiences, and habits have a major influence on what we see, hear, understand, believe, and remember.
- Competence in listening and observing requires conscious effort, an awareness of factors influencing the process, and an understanding of ourselves and our own capabilities, needs, attitudes, values, and goals.

SUMMARY

In this chapter, our focus has been on the nature of information reception, and the processes involved in sensing and making sense of the people, objects, and circumstances in our environment. Individuals play an active role in this process though they may have little awareness that it is taking place.

Selection, interpretation, and retention are primary facets of information reception. Collectively, they are the processes by which we create, transform, and use information to relate to our environment and one another.

Selection involves the selective attention to particular environmental information sources from all those to which an individual is exposed. Interpretation consists of the transformation of those messages into a form that has value and utility for the individual. Retention involves short- and long-term, semantic and episodic, memory. In actual operation, selection, interpretation, and retention are very much interrelated activities.

A number of factors influence selection, interpretation, and retention. Many of them have to do with the receiver and his or her needs, attitudes, beliefs, values, goals, capabilities, uses, style, experience, and habits.

Other factors that influence information reception have to do with messages—their origin, mode, physical characteristics, novelty, and organization. Sources also have an impact on reception, through their proximity, attractiveness, credibility, motivation, intention, delivery, status, power, and authority. Message reception may also be affected by factors related to technology and the environment.

ENDNOTES

1. See Stuart M. Albert, Lee Alan Becker, and Timothy C. Brock, "Familiarity, Utility, and Supportiveness as Determinants of Information Receptivity," *Journal of Personality and Social Psychology*, Vol. 14, 1970, pp. 292–301. D. E. Broadbent, "A Mechanical Model for Human Attention and Immediate Memory," *Psychological Review*, Vol. 64, 1957, pp. 205–215. Robert T. Craig, "Information Systems Theory and Research: An Overview of Individual Information Processing," in *Communication Yearbook 3*. Ed. by Dan Nimmo (New Brunswick, NJ: Transaction, International Communication Association, 1979), pp. 99–120. D. Deutsch and J. A. Deutsch, "Attention: Some Theoretical Considerations," *Psychological Review*, Vol. 70, 1963, pp. 80–90. Lewis Donohew and Philip Palmgreen, "An Investigation of 'Mechanisms' of Information Selection," *Journalism Quarterly*, Vol. 48, 1971, pp. 624–639. Lewis Donohew and Philip Palmgreen, "Reappraisal of Dissonance and the Selective Exposure Hypothesis," *Journalism Quarterly*, Vol. 48, 1971, pp. 412–420. Anne M. Treisman, "Strategies and Models of Selective Attention," *Psychological Review*, Vol. 76, No. 3, 1969, pp. 282–299. Sally Planalp and Dean E. Hewes, "A Cognitive Approach to Communication Theory: Cognito Ergo Dico?" in *Communication Yearbook 5*. Ed. by Michael Burgoon (New Brunswick, NJ: Transaction, 1982), pp. 49–78. Klaus Krippendorff, "The Past of Communication's Hoped-For Future," *Journal of Communication*, Vol. 43, 1993, pp. 34–44.

2. Samuel L. Becker, "Visual Stimuli and the Construction of Meaning," in *Visual Learning, Thinking and Communication*. Ed. by Bikkar S. Randhawa (New York: Academic Press, 1978), pp. 39–60.

3. Broadbent, 1957.

4. Craig, 1979, p. 102.

5. See Norman F. Dixon, *Preconscious Processing* (London: Wiley, 1981).

6. The issue of *what* is recalled under hypnosis and drugs is relatively controversial. While it was long believed that the information remembered was in its "original, unaltered" form, recent studies have suggested that often it is a transformed, elaborated, and often distorted version, changed by time and circumstance. For a discussion of these issues, see Elizabeth Loftus, *Memory* (Reading, MA: Addison-Wesley, 1980), pp. 54–62.

7. Craig, 1979, p. 103.

8. Morton Hunt, *The Universe Within* (New York: Simon & Schuster, 1982), p. 85.

9. Hunt, 1982, p. 86.

10. Hunt, 1982, p. 86.

11. For a more detailed description of information-processing stages and dynamics see Geoffrey R. Loftus and Elizabeth F. Loftus, *Human Memory: The Processing of Information* (Hillsdale, NJ: Lawrence Erlbaum), 1976; and Peter H. Lindsay and Donald A. Norman, *Human Information Processing* (New York: Academic, 1977).

12. Hunt, 1982, p. 104.

13. G. Loftus and E. Loftus, 1976, p. 8. The authors provide a useful overview and model of information processing and memory in their "Introduction." See also Hunt, 1982, especially Ch. 3, and Elizabeth Loftus, 1980, especially Ch. 2.

14. G. Loftus and E. Loftus, 1976, p. 8.

15. George Mandler, *Cognitive Psychology: An Essay in Cognitive Science* (Hillsdale, NJ: Lawrence Erlbaum, 1985), pp. 92–94. Lists of distinguishing characteristics are presented here in shortened form.

16. E. Tulving, *Elements of Episodic Memory* (Oxford, England: Oxford University Press, 1983). See discussion in Mandler, 1985, pp. 106–107; and Gillian Cohen, *Memory in the Real World* (Hillsdale, NJ: Lawrence Erlbaum, 1989), pp. 114–115.

17. Cohen, 1989, pp. 114–115.

18. Cohen, 1989, pp. 114–115.

19. Based on a listing and discussion by Cohen, 1989, pp. 217–221.

20. One of the most widely cited classifications in recent years was provided in the writings of Abraham Maslow, "A Theory of Human Motivation," *Psychological Review,* Vol. 50, 1943, pp. 370–396. The framework differentiates between basic biological needs and "higher order" psychological and social needs.

21. Maslow, 1950.

22. Maslow, 1950.

23. See Elihu Katz, Jay G. Blumler, and Michael Gurevitch, "Utilization of Mass Communication by the Individual," in *The Uses of Mass Communications,* Jay G. Blumler and Elihu Katz, eds. (Beverly Hills, CA: Sage, 1974), pp. 22–23; and Alan M. Rubin, "Audience Activity and Media Use," *Communication Monographs,* Vol. 60, 1993, pp. 98–105.

24. Lawrence R. Wheeless, "The Effects of Attitude, Credibility, and Homophily on Selective Exposure to Information," *Speech Monographs,* Vol. 41, April 1974, pp. 329–338.

25. Cf. Philip Zimbardo, *Shyness* (Reading, MA: Addison-Wesley); James C. McCroskey, "Oral Communication Apprehension: A Summary of Recent Theory and Research," *Human Communication Research,* Vol. 4, 1977, pp. 78–96; Gerald M. Phillips and Nancy J. Metzger, "The Reticent Syndrome: Some Theoretical Considerations about Etiology and Treatment," *Speech Monographs,* Vol. 40, 1973; James C. McCroskey, "The Communication Apprehension Perspective," in *Avoiding Communication: Shyness, Reticence, and Communication Apprehension.* Ed. by John A. Daly and James C. McCroskey (Beverly Hills, CA: Sage, 1984), pp. 12–38

26. Loftus, 1980, pp. 24–25.

27. Loftus, 1980, pp. 24–25.

28. Nan Lin, *The Study of Human Communication* (New York: Bobbs-Merrill, 1973), pp. 44–46.

29. Wheeless, 1974.

30. Carl I. Hovland and W. Weiss, "The Influence of Source Credibility on Communication Effectiveness," *Public Opinion Quarterly,* Vol. 15, 1951, pp. 635–650; for a discussion of the role of credibility in communication see James C. McCroskey, *An Introduction to Rhetorical Communication* (Englewood Cliffs, NJ: Prentice Hall, 1986), especially Ch. 4.

31. The way we explain behavior to ourselves is the focus of work in an area called *attribution theory.* See David R. Seibold and Brian H. Spitzberg, "Attribution Theory and Research: Formalization, Review, and Implications for Communication," in *Progress in Communication Sciences,* Vol. 3. Ed. by Brenda Dervin and M. J. Voight (Norwood, NJ: Ablex, 1981), pp. 85–125.

32. "What Is TV Doing to America?" *U.S. News and World Report,* August 2, 1982, p. 29.

33. Bill Carter, "Two Upstart Networks Getting Black Viewers," *New York Times,* Oct. 7, 1996, p. c16.

34. *Television and Behavior: Ten Years of Scientific Progress and Implications for the Eighties,* Vol. 1: Summary Report (Rockville, MD: National Institute of Mental Health, 1982), p. 24.

35. *Television and Behavior,* 1982, p. 26.

36. Hunt, 1982, pp. 119–121.

Verbal Messages

IN THIS CHAPTER

Why . . .
- Language and reality are sometimes mistaken for one another.
- We follow rules when we engage in conversations.
- Stereotypes about which gender is most talkative are misleading.
- Verbal messages say as much about our relationships as they do the topic of conversation.
- Metacommunication is important.

Message Production
- An Illustration

Encoding and Decoding

Process- versus Meaning-Centered Models of Communication

The Nature of Language
- Physiological Factors
- Cognitive Factors

Language Acquisition

Representation
- Language and Reality
- Limitations of Language for Representation

Conversation
- Negotiation of Meanings
- Rules and Rituals

- Language and Gender
- Content and Relationship
- Metacommunication

Social and Public Communication

- Production and Distribution of Social Realities

Implications and Applications

Summary

MESSAGE PRODUCTION

Producing messages is as fundamental to our lives as receiving them. Virtually every aspect of our behavior—our language, tone of voice, appearance, eyes, actions, even our use of space and time—is a potential source of information that may be selected for attention, interpreted, remembered, and acted upon by others.

An Illustration

As a way to introduce the topic of message production, consider the following scenario involving a job interview:

It's time to get serious about finding a job. A friend calls your attention to an advertisement online for a position that sounds interesting at a company whose name you recognize. You prepare a resume and send it off with a cover letter.

Several days later you get a call and an interview is scheduled.

You decide that it's wise to spend time preparing. You gather some information on the organization and plan what you'll say if they ask why you want the position and why you are not working now. You also make up a list of questions you would like to ask them and give some thought to the kind of impression you would like to create.

When the day of the interview arrives, you dress well and arrive a few minutes early. You feel well-prepared and are ready to make a good impression. When the interviewer arrives, you greet her enthusiastically with "Hello. How are you?", shake her hand, and take a seat next to the desk. You take a deep breath, hoping that will help you relax.

As the questions begin to come, you try to respond in a way that will lead the interviewer to see you as comfortable yet not overly informal, interested but not overly assertive, composed yet spontaneous, self-assured but not arrogant, interested in the job but not desperate.

After what seems like about an hour, she says she has no more questions, and asks if you do. You inquire about starting salary, opportunities for advancement, and benefits—questions you selected because they would yield information you needed, while creating the impression of competence and alertness.

After brief responses, she thanks you for coming, and indicates that she will be in touch with you as soon as all the applicants for the position have been considered. You respond, "Thanks," get up, and leave.

Now let's examine the situation from the organization's point of view: The task of finding a qualified person was initiated long before the interview, with the collection of information and the preparation of the job description and advertisement. In a more general sense, the recruitment process actually began with the firm's advertising and public relations efforts over the years.

After screening many applications, the list of people to be interviewed was finalized. The goal of the interview itself was to create a positive, yet realistic, impression of the organization and the job and to evaluate candidates' suitability for the position.

Questions were asked from a standardized interview guide. They were designed to help probe candidates' technical qualifications, while giving the interviewer a sense of how much "homework" applicants had done to prepare for the interview, how composed and confident they were, how they approached problems, how they dealt with people, and how they felt about themselves. Typical interview questions include:

- How did you learn about the position?
- How much do you know about the company?
- Where did you go to school?
- What was your major? Why did you select that field?
- What experience have you had that is relevant to this job?
- What are your greatest strengths and weaknesses?
- What are you looking for in this position?
- What questions do you have about the job?
- What are your long-term career objectives?

ENCODING AND DECODING

In a situation such as the one described, each party is putting forth a good deal of effort to provide information and to create particular kinds of impressions. The individuals involved have specific goals in mind and communicate in ways designed to achieve them. This process—converting an idea into a message—is termed *encoding*. Some of the messages that become significant for others are intentionally encoded. Our hope is that the individuals for whom our messages are prepared will *decode* them—translate the message into an idea—more or less as we intend.

Even in circumstances like the job interview discussed previously—where participants have a clear idea of the meaning they want to convey through their messages—they are also likely to communicate information that is unintended. This happens no matter how well we plan or rehearse. An inappropriate greeting, evasiveness in answering a question, a shaky voice, an abrupt change of topic, a misused word, a poorly constructed phrase, the lack of eye contact, or a sweaty brow can easily have as much—or more—impact as the messages we try to encode intentionally.

The messages we produce fall into two broad categories: verbal and nonverbal. In this chapter, we will examine verbal messages in some detail. Nonverbal messages are the focus of the next chapter.

PROCESS- VERSUS MEANING-CENTERED MODELS OF COMMUNICATION

As we discussed in Chapter 3, many of the major models of communication emphasize the process of communication. These models focus on message transmission and are concerned with the channel, sender, receiver, noise, and feedback. Such models, and some of our discussion of verbal messages, focus on sending and receiving a message. Looking at communication in this way has several advantages. The models allow us to examine how messages may get lost or distorted in the communication process and how receivers may miss the message sent. For example, the phrase "brick red" may be used by someone interested in fashion. Someone uninterested in fashion may differentiate red from orange, but not attach specific labels to distinct shades of red. If someone uses a very specific color label, he or she may be greeted by a blank stare from others who are not concerned about this type of distinction.

Another view of communication focuses on communication as the generation of meaning. John Fiske describes this model by saying:

> For communication to take place I have to create a message out of signs. This message stimulates you to create a meaning for yourself that relates in some way to the meaning that I generated in my message in the first place. The more we share the same codes, the more we use the same sign systems, the closer our two "meanings" of the message will approximate.[1]

Note that this definition relies on concepts such as signs, codes, and meaning. In this view, messages are constructed of signs which produce meaning in interaction with receivers.[2] Codes are the systems into which signs are organized. This view emphasizes the meaning while the process model emphasizes the sender and receiver.

The theories we discuss in this chapter are examples of both the process and meaning-centered views of communication. Both viewpoints contribute to our understanding of the phenomenon of communication.

THE NATURE OF LANGUAGE

Verbal messages make use of alphanumeric language, one of humanity's most impressive accomplishments. About 10,000 distinct languages and dialects are in use today, and each is unique in some respects.[3] There are also a number of commonalities among languages. All spoken languages, for instance, make use of a distinction between vowels and consonants, and in nearly all languages the subject precedes the object in declarative sentences.[4] Every language has an identifiable pattern and set of rules relative to:

- *Phonology.* The way sounds are combined to form words
- *Syntax.* The way words are combined into sentences
- *Semantics.* The meanings of words on the basis of their relationship to one another and to elements in the environment
- *Pragmatics.* The way in which language is used in practice

Physiological Factors

Some general similarities among languages may be the result of a common ancestry. Major similarities, however, appear to be more the result of human physical and mental capacities. Although a number of animal species can produce auditory messages, even primates with their ability for vocalization lack the basic physiological capacity of humans.

As shown in Figure 5.1, the human larynx located at the upper end of the trachea or windpipe is strengthened by cartilage that supports the vocal cords. When air from the lungs passes over the vocal cords with a greater force than occurs during normal breathing, the cords vibrate. The vibrations that result are

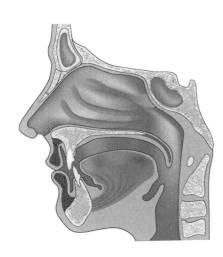

Figure 5.1
Human Sound Production The larynx is located at the upper end of the trachea or windpipe. Air passing through the vocal cords causes vibrations that produce human voice patterns. Tightening of the vocal cords produces high-pitched sounds; loosening the cords results in a lower pitch.
© Yoko Design, 2014. Shutterstock, Inc.

called *voicing*. As the vocal cords are tightened, the pitch of the voice rises; as they are loosened, the pitch lowers. The position of the tongue provides additional variation in sound production. As the air is projected with voice-producing force, it is affected by the vocal cords and the tongue, as well as by the lips, mouth, teeth, and jaw.

The position of the tongue, lips, and jaw are the primary factors involved in the creation of the vowel sounds in English. When the out-flowing breath creates friction against the teeth, lower lip, or the upper parts of the mouth or tongue, sounds such as the American English pronunciation of f, v, s, z, th, sh, and zh are produced. If the breath is stopped momentarily by movement of the lower lip or some part of the tongue, another sort of friction results, creating sounds such as that of p, b, t, d, k, and g. When the breath is rapidly and intermittently stopped, trills or flips result, which are associated with the pronunciation of rr in Spanish, and tt in words such as butter or letter in English. If the breath stream is stopped in the mouth such that it is forced through the nasal passages, the result is a nasal sound common to French and to the English pronunciation of b, m, d, n, and g.[5] Sounds of letters are combined to form words, and words to form phrases and sentences.

Cognitive Factors

Human physiology only partially explains the workings of the communication process. Controlling these mechanisms are the brain and nervous system, which enable us to sense, make sense of, and relate to our environment and one another. Here, the differences between humans and other animals are striking.

One example will help to illustrate this point. Studies of chimps and gorillas who have been taught American sign language indicate clearly that primates can be taught to use language. However, the total vocabulary of the most successful of these "students" was four hundred words. In contrast, the average human has a vocabulary nearly two hundred times that large.[6]

Findings from neurophysiological research have pointed to the importance of particular areas of the brain for linguistic functioning. Especially important in this regard are *Broca's Area* and *Wernicke's Area,* both of which are located in the left half or hemisphere of the brain.[7] See Figure 5.2. Research suggests that ideas or feelings that an individual wishes to vocalize are translated into an appropriate auditory pattern in Wernicke's Area and then transmitted to Broca's Area, which activates the electrical impulses needed to mobilize the voice-producing

Figure 5.2
Left Hemisphere of the
Human Brain
© okili77, 2014. Shutterstock, Inc.

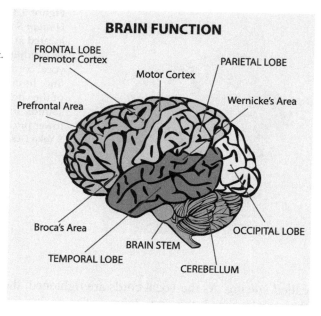

mechanisms and to create the intended vocalization.[8] This conclusion is supported by studies that have shown that damage to Broca's Area of the brain disturbs the production of speech but has much less impact on comprehension, whereas damage to Wernicke's Area disrupts all aspects of language use.[9]

LANGUAGE ACQUISITION

A good deal of attention has been devoted to determining precisely how and when we first develop competency in the use of language. Some linguists contend that the basic structure of language is innate in humans and that a child needs to learn only the surface details of the language spoken in his or her environment. Others see language acquisition as a part of the general development of the individual.[10] Both groups agree that interaction between the individual and the environment is essential to linguistic competence. Studies have demonstrated that without the capacity and opportunity to talk with others, no language capability develops.[11]

There are two broad perspectives on language development—the psycholinguistic approach and the sociolinguistic approach:[12]

1. *The psycholinguistic approach.* Early utterances—*protowords* (the forerunners of words) and words themselves—are based on a child's personalized understanding of the world. Language is a means for the expression of meanings he or she has learned.
2. *The sociolinguistic approach.* Language development occurs when a child experiences a need to communicate. Language is learned through social interaction and is a means for accommodating the demands of social life.

Studies of the first few months of life suggest that language acquisition begins with random "coos" and "giggles" in the presence of family members and other familiar persons, as illustrated in Figure 5.3. At age six to nine months, the "coos" and "giggles" are replaced by babbling sounds; and by eighteen months, most children can form a few simple words—dada, papa, mama, or nana.[13]

The speech patterns of others in the environment are important during this stage and throughout language acquisition. Generally, the speech of those

Child's Age	Coordination		Language
4 months	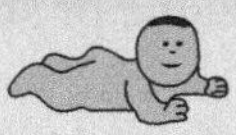	Holds head up.	Coos and chuckles when people play with him/her
6 to 9 months		Can sit alone and pull himself/herself up into a standing position.	Babbles continually, sounding like this: "gagagag; yayayaya; dadadada."
12 to 18 months		First stands alone, then walks along furniture, and, finally, walks alone.	Uses a few words, follows simple commands, and knows what "no" means.
18 to 21 months		Walking looks stiff and jerky, sits in a chair, can crawl down stairs, and throw a ball (clumsily).	Understands simple questions and begins to put two or three words together in sentences.
24 to 27 months		Runs well, but falls when making a quick turn. Can also walk up and down stairs.	Uses short sentences composed of words from a 300–400 word vocabulary.
30 to 33 months		Has good hand and finger coordination and can manipulate objects well.	Vocabulary increases in size, and three and four word sentences are prevalent; language begins to sound adult like.
36 to 39 months		Runs smoothly and negotiates sharp turns; walks stairs by alternating feet; can ride a tricycle, stand on one foot (briefly), and jump twelve inches in the air.	Talks in well-formed sentences, following rather complex grammatical rules; others can generally understand what he/she is talking about.

Figure 5.3
The Development of Language Skills
Edited by Frank Smith and George A. Miller, The Genesis of Language: A Psycholinguistic Approach, *Figure: The Development of Language Skills,*
© *1966 Massachusetts Institute of Technology, by permission of The MIT Press.*

who care for and speak to a child differs from adult language use. Vocabulary is simplified; intonation patterns are exaggerated; sentences are simple; frequent questions are asked by mothers; and frequent assertions are made by fathers.[14] This phenomenon is known as child directed speech.[15]

During the earliest stages of language development children use single words to label, assert, or question.[16] In addition to describing an important person, for example, "mama" may be used as an assertion, "Mama!" may mean, "I want you!" or "I need you, now!" Posed as a question, "Mama?" is a way of saying, "Where are you?" or "Will you come help me?" or "Is that you?" By the time most children reach the age of two, they are able to use language to express any number of meanings such as:[17]

- *Nomination.* Naming
- *Recurrence.* Acknowledging recurrence or reappearance
- *Denial.* Rejecting an idea
- *Nonexistence.* Acknowledging the absence or disappearance of something or someone

- *Rejection.* Preventing an activity or appearance of something or someone
- *Location.* Specifying the relationship between two objects
- *Possession.* Associating an object with someone or something
- *Attribution.* Relating objects to one another
- *Experience + experiences.* A living thing affected by an event
- *Action + actor.* A living thing receives the force of an action
- *Action + object.* An object affected by an action or activity

As illustrated in Figure 5.3, when a child reaches the age of two and beyond, he or she begins to form two-word sentences: "The two-word stage is a time for experimenting with many binary semantic-syntactic relations such as possessor-possessed ("Mommy sock"), actor-action ("Cat sleeping"), and action-object ("Drink soup").[18]

Although the child's vocabulary is growing, words are being used primarily to define specific, concrete actions and objects. A "car" may be understood as "a way to go to the store," and a "jack-in-the-box" is "what plays music and pops up." From this point on, a child's vocabulary and ability to form sentences progresses rapidly. Before youngsters are three, most are able to use their three-hundred to four-hundred word vocabularies to create well-formed sentences of three, four, and more words.[19]

As a child grows older, his or her phonetic, syntactic, semantic, and pragmatic skills develop. Words are used in increasingly more abstract ways. Whereas "dog" to the toddler meant "my dog Spot," to the youngster it may refer to "my dog Spot and John's dog Rusty." And in later stages of development, "dog" becomes "a kind of pet" and later "a specific kind of four-legged animal."

What began as the use of words and sentences to refer to things that are immediate and tangible gradually evolves to a capability for referring to ideas and objects that are abstract or distant. Thus, as a child develops increasing skill in the use of language, the linkage between his or her words and the particular events of the immediate surroundings becomes progressively more remote. For an adult, any word's meaning is an abstraction based on a lifetime of experiences.

Language is an incredibly powerful tool. We use language not only in vocal but also in written form, not only in single sentences but in lengthy documents and databases, not only face-to-face but also in situations involving communication technologies. We can classify the major everyday uses of language into three categories: (1) Representation; (2) Conversation; and (3) Social and Public Communication.

REPRESENTATION

Language and Reality

At the most basic level, language enables us to name and symbolically represent elements in our world. Ferdinand de Saussure, a noted linguist, maintains that the relationship between the word (the "signifier") and the object it represents ("the signified") is an arbitrary one. With the exception of a few onomatopoeic words like "whoosh" and "clang," there is no intrinsic connection between the objects and the "signs" we use to refer to them. Some of the labels refer to the tangible and concrete—friends, teachers, books, courses, reading, and writing. Language also provides the means through which we represent abstract concepts—friendship, learning, love, knowledge, freedom. Through language, we are able to manipulate symbols in our thinking. We can create, test, and refine our theories or understandings of the world.

The relationship between language and the "reality" it represents is complex.

> In the Middle Ages, for example, the word *Abracadabra* was believed to be capable of curing fever. Apparently, the first prescription for its use came from a poem on medicine by Quintus Serenus Sammonicus, a doctor who accompanied the Roman Emperor Severus on an expedition to Britain in 208 AD. The word was to be written on a triangular piece of paper. The sheet of paper was to be worn on a piece of flax around the patient's neck for nine days and then thrown backwards over the shoulder into a stream that ran eastward. Presumably, when the word disappeared, so would the ills of the patient.[20]

The words and concepts we have available to represent experience guide us toward particular ways of understanding reality. In English, a common arrangement of nouns and verbs is:

subject → verb → object

Two examples are: "Bill likes Mary," or "You make me mad." The pattern is "one person or thing causing another person or thing." Implicit in the form is a sense of one-way causality—the subject (noun) causes (verb) the outcome in the object (noun). Patterns of representational language use are more than just ways of talking. They imply and encourage ways of thinking—in this instance, they encourage us to see things in terms of "this" causing "that."

According to the *Sapir–Whorf hypothesis,* language "is not merely a reproducing instrument for voicing ideas but rather is itself the shaper of ideas. . . . We dissect nature along the lines laid down by our native language."[21] For example, although colors occur on a continuous spectrum without natural divisions, we classify this spectral band into discrete sections (such as blue versus green). Everyone who speaks the same language agrees on these labels. While many languages classify colors in the same way English does, some languages divide the spectrum differently. A person's ability to remember a particular color correlates to the codeability of a word for that color in the speaker's language.

Although the language system available to us has a major impact on our perceptions, our ability to understand external reality is not controlled entirely by our language.[22] The realities which confront us have a great impact on our language and the patterns we develop and use. In a society in which people's survival depends upon fishing, for instance, the language will include many words and phrases that capture subtleties of weather, the sea, boats, and fishing. These subtleties are absent in the common language of more technologically-oriented societies in which computer and electronics terminology abound. Similarly, the language used by an engineer to describe the structures of the world may be difficult to comprehend by a friend who is a lawyer or a psychologist.

The use of language is such a basic and subtle aspect of human life that its representational and "artificial" nature are often overlooked. This is especially so when particular language use patterns are widely shared. As long as others seem to share our meaning, we believe that representation and "reality" are the same. Unfortunately, there are many instances where we *assume* our words are being understood and their meanings shared when they may not be. Researchers have shown that even terms like "always," "often," and "rarely," when used by health professionals in the context of laboratory reports, are subject to a wide range of interpretation. A study of physicians and health care administrators in several settings showed that estimates of the meaning of "always" varied from 60 percent to 100 percent. For "sometimes," estimates ranged from 0 to 90 percent; and for "rarely," meanings varied from 0 to 95 percent.[23]

Generally, language seems to work "as if it were real." Most often, when we ask someone to pass the salt, their arm extends, grasps a salt container, and, without much difficulty at all, places the salt container in front of us. But there are also a number of circumstances in life which remind the reflective person that an uncritical belief in the "reality of language" can lead to difficulties. Getting a message through to someone who should quit smoking, lose weight, drive more carefully, or "turn over a new leaf" is a much more difficult proposition.

Similarly, a man saying that he is "in love" may not tell us all that much about the way he feels, how he will behave, or what he really thinks about the concept and the person to whom his words refer. We use the words "I do," for example, to seal the bonds of marriage. Although these two words have great symbolic value to the parties involved at that moment, the stability of the marriage will depend not upon the words but upon the behaviors and ideologies to which they refer.

Beyond the problems that arise from confusing words with the people, behaviors, actions, or ideas to which they refer, additional complexity in language results because in actual use words seldom represent the same things to two different people. As noted earlier, the meanings each of us attaches to words and phrases depend on our experiences. As a consequence, the meanings of words are subjective and, to some extent, unique to each individual. The following exchange illustrates the point:

> *Lynn:* (9:00 in the morning) Marty, I need that breakdown on the Johnson deal that you've been working on for this afternoon's meeting.
>
> *Marty:* Okay, Lynn, you'll have it soon.
>
> *Marty:* Sally, that memo for sales has got to go out this morning.
>
> *Sally:* I'll get it right out.
>
> *Lynn:* (4:30 that afternoon) Marty, where's that information you promised to get me this afternoon?
>
> *Marty:* You should have had it this morning. I asked Sally to get it right over to you.
>
> *Lynn:* Well, it's not here and you know this isn't the first time something like this has happened . . .

As a result of the day's events. Marty has accumulated more evidence that Sally is incompetent. Lynn has decided once and for all that she simply can't count on Marty, and Sally is convinced that Marty is always looking for a reason to criticize her. Although all of these conclusions may be justified, it is also quite possible that at least a partial explanation of what occurred is to be found in the words and phrases each person used and how they were interpreted. Initially, Lynn indicated to Marty that she needed the information for the afternoon meeting. Marty told Sally that it had "to go out this morning." But what did "go out this morning" mean? To Sally, who sent it out at 11:00 A.M. through the interoffice mail system—it meant *go out* this morning. To Lynn and Marty it meant *be delivered* this morning.

The same kind of difficulties arise in many other settings. For instance, hour after hour is spent in labor negotiations, arguing over the precise terminology to be used in a contract. Seemingly innocent words like "should," "will," "are," or "may" can become very problematic in these circumstances. See Figure 5.4.

Figure 5.4
Minor differences in word choice—such as "may be" versus "is" in the signs shown—may have a substantial impact on the significance a message will have.
© Jim Lambert, 2014. Shutterstock, Inc.

Limitations of Language for Representation

Although language functions successfully in many interactions, a group of scholars known as general semanticists caution that several characteristics of language limit its usefulness.[24]

The Principle of Nonidentity (A is not A).   The principle of nonidentity reminds us that words are not the same order of "stuff" as the "realities" to which they refer. The world is constantly changing, while the language available for making sense of it may not. The reverse may also occur when language changes but the reality it refers to doesn't.

A dramatic illustration of the representational limitations of language—and the manner in which these limitations can be overcome—is provided by the New Revised Standard Version of the Bible. The 1990 version was an update of the 1952 version, both of which are descendants of the 1611 *King James Bible*. Changes in this edition aim to make language clearer, more contemporary, and more gender- and racially sensitive, as shown in Box 5.1 (p. 138).[25]

BOX 5.1 • *Changing Language in the Bible*

Mathew 4:4
    1952 Version: "Man does not live by bread alone."
    1990 Version: "One does not live by bread alone."
II Corinthians 11:25
    1952 Version: "Once I was stoned."
    1990 Version: "Once I received a stoning."
Song of Solomon 1:5
    1952 Version: "I am very dark, but comely."
    1990 Version: "I am black and beautiful."

Source: Ari L. Goldman, "New Bible: 'He' Goes the Way of All Flesh," *New York Times*, Sept. 28, 1990, p. A10.

As another example: who would have imagined fifty years ago that advances in electronics would mean that words like *hard drive mouse, DVD, CD,* or *MP3* would become household terms for so many of us?

The Principle of Non-Allness (A is not all A). The principle of non-allness asserts that "the map is not the territory"—our language can never represent all of the object, event, or person to which we are referring. As Anatol Rapoport explains:

> . . . no matter how good a map you make, you cannot represent all of the territory in it. Translated into terms of language, it means that no matter how much you say about some "thing," "event," "quality," or whatnot, you cannot say all about it.[26]

The Principle of Self-Reflexiveness. The principle of self-reflexiveness calls attention to the problems that can arise when we use language to talk about our use of language. When we use concepts to talk about concepts, we become increasingly abstract and move progressively into the world of words and away from the world of the tangible.

For example, our self-reflexive capability allows us to label ourselves "successes" or "failures" as if these were actual characteristics that have an existence apart from our representations of them. We may easily forget that one cannot *be* a success or failure but can only be *seen* or *interpreted* as such by someone.

CONVERSATION

Negotiation of Meanings

As we noted at the beginning of this chapter, we can also look at language from a social and interactional perspective. Through language we are able to coordinate our own activities with those of others, to undertake joint projects, to discuss and solve problems, and to share in the pursuit of personal and social needs.

From an interactional perspective, language is a tool for the negotiation of meanings between and among individuals. When we create a spoken or written message, our language serves as the medium to convey our representations. It is our means of projecting ourselves and our ideas into the environment.

As we have discussed previously, the messages we encode are based on meanings influenced by our own experiences, needs, and goals; and, to some extent at least, we are each unique in these terms. When others decode our messages, they do so in terms of the meanings our words have for them—based on their experiences, needs, goals, and capabilities. When people talk about their feelings about "dogs," they, of course, are using the word *dog* to refer to the "dogs-of-their-experience" as they are relevant to the current conversation. When we decode the message, we do so in terms of the "dogs-of-our-experience." See Figure 5.5.

Thus, in any conversation (or written exchange), language serves as a medium through which individuals: (1) code and externalize meanings, and (2) decode and internalize meanings. As the interaction continues, language serves as the channel through which interactants may: (3) discover discrepancies and/or similarities in their meanings, and (4) negotiate a mutuality of meaning appropriate to the purposes at hand. In some circumstances, we may be able to get along fine in a discussion about dogs if one person is thinking of a poodle and the other person is thinking about a pit bull. In other situations, a greater level of mutual understanding would be essential.

Rules and Rituals

Do you get out your cell phone as soon as you leave class? We take our ability to converse with others very much for granted, so much so that it may seem like quite a simple activity. Clearly, this is not the case. As communication researcher Margaret McLaughlin indicates, our ability to engage in conversation presupposes that we have and can use an incredible amount of knowledge:

> . . . not only what we might call *world knowledge* (that groceries cost money, that parents love their children, that dogs bite, etc.), but also more specific knowledge bases, such as the rules of grammar, syntax, etiquette, and so on, as well as specifically *conversational rules* such as "When someone has replied to your summons, disclose the reason for the summons," and "Before saying good-bye to a telephone caller, reach agreement that all topical talk is completed." What is fascinating about conversation is that the ordinary person rarely reflects upon the vastness of the knowledge store that is required to carry it on.[27]

A *rule* is a prescription, regulation, or requirement. Some rules are obvious and explicit—like the rules of tennis, traffic regulations, or the requirements for membership in a formal group or organization. Other rules are implicit and subtle, like tennis etiquette, or the informal norms and practices expected of members of a group or organization. *Conversational rules* are those largely implicit and subtle regulations that guide our behavior in verbal interaction. They describe how one must, should, or should not behave in interactions with others.[28] Conversational rules facilitate cooperative effort, help to structure and

"I can't think of a better companion than a dog. They are faithful, kind, affectionate. . . Sunshine is like a member of the family."

"I'd never think of going out at night without my dog by my side."

"DOG"

"I've never cared much for dogs as pets."

"I agree, dogs make great pets."

Figure 5.5
In everyday usage, we speak and hear based on the meanings words have for us.
© Scorpp, 2014. Shutterstock, Inc., © Erik Lam, 2014. Shutterstock, Inc., © Eric Isselee, 2014. Shutterstock, Inc., © Charlie Bard, 2014. Shutterstock, Inc.

regularize interaction, provide a basis for predicting patterns of communication, and guide us in interpreting the actions of others.

Communication scholars have identified a number of rules that guide our behavior in conversations. We can group these rules into the following categories:[29]

- *Cooperativeness.* Be sincere and make your contributions reasonable, given the agreed-on purpose of the conversation.
- *Informativeness.* Make your contributions as informative as possible or necessary.
- *Responsiveness.* Take account of and be responsive to the informational needs of others.
- *Interactiveness.* Share responsibility with other interactants for guiding and managing the conversation.
- *Conformance.* Know and follow accepted conversational practices. Inform others when you violate a rule.

Cooperativeness.   Without some degree of cooperativeness and willingness to commit to interaction, conversation is impossible. H. Paul Grice, an important contributor to our understanding of conversational rules, called this general rule the *cooperative principle,* out of which flows other maxims of cooperation:[30]

- Don't state the obvious, or restate what others already know.
- Don't be superfluous—don't say too much.
- Make your comments relevant to the topic at hand.

Informativeness.   Conversation also normally involves a commitment to be informative:

- Don't knowingly mislead or say something you believe is false.
- Don't exaggerate or say more than you know.
- Don't withhold or say less than you know.

Responsiveness.   The obligation to be aware of and accommodating to the needs of other interactants involves inferring and responding to other's knowledge and beliefs, responding to questions and requests for information, using a manner and tone that takes account of the needs of other interactants, being clear, being courteous, and avoiding excessive boasting and self-promotion.

Interactiveness.   Interactiveness also refers to rules governing the management of the conversation. These commitments have to do with conversational sequences and rituals, including:

1. *Initiating interaction.* Initiating conversations and/or responding to the initiation efforts of others. If, for example, I say: "How are you?" the expectation is that you will participate in the initiation ritual by responding and will do so along the lines of: "Fine, and you?"
2. *Establishing a conversational agenda.* Participating in the process of setting the agenda for discussion such as in a meeting. If, for example, I say: "I guess our main topic of discussion today is how to update our advertising," the expectation is that you will either agree with the agenda as defined and allow it to guide the conversation or disagree and take the lead in suggesting another agenda.

3. *Turn taking as the conversation progresses.* Sometimes called *interaction management.* This is the expectation that people will "take turns" in speaking as a conversation progresses, avoiding monopolizing the discussion and nonparticipation.

4. *Topic shifting.* Changing topics and/or responding to the topic changes of others. The expectation is that topic changes are suggested and agreed to or explicitly negotiated, rather than unilaterally imposed. If you are in the middle of an enthusiastic description of a recent trip to Europe, it is expected that the other person will not interrupt in the middle of your statement and begin talking about a course he or she is thinking of taking. Rules call for the other person to work to produce a gradual, "natural" transition in the topic or to wait until a natural break in the conversation occurs or to introduce a transition that is responsive to you. Thus, he or she might say: "Your talking about the trip reminds me of a new course I learned about while you were away. I really want to tell you about it. It sounds interesting."

5. *Closing.* Terminating conversations and responding to termination initiatives by others—sometimes called *leave-taking.* The expectation is that leave-taking occurs by mutual agreement. That is, it is expected that someone will not get up and walk away while you're in the middle of talking about your trip. As with openings, there are a number of conversational rituals and conventions associated with conversational closings. Thus, a closing like, "OK, then, take care," and a response, such as, "You, too!" serve to signal the desire of the initiator to terminate conversation and provide a standardized way of dealing with what would otherwise be an ambiguous and potentially awkward circumstance.

Conformance. Conformance refers to our obligation to adhere to conversation rules or to provide an explanation when a violation occurs. The expectation is that we will follow rules in our conversations. When violations occur, the consequences are frequently negative. They may include confusion, frustration, misunderstanding, a loss of trust or friendliness among conversants, or a reinterpretation of the value and goals of the conversation by one or more of the parties involved.

There are any number of circumstances in which we violate rules. We may shift a topic abruptly, get up to leave in the middle of a conversation, exaggerate or understate, or say things we don't mean. There may be good reasons for these actions. When rule violations occur, we are expected to explain the reason for the violation. For instance, when you must interrupt or exit a conversation abruptly, an explanation that you just realized you're late for class, together with an apology, will help to excuse the rule violation.

One of the most blatant examples of rule violation happens when one interactant knowingly engages in deception. In such a circumstance, the informativeness rule and, hence, the sharing of information, have been undermined. When all other rules are followed, efforts to deceive may be quite successful. For instance, we may find ourselves persuaded by a cooperative, responsive, and interactive salesperson, even when some of the information provided about a product is incorrect. One of the reasons this occurs, of course, is that we are often better able to make accurate judgments about whether conversational rules are being followed than whether we are being told the truth. If deception is detected, it is likely to have a substantial impact on the conversation and the meanings which result. The consequences of an attempt at deception will depend on the topic, the nature of the relationship between conversants, and the situation.

In some situations, individuals may say things that are untrue, but without the goal of deception. For example, we may say, "That dress looks great on her," but if we are being sarcastic and don't intend our message to be taken literally, we can indicate this through tone of voice or facial expressions.

Rules and the significance of rule violations depend a lot on the situation or context. Our expectations may differ depending on whether we are talking with an intimate friend or a stranger, a child or an adult, a member of the same or opposite sex, a salesperson or a member of the clergy, one other person or several others. Thus, contextual, gender, ethnic, racial, and cultural differences may all have an impact on conversational protocol.

Language and Gender

In most cultures, individual communication behaviors are used by both men and women. For example, men and women may smile to indicate pleasure or raise their voices to indicate anger. According to one estimate, men and women overlap in their communication actions 99 percent of the time.[31] On the other hand, there are scholars who believe that men and women learn to speak differently and that men and women have internalized different norms for conversation.[32] According to this view, men tend to adopt a more competitive style in conversation while women tend to adopt a more cooperative mode. Because gender is the social construction of masculinity and femininity within a culture, these differences may vary by culture. The areas in which differences have been noted by some researchers include: initiation, conversational maintenance and question asking, argumentativeness, and lexical and phonological characteristics.[33]

Initiation.   Women generally spend more time initiating conversations than men. However, topics introduced by men are more likely to be taken note of and carried on by other interactants. The following exchange at a restaurant illustrates a familiar pattern:[34]

> *Maureen:* What are you going to order?
> *Tom:* The bacon burger.
> *Maureen:* That sounds good. I think I'll have the chicken salad.

After the order is taken, and a moment of silence. . . .

> *Maureen:* I went to the mall yesterday to look for a dress for my sister's wedding.
> *Tom:* Yeah?
> *Maureen:* But I couldn't find anything I liked. I guess I'll have to keep looking around.
> *Tom:* (No response.)

As Lea Stewart and colleagues explain: "This example illustrates one way that men may inhibit conversations with women, by giving minimal responses such as 'yeah' or 'oh' to topics introduced by women."[35]

Conversational Maintenance and Question Asking.   Women generally spend more time and effort facilitating the continuation of conversation, as is well illustrated in the restaurant dialogue discussed previously. Researchers have also found that when they analyzed tapes of actual conversations, 70 percent of the questions asked by interactants were posed by women.[36]

Argumentativeness. *Argumentativeness* is defined as a stable trait that predisposes an individual in communication situations to advocate positions on controversial issues and to verbally attack the positions that other people take on these issues.[37] In general, men score higher on measures of argumentativeness than women.[38] Although women are able to use this communication strategy when appropriate, they are more likely to believe that arguing is a strategy for dominating and controlling another person.[39]

Lexical and Phonological Characteristics.   Not surprisingly, studies show that women use a larger vocabulary to discuss topics about which they have greater interest and experience. And, conversely, in areas where men have greater expertise, their vocabularies are broader. There are also differences in the adjectives used by the two sexes. Robin Lakoff has noted that words like *adorable, charming, sweet,* and *lovely* are more likely to be used by women, while men are more apt to use terms such as *nice, good,* or *pretty.*[40] Studies suggest that women use intensifying adverbs more than men—for example, "I *really* enjoyed the book," or "I'm *so* disappointed."

Content and Relationship

Whether we use our words in a planned, intentional way or in a less systematic, unintentional fashion, verbal messages provide potential information of two types: (1) information about *content*—the topic under discussion, and (2) information about *relationships*—about the source and how the source regards the intended recipient(s).[41] A written or spoken presentation designed to convince us to vote for a particular candidate, for instance, includes *content* about the candidate, his or her qualifications, campaign promises, and potentials. Also, the presentation provides messages as to the level of preparation, interest, education, intelligence, attitudes, beliefs, mood, and motives of the speaker. And the speech may provide clues as to how the speaker regards the intended audience. Does the speaker "look down" on the audience? Does he or she consider them to be powerful, authoritative, educated? Does he or she fear or resent them?

To further clarify this distinction, consider the following statement:

Marge: Carol is an incompetent and uncaring person!

From a content point of view, Marge is indicating that there are some things about Carol that bother her. Beyond that, Marge may also be providing some clues about herself. She seems to feel quite strongly about Carol. Perhaps she is a fairly outspoken individual. Perhaps she is judgmental and intolerant of individual differences. Perhaps she is just jealous or envious of Carol.

In her communication about Carol and herself, Marge may also be providing clues to how she regards the person to whom she is speaking. It is likely that Marge sees herself as being, or wanting to be seen as being, closer to the person she's talking to than she is to Carol. It is also probable that Marge assumes the listener is closer to her than to Carol. One could also infer that she trusts the listener, that she simply doesn't care who knows how she feels about Carol, or that she is pursuing a specific personal motive. At the least, we can safely assume that Marge has some reason for wanting to share her reaction with the listener. No matter what her intent is, however, her message has both a content and relationship component.

Consider two more examples:

1. **Daddy:** (Following the sound of breaking glass) Marc.
   Marc: Daddy, I didn't do it. Honest.
2. **Ed:** Mary, I want to talk to you.
   Mary: Ed, I know what you're going to say. I'm sorry, I never intended for you to get hurt . . . It just happened.

In all respects except the content, these two exchanges are quite similar. In each instance the first speaker is really saying very little from a topical point of view. In fact, in both cases, the individuals that initiate the conversation provide no information that identifies a topic for discussion. The second speakers, however, provide the basis for a number of inferences. Both Marc and Mary seem to assume they are being asked about a particular act, even though this is not necessarily the case. They respond *defensively*—as though they have been attacked. Their responses, perhaps motivated by guilt, fear, or both, are messages from which one could infer something about their feelings and attitudes. Their messages also provide the basis for inferences as to how they feel about the other person. Both Marc and Mary are concerned about their relationships, by necessity or choice. For whatever reasons, both seem to see themselves in a "one-down" or inferior position, in which they must justify, explain, and/or seek forgiveness or approval from Daddy or Ed.

Let's examine a slightly more complicated situation:

Bill: My wife and I are really excited. We've got a chance to go to Las Vegas this weekend on a special half-price package on the Internet. It wasn't really the time we had picked to go, but we just can't pass it up . . . Doubt we'll ever have a chance to go so cheaply again.

Todd: I considered going, but with my job the way it is, I decided it's not smart to spend money on travel this year.

In the brief exchange, Bill is providing information about the prospect of an upcoming trip. He's also explaining that it will cost only half the normal amount. The fact that Bill is talking about the trip at all may suggest that he's the type of person who enjoys sharing his excitement. Or he may be boasting; perhaps he is seeking attention or recognition.

By explaining that he got a special price, Bill may provide a clue that he wishes to be seen as clever, shrewd, or economical. Or, alternatively, his message may suggest that he is the kind of person who feels the need to justify or apologize for his good fortune. The decision to share his plans with Todd suggests that Bill cares about or values Todd, or that he wants to impress Todd, or to solicit support or encouragement.

Todd says that he does not think it is a smart time to spend money on a trip. Beyond this, his response may provide a clue that he is unwilling to share in Bill's excitement. He may be jealous. Or he may fail to detect Bill's excitement. Todd's response also may suggest that he wishes to be seen as more rational than Bill—at least in this instance. From a relationship perspective, it seems that he feels no obligation to acknowledge or contribute to Bill's excitement and has no particular interest in providing an audience for further discussion of Bill's trip.

While the content aspect of an utterance is generally fairly straightforward to discern, it may be harder for interactants to be confident about their understanding of the relationship aspect. Nonetheless, all utterances can be, and generally are, understood at both content and relationship levels.

Thus, language not only communicates something *about* a relationship, it also helps to create the relationship. For example, we are more likely to feel close to someone who discloses a very personal feeling to us. That person trusts us enough to share a hidden feeling, and we reciprocate by deepening our friendship.

Metacommunication

Sometimes we engage in conversations about our conversation; or to put it differently, we communicate about communication. This is termed *metacommunication*.[42]

1. *Brenda:* Matt, let's go to a movie tonight.
2. *Matt:* Oh, I don't know, Brenda. Can we talk about it later?
3. *Brenda:* That's becoming a pattern around here, Matt. You never want to carry a discussion through to a conclusion.
4. *Matt:* The pattern *I see* is the one where you refuse to end a conversation until you've gotten the decision you want.
5. *Brenda:* Same old story. You can't handle any negative feedback. One small criticism, and you get so defensive.

In the first exchange above—(1) and (2)—Matt and Brenda are discussing the possibility of going to a movie. With Brenda's response (3), there is a shift from talking about the movie to talking about the way Matt responded. In his next response (4), Matt comments on Brenda's communication. Brenda continues the process of metacommunication as she replies (5), carrying forth a fairly common pattern of communication.

Of course, metacommunication can be used in a positive way in a relationship, too. Consider this conversation:

1. *Sally:* Jim, let's go to a movie tonight.
2. *Jim:* Oh, I don't know, Sally. Can we talk about it later?
3. *Sally:* That doesn't really sound like you, Jim. Is everything okay?
4. *Jim:* I got some bad news at work today and don't feel like going out.
5. *Sally:* What's wrong? Can I help?

In this instance, Sally and Jim begin by discussing going to a movie (1 and 2), but Sally interprets Jim's reply as atypical and asks him about it (3). This metacommunication leads Jim to disclose his bad news (4), and then Sally asks for more information (5).

SOCIAL AND PUBLIC COMMUNICATION

Production and Distribution of Social Realities

Language is the primary means used for social and public expression. We are confronted by public speeches on all topics, as well as by news, entertainment, advertisements, e-mail, and public relations messages. These messages are a pervasive part of the environment in which we live. Messages and meanings which are widely distributed and popularized through public communication become accepted realities. As communication scholar Lee Thayer explains:

> What is uniquely characteristic of human communication . . . is the fact that (human) . . . sophistication . . . has made possible the emergence and evolution of a purely communicational environment or reality . . . i.e., an environment or reality comprised of anything that can be and is talked about. Whatever can be talked about comprises a reality in the sense that it must be adapted to and dealt with in much the same way as that reality which is subject to sensory validation (the physical environment).[43]

Thus, it is largely through social and public communication that the shared realities of language and meanings are created, perpetuated, reaffirmed, or altered. The familiar story of "The Emperor's New Clothes" (Box 5.2) gives us insight into the powerful and pervasive nature of the basic process by which this happens. Messages are produced, distributed, believed, used, socially accepted, and eventually take on an objective reality that is seldom questioned.

IMPLICATIONS AND APPLICATIONS

- Language is the primary means of recording information for ourselves, and for producing and transmitting messages for others.
- Our use of language provides messages from which inferences are drawn about our interest in a particular topic, attitudes, education, mood, motives, age, personality, concepts of ourselves, and our regard for our listeners, readers, or viewers.
- Verbal messages may be either oral or written. Written messages (whether in print or electronic formats) are well-suited to situations in which we desire a high degree of control and predictability over the message that is produced and transmitted, or in which a document or record of communication is required. However, compared to oral communication, written message sending and feedback require more time; and it is sometimes more difficult to change one's position once it has been committed to writing. Oral messages create a sense of spontaneity and provide for instantaneous feedback and adjustment of one's position or approach. They leave no document behind, which can be an asset in some circumstances and a liability in others.
- Our words and concepts are our tools for labeling the people, objects, and events around us.
- There are many circumstances in life which remind us of the dangers of reacting to words as if they were the objects, people, or events to which they refer.
- Our representations are seldom, if ever, neutral or value free. They are influenced by our ways of thinking, and, in turn, they guide our thinking. Sometimes the influence is liberating; sometimes it constrains us. For instance, when we use sentences in which the structure is noun → verb → noun, we are more likely to think about the world, and communication, in cause-and-effect terms.
- The labels we use for ourselves—such as intelligent, attractive, poor, or unhappy—direct our thinking about ourselves down particular paths and not others. Likewise, the labels we use for other people—rich, uncaring, friendly, or aggressive, for instance—also guide our ways of thinking about people in particular ways, while discouraging other ways of viewing them.

BOX 5.2 • *The Emperor's New Clothes*

In the great city in which he lived many strangers came every day. One day two rogues came. They said they were weavers, and declared they could weave the finest cloth anyone could imagine. Their colors and patterns were unusually beautiful, they said, and explained that the clothes made of the cloth possessed the wonderful quality that they became invisible to anyone who was unfit for the office he held or was not very bright or perceptive.

"Those would be most unusual clothes!" thought the Emperor. "If I wore those, I should be able to find out what men in my empire are not fit for the places they have; I could tell the clever ones from the idiots." He asked the men to begin weaving immediately.

They put up two looms, and pretended to be working. They at once demanded the finest silk and the costliest gold; this they put into their own pockets, and worked at the empty looms till late into the night.

After a few weeks passed, the Emperor said to himself, "I should like to know how far they have got on with the cloth." But he felt quite uncomfortable when he thought that those who were not fit for their offices could not see it. He believed, of course, that he had nothing to fear for himself, but he preferred first to send someone else to see how matters stood.

"I will send my honest old Minister to the weavers," thought the Emperor. "He can judge best how the cloth looks, for he has sense, and no one understands his office better than he." So the good old Minister went out into the hall where the two rogues sat working at the empty looms.

"Mercy!" thought the old Minister, and he opened his eyes wide. "I cannot see anything at all! Can I indeed be so stupid? Am I not fit for my office? It will never do for me to tell that I could not see the cloth."

"Haven't you anything to say about it?" asked one of the rogues, as he went on weaving. "It is charming—quite enchanting!" answered the old Minister, as he peered through his spectacles. "What a fine pattern, and what colors! Yes, I shall tell the Emperor that I am very much pleased with it."

The Emperor soon sent another honest officer of the court to see how the weaving was going on, and if the cloth would soon be ready. He fared just like the first: he looked and looked. "Isn't that a pretty piece of cloth?" asked the two rogues; and they displayed and explained the handsome pattern which was not there at all.

"I am not stupid!" thought the man. "Yet it must be that I am not fit for my office. If that is the case, I must not let it be noticed." And so he praised the cloth which he did not see, and expressed his pleasure at the beautiful colors and charming pattern. "Yes, it is enchanting," he told the Emperor.

All the people in the town were talking of the gorgeous cloth. The Emperor wished to see it himself while it was still upon the loom. With a whole crowd of chosen men, among whom were also the two honest statesmen who had already been there, he went to the two cunning rogues.

"Isn't that splendid?" said the two statesmen, who had already been there once. "Doesn't your Majesty approve of the pattern and the colors?" And they pointed to the loom, assuming that the others could see the cloth.

"What's this?" thought the Emperor. "I can see nothing at all! That is terrible. Am I stupid? Am I not fit to be Emperor?" He said aloud, "Oh, it is very beautiful! It is our highest approval." He nodded in a contented way, and gazed at the loom. . . .

The fable of "The Emperor's New Clothes" provides an excellent, though exaggerated, illustration of the process by which our realities are created through language.

- In our conversations we expect others to follow a number of rules and rituals—regarding social initiation, turn taking, agenda setting, topic shifts, and leave-taking, for instance. We tend to think little about conversational rules until they are violated. When rules are broken, they often have a great impact on the conversation, on our impression of the rule breaker, and on our concept of the relationship.
- In some instances, women and men use language differently, as a consequence of different patterns of experience. Women are more forthcoming as conversation initiators, question askers, and conversation maintainers. Men may be more argumentative and may work harder to maintain control of conversations.
- Our verbal messages to others, and theirs to us, do two things simultaneously: (1) they relate specific content; and (2) they establish, comment on, reinforce, or alter relationships.
- As we engage in social or public communication, we take part in creating, distributing, reinforcing, or altering the meaning of language and the rules for its use.

SUMMARY

Through our words, sentences, tone, appearance, actions, and other behaviors, we produce messages that are potentially significant sources of information for others. Some of the messages we encode intentionally, others more by accident. Decoding occurs when our messages are attended to and interpreted.

Most of our purposefully-created messages involve the use of language. Languages are similar to one another in several respects. All have rules relative to phonology, syntax, semantics, and pragmatics. Still more basic similarities result from the physiological and cognitive capacities of humans. The physiology of human speech is more advanced than that necessary for vocalizations in other species, and the differences between human mental abilities and those of other animals are even more pronounced. Particular areas of the brain—*Broca's Area* and *Wernicke's Area*—both of which are located in the left hemisphere, are thought to be critical to language use.

Our capacity for language develops from the time we are infants through a progressive series of stages. As adults, we use language not only to refer to the immediate environment as does the child, but also to record, describe, assert, express emotion, question, identify ourselves, entertain, defend, and accomplish a number of other purposes.

Language plays a central role in human interaction in terms of representation, conversation, and social and public communication. At the most basic level it is our means for representing and labeling elements of our environment and one another.

By means of language we negotiate understandings through conversation. Understanding the nature of conversation requires an awareness of the influence of rules and rituals, language and gender differences, content and relationship messages, and meta-communication. Additionally, language provides the medium through which social and public communication take place and the means through which shared communication realities are created.

ENDNOTES

1. John Fiske, *Introduction to Communication Studies* (New York: Methuen, 1982), p. 43.

2. Fiske, 1982, p. 3.

3. William S-Y Wang, "Language and Derivative Systems," in *Human Communication: Language and Its Psychobiological Basis.* Ed. by William S-Y Wang (San Francisco: Freeman, 1982), p. 36.

4. Wang, 1982, p. 36.

5. Harold Whitehall, "The English Language," in *Webster's New World Dictionary of the American Language* (Cleveland: World, 1964), pp. xv–xxix.

6. Morton Hunt, *The Universe Within* (New York: Simon and Schuster, 1982), pp. 36–37.

7. What is named Broca's Area is based on the pioneering research by Paul Broca during the late 1800s. Wernicke's Area is named for German neurologist Karl Wernicke, who is acknowledged as the first to discover that damage to that section of the left hemisphere would lead to difficulties in speech comprehension. For a detailed discussion of the history and significance of this work to neurophysiology and speech, see *Left Brain, Right Brain,* by Sally P. Springer and George Deutsch (San Francisco: Freeman, 1981); "Specializations of the Human Brain," by Norman Geschwind in *Scientific American* (September 1979); Ross Buck, "Spontaneous and Symbolic Nonverbal Behavior and the Ontogeny of Communication," in *Development of Nonverbal Behavior in Children.* Ed. by R. S. Feldman (New York: Springer-Verlag, 1982), pp. 29–62; and an overview provided by Hunt, 1982.

8. Norman Geschwind, "Specializations of the Human Brain," in Wang, 1982, pp. 113–115.

9. Geschwind, 1982, p. 112. Also see discussion in Hunt, 1982, pp. 33–36.

10. Breyne Arlene Moskowitz, "The Acquisition of Language," in Wang, 1982, p. 122.

11. Moskowitz, 1982, p. 123.

12. Judith Coupe and Juliet Goldbart, *Communication before Speech* (London: Croon Helm, 1988), pp. 20–21.

13. The summary of stages in language acquisition is based upon an in-depth discussion provided in Barbara S. Wood, *Children and Communication* (Englewood Cliffs, NJ: Prentice Hall, 1976), pp. 24–27, adapted from Eric Lenneberg, "The Natural History of Language," in *The Genesis of Language.* Ed. by Frank Smith and George A. Miller (Cambridge, MA: MIT Press, 1968), p. 222. See also, Moskowitz, 1982.

14. Moskowitz, 1982, p. 123.

15. Jean Berko Gleason, "Sex Differences in Parent–Child Interaction," in *Language, Gender, and Sex in Comparative Perspective.* Ed. by S. U. Philips, S. Steele, and C. Tanz (Cambridge, England: Cambridge University Press, 1987), p. 191.

16. Wood, 1976, pp. 112–113.

17. Adapted from Coupe and Goldbart, 1988, p. 25. Based originally on L. Leonard, "Semantic Considerations in Early Language Training," in *Developmental Language Intervention.* Ed. by K. Ruder and M. Smith (Baltimore: University Park Press, 1984).

18. Moskowitz, 1982, p. 125.

19. Wood, 1976, pp. 25–26.

20. Richard Cavendish, *Man, Myth, and Magic, Volume 1* (New York: Marshall Cavendish, 1970).

21. Benjamin L. Whorf, *Language, Thought and Reality* (Cambridge, MA: MIT Press, 1956), p. 206.

22. Peter Farb, *Word Play* (New York: Bantam Books, 1978), p. 213.

23. William O. Robertson, "Quantifying the Meanings of Words," *Journal of the American Medical Association,* Vol. 249, No. 19, 1983, pp. 2631–2632.

24. See discussion by Richard Budd in "General Semantics," in *Interdisciplinary Approaches to Human Communication.* Ed. by Richard W. Budd and Brent D. Ruben (Rochelle Park, NJ: Hayden, 1979). Reprinted by Transaction Books, New Brunswick, NJ.

25. Ari L. Goldman, "New Bible: 'He' Goes the Way of All Flesh," The *New York Times,* Sept. 28, 1990, p. A10.

26. Anatol Rapoport, "What Is Semantics," in *The Use and Misuse of Language.* Ed. by S. I. Hayakawa (New York: Fawcett, Premier Books, 1962), pp. 19–20.

27. Margaret McLaughlin, *Conversation: How Talk Is Organized* (Newbury Park, CA: Sage, 1984), pp. 13–14.

28. Adapted from Susan Shiminoff, *Communicative Rules: Theory and Research* (Beverly Hills, CA: Sage, 1980); see discussion in McLaughlin, 1984, p. 16.

29. Adapted from Mark Ashcraft, *Human Memory and Cognition* (Glenview, IL: Scott, Foresman, 1989), pp. 447–467, especially the framework presented on p. 459. Based on the framework developed by H. Paul Grice, "Logic and Conversation," in *Syntax and Semantics, Vol. 3: Speech Actions.* Ed. by P. Cole and J. L. Morgan (New York: Seminar Press, 1975), pp. 41–58. And D. A. Norman and D. E. Rumelhart, *Explorations in Cognition* (San Francisco: Freeman, 1975); Ronald Wardhaugh, *How Conversation Works* (Oxford, England: Blackwell, 1985); and McLaughlin, 1984.

30. Grice, 1975; see discussion in Stephen W. Littlejohn, *Theories of Human Communication,* 5th ed. (Belmont, CA: Wadsworth, 1996), p. 91.

31. D. J. Canary and K. S. Hause, "Is There Any Reason to Research Sex Differences in Communication?", *Communication Quarterly,* Vol. 41, 1993, p. 129.

32. Jennifer Coates, *Women, Men and Language* (New York: Longman, 1986); Deborah Tannen, *You Just Don't Understand: Men and Women in Conversation* (New York: William Morrow, 1990).

33. The framework and research summary presented in this section is based on Lea P. Stewart, Pamela J. Cooper, Alan D. Stewart, and Sheryl A. Friedley, *Communication and Gender,* 4th ed. (Boston: Allyn and Bacon, 2003), pp. 37–61. See also discussion in John Pfeiffer, "Girl Talk—Boy Talk," *Science,* Vol. 6, No. 1, Feb. 1985, pp. 58–63.

34. Based on dialogue provided Stewart, et al., 2003, p. 49.

35. Stewart, et al., 2003, p. 49.

36. P. M. Fishman, "Interaction: The Work Women Do," *Social Problems,* Vol. 25, pp. 397–406, 1978, discussed in Pfeiffer, 1985.

37. D. A. Infante and A. S. Rancer, "A Conceptualization and Measure of Argumentativeness," *Journal of Personality Assessment,* Vol. 46, 1982, pp. 72–80.

38. D. A. Infante, "Inducing Women to Be More Argumentative: Source Credibility Effects," *Journal of Applied Communication Research,* Vol. 13, 1985, pp. 33–44.

39. A. M. Nicotera and A. S. Rancer, "The Influence of Sex on Self-Perceptions and Social Stereotyping of Aggressive Communication Predispositions," *Western Journal of Communication,* Vol. 58, 1994, pp. 283–307.

40. Robin Lakoff, *Language and Woman's Place* (New York: Harper & Row, 1975).

41. Paul Watzlawick, Janet H. Beavin, and Don D. Jackson, *Pragmatics of Human Communication* (New York: Norton, 1967), pp. 51–52.

42. Watzlawick, et al., 1967, pp. 53–54.

43. Lee Thayer, "Communication—Sine Qua Non of the Behavioral Sciences," in Budd and Ruben, 1979. Reprinted by Transaction Books, New Brunswick, NJ.

CHAPTER
6

Nonverbal Messages

IN THIS CHAPTER

Why . . .

- Nonverbal messages are often more important than verbal ones.
- Most of us know so little about nonverbal communication.
- Paralanguage can be more influential than language.
- Eye contact is influential in relationships.
- Your seating position in a classroom may predict your grade.

Similarities between Verbal and Nonverbal Communication

- Rule-Governed
- Intentionality
- Common Message Functions

Differences between Verbal and Nonverbal Communication

- Awareness and Attention
- Overt and Covert Rules
- Control
- Public versus Private Status
- Hemispheric Specialization

Paralanguage

- Vocalic Forms
- Written Forms

The Face

- Eye Gaze
- Pupil Dilation

The Body

- Hair
- Physique
- Dress and Adornment
- Artifacts

Gestures—Kinesics

- Inherited, Discovered, Imitated, and Trained Actions
- Origins of Gestures
- Types of Gestures

Touch—Haptics

Space—Proxemics

- The Physical Environment

Time—Chronemics

- Timing
- Timeliness

Messages and Meanings: MS ≠ MR

Implications and Applications

Summary

Kim walks over to a row of unoccupied chairs, places the briefcase and purse she is carrying on the seat to her right, and situates a bag with a picture of Mickey Mouse near her on the floor. She begins to leaf through the pages of *The Wall Street Journal,* glancing periodically at her watch and the monitor listing incoming flights. She checks her cell phone and sighs.

After about five minutes have passed, a middle-aged man dressed in a three-piece suit with a carry-on bag over his shoulder walks over and takes a seat directly across from her. As Kim glances up, her eyes catch his. He smiles, and she looks away. Kim concentrates her attention on the newspaper in front of her, but senses that the man is still staring. Finally, she notices him get up and walk away.

Several minutes later he reappears, walks over to the seat next to her and sits down without saying a word. Seconds later, Kim picks up her briefcase, the newspaper, and shopping bag and walks rapidly toward the concourse. Shortly thereafter, the man gets up and heads off in the same direction.

Though no words are spoken in this scenario, the individuals' appearance, facial expressions, dress, actions, use of space and time provide important cues that are interpreted and acted upon. Based on the man's smile, eye contact, and physical movement, Kim concludes that the onlooker is taking more than a casual interest in her and removes herself from the situation.

You have probably also formed initial impressions of the two individuals based on nothing more than the sparse description of their nonverbal behavior. For instance, you may have concluded that Kim is

- Carrying items she purchased at a Disney store or theme park
- Very conscious of the time

- Waiting for a plane
- Employed in a professional position

The man in the three-piece suit, you may assume to be

- Traveling
- Interested in initiating contact with Kim
- Employed in business or a profession

The formation of your reactions to the characters—and theirs to one another—based on nonverbal cues is not unique to this situation. Particularly in circumstances where we are forming first impressions, or where there are conflicts between words and actions, nonverbal messages are often far more influential than verbal ones. In fact, researcher Albert Mehrabian suggests that where we are confused about how we feel about another person, verbal messages account for only 7 percent of our overall impression and the rest are accounted for by nonverbal factors.[1] Thus:

Total Feeling = 7% Verbal Impact + 38% Vocal Impact + 55% Facial Impact

Although some researchers disagree with these numbers, it is clear that nonverbal codes are very influential. A great many nonverbal factors contribute to the global impressions people form. Sometimes impressions are accurate; often they are incorrect, exaggerated, or incomplete. In the situation just described, our first impressions may be correct. However, a number of other interpretations are possible. The Mickey Mouse bag may have been given to Kim to carry several reports from her office. The frequent glances at her watch could have simply been a nervous gesture, and she may have been leafing through *The Wall Street Journal* for no better reason than she found it on the chair next to her. She might have been passing time before going to work at one of the shops in the airport. Or perhaps she was a plainclothes airport security guard.

The man in the suit may have been interested in establishing a personal relationship or simply a friendly person with no intentions that involved Kim. His actions may have been a response to hers, or any apparent connection could have been coincidental. Or, *he* may have been a member of the security staff with questions about the contents of the Disney bag and growing suspicions about Kim's very nervous behavior.

Even from this simple example, three important characteristics of nonverbal communication are apparent:

1. A number of factors influence nonverbal communication.
2. Nonverbal messages generally have a variety of meanings.
3. The interpretation of nonverbal communication depends on the nonverbal messages themselves and also on the circumstance and the observer.

SIMILARITIES BETWEEN VERBAL AND NONVERBAL COMMUNICATION

Rule-Governed

Rules can be identified in nonverbal, as well as in verbal, messages. Some of these patterns pertain to the production of nonverbal messages and to the ways in which emotions are displayed. Still others are necessary to comprehend the significance of messages.

Rules associated with the creation of many nonverbal behaviors—a handshake, for instance—are similar to phonetics. Rules prescribing the appropriate sequence of nonverbal cues relative to one another—in meeting someone for the first time, for example—are a type of syntax. There are also general semantic patterns for many nonverbal behaviors that can be identified, and there are conventions as to when and how particular cues are to be used—a kind of pragmatics of nonverbal communication.

As with verbal messages, some nonverbal patterns are common to the behavior of all individuals. In facial expressions, for instance, studies suggest that there is a predictable relationship among emotions such as happiness, sadness, anger, disgust, surprise, or fear, and distinctive movements of facial muscles regardless of a person's personal and cultural background.[2] Gestures, such as head nodding, which we associate with "yes" and "no," as well as crying or laughing also seem to be universal, though their precise meanings may not be. But there are a great many more patterns that are unique to particular individuals, groups, regions, occupations, or cultures.

Intentionality

Most often, language is consciously used by people for the purpose of sending messages. This is the case in spoken, and especially written, communication. This is also often the case with nonverbal communication. We may consciously use particular facial expressions, gestures, and dress on a first date, job interview, or a group meeting, with the intention of creating a desired effect.

Both verbal and nonverbal messages may also be produced and transmitted unintentionally Unintentional cues, like lowering your eyebrows and tightening your lips in anger when trying to appear kind and understanding of a friend's rudeness, can have as much information value as poor word choice or confusing sentences.

Common Message Functions

Verbal or nonverbal behavior may bear any one of several relationships to one another:[3]

- Messages may be *redundant* and duplicate one another, as when a person says, "I am going to sit down," and then walks over to a chair and sits.
- They can also *substitute* for one another, as when a handshake substitutes for "Hello, it's nice to meet you."
- Verbal and nonverbal messages may be *complementary,* as when an individual smiles and says, "Come in, I'm glad to see you."
- A verbal or nonverbal code may also be used to add *emphasis* to the other, such as making a fist to underscore a point being made verbally.
- Verbal and nonverbal codes can also be sources of *contradiction,* as would be the case if we were told how interested another person was in hearing our thoughts, while the "listener" stared across the room at a member of the opposite sex.
- Both types of codes can be used for *regulation*—controlling the communication process, determining who will speak, for how long, and even when changes in topic will occur.

DIFFERENCES BETWEEN VERBAL AND NONVERBAL COMMUNICATION

Awareness and Attention

During the last several decades nonverbal communication has emerged as an area of extensive scholarly study and a topic of popular articles and books. But verbal communication continues to receive more attention.

This emphasis is most apparent when we consider the manner in which training in the two areas is handled in schools. Proficiency in communicating information through verbal messages is, in fact, considered to be so important that it is regarded as one of "the basic skills"; and great effort is expended to ensure that we are taught rules of pronunciation, syntax, semantics, and pragmatics as a part of our formal education. Theory and practice in the written and oral use of language are provided at virtually all educational levels.

By comparison, nonverbal skills receive little attention in most schools. Music, art, and physical education are generally included as part of the curriculum. However, no proficiency training comparable to composition, literature, or public speaking is provided for the nonverbal competencies that are so vital to human communication.

At home, attention is paid to dress, personal habits, and other forms of nonverbal messages that would get someone labeled as unpopular, dangerous, or even unappealing. However, most of these nonverbal "lessons" learned at home have to do with avoiding these negative attributions.

Overt and Covert Rules

One of the explanations for the relatively greater emphasis placed on verbal communication is that in all cultures there are *overt rules* and structures for language and language use. As a result, this information is provided in various sources. Nothing comparable exists for nonverbal communication. There are no nonverbal dictionaries or style manuals. And, other than books on etiquette, fashion, and body language, there are no guides to nonverbal usage.

We learn the *covert rules* of nonverbal communication more indirectly, through observation, and subtle—and sometimes not so subtle—patterns of reward and punishment.[4] Thus, we "know the rules" for greeting and expressing affection to others nonverbally—when to shake hands, for how long, how hard to squeeze the other person's hand, and when hugs and kissing are appropriate—but these rules are covert and not as universally agreed on. Few of us are conscious of their role in governing our behavior or are able to articulate the rules involved.

Control

While we devote considerable attention to managing our nonverbal communication in some situations, we are often more successful in controlling our verbal messages. If the goal is to convey our competence or grasp of a situation, for example, most of us are better able to control the impression we create verbally than nonverbally. Through planning and rehearsal, we will probably be able to gain predictability regarding the messages we will send verbally. However, despite our best efforts to manage our nonverbal behavior, nervousness or embarrassment may be quite apparent through *nonverbal leakage* (nonverbal behavior that contradicts our verbal messages)—a trembling voice or sweaty palm, for instance.

Public versus Private Status

Language usage patterns have long been regarded as a topic that is appropriate for public discussion and scrutiny. Teachers, parents, or friends are generally quite willing to ask us questions when they don't understand what is being said or to comment when they disagree. However, matters relating to our appearance, gestures, mannerisms, and body positions are generally considered private, personal, and even taboo topics, and are therefore far less likely topics of open discussion, analysis, or critique.

Recently the rules for discussing appropriate nonverbal behaviors have changed, especially for public figures. A great deal of attention is paid to various parts of movie stars' bodies or wardrobes. And everything is being "made over" from faces to hips to houses.

Hemispheric Specialization

Another major difference and a topic of scholarly interest is the location in the brain in which nonverbal activities are centered. As we noted, the left hemisphere of the brain is thought to play a predominant role in language processes.[5] Other activities which require the sequential processing of information, such as mathematics, seem also to rely heavily on the left hemisphere. The right hemisphere is of special significance in the recognition of faces and body images, art, music and other endeavors where integration, creativity, or imagination are involved.[6]

Studies show that some individuals with damage to the right hemisphere have difficulty with location and spatial relationships, recognition of familiar faces, or recognition of scenes or objects. Other research, which argues convincingly in favor of right-hemisphere specialization, has shown that even where damage to the language centers in the left hemisphere is so severe that the patients may have difficulty speaking, the ability to sing is often unaffected.[7] People with severe stutters can often sing without difficulty, too.

In the remainder of this chapter, we will examine four channels of nonverbal cues:

- Paralanguage
- Face
- Body
- External cues—space and time

PARALANGUAGE

We've all heard the phrase, "It's not what you said, but how you said it." What we say—using words, phrases, and sentences—is obviously important to communication. However, the way we use language can be even more important than our words as sources of information. *Paralanguage* refers to any message that accompanies and supplements language. Technically speaking, any supplemental nonverbal message can be viewed as an instance of paralanguage.

Vocalic Forms

One focus of our discussion of paralanguage will be on *vocalics*—auditory messages, other than words, created in the process of speaking.[8] Vocalics, which include pitch, rate of speech, rhythm, coughs, and giggles, nasality, pauses, even silence, are very significant sources of impressions in face-to-face communication.[9] Recall that Mehrabian found that when an individual is confused in his or her feelings about another person, vocal messages accounted for 38 percent of the impression that is formed.[10]

Long before children develop skill in language use, they have a familiarity with the tonal pattern of the language in their surroundings. Studies suggest that from the tonal contours of the babbling, it is possible to identify the language environment in which a child lives, even as early as the second year of life.[11] The paralinguistic patterns acquired by children reflect not only the language patterns of the region in which they are being raised but also the unique patterns of family and friends.

With spoken language, paralinguistic cues such as loudness, rate of speaking, tone, interjections, pitch variation, and use of pauses can have a major influence on whether and how one reacts to the individual and his or her verbalizations. On the basis of pitch, for example, we are able to determine whether a particular utterance is a statement or a question, a serious comment, or a sarcastic barb. Whether the word *really* spoken orally is interpreted as "Really?" or "Really!" is determined through paralanguage rather than through the word itself. In the same way, we decide whether, "That's beautiful," is to be taken literally or to mean quite the opposite.

Pitch is also the difference between whether "Can I help you?" creates a positive or negative impression. Spoken with a raised pitch at the end of the sentence, the sense is one of politeness and genuine interest. The same words, spoken in a monotone are likely to be taken as rudeness and disinterest.

Interjections (*nonfluencies*)—such as "like" "a" "huh" "so" or "you know"—and stuttering may also have an impact upon the way an utterance is interpreted. Remember the teacher who inserted "um" between every other word? Consider the potential difference in the impressions and likely impact created by each of the following:

- *Sam:* Like do you want to like go now or like later?
- *Shawna:* Do you want to go now or later?

Although the words used are essentially the same, the meanings we would attach to these two messages, and the inferences we would draw about their sources, are likely to be very different. Based on first impressions, would you rather hire Sam or Shawna to represent your company to the public? Who would you prefer to date?

As suggested by previous examples, paralanguage provides a basis for inferences about a speaker, as well as having a potential influence on the impact of the content of the message. Rate of speed and accent, for example, can provide the basis for inferences as to nationality, the region of the country in which the person was raised, and other characteristics associated with stereotypes about the geographic locale. The stereotypical linguistic patterns of the "fast-talking New Yorker" or "the slow-speaking Southerner," are often associated with behavioral, as well as geographic, characteristics. Paralanguage can also provide the basis for assumptions about the speaker's educational level, interest in the topic, and mood. Moreover, tone, pitch, rate of speech, and volume provide clues as to an individual's emotional state.

In some languages, paralanguage is even more essential to communication than it is in English. In Chinese, tones determine the meaning of words. Standard Chinese has only four tones: falling, rising, level, and dipping (or falling and then rising).[12] Changing the tone has the same kind of effect on the meaning of a word as changing a vowel or a consonant would in English.

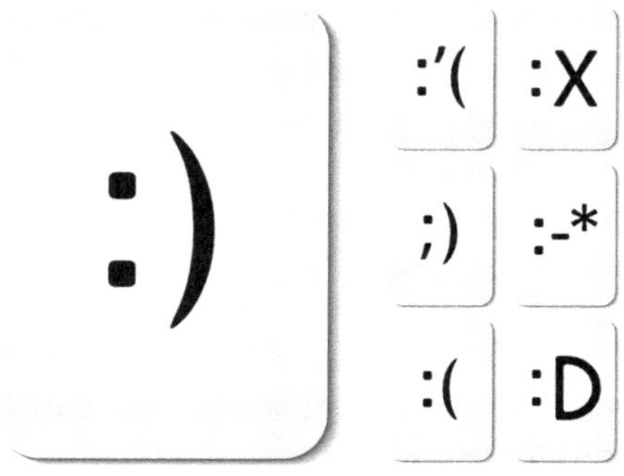

Figure 6.1
Emoticons are useful in e-mail and text messaging.
© cTermit, 2014.Shutterstock, Inc.

Written Forms

Up to this point we have been discussing paralanguage as it relates to *spoken* language. The form of a word or statement is also important to interpretation in *written* language use. The visual appearance of written materials, in terms of punctuation, spelling, neatness, the use of space for margins and between words, whether the document is printed or handwritten, and even the color of ink are likely to influence the reader's reaction to the words and its source.

In written language, paralinguistic cues serve as a basis for generalized inferences as to how educated, careful, respectful, or serious a person is, and may provide clues as to his or her mood or emotions at the time of writing. These in turn, may affect the way others think about and relate to the author.

The use of paralinguistic cues is evident in the conventions developed for appropriate communication via e-mail. For example, using capital letters is considered SHOUTING. Emoticons are useful in e-mail and text messaging. Combinations of punctuation marks indicate smiling :-) or winking ;-), for example. See Figure 6.1.

THE FACE

Generally speaking, we react to a person's face holistically. See Figure 6.2. That is, when we look at someone's face, we get an overall impression and seldom think of the face in terms of its distinctive features. Yet as nonverbal communication researcher Mark Knapp explains

> The human face comes in many sizes and shapes. Faces may be triangular, square, and round; foreheads may be high and wide, high and narrow, low and wide, or protruding; complexions may be light, dark, smooth, wrinkled, or blemished; eyes may be close or far apart, or bulging; noses may be short, long, flat, crooked, "hump-backed," or a "ski slope"; mouths may be large or small with thin or thick lips; and cheeks can bulge or appear sunken.[13]

Beyond their significance in contributing to one's overall appearance, facial expressions serve as message sources in their own right, providing probably the best source of information as to an individual's emotional state—happiness, fear, surprise, sadness, anger, disgust, contempt, and interest.[14] Our feelings are often, as the adage suggests, "written all over our faces." It has been estimated that our faces are capable of creating 250,000 expressions. Nevertheless, we don't actually show that many. Researchers estimate there are only about 44 distinct ways in which facial muscles move (see Figure 6.3).

Figure 6.2
Could these children look
any happier?
© Tom Wang, 2014.
Shutterstock, Inc.

Researchers also believe that the role of the face in relation to emotion is common to all humans. Describing what has been called a "neurocultural theory of facial expression," Paul Ekman explains: "What is universal in facial expressions of emotion is the particular set of facial muscular movements when a given emotion is elicited."[15] The specific events and circumstances that *trigger*

Figure 6.3
In addition to contributing to overall appearance, one's face provides the basis for inferences as to one's emotional state, age, mood, interest level, personality, and reaction to events and people.
© Piotr Marcinski, 2014. Shutterstock, Inc., © Ivy Photos, 2014. Shutterstock, Inc., © ollyy, 2014. Shutterstock, Inc., © ollyy, 2014. Shutterstock, Inc., © ollyy, 2014. Shutterstock, Inc., © ArtFamily, 2014. Shutterstock, Inc., © Daniel M. Ernst, 2014. Shutterstock, Inc.

emotions vary from one individual and culture to another.[16] And the customs and rules guiding the *display rules* of particular emotions also may vary from person to person, and culture to culture. Yet, for any emotion, exaggeration, understatement, and masking (deception) may occur.[17] An employee might exaggerate or mask an emotion of disappointment with a smile, for example, when learning that a promised "generous raise" only amounts to 25 cents per hour.

Eye Gaze

Probably the most influential features of the face in terms of communication are the eyes. As Ellsworth notes:

> Unlike many nonverbal behaviors having a potential cue-value that is rarely realized, such as foot movements, [or] subtle facial or postural changes, a direct gaze has a high probability of being noticed. For a behavior that involves no noise and little movement, it has a remarkable capacity to draw attention to itself even at a distance.[18]

As significant as eye behavior is to human communication, most of us are relatively unsophisticated in our awareness of eye behaviors and our ability to characterize them with any precision. Among those who study this facet of our nonverbal behavior, a number of terms have been advanced that assist in description:[19]

- *Face contact.* Looking at a person's face
- *Eye contact (or eye gaze).* Looking at a person's eyes
- *Mutual gaze.* Mutual gazing by two individuals at one another's face
- *One-sided gaze.* One person looking at another's face, but the behavior is not reciprocated
- *Gaze avoidance.* One person actively avoiding another's eye gaze
- *Gaze omission.* One individual failing to look at another, but without the intention of doing so

As children, we have heard many times that "it's not polite to stare"; and, as adults, there are frequent reminders of the "rule." If one stops at a traffic light, and the person in the next car looks interesting, one may "steal a glance"; but one is careful not to appear to stare. Similarly, while waiting in line at a grocery store, or sitting in a restaurant or other public place, we may casually glance at the people around us, but at the same time we should try to appear as though we are not noticing the other people at all.

Actually, the rule that we apply as adults is, "It's not polite to stare at people you don't know very well, unless you can do so without having them notice you." When and if we are noticed, we pretend not to have been looking, unless the intent is to violate the other's expectations.

The rules for eye contact with friends and acquaintances are quite different from those for strangers. When conversing verbally with even a casual acquaintance, some degree of mutual eye gaze is customary. "Looking" may help in grasping the ideas being discussed and is an indication of attention and interest. Among close friends, extended eye contact is not only acceptable, but is expected. In the case of intimate friends and lovers, prolonged glances may be exchanged periodically even when no accompanying words are spoken.

There are a number of other situations where eye glances are optional. For instance, when a speaker such as a teacher asks a question of a large audience, each member of the group may choose to engage or avoid the glance of the speaker. Generally, the likelihood of being called on to answer a question is considerably greater if one looks at the speaker than if one looks away.

At what and whom we look, for how long, under what circumstances, whether the gaze is one-sided or mutual, and whether we are engaged in gaze omission or gaze avoidance, provide the basis for inferences as to our focus of attention, interests, intentions, and even attitudes. Looking may be a matter of observing, orienting, inspecting, concealing, avoiding, or searching for pacification.[20]

Researchers have demonstrated that a primary function of eye gaze, or the lack thereof, is to regulate interaction. Eye contact serves as a signal of readiness to interact, and the absence of such contact, whether intended or accidental, tends to reduce the likelihood of such interaction.[21] Other studies suggest that eye gaze also plays an important role in personal attraction. Generally speaking, positive feelings toward an individual and high degree of eye contact go together. Perhaps for this reason, we often assume that people who look our way are attracted to us. Studies indicate, further, that individuals who engage in high levels of eye gaze are typically seen as more influential and effective in their dealings than others.

A number of factors have been shown in research to be related to the extent of eye gaze, including distance, physical characteristics, personality, topic, situation, and cultural background.[22] Based on this research, one can predict that, generally, more eye contact will occur when one is physically distant from others, when the topic being discussed is impersonal, and when there is a high degree of interest in the other person's reactions. Greater eye contact also occurs when one is trying to dominate or influence others, comes from a culture that emphasizes eye contact during conversation, is generally outgoing, striving to be included, listening rather than talking, or when one is dependent on the other person.[23]

One would expect less gazing between people who are physically close, when intimate topics are being discussed, when there are other relevant objects or people nearby, or when someone is not particularly interested in another's reactions or is embarrassed. Similarly, if an individual is submissive, shy, sad, ashamed, attempting to hide something, or of higher status than the person with whom he or she is talking, less eye contact is also likely.[24] Obviously, these are generalities which may not apply in a given circumstance.

Eye gaze is one area of nonverbal communication in which there are many cultural differences. For example, a student from Greece commented that in his culture it is considered polite to maintain direct eye contact while listening to someone talk. His North American friends continually ask him if something is wrong because they feel he is "staring at them." In some cultures, it is considered respectful to look down when a person in authority is speaking. In North America, however, parents often criticize their teenagers for not listening to them if they are not looking at them.

Pupil Dilation

The pupils of the eye can be an indication of interest or attraction. See Figure 6.4. As we look at people or objects that are seen as appealing, the pupils tend to enlarge; and, in at least some experimental settings, there is evidence that pupil size can be a factor in judgments of a person's attractiveness. In these studies, pictures of females with enlarged pupils were consistently rated as more attractive by males than were those of women with small pupils.[25]

Figure 6.4
Research suggests that when we look at an individual or object that is of interest or is seen as attractive, our pupils dilate.
© Serg Zastavkin, 2014. Shutterstock, Inc.

The extent to which pupil size is actually a useful source of information is still a question. Particularly in a culture such as ours, in which we stand so far apart during most conversations, it is difficult to discern the size of another person's pupils, even when making an effort to do so. In Middle Eastern cultures, however, where the standard distance separating people during conversations is much smaller, information based on pupil size may be more usable.[26]

THE BODY

It is said that "Beauty is only skin-deep," and "You can't judge a book by its cover." However, there is little doubt that, particularly when other sources of information are lacking, "surface-level" information plays a critical role in human communication.

Appearance is probably the single most important information source in the formation of initial impressions. Perhaps the most dramatic evidence of the importance of appearance comes from studies of dating preferences, in which perceived attractiveness was more important than such factors as religion, race, self-esteem, academic achievement, aptitude, personality, or popularity, in determining how well individuals would like one another. Evidence from other studies suggests that physical attractiveness is not only important to dating preferences but also is often a predictor of how successful, popular, sociable, sexually attractive, credible, and even how happy people are.[27]

A number of factors contribute to appearance, among them one's *hair, physique, dress, adornment,* and *artifacts.*

Hair

Hair and beard length, color, and style also are important nonverbal message sources. These factors contribute to overall attractiveness and may also serve as the basis of inferences as to one's personality, age, occupation, attitudes, beliefs, and values.

Physique

Physique includes body type, size, and shape. Studies have suggested, for example, that inferences may be drawn about personality based on *somatype—* body shape and size. People who appear to be "soft," "round," and overweight (endomorphs) may be assumed to be affectionate, calm, cheerful, extroverted, forgiving, kind, soft-hearted, or warm. People who appear to be muscular, bony, and athletic-looking (mesomorphs) may be stereotyped as active, argumentative, assertive, competitive, confident, dominant, optimistic, or reckless; and people who are tall and thin in appearance (ectomorphs) may be assumed to be aloof, anxious, cautious, cool, introspective, meticulous, sensitive, or shy. Although most studies find a match between particular physical traits and people's *perceptions,* there is little correlation between somatypes and actual behavioral characteristics.

One's height alone may also provide the basis for stereotyping. For males in our culture, greater height is often associated with positive qualities, while, beyond a certain point, the opposite is the case for females. Where these biases operate, they may be a consequence of primitive, subconscious reactions. Height plays an interesting role in politics and other aspects of society, for example:[28]

- All U.S. presidents except for James Madison (5 foot 4) and Benjamin Harrison (5 foot 6) have been taller than the average height of men of their time.
- Richard Nixon was perceived by his supporters to be taller than John F. Kennedy. Kennedy's supporters believed he was taller. Both men were actually six feet tall.
- Every inch taller a man is than average equates to an average of $600 more per year in salary.
- In 1973, the U.S. Civil Service Commission eliminated height and weight requirements that discriminated against women applying for police, park service, and fire fighting jobs.

Dress and Adornment

Dress fulfills a number of functions for us as humans, including decoration, physical and psychological protection, sexual attraction, self-assertion, self-denial, concealment, group identification, and display of status or role.[29] Cosmetics, jewelry, eyeglasses, tattoos, hair weaves, false eyelashes, and body piercings serve many of these same ends.

Nonverbal communication scholar Dale Leathers writes: "Our social identity and image is defined, sustained and positively or negatively modified by communication through appearance."[30] Dress is the major facet of appearance through which we can exercise control over communication. We generally assume that people make conscious choices about what they wear and therefore take their dress to be an important source of information about them.[31]

Dress and adornment are noteworthy and often utilized as the basis for judgments as to gender, age, approachability, financial well-being, social class, tastes, values, and cultural background. See Figure 6.5.

Badges of various kinds also provide information about a person's identity, status, or affiliations. Often dress serves as an occupational badge, as is generally the case with police officers, nurses, doctors, clergy, military personnel, and members of particular athletic teams. In such instances, the "costume" people wear is designed, standardized, and used to make their occupation easy to determine. The "uniforms" of college students, business-people, or factory workers may serve much the same function, though they are not necessarily intended to do so.

Other badges are hats, shirts, sweatshirts, or jackets that bear the name of an individual, school, employer, manufacturer, favorite auto, or musical

Figure 6.5
In addition to providing a source of basic information such as age, gender, occupation, and group affiliation, dress also often plays a critical role in first impressions.
© mimagephotography, 2014. Shutterstock, Inc., © auremar, 2014. Shutterstock, Inc., © Paul Hakimata Photography, 2014. Shutterstock, Inc.

performer. Specialized jewelry such as a fraternity or sorority pin, a wedding or engagement ring, or a necklace with a name or religious symbol, may also serve to provide information as to one's identity, status, group, or organizational affiliation.

In an interesting study, nonverbal researchers Mark Frank and Thomas Gilovich found that what we wear influences not only others' behavior but also our own.[32] They discovered that, reflecting the notion that "bad guys wear black," professional football and ice hockey teams that wear black uniforms were penalized more. Teams that changed their uniforms to black had an increase in penalties. Judges rated the same behavior as "more illegal" when performed by a player in a black uniform. Finally, when students put on black uniforms they chose to play more aggressive games than when they put on white uniforms.

Artifacts

We surround ourselves with artifacts—toys, technology, furniture, decorative items, and so on. Our cars and homes are also artifacts—objects—that provide additional messages from which others may draw inferences about our financial resources, aesthetic preferences, personality, status, or occupation. A particular credit card, briefcase, or a business card may serve as artifactual cues to which people react as they form impressions based on our appearance.

GESTURES—KINESICS

Movements of body, head, arms, legs, or feet—technically labeled *kinesics*—also play an important role in human communication. Studies suggest that we progress in the development of our capacity for gesturing through four basic stages.[33] In the first stage, from birth to three months, irregular, jerky movements of the entire body indicate excitement and distress. In the next stage, three to five months, the infant is able to move the entire body more rhythmically, in patterns associated with anger and delight. In the third stage, five to fourteen months, children develop specialized gestures such as making faces, head turning, and poking. Between the ages of fourteen and twenty-four months, the child is able to express affection for particular people, as well as joy and jealousy, through contact movements such as poking, hitting, and caressing.

Gestures, as well as other cues, may either be *purposeful*—messages which are intended to achieve a particular purpose—or *incidental* and *unintended*. Some gestures may be used as complements for language, such as if we shake our head back and forth while saying "no," when asked a question. In other instances we use gestures in place of words. A shrug of the shoulders, for instance, is used to indicate confusion or uncertainty, a frown and slow horizontal back-and-forth motion of the head to indicate frustration or annoyance, or the circle sign made by the thumb and the forefinger to mean "OK."

Inherited, Discovered, Imitated, and Trained Actions

Desmond Morris, an anthropologist, suggests that gestures are acquired through *inheritance, discovery, imitation,* and *training*.[34] Examples of actions that are inborn include the sucking response of the baby and the use of body contact gestures as a part of courtship.

Some gestures we discover as we identify the limitations and capabilities of our bodies. The way people cross their arms is an example. There is little variation from one culture to another, but there are differences between individuals within any one culture, and each individual tends to be fairly consistent over time. Some of us fold left hand over right, and others right over left. Regardless of which we have become accustomed to, it is difficult to reverse the pattern without considerable effort, as shown in Figure 6.6.[35]

We acquire many of our gestures unknowingly from the people around us as we grow up. The typical handshake, for instance, is acquired through imitation, as are many other greeting forms and cultural and subcultural mannerisms.

Actions such as winking, playing tennis, jumping on one foot, whistling, or walking on one's hands, require active training in order to master. The wink, for example, taken so much for granted by the adult, is a formidable challenge for a child. Like other trained actions, substantial observation and systematic effort is required to master it.

Origins of Gestures

It is interesting to speculate on the origins of human gestures. Some gestures displayed by adults seem to be carried over from our activities as children.

Figure 6.6
Folding one's arms can be considered a *discovered action.* Cross your arms. Now reverse them. How does that feel?
Source: Desmond Morris, *Manwatching* (New York: Abrams, 1977).
© OPOLJA, 2014. Shutterstock, Inc., © pio3, 2014. Shutterstock, Inc.

Smoking, pencil chewing, nail biting, candy and gum chewing, and "emotional eating" may well have their roots in our early feeding experiences when oral satisfaction was associated with safety and security.

Other gestures may have cultural origins. Kissing may have its roots in the feeding habits of our ancestors. At early points in human history, mothers apparently fed their young by chewing food in their mouths first and then passing the food to their child's mouth in a gesture which very much resembles the tongue-kissing of adult lovers today.[36]

Another gesture, the horizontal head shaking which we use to say "no," may well have its origins in the infant's side-to-side head shaking gesture indicating he or she wants no more milk from the mother's breast, a bottle, or a spoon.[37]

Types of Gestures

There are many ways of classifying gestures. An extensive list provided by Morris includes the following.[38]

Baton Signals and Guide Signs.   One type of gesture, the *baton signal,* is used to underscore or emphasize a particular point being made verbally. Examples of baton signals include a downward clipping motion of the hand, a forward jabbing movement of the fingers and hand, and the raised forefinger. Another similar kind of gesture is the *guide sign,* by means of which we indicate directions to others, as when we point, direct, or beckon another person nonverbally.

Yes–No Signals.   *Yes–no signals* are another category of gesture. Movements of the head are the primary means for creating these signals. While many gestures are unique to one or several cultures, the vertical, "yes" head nod appears to be fairly universal. Even though we might assume that the meaning of the "yes" nod is fairly specific, there are a number of variations:

> *The acknowledging nod.* "Yes, I am still listening."
>
> *The encouraging nod.* "Yes, how fascinating."
>
> *The understanding nod.* "Yes, I see what you mean."
>
> *The agreeing nod.* "Yes, I will."
>
> *The factual nod.* "Yes, that is correct."[39]

The "no" gesture, of course, consists of a horizontal movement of the head. In many parts of the world a side-to-side swaying of the head is also used to say "maybe yes, maybe no." In addition to the head, the hand and fingers can also be used to express yes–no signals. For instance, in North American culture a shaking of the forefinger from side to side is a way of saying "no." Similarly, forming a circle with the thumb and forefinger can often mean "yes," or "ok," though this meaning varies from culture to culture. See Figure 6.7.

Again it is important to recognize the existence of cultural differences. For example, a quick upward nod of the head can mean "no" in Greece.

Greetings and Salutation Displays.   The most familiar greeting forms are the handshake, embrace, and kiss by which we signal our pleasure at someone's arrival or the significance of their departure.

There are several stages in the greeting or salutation process. The first phase is the *inconvenience display:*

Figure 6.7
A circle sign made with the thumb and forefinger illustrates how the significance of a single gesture can vary substantially from one culture to another. In England and North America, the sign means, "okay." For the French, it signifies "okay" when the gesture is made while smiling. If it is accompanied by a frown, it is taken to mean "worthless" or "zero." In Japan, the same sign is often used as a sign for "money."
Source: Desmond Morris, *Manwatching* (New York: Abrams, 1977).
© Alexy Boldin, 2014. Shutterstock, Inc.

To show the strength of our friendliness, we "put ourselves out" to varying degrees. We demonstrate that we are taking the trouble. For both host and guest, this may mean "dressing up." For the guest it may mean a long journey. For the host it may entail a bodily shift from the center of [the] home territory. The host may make an effort to meet a guest like when a head of state formally welcomes another head of state at an airport or when a brother drives to the airport to greet his sister returning from abroad. This is the maximum form of bodily displacement that a host can offer. From this extreme there is a declining scale of inconvenience, as the distance traveled by the host decreases.[40]

The second stage is the *distant display*. From the moment the guest and host see each other, they can indicate the other's presence by several other gestures including a smile, eyebrow flash, head tilt, wave, and sometimes an outstretching of arms indicating an upcoming embrace. As the two individuals approach one another, they signify pleasure at the other's presence by hugging, squeezing, patting, kissing, or pressing their checks together, perhaps with extended eye contact, laughing, smiling, or even crying. The particular greeting used depends on a number of factors including the nature of the relationship, the situation in which they are meeting one another, the length of time that has passed since they have seen one another, and the extent of change in either person's status since they were together.

Tie Signs.   The *bonding* or *tie sign* is a category of gesture through which individuals indicate that they are in a relationship. In much the same way that wedding rings, fraternity or sorority pins, or matching clothing suggest the existence of a relationship between two or more people, certain gestures serve the same purpose. Handholding, linked arms, a single drink shared by two people, close physical proximity when sitting or walking, and the simultaneous sharing of objects of all kinds provide cues about the individuals and the nature of their relationship. See Figure 6.8.

Isolation Gestures.   Other common gestures are body positionings such as crossing arms or legs, through which we conceal or block portions of the body from view. In some instances, *isolating gestures* may serve as intentional

Figure 6.8
Even when no words are spoken, nonverbal cues often provide clues as to who "goes with" whom in any given situation.
© Olesia Bilkei, 2014. Shutterstock, Inc.

messages, though more often they are less purposeful. These and other gestures, including hugging oneself, supporting the chin or cheek with an arm, or touching one's mouth, may signal discomfort or anxiety, even though we may be unaware of these feelings.[41] According to Paul Ekman, these adaptors or manipulators tend to increase with anxiety.

Other Gestures.   Gestures also play a major role in courtship, mating, and sexual affairs. In addition to hand holding, kissing, petting, and forms of sexual contact, *preening behavior*—for instance, stroking one's hair, adjusting makeup or clothing in the mirror, or stroking one's own arms or legs—can also play a role in sexual attraction.[42]

In religion, gestures have significant functions. Kneeling, standing at appropriate times, bowing, and folding one's hands in prayer are symbolic means through which people participate in the central rituals of any faith.

TOUCH—HAPTICS

When a gesture is extended to the point where physical contact is involved, tactile messages are created. For humans the significance of tactile messages, also known as *haptics,* begins well before birth in the prenatal contact between mother and infant. From the first moments of life, touch is the primary means by which children and parents relate to one another. Through this tactile mode, feeding takes place and affection is expressed.

During the early years of our development, touch continues to be the central means for expressions of warmth and caring among family members and close friends. Beginning with the preschool and elementary years, physical contact also takes on a role in play and sports and, particularly among boys in our culture, fighting. During this period, we also learn the significance of tactile messages in greeting rituals such as the handshake, hug, and kiss.

In the teenage and preadult years, touching takes on increasing significance in expressions of warmth, love, and intimacy. Tactile messages are important in athletic endeavors, in the actual activity of the sport, and in the pats and slaps of assurance and encouragement among players and coaches. For some, the role of touch in aggression continues during this period. Among adults, most physical contact is associated with (1) informal greetings and gestures of departure between friends and colleagues, (2) expressions of intimacy and sexual activities, and (3) expressions of hostility and aggression.

Two of the interesting facets of tactile messages are their power and their inherent ambiguity. In health care settings, one of the sources of discomfort for many patients is the fact that examinations and treatment involve being touched by relative strangers in a manner that we normally associate with intimate relations.

Recent innovations in technology have helped to link our sense of touch with our ability to communicate verbal messages. For example, the tactile graphic display allows Web surfers with vision impairment to feel images from the Internet much in the same way words can be represented in Braille.[43]

Levels of contact and comfort with touching vary to some extent from one culture to another. In some Asian or African cultures, for example, male friends may walk down the street hand-in-hand as they talk. In Middle Eastern cultures, casual acquaintances stand so close together when talking that North Americans may assume they are intimates. By comparison, the United States is a low-contact culture. In general, North Americans go to great lengths to avoid touching whenever possible. In an elevator or crowded shopping mall, for instance, we generally touch strangers only when absolutely necessary and then often with discomfort.

Depending on the circumstance, people involved, and the culture, touch may lead us to react with considerably more intensity than we would to verbal or other nonverbal cues. Touching another person without his or her consent is regarded in many societies as far more disturbing than verbal abuse or obscene gestures.

SPACE—PROXEMICS

The use of space, *proxemics,* plays an important role in human communication. To some extent the intensity of tactile messages occurs because we have well-defined expectations as to how much personal space we will have around us. When our *personal space,* the *portable territory* we carry with us from place to place, is invaded, we respond. Being bumped unnecessarily in an elevator, having a beach towel walked across or practically shared by a stranger, or being unnecessarily crowded while shopping generally cause us discomfort for this reason. Our response is to readjust our own position to regain the amount of space we think we need. Research suggests that in some instances the extreme violation of personal space over time, such as occurs in hysterical crowds and very high density neighborhoods, can lead to extreme reaction, frustration, and even aggression.

Edward Hall has done much to broaden our understanding of the way space is used during face-to-face conversations.[44] Hall found that the distance between interactants varied predictably depending on the setting and the content of conversation:

- *Public conversations.* 12 feet to the limits of visibility
- *Informal and business conversations.* 4 to 12 feet
- *Casual conversations.* 1½ to 4 feet
- *Intimate conversations.* 0 to 18 inches

Fluctuations in each category depend on a number of factors: the culture in which the conversation takes place, the ages of the interactants, topic being discussed, setting, nature of the relationship, attitudes and feelings of the individuals, and so on.[45] See Figure 6.9.

The use of space and position is also important in seating. In a group situation, for instance, certain positions are more often associated with high levels of activity and leadership than others. Being in front of a group, separated

Figure 6.9
Body positioning and the way space is used play important roles in human interaction.
© Antonio Guillem, 2014. Shutterstock, Inc., © Peter Bernik, 2014. Shutterstock, Inc., © szefei, 2014. Shutterstock, Inc.

more from the group as a whole than are any of the individual members from one another, affords the isolated individual a position of distance and authority. Examples are a teacher in front of a class, a judge in front of the court, a religious leader at the front of the church, and so on.

A person's position within a large room—a classroom, for example—can also have an influence on verbal behavior. In typical classes, over 50 percent of the comments are initiated by class members located in the front and center positions within the room, referred to as the "participation zone." For many individuals, position is the most influential factor explaining their participation.[46]

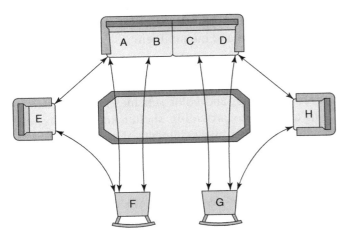

Figure 6.10
The arrangement of furniture and seating patterns play an important role in the level and direction of conversation. All other things being equal, the pairs marked by arrows would engage in the most frequent conversation. Those persons seated on the couch would be least likely to engage in interaction.
From *Public Places and Private Spaces: The Psychology of Work, Play and Living Environment* by Albert Mehrabian. Copyright © 1976 by Basic Books, Inc. Reprinted with permission of Basic Books in the format Republish in a book via Copyright Clearance Center.

In smaller groups, particularly where furniture is involved, the head of the table is traditionally a position of leadership, honor, respect, and power. See Figures 6.10 and 6.11. In a conference room, a similar association often exists with the person sitting at the head of a table. Some researchers have found, for instance, that in experimental jury deliberations, the person sitting at the head of the table was chosen much more often as leader than people in other positions.[47] Our positions relative to others, whether in silence or active conversation,

Conversation	60%	27%	13%
Cooperation	68	13	19
Co-action	18	32	50
Competition	12	23	65

Conversation	45%	36%	12%	1%	4%	2%
Cooperation	23	13	42	8	10	4
Co-action	8	8	10	21	34	19
Competition	6	22	7	40	19	6

Figure 6.11
In studies of relationships and seating preference, Robert Sommer and M. Cook asked students to indicate how they would prefer to situate themselves for each of the following situations:
(1) *Conversation:* Casual discussions for a few moments before class.
(2) *Cooperation:* Sitting and studying together for a common exam.
(3) *Co-action:* Sitting and studying for different exams.
(4) *Competition:* Competing to see which person would be first to solve a series of puzzles.
Students were asked to indicate their preferences for round and rectangular tables, each with six possible seating positions. The results of the two studies are shown under the diagrams.
Source: "Experiments on Orientation and Proxemics" by Mark Cook, *Human Relations*, Vol. 23, No. 1, pp. 61–76. Copyright © 1970 by The Tavistock Institute. Reproduced with permission of Sage Publications Ltd. in the format republish in a book/journal via Copyright Clearance Center.

standing or sitting, can be a significant factor in shaping communication and in contributing to others' impressions of us and ours of them.

The Physical Environment

Our buildings, furniture, decor, lighting, and color schemes are the result of human decision making. In addition to providing shelter and housing, and facilitating our various activities, the man-made elements of our physical environment also serve a number of informational functions—some intentionally, many by accident.

Whether one thinks of the arrangement of furniture and the selection of wall hangings in one's own apartment, the design and furnishing of an elegant restaurant, the layout of a shopping mall, or the architecture of a massive airport complex, all have much in common in terms of communication.

Directing Behavior.   Each environment with its furniture, decor, and color serves as a source of information that may have an impact on the people present. Some of the information is "designed-in" by the architect or designer to shape the way the environment or its parts are used. Sidewalks in a park, for example, direct our movement as we walk about. Similarly, chairs used in some fast-food restaurants are designed to be comfortable for only a short period of time and may well influence our decisions about how long to remain in the environment.

Provide Symbolic Value.   Structures and their contents, by virtue of their size, shape, use of space, and decor, may also have symbolic significance for us. Religious buildings and their contents, for example, are often symbolic by their very nature. Large rooms with high ceilings, stained glass windows, dimly-lit interiors, deep colors, and sacred books and objects, each have information value to those who use the environment.

The symbolic properties of houses of worship have their parallels in shopping malls, parks, restaurants, as well as in the structure and decor of homes and apartments. The differences, for instance, between dining in a candlelit room with elegantly upholstered armchairs and soft dinner music compared to the experience of having dinner at the counter of a truck stop or diner are quite substantial. See Figure 6.12.

Figure 6.12
The objects of our physical environment also serve as nonverbal information sources, providing clues as to how they are to be understood, related to, and whether and how they are to be used.
© kathmandupphotog, 2014. Shutterstock, Inc., © Pawel Kowalczyk, 2014. Shutterstock, Inc.

Regulating Interaction. Environments may also provide the basis for information that regulates—encourages or discourages—interaction. The study carrels of the library, for example, serve to separate and isolate their users, discouraging interaction, while a business office with no private offices or partitions encourages interchange. In a similar sense, a classroom with permanently attached chairs contributes to "one-way" message flow. Robert Sommer provides the following description of the typical classroom and its impact.

> The American classroom is dominated by what has been called the rule of two-thirds—two-thirds of the time someone is talking and two-thirds of the time it is the teacher, and two-thirds of the time that the teacher is talking, she is lecturing, giving directions or criticizing behavior. Movement in and out of classrooms and the school building itself is rigidly controlled. Everywhere one looks there are "lines"—generally straight lines that bend around corners before entering the auditorium, the cafeteria, or the shop. . . . The straight rows tell the student to look ahead and ignore everyone except the teacher, the students are jammed so tightly together that psychological escape, much less physical separation, is impossible. The teachers have 50 times more free space than the students with the mobility to move about. . . . The august figure can rise and walk among the lowly who lack the authority even to stand without explicit permission. Teacher and children may share the same classroom but they see it differently. From a student's eye level, the world is cluttered, disorganized, full of people's shoulders, heads, and body movements. [The student's] world at ground level is colder than the teacher's world. [The teacher] looms over the scene like a helicopter swooping down to ridicule or punish any wrong-doer.[48]

TIME—CHRONEMICS

The use of time and timing—*chronemics,* as it is technically designated—is another critical, and often overlooked, factor in communication. In fact, the reactions to our words and deeds may depend far more on *when* we speak or act, than on the content of the action.

Timing

Timing plays a role in interaction at two levels of analysis: (1) micro and (2) macro. Micro-conversational time-use characteristics include the speed at which we talk, the number and extent of pauses and interruptions, our "talk-to-silence" ratio, and our patterns of conversational "turn taking." These factors can play an important role in terms of message transmission, reception, and interpretation; and each also serves as a basis for the formation of impressions about the individuals involved. Too little talking, for instance, can be read as disinterest, shyness or boredom, whereas too much can be construed as aggressiveness, self-assuredness, presumptuousness, overconfidence, or rudeness.

At the macrolevel are our more general decisions as to whether to even engage in conversation at a particular point in time. It comes as no surprise to anyone who has ever asked for a raise or to borrow the family car that there are certain times that are better than others for presenting ideas or suggestions. The decisions people make about when to speak and when to be silent, when they have said too much and when too little, when to "speak their piece" and when to "keep it to themselves" are among the most critical decisions they make relative to communication.

Timeliness

Sayings like "Time is money," "Never put off until tomorrow what you can do today," "A stitch in time saves nine," and "The sooner the better" reflect the common North American view that time is a precious commodity. The faster we can get something done, the less time we "waste."

Our "time-is-money" philosophy shows up in a great many of our activities. We find ourselves rushing to meet deadlines, keep appointments, avoid waste, and increase productivity. We drive as fast as we legally can, so we'll get where we're going quicker. When we have an appointment with someone, we like to get business transacted in as little time as possible so we can move on to the next task. We want to leave work "on time" whenever possible to hurry home. En route every red light, wait at a pedestrian crossing, or slow-moving car is an annoyance as we rush home. We want to get home quickly to relax and enjoy our "leisure time."

Given the significance of time in our daily lives, it is not surprising that our use of it can have an important impact on behavior. Being "early" or "late" is a message. The meaning provided by such messages varies depending on a number of factors, including the amount of time we are early or late, the purpose of an appointment, the length of the relationship between the people involved, the relative status of the parties involved, and the orientation toward time of each of the individuals.

Being fifteen minutes late for a job interview can lead to the cancellation of the appointment, while being fifteen minutes late for a party may result in being embarrassingly "early." Being late for a business meeting carries different consequences than being late for a social engagement. Arriving an hour late—even with a good reason—for a first date will probably be reacted to differently than being as late for dinner with one's spouse. In such circumstances, timeliness and the use of time—being on time, late, or early—may be as significant a source of information to other persons as whatever one does or says after arriving.

There are very significant intercultural differences in the use of time. In Latin America and the Middle East, one can arrive at a time that a North American or Canadian would consider "late," and still be considered "on time" or even "early." Business executives and travelers must learn about, understand, and respect these cultural differences when in other countries.

MESSAGES AND MEANINGS: MS ≠ MR

We have seen how verbal and nonverbal behaviors play a pervasive role in human communication. Individuals create verbal and nonverbal messages that can and often do become significant to others. Sometimes the behaviors are intentional, as with a planned speech or the wave of a hand. Often they are accidental, as with a blush or an avoidance of eye contact in embarrassment.

The process of verbal, and especially nonverbal, message making seems automatic. Both occur as a natural and basic part of human activity. The nonverbal and verbal behaviors of any one individual can be seen as contributing to the vast array of information in the symbolic environment that surrounds us at any point in time.

It is important to keep in mind that the presence of particular verbal or nonverbal messages in the environment provides little or no assurance that they will be attended to or interpreted in a particular way. Bill tells Mary "I love you." Mary says, "I love you, too." Each has heard the verbal message provided by the other, and the words each are saying are the same. Can we assume the message has the same meaning for both Bill and Mary? Not necessarily. Whether we think in terms of ourselves as "senders" or "receivers" of messages in a relationship, group, organization, society, or mass audience, messages sent (intentionally or not) do not necessarily equal messages received. Common messages do not necessarily result in shared interpretation. Maybe Bill and Mary have the same meanings in mind. Or, perhaps, Bill means he wants to get married, while Mary means she wants to go out only with Bill.

The same distinction between message and meaning is important in the realm of nonverbal codes: Eye engagement intended as a sign of interest by one person may be read as aggressiveness by another; a gesture interpreted as an isolation gesture by one person may be regarded as a way of keeping warm in a cold room to others. Verbal and nonverbal behaviors are *sources* of meaning, but they are not, in and of themselves, meaningful, with the possible exception of facial expressions that accompany emotions.

Situational and topical considerations can also be important. Nonverbal communication researcher Mark Frank explains that people often prefer to receive admissions of affection in person rather than in a letter or on the phone. In a face-to-face situation, we can see how the other person "really" feels because we can observe their nonverbal behaviors. The same principle applies to relationship breakups, too.[49]

The meanings of verbal and nonverbal messages depend not only on the messages that are available but also on our individual ways of processing information and on our social interactions with others. Whether we regard a particular person as attractive or intelligent will depend minimally on: (1) the nonverbal and verbal behaviors of the person in question; (2) the way we personally attend to and interpret those behaviors; and (3) the social interactions with our peers and other members of our society that have helped to define and shape our notion of what constitutes attractiveness or intelligence.

To determine the meanings of particular messages, we have to look beyond the verbal and nonverbal messages to the processes involved in information reception. We must look also to the relationships, groups, organizations, cultures, and societies, which provide the contexts in which verbal and nonverbal messages are created, shared, and interpreted.

IMPLICATIONS AND APPLICATIONS

- Paralanguage, appearance, gestures, touch, space, and time are important sources of information in a wide range of situations.
- Our nonverbal behaviors are governed by rules we have learned through experience over the course of our lifetime.
- We are largely unaware of the rules that guide our nonverbal behaviors and our reactions to them.
- When others violate nonverbal rules, we generally have global, overgeneralized, sometimes emotional reactions. For instance, a person may be perceived to be a wimp if he or she doesn't squeeze firmly enough while shaking hands, or we may feel angry when someone is continually late for appointments.
- We are generally aware of only a small percentage of the nonverbal messages we create and convey in any situation.
- Some facets of nonverbal communication, such as dress, greetings, and time, we can easily manage if we choose to do so. Others, like paralanguage, eye contact, gestures, and the use of space can be managed with effort and practice. Still others—a blush of embarrassment or a nervous gesture—we may be unable to control.
- Nonverbal competence requires awareness of and attention to the patterns of communication, and conscious effort to be sensitive to the impact of our nonverbal behavior on others.

SUMMARY

Nonverbal behavior plays an important role in human communication. There are a number of similarities between verbal and nonverbal communication. They: (1) are rule-governed; (2) make possible the production of unintended, as well as purposeful messages; and (3) share a variety of message functions in common.

There are also key differences: (1) Compared to language, there has been a lack of awareness and attention to nonverbal cues and their impact on behavior; (2) nonverbal communication involves rules which are primarily covert rather than overt; and (3) verbal message processing is thought to occur primarily in the left hemisphere of the brain, while the right hemisphere is essential for processing information related to nonverbal activity.

Paralanguage, appearance, gestures, touch, space, and time are six primary sources of nonverbal messages. Appearance plays an important role in interpersonal relations, particularly in initial impressions. Dress, adornment and physique are facets of appearance that serve as potential information sources. The face is a central aspect of one's appearance, providing the primary source of information as to one's emotional state. Hair is also a message source.

The eyes are perhaps the most important component of the facial system in terms of communication. Based on direction and duration of eye gaze, or the absence thereof, cues are provided that serve as the basis of inferences as to interest, readiness to interact, and attraction. Pupil size may also be important.

Gestures are potential sources of information. Among the most common types of gestures are: baton signals and guide signs, yes–no signals, greetings and salutation displays, tie signs, and isolation gestures.

Touch is another source of messages that plays a central role in greetings, the expression of intimacy, and acts of aggression. The intensity of reactions to tactile cues is suggestive of the importance of space in communication. When our personal space is invaded in other than intimate relationships, discomfort—and often a "fight or flight" reaction—results.

The significance of spatial cues is also apparent in seating patterns. Certain seating positions may be associated with high levels of participation and leadership. The nature and placement of elements in the physical environment—furniture, decor, lighting, and color schemes—also generate messages that are potentially significant to behavior. They often provide cues that influence their use, symbolic value, and interaction patterns.

Time, timing, and timeliness can also be significant in the communication process. The way time is shared in conversations, for instance, can be a source of information that is even more influential than the content of those discussions. Timeliness—being "late" or "early"—can itself be a potential information source. Substantial cultural variations exist.

Our verbal and nonverbal behaviors—some intentionally enacted—create a pool of messages that is part of the environment that surrounds us. The presence of verbal and nonverbal messages provides no assurance that they will be attended to or be of particular significance to individuals within that environment. Messages sent (intentionally or not) do not equal messages received.

ENDNOTES

1. Albert Mehrabian, *Silent Messages* (Belmont, CA: Wadsworth, 1971), pp. 42–47; and *Nonverbal Communication* (Chicago: Aldine-Atherton, 1972), pp. 181–184.

2. See Paul Ekman, Wallace Friesen, and P. Ellsworth, *Emotion in the Human Face: Guidelines for Research and an Integration of the Findings* (New York: Pergamon Press, 1972); Paul Ekman, "Universal and Cultural

Differences in Facial Expressions of Emotions," in *Nebraska Symposium on Motivation*. Ed. by J. K. Cole (Lincoln: University of Nebraska Press, 1972), pp. 207–283; and the discussion of these and other related works in Robert G. Harper, Arthur N Wiens and Ioseph D. Matarazzo, eds., *Nonverbal Communication: The State of the Art* (New York: Wiley, 1978), p. 212.

3. For a detailed discussion on functions of nonverbal cues, on which this summary is based, see Judee K. Burgoon and Thomas Saine, *The Unspoken Dialogue: An Introduction to Nonverbal Communication* (Boston: Houghton Mifflin, 1978), pp. 10–14.

4. We are indebted to Valerie Manusov for suggesting the distinction between covert and overt rules in discussing nonverbal and verbal communication.

5. Robert E. Ornstein, *The Psychology of Consciousness* (San Francisco: Freeman, 1977), pp. 20–21. See more detailed discussion in Sally P. Springer and George Deutsch, *Left Brain, Right Brain* (San Francisco: Freeman, 1981), and Norman Geschwind, "Specializations of the Human Brain," *Scientific American*, September, 1979, pp. 180–182.

6. Springer and Deutsch, 1981.

7. Springer and Deutsch, 1981, p. 15.

8. Burgoon and Saine, p. 80.

9. See discussion in Burgoon and Saine, 1978, pp. 80–84.

10. Mehrabian, 1972, pp. 181–184.

11. William S-Y Wang, "The Chinese Language," in *Human Communication: Language and Its Psychobiological Bases* (San Francisco: Freeman, 1982), p. 58.

12. Wang, 1982, p. 58.

13. Mark L. Knapp and Judith A. Hall, *Nonverbal Communication in Human Interaction*, 5th ed. (Belmont, CA: Wadsworth, 2002), p. 305.

14. Knapp and Hall, 2002, p. 308.

15. Ekman, Friesen, and Ellsworth, 1972, p. 50.

16. Ekman, 1972, p. 216.

17. See discussion in Harper, et al., 1978 pp. 98–105; and Ekman, 1972.

18. P. C. Ellsworth, "Direct Gaze as a Social Stimulus: The Example of Aggression," in *Nonverbal Communication of Aggression*. Ed. by P. Pliner, L. Krames, and T. Alloway (New York: Plenum, 1975), pp. 5–6.

19. Harper, 1978, p. 173.

20. G. Nielsen, *Studies of Self-Confrontation* (Copenhagen, Denmark: Munksgaard, 1962).

21. An excellent summary of research findings on the functions and perceived impact of eye gaze is provided in Harper, 1978, pp. 181–215.

22. See discussion in Knapp and Hall, 2002, pp. 349–355.23. Knapp and Hall, 2002, p. 361.

24. Knapp and Hall, 2002, pp. 355–358.

25. A discussion of research on pupil dilation by E. H. Hess, *The Tell-Tale Eye* (New York Van Nostrand Reinhold, 1975); and E. H. Hess, A. L. Seltzer, and J. M. Shlien, "Pupil Responses of Hetero- and Homosexual Males to Pictures of Men and Women: A Pilot Study," *Journal of Abnormal Psychology*, Vol. 70, 1965, pp. 587–590. A useful summary is provided in Knapp and Hall, 2002, pp. 366–369, and Desmond Morris, *Man-watching* (New York: Abrams, 1977), pp. 169–172.

26. Edward T. Hall, "Learning the Arabs' Silent Language," *Psychology Today*, August 1979, pp. 47–48.

27. Knapp and Hall, 2002, pp. 180–181.

28. John S. Gillis, *Too Tall, Too Small* (Champaign, IL: Institute for Personality and Ability Testing, 1982); and Kim Painter, "How Bush, Dukakis Measure Up in '88," *USA Today*, Vol. D4, Sept. 22, 1988.

29. Knapp and Hall, 2002, p. 208.,

30. Dale G. Leathers, *Nonverbal Communication Systems* (Boston: Allyn and Bacon, 1976), p. 96.

31. Valerie Manusov, unpublished notes on nonverbal communication, January 1991.

32. Mark G. Frank and Thomas Gilovich, "The Dark Side of Self and Social Perception: Black Uniforms and Aggression in Professional Sports," *Journal of Personality and Social Psychology*, Vol. 54, 1988, pp. 74–83.

33. A discussion of research and writings on the development of nonverbal capabilities in children is provided in Barbara S. Wood, *Children and Communication* (Englewood Cliffs, NJ: Prentice Hall, 1976), pp. 194–200.

34. Morris, 1977, pp. 17–23. The term *imitated actions* is used to refer to what Morris has labeled *absorbed actions*.

35. Morris, 1977, pp. 16–17.

36. Morris, 1977, p. 52.

37. Morris, 1977, pp. 68–69.

38. The discussion of baton signals, yes–no signs, guide signs, salutations displays, tie signs, and isolation gestures is based on the work of Morris, 1977, pp. 56–100.

39. Morris, 1977, p. 68.

40. Morris, 1977, p. 79.

41. See Morris' discussion of "barrier signals," 1977, pp. 133–135, and "auto contact behaviours" pp. 102–105.

42. Knapp and Hall, 2002, p. 229.

43. "New Device Enables Blind to 'Feel' Electronic Images," *Education USA*, Vol. 44 (23), November 11, 2002, p. 12.

44. See discussion of personal space provided in *The Silent Language*, Edward T. Hall (New York: Doubleday, 1959), especially Chapter 10.

45. A useful discussion of the work of Edward Hall and others in the area of personal space is provided in Knapp and Hall, 2002, pp. 152–161, and Burgoon and Saine, 1978, pp. 92–97.

46. A summary of research on position and participation is provided in Knapp and Hall, 2002, pp. 109–114.

47. F. Strodtbeck and L. Hook, "The Social Dimensions of a Twelve Man Jury Table," *Sociometry*, Vol. 24, 1961, pp. 297–415.

48. Robert Sommer, *Personal Space* (Englewood Cliffs, NJ: Prentice Hall, 1969), p. 99.

49. Mark G. Frank, unpublished notes on nonverbal communication, December 1996.

CHAPTER

7

Relationships

IN THIS CHAPTER

Why . . .

- People riding on elevators are engaged in interpersonal communication even if they don't speak.
- Both short- and long-term relationships have advantages.
- Breaking up isn't always hard to do.
- Intimate communication is important to health.
- Pets make good relationship companions.

Interpersonal Communication and Relationships

Types of Relationships

- Dyadic and Triadic Relationships
- Task and Social Relationships
- Short- and Long-Term Relationships
- Casual and Intimate Relationships
- Dating, Love, and Marital Relationships
- Family Relationships

The Evolution of Relationships

- Stage One: Initiation
- Stage Two: Exploration
- Stage Three: Intensification
- Stage Four: Formalization
- Stage Five: Redefinition
- Stage Six: Deterioration

Relational Patterns

- Supportive and Defensive Climates
- Dependencies and Counterdependencies
- Progressive and Regressive Spirals

Factors That Influence Patterns

- Stage of Relationship and Context
- Interpersonal Needs and Styles
- Power
- Conflict

Implications and Applications

Summary

> For months you have wanted to get together to try to work things out. You think your ex feels the same way. What's needed is calm and rational conversation. You want to make clear how much the relationship matters and to try to recapture what's been lost. Minutes into the encounter, another argument begins. Your ex thinks he or she is right; you are convinced you're right. He or she yells; you yell back even louder, as each of you tries—in vain—to get one another to understand.

Participation in relationships with friends, family members, intimates, roommates, siblings, employers, and peers is basic to life. Situations like the one above are, unfortunately, not all that uncommon. They remind us that productive relationships are as challenging to develop and maintain as they are important to us.

Communication is the basic ingredient in social life, and an understanding of it can be a very powerful tool for fostering positive and productive relationships of all kinds.

The concepts of *communication* and of *relationship* are intertwined in several basic ways. First, as we have seen, one of the most fundamental outcomes of human communication is the development of social units; and no such units are more central to our lives than relationships. Second, our relationships—with parents, relatives, friends, intimates, and colleagues—are essential to our learning, growth, and development. Third, it is within relationships of one sort or another that most of our purposeful communication activities take place.

INTERPERSONAL COMMUNICATION AND RELATIONSHIPS

What is a *relationship*? Sometimes the term *relationship* is used as a way of talking about a friendship we regard as particularly significant. Relationships may involve emotional or sexual intimacy. Relationship is also used more generally to refer to other one-to-one social units, such as those composed of a teacher and student, parent and child, employer and employee, or doctor and patient.

Although most people agree that friendships, intimate arrangements, or other social groupings qualify as relationships, few people would use this term to describe passengers riding on an elevator or strangers passing on a crowded street. From the point of view of communication, however, these also can be thought of as relationships, and analyzing these units provides valuable insights into other, more complex, human relationships.

In the most basic sense, a *relationship* is formed whenever reciprocal message processing occurs: that is, when two or more individuals mutually take account of and adjust to one another's verbal or nonverbal behavior. This reciprocal message processing, which we can call *interpersonal communication*, is the means through which relationships of all types are initiated, develop, grow, and sometimes deteriorate.

One of the simplest relationships is that created by people passing one another on a crowded sidewalk. In order for two individuals to negotiate past each other without bumping, each must process information relative to the other's presence, location, direction, and rate of movement. The individuals involved must use this information to guide their action in order to pass without colliding. In this simple situation all the essential elements of any relationship are in operation.

A slightly more complex example is provided by people riding on an elevator, as depicted in Figure 7.1. When alone in an elevator, most of us stand to the rear, often in the center. Typically, as a second person enters, we move to one corner or another, leaving the remaining corner for the newly arriving passenger. In so doing, we initiate a simple relationship as we take note of and adjust our behavior—movements, gestures, and position—relative to one another. With little conscious awareness, reciprocal message processing and mutual influence have taken place, as we define and redefine the territory available for our use.

As a third person enters the elevator, further adjustments are likely to occur as the social unit shifts from a two-person relationship to one composed of three individuals. Readjustments of this kind provide observable evidence that reciprocal message processing is taking place and that a relationship has been formed.

Whether our point of reference is strangers passing on the street or an intimate, enduring friendship, the basic dynamics involved in the formation and evolution of relationships are quite similar. In each circumstance, we enter the

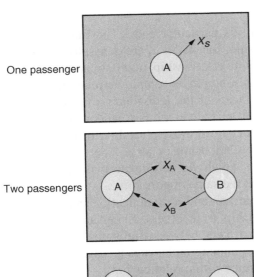

Figure 7.1
In a very basic sense, a relationship is formed among passengers on an elevator as the individuals adjust their behavior relative to one another, based on an awareness of one another's presence.

relationship behaving toward other people on the basis of the personal theories and representations we have acquired through previous experience. As relationships develop, a mutual influence occurs as we adopt or create *joint*, or *relational, communication rules*. These rules guide, shape, and, in a sense govern the particular social unit from its initiation through the various stages of development to its eventual termination, in much the same ways as personal representations guide an individual's behavior.

In the case of strangers passing on the street, the information-processing rules the individuals use are relatively simple; and the relationship itself is short-lived. By contrast, intimate relationships between people who have lived or worked together for many years can be exceptionally complex.

We are unaware of many of the relationships of which we are a part. Very often, we are taking account of and being taken account of, influencing and being influenced, without awareness or intention.

TYPES OF RELATIONSHIPS

In this chapter, the primary focus of our discussion will be on those relationships of which we are aware and which we intentionally form and maintain. Relationships of this kind can be classified in terms of a number of factors, including the number of people involved, the purpose of the relationship, its duration, and the level of intimacy attained.

Dyadic and Triadic Relationships

The vast majority of our relationships are *dyads*—two person units. As children, our first contacts with others are dyadic, and it is not until we reach the age of six to twelve years that we are able to engage in conversation with several people at the same time.[1] As adults, we are members of a large number of different dyads, such as roommates, best friends, spouses, or co-workers.

As William Wilmot notes in *Dyadic Communication*, each of the many dyads in which we participate is unique in a number of respects.[2]

1. Every dyadic relationship fulfills particular ends. The functions served by a teacher–student relationship, for instance, are generally quite different from those of a husband–wife relationship; and both are distinct from those served by doctor–patient or employee–employer relationships.
2. Each dyad involves different facets of the individuals who participate in them. The demands placed on an individual as a student in a teacher–student relationship are different from those placed on that same person as a wife in a husband–wife relationship or as a supervisor in a work relationship. No two dyads in which we participate make precisely the same demands on us or present the same opportunities.
3. In any dyad, unique language patterns and communication patterns develop that differentiate that relationship from others. Slang and "in-phrases" among friends, terms of endearment between intimates, and ritualized greetings and work place jargon among colleagues are the result of these ongoing communication dynamics within relationships.

Although the majority of the relationships in which we participate involve two people, we also often find ourselves in social units composed of three or four people, and these relationships may get very complex, as the popular television show *Grey's Anatomy* demonstrates.

Triads—three-person relationships—differ from dyads in several respects, particularly in their complexity. In dyads, reciprocal message processing takes place between two people. With triads, there are six possible message-processing pairings: person 1 with person 2, person 1 with person 3, person 2 with person 3, persons 1 and 2 with person 3, persons 1 and 3 with person 2, and persons 2 and 3 with person 1.[3]

Beyond the increased complexity resulting from more possible pairings, triads differ from dyads in several additional respects. One of these is intimacy. While it is possible for members of triads (or larger groups) to develop very close relationships, there is generally a greater potential for intimacy when interaction is limited exclusively to two people.

Intimacy is a difficult concept to define, however. Traditionally, communication scholars have discussed intimacy in terms of amount and depth of self-disclosure. For example, a friendship was seen as intimate if the individuals told each other their most personal secrets. More recent evidence suggests that intimacy may result from participating in activities together as well as from disclosing highly personal information.[4] Intimate relationships based on mutual participation in activities may be particularly important for males. Although many men may enjoy doing things together while many women may enjoy talking together, this does not mean that men do not confide in each other and that women do not share activities.

Second, in relationships of more than two people, differences of opinion can be resolved by voting to determine the majority opinion. In dyads, negotiation is the only means of decision making available. A further distinction is that triads and larger groups have somewhat more stability than dyads. When only two people are involved in a relationship, either party has the power to destroy the unit by withdrawing. In triads, and larger social units, the withdrawal of one party may have a marked impact on the unit, but it will not necessarily lead to its termination.

Finally, it is rare that triads operate such that all parties are equally and evenly involved. Typically, at any point in time, two members of the relationship are closer to one another or in greater agreement than the other party or parties. The result is often the formation of coalitions, struggles for "leadership," and sometimes open conflict. Because of this, some authors have argued that there is actually no such thing as a triadic or quadratic relationship, but rather that such units are better thought of as a dyad plus one, or two dyads.[5]

Task and Social Relationships

In addition to thinking about relationships in terms of the number of people involved, we can also look at the primary purpose for their formation. Many relationships are developed for the purpose of *coordinated action*—completion of a task or project that one individual could not manage alone. A simple example of this type of relationship is one person holding on to a board while another person saws off a piece.

The relationships created between a taxi driver and passenger or between an athletic trainer and athlete, provide other illustrations of two individuals working together to accomplish a specific task.[6] Social units composed of colleagues at work, employer and employee, leader and follower, doctor and patient, teacher and student, therapist and patient, are additional examples of *task relationships* that play a major role in our lives.

In some situations, accomplishing a task is of secondary importance or perhaps of no significance whatsoever. In such circumstances, *personally-* or *socially-oriented goals* take precedence. Making a new acquaintance, having coffee with a friend, and spending time chatting periodically with a co-worker during lunch serve a number of important functions, even though they are not essential to the completion of a task. *Social relationships* can provide a means of diversion, recreation, intimacy, or companionship. They may also be a way of avoiding isolation or loneliness, confirming our own sense of worth, giving and receiving affection, or comparing our views and opinions to those held by others.[7]

Individuals may be willing to devote more or less time, energy, and commitment to a relationship, depending on whether they see it as essentially task or socially oriented. As a result, the communication patterns that develop will often vary substantially depending on how the members regard their purpose for participating in a given relationship in the first place.

Short- and Long-Term Relationships

Longevity is another factor that has a significant bearing on the nature of relationships. Most of us are engaged in at least several *long-term relationships* with members of our immediate families, relatives, intimates, and friends. We also participate in the formation and/or maintenance of any number of *transitory relationships*—an exchange of smiles and glances while walking down a hallway, a wave and hello to a familiar face in the neighborhood, or an exchange of pleasantries with a clerk in a store.

Between these two extremes are relationships of varying duration. In general, the older a relationship, the more the investment we have made in it, and the greater the investment we are willing to make in order to preserve it. A substantial investment in long-term relationships makes us willing to maintain them with investments that are greater than those we would make in a newly formed relationship.

With short-term relationships there is little history, generally fewer personal consequences should the relationship not progress, and relatively little personal involvement. In such circumstances, we are far less locked into particular identities, and much less constrained by past actions and the images others may have of us. In many instances, short-term relationships can be attractive and functional precisely because they are seen as allowing greater personal flexibility and requiring less investment, commitment, and follow-through. See Figure 7.3.

Figure 7.2
Friendships serve important functions in our lives.
© Syda Productions, 2014. Shutterstock, Inc.

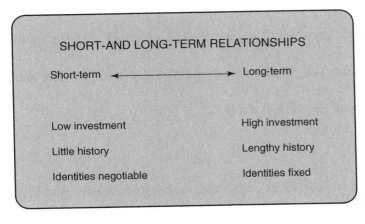

Figure 7.3

Casual and Intimate Relationships

Relationships can also be characterized in terms of their "depth" or level of intimacy. At one extreme are relationships between acquaintances. At the other extreme are relationships between intimates. Casual relationships between friends and colleagues fall near the center between these two extremes.

In general, relationships between acquaintances are characterized by impersonal and ritualized communication patterns. The following exchange of pleasantries is typical of such relationships:

> *Eric:* Hello. How are you?
>
> *Pam:* Fine, thanks, and you?
>
> *Eric:* Good.
>
> *Pam:* It's a beautiful day today, isn't it?
>
> *Eric:* Sure is.
>
> *Pam:* How's the family?
>
> *Eric:* Everyone is fine. How's yours?
>
> ***And so on.***

Disclosure.   The specifics of the exchange are impersonal and ritualized in the sense that either person could—and probably would—make the same remarks to anyone. There is little that suggests the uniqueness of the relationship to either individual. Further, in such a conversation, there is a lack of *self-disclosure, other-disclosure*, or *topical disclosure*.[8] That is, neither person is disclosing much information about his or her own opinions or beliefs at other than a surface level, and there is an obvious absence of personal feeling being expressed.

In more intimate relationships, individuals may share some of their private concerns about life, death, illness, and their feelings about other people and themselves. An exchange between people who have attained greater intimacy would contrast markedly with the previous exchange:

> *Eric:* Hello. How are you?
>
> *Pam:* Not that great, to be honest.
>
> *Eric:* What's the matter?
>
> *Pam:* I went for a routine check-up last week, and the doctor found a tumor.

Eric: How serious is it?

Pam: They don't know yet. The test results aren't back, but I'm really afraid.

Eric: I don't blame you. It scares me even hearing about it. Do you want to talk?

Pam: I really think I need to, if it's O.K.

Eric: Of course it's O.K. . . .

And so on.

Contrasted with the earlier example, this exchange is neither ritualized nor impersonal. A high degree of topical-disclosure, other-disclosure, and self-disclosure is involved. The interaction is also distinctive. It seems unlikely that either person would be participating in precisely the same kind of discussion with many other individuals, which suggests the uniqueness of this relationship.

A good deal of research has been conducted on self-disclosure. Findings include:[9]

- Disclosure increases with increased intimacy.
- Disclosure increases when rewarded.
- Disclosure increases with the need to reduce uncertainty in a relationship.
- Disclosure tends to be reciprocated.
- Women disclose more to individuals they like.
- Men disclose more to individuals they trust.
- Disclosure is regulated by rules of appropriateness.
- Attraction is related to positive disclosure but not to negative disclosure.
- Negative disclosure occurs with greater frequency in highly intimate settings than in less intimate ones.
- Relationship satisfaction is greatest when there is moderate—rather than a great deal of or very little—disclosure.

Relationships of different levels of intimacy have varying values for us. As Erving Goffman and other writers have noted, the ritualized exchanges that characterize casual acquaintances permit us to maintain contact with a large number of individuals with a minimum of effort and conscious attention. Such exchanges are a way of saying: "Hello, I see you. It seems to me it is worth acknowledging you. I want you to know that. I hope you feel the same way, too." Ritualized conversation is also important because it is generally the first step in developing closer relationships.

Intimate relationships, by contrast, require a substantial investment of time and effort. They can, however, provide opportunities for personal and social growth that may well be impossible to derive in any other way. They afford a context of trust in which individuals can express themselves candidly. Intimate relationships also encourage a greater degree of continuity and honesty than in other relationships, and allow us to openly explore and apply the insights gained over a period of time.

Intimate relationships may have physical benefits as well as emotional ones. In his book, *The Broken Heart: The Medical Consequences of Loneliness*, James Lynch cites research that indicates that the absence of intimate relationships can have negative medical consequences. Studies have shown that a continual state of loneliness, the absence or death of parents during the early years of childhood, or the loss of a loved one are significant factors contributing to the likelihood of premature death. This work vividly underscores the critical role of intimate relationships in our lives.[10]

Some studies suggest that having a relationship with a pet may serve the same beneficial role as significant human attachments in times of stress, providing not only a source of companionship but an aid to health and relaxation.

Are all pet relationships equally effective in this regard? Apparently not. Dogs seem to make better relationship partners than cats or birds. Studies show that dog owners with high levels of stress visited their physicians less frequently than similarly stressed people without dogs. This result did not occur for the owners of cats and birds.[11]

What is it, exactly, that dogs do in relationships that apparently makes them such ideal partners? Some dogs provide protection. But this is certainly not the case with the majority of pet dogs. Even if they lack the ability to protect their owners, they may still be wonderful companions. They exhibit a number of the qualities that are highly valued in human companions. Dogs are perceived by their owners to be attentive, interested, trusting, loyal, and tolerant. They are nonargumentative and seem, at times, able to demonstrate compassion and empathy. Some dogs are even masters of good eye contact. Collectively, these are many of the characteristics we value in friends and human companions; such behavior provides a sense of security and reassurance and confirms our sense of worth.

Dating, Love, and Marital Relationships

Communication obviously plays a very important role in dating, love, and marital relationships. The initial attraction and encounters that lead to dating, love, and marriage begin as casual contacts and develop through stages of increasing intimacy.

As Edwin Thomas explains:

> Talking is one of the primary activities marital partners engage in together and most couples spend enormous amounts of time talking to each other. Communication between marital partners is vitally important for individual well-being and mutual harmony. It reflects difficulties and strengths in the marriage and in other areas of life and sets the stage for future marital satisfaction or discord.[12]

Communication researcher Michael Beatty points out that early in the development of dating and love relationships, couples often overlook or avoid discussions of potential problems and conflicts.[13] They may assume that conversing about problems and the expression of conflict or anger will necessarily be destructive. As difficulties become great, pressure to address these issues increases. Couples lacking a tradition of disclosure and openness in dealing with one another and their relationship may decide that breaking up is the only logical alternative.

On the other hand, couples who are willing and able to converse with one another about their relationship, its evolution, and its problems may achieve more satisfying and effective relationships. Through conversation:

- Partners are able to anticipate or deal with potential problems at an early stage.
- Partners have the benefit of knowing how each other perceives and feels about the relationship, its development, and each other's contribution to it.
- Partners have the opportunity to work together to meet challenges and solve problems.
- Partners can monitor the relationship, and that process will provide an additional source of intimacy and commonness between them.

RESEARCH PROFILE

Disclosure of Personal Information • Kathryn Greene

People disclose information in a variety of contexts including interpersonal relationships and healthcare settings. Professor Greene's research demonstrates the importance of disclosing information about relevant topics such as HIV/AIDS.

• • •

Many college students are exploring relationships in the process of dating and meeting many new people. One issue that arises in dating or meeting new people generally is what information to share with this person, especially as it relates to health. My research focuses on the area of privacy and disclosure of HIV diagnoses. This work examines how people balance competing needs to disclose and protect privacy. Overall, my research indicates that people choose to disclose an HIV diagnosis to those they feel close to, when they expect a positive response to sharing the information, when they need support, and only after they have adjusted to the diagnosis. These decisions to disclose to family members, children, and partners are especially difficult.

Some of my research examines attitudes toward privacy, and other work examines disclosure behavior or intentions to disclose. For example, I conducted interviews with African American pregnant teenage women

with HIV about how they choose to share their diagnosis. This research on disclosure and health also provides added understanding about how risk decisions are made, for example the roles of stigma, relational variables, and the family. My most recent project in this area is described in a co-authored book, *Privacy, Disclosure of HIV/AIDS in Interpersonal Relationships: A Sourcebook for Researchers and Practitioners* (Lawrence Erlbaum, 2003). This particular line of research is expanding to include examination of the role of stigma in health decision making. Other emerging research focuses on the role of social and personal relationships in the context of health conditions. My research explores factors such as social support, coping, and disclosure in relationship management.

The value of this research examining privacy, disclosure, and stigma is particularly apparent in the application to HIV and AIDS. Because people with HIV need support and also can transmit the virus to partners, studying disclosure has potential benefits in multiple ways. Disclosing can help people access support, can possibly protect someone from contracting HIV, yet it is risky to tell others. To help apply the knowledge gained through research, I work with various local and regional HIV service organizations and several school districts and health departments on issues related to communication and disclosure.

Family Relationships

Families, and our images of families, are based on, formed, and maintained through communication. Family members and family relationships simultaneously influence and are influenced by each other.[14]

Historically, families have been defined from three perspectives: structural, psychosocial task, and transactional.[15] *Structural* definitions are based on the presence or absence of certain family members (for example, parents and children) and distinguish between families of origin, families of procreation, and extended families. *Psychosocial task* definitions are based on whether groups of people accomplish certain tasks together (for example, maintaining a household, educating children, and providing emotional and material support to each other). *Transactional* definitions are based on whether groups of intimates through their behavior generate a sense of family identity with emotional ties and an experience of a history and a future.

Communication scholars Ascan Koerner and Mary Ann Fitzpatrick argue that some families exhibit a *conversational orientation* in which they create an atmosphere in which all family members are encouraged to voice their opinions about a wide range of topics. These families believe that open and frequent sharing of information is essential to an enjoyable and rewarding family life. Families exhibiting a *conformity orientation* create a communication climate that is characterized by homogeneity of attitudes, values, and beliefs. This type of orientation is usually associated with a more traditional family structure.[16]

These orientations lead to four different types of families:[17]

- *Consensual* families are high in both conversation and conformity orientation. Their communication is characterized by an interest in open communication and exploring new ideas as well as a desire to preserve the existing hierarchy within the family.
- *Pluralistic* families have a high conversation orientation and low conformity. They are more likely to engage in open, unconstrained discussion among all family members about a variety of topics.
- *Protective* families are low on conversation orientation and high on conformity orientation. Their communication is more likely to emphasize parental authority with parents believing they should make all the decisions for their children.
- *Laissez-faire* families are low in both conversation and conformity orientations. They have relatively little interaction among family members. Parents exhibit relatively little interest in their children's decisions and do not appear to value communicating with them.

The relationship between mass media and family communication is highly interdependent and complex.[18] Communication researcher Barbara J. Wilson reminds us how family life may be organized, structured, and defined in part by the mass media, particularly television. In many families, the architecture of the house, meal times, and even conversations are structured around television. Television and other media, such as the Internet, have the potential to enhance family interaction if, for instance, they bring families together in a shared social space and foster a feeling of togetherness. In this way, as families structure their activities around the media, the technologies themselves become part of how family members negotiate their social reality. Media also play an important role in shaping one's beliefs and expectations of family life. On the other hand, family conflict can also arise over mass media, for example, when family members argue over the remote control or who will have access to the computer to check their e-mail.

Communication within families is influenced by many factors including culture, race, and ethnicity. Research based on European American families does not necessarily generalize to non–European American families.[19] But ethnicity is a good predictor of family communication only when we study people who

Figure 7.4
Nonverbal cues provide information about the nature of relationships.
© iofoto, 2014. Shutterstock, Inc.

identify with their ethnic groups and maintain ethnic cultural practices. Given the increasing number of blended families, traditions common to members of particular groups are being adopted by others, which creates more diverse communication patterns for many families.

THE EVOLUTION OF RELATIONSHIPS

Whether relationships are dyads or triads, task or socially oriented, short- or long-term, casual or intimate, the dynamics by which they are initiated, develop, and eventually deteriorate and terminate are quite similar in terms of communication.[20]

Stage One: Initiation

The initial stage in the formation of any relationship involves *social initiation* or *encounter*. In this phase, two or several individuals take note of and adjust to one another's behavior. Often the initial messages to which the individuals adjust are nonverbal—a smile, glance, handshake, movement, or appearance. Should the relationship continue, progressive reciprocity of message processing occurs. One person notices the other's actions, position, appearance, and gestures. The second person reacts, and those reactions are noted and reacted to by the first person, whose reactions are acted on by the second person, and so on.

During the early stages of a relationship, the individuals involved operate in terms of the personal theories, representations, and communication habits they bring with them from previous experiences. As interpersonal communication progresses, each begins to acquire some knowledge of the other's ways of sensing, making sense of, acting, and reacting. Gradually, through combination, recombination, blend, mutation, compromise, and unspoken negotiation, the joint rules by which their particular relationship will operate begin to emerge.

As we encounter another person and initiate a relationship, we have two concerns—being perceived positively by the other person and evaluating the other person. Most people want to be perceived by others as worthy human beings, and, therefore, we try to act in a manner we believe will be seen favorably by the other person. Most job applicants, for example, will not put their feet on the interviewer's desk or chew gum during a job interview. In general, we believe that a person who puts feet up on a desk and chews gum does not understand the rules of the workplace, is not showing respect to the interviewer, and, therefore, won't be a good employee. The gum-chewer might be a brilliant accountant, but probably will not get past the first interview.

We make evaluations in a similar manner in other types of relationships, too. For example, we have often heard people refer to others as "my type" or "not my type." This means that some individuals have an idea of the characteristics (often physical) of a person who will make a good relationship partner, and they look for that type of person to date. Good friends sometimes know that this particular pairing will eventually lead to relationship disaster, but are powerless to stop someone from getting into yet another bad relationship.

Stage Two: Exploration

The second stage of relational development, *exploration*, picks up shortly after the initial encounter, as the participants begin exploring potentials of the other person and the possibility of further pursuing the relationship. In this phase we gather information about the other person's style, motives, interests, and values. This knowledge serves as the basis for assessing the merits of continuing the relationship.

This stage may be characterized by small talk—but the importance of this talk is anything but small. All relationships begin with the participants trying to find out information about each other. Beyond observing what a person looks like from the outside, we need to know what the person is like "on the inside" in order to feel comfortable talking about topics of more depth than the weather or the score of the last football game. Sometimes this conversation is difficult because we really don't know what the other person likes to talk about. Sometimes this conversation is formalized, as in a job interview in which the interviewer has a set list of questions to ask of each applicant, or in an examination at the doctor's office that involves a specific list of questions in order to make a diagnosis.

Although exploration may be hard work, it is often enjoyable to get to know another person and to hear what he or she has to say about particular topics. Future conversations get easier as we learn more about people and get to know their likes and dislikes better.

Stage Three: Intensification

If the relationship progresses, it moves into a third phase, which Mark Knapp and Anita Vangelisti have labeled the *intensifying* stage.[21] In reaching this level, the participants have arrived at a decision—which they may or may not verbalize—that they wish the relationship to continue. As the relationship progresses, they acquire a good deal of knowledge about each other and, at the same time, create a number of joint rules, a shared language, and characteristic relational rituals. A relationship at this stage may stall, deteriorate, or continue to develop.

At this stage of a relationship, people often consider themselves "close friends." People at this stage are more likely to share deeper secrets (such as their fear of failure or past drug use), to use more personal terms or nicknames for each other, and to develop symbols that have a private meaning. For example, items that were bought together (like a favorite lamp or chair) or events that were shared (like getting soaked in a rainstorm while waiting for a taxi) are used as the basis for intimate conversations.[22] We also intensify our relationships nonverbally by touching each other more frequently and in more intimate ways.

Figure 7.5
Relationship stages are reflected in nonverbal as well as verbal behavior patterns.
© karelnoppe, 2014. Shutterstock, Inc.

Stage Four: Formalization

Should the relationship progress further, some formal, symbolic acknowledgement binding the individuals to one another is common. In the case of a love relationship, the formal bonding may take the form of engagement or wedding rings. With an individual being hired for a job, the employee and employer may sign a contract. Where two persons are entering a business partnership, the relationship may be formalized by ratifying legal agreements.

During this stage, the individuals advance in their joint creation of relational rules, including the development of shared symbols and preferred and characteristic patterns of conversing. The meanings of these verbal and nonverbal behaviors become standardized. Over time, the relationship develops a distinctiveness that distinguishes it in subtle and not-so-subtle ways from the many other relationships in which the individuals have been involved.

Formalization is a very important stage in any relationship. This is the stage in which people announce to the world that they are committed to each other. This commitment may be indicated nonverbally (for example, with an engagement ring) or by referring to a person in a different way (for example, "this is my fiancé").

Although the beginning of this process may be very exciting (such as planning a wedding or getting a first job), the relationship can develop repetitive communication patterns. These patterns may be positive or negative. For example, some couples may enjoy greeting each other in the same way every day when they return from work ("So how was your day?") while others find that they have the same fight ("Why are you always late?") over and over again.

Stage Five: Redefinition

With the passage of time, people inevitably grow and develop, creating pressure for change on the other person in the relationship, as well as on the relationship itself. As a consequence, a need for redefining some of the joint rules of the relationship often arises. There are many classic illustrations of these types of situations: perhaps a teenager no longer wants to be so closely supervised by his or her parents, or an employee wants more latitude on the job than when first hired. In each instance, changes in the individuals place strains on their relationships and on the accepted and often difficult-to-change rules and patterns that have developed.

Sometimes the needed redefinition is a very gradual, natural, and easily manageable part of the evolution of a relationship. In other instances, when change is too rapid or extreme, or resistance too great, a deterioration process begins. The couple who fights about one partner's chronic lateness may resolve their difficulties by agreeing to meet in a location in which the prompt partner can do something while waiting for the other person. An employer with an employee who is chronically late may file a formal reprimand and warn the person that his or her job is in jeopardy if the behavior does not change.

Stage Six: Deterioration

Initially, the deterioration may go unnoticed, as people in a relationship begin more and more to "go their own ways" physically and symbolically. Things that once were shared no longer are. Words or gestures that once mattered no longer do. Once-glowing prospects for the future at a particular job become blurred and faded. Rules that grew naturally in a love relationship during its development now seem confining and are followed with resignation.

Figure 7.6
Symbols and Rituals of
Bonding
© Ioannis Ioannou, 2014.
Shutterstock, Inc.

Once the deterioration process has reached this point, it is quite likely that the relationship is headed for dissolution, as the behaviors of each person come to make less and less difference to the actions and reactions of the other. Physical separation and the dissolution of any remaining legal or contractual obligations are the final steps in the often painful process of terminating a relationship.

Communication researcher Steve Duck has identified four phases in the dissolution process, which can be summarized as follows:[23]

"Self-Talk" Phase

- Focusing on the other partner's behavior
- Evaluating our own contribution and adequacy in the relationship
- Emphasizing negatives of the relationship
- Considering withdrawal
- Identifying positive aspects of alternative relationships

Interpersonal Communication Phase

- Deciding to confront the problem openly
- Confronting
- Negotiating and discussing
- Exploring possibilities for repair and reconciliation
- Assessing costs of withdrawal or reduced intimacy
- Separating

Group and Social Communication Phase

- Agreeing with the partner as to how to relate to one another following dissolution of the relationship
- Initiating gossip/discussion in social groups
- Constructing and telling face-saving and blame-placing stories and accounts of what happened
- Considering and dealing with the effects on our other social groups

"Grave Dressing" and Public Communication Phase

- "Rebounding"
- Replaying, analyzing, and moralizing—postmortem replay of events
- Distributing our own version of the break-up story publicly

Relationships do not necessarily move through these stages in an orderly way. They may stall in any one stage, back up and go forward again, or stop at one point for an extended period of time.

RELATIONAL PATTERNS

As relationships evolve, characteristic communication patterns develop. These relational patterns are the result of joint rules that have developed between the people involved. In this section, we will briefly consider four of the most common of these communication patterns: (1) supportive and defensive climates; (2) dependencies and counter-dependencies; (3) progressive and regressive spirals; and (4) self-fulfilling and self-defeating prophecies.[24]

Supportive and Defensive Climates

"I appreciate how supportive you were last night when I was upset."

"Do you have to criticize and judge everything I do?"

"I wish you would appreciate me more."

"It seems as though you find fault with me no matter what I say or do."

"You're being so defensive!"

The orientations of individuals within relationships and their patterns of communicating with one another create the climate of communication. Climates and individual behaviors can be characterized along a continuum from highly *supportive* to highly *defensive*. Each statement above is a comment on how supportive or defensive the speaker perceives another person—and the relationship overall—to be at a particular point in time.

There are a number of communication behaviors that tend to create and maintain defensive climates within relationships:[25]

- *Evaluating.* Judging other's behavior
- *Controlling.* Striving to control or manage other's behavior
- *Developing strategy.* Planning techniques, hidden agendas, and moves to use in relationships, as you might in a chess game
- *Remaining neutral.* Remaining aloof and remote from others' feelings and concerns
- *Asserting superiority.* Seeing and expressing yourself as more worthy than others
- *Conveying certainty.* Assuming and acting as though you are absolutely certain in your knowledge and perceptions

In contrast, the following behaviors are seen as contributing to a supportive climate:

- *Describing.* Describing rather than judging or evaluating the other person's behavior
- *Maintaining a problem orientation.* Focusing on specific problems to be solved
- *Being spontaneous.* Dealing with situations as they develop, without a hidden agenda or "master plan"
- *Empathizing.* Looking at things from the other person's viewpoint
- *Asserting equality.* Seeing and presenting ourselves as equal to others
- *Conveying provisionalism.* Maintaining a degree of uncertainty and tentativeness in our thoughts and beliefs

Dependencies and Counterdependencies

The dynamics of dependency and counterdependency are prevalent in many relationships at various points in time. A *dependency relationship* exists when one individual in a relationship who is highly dependent on another for support, money, work, leadership, or guidance generalizes this dependency to other facets of the relationship.

The classic example of this kind of relational dynamic develops between children and their parents or, in some cases, between therapists and their patients.[26] In both instances, one individual has particular needs or goals that are being met by the other individual or individuals in the relationship. The dependent pattern may become more generalized, so that one person comes to rely on the other in a broad range of circumstances that are unrelated to the original basis for dependency. When this occurs, a dynamic is set in motion that can have farreaching impact and consequences for the individuals as well as the relationship. Whether people are discussing politics, sex, or religion, whether they are trying to decide where to eat or where to live, the dependent person comes to take cues from the other, on whom he or she has learned to rely, as the following conversation might suggest:

Alice: I think we should go to The Tavern for lunch. How does that sound?

Jenny: Fine.

Alice: Come to think of it, The Tavern is likely to be crowded at this hour. How about the Corner Grill?

Jenny: Sure, that sounds great, too.

In other relationships, or in the same relationship at other points in time, the dependency is in the opposite direction. In these circumstances, one individual relates to the other not as a dependent but, instead, as a *counterdependent*. While the dependent individual complies with the other person in the relationship across a broad range of topics, the counterdependent person characteristically disagrees, as the following scenario illustrates:

Alice: I think we should go to The Tavern for lunch. How does that sound?

Jenny: I'm tired of The Tavern.

Alice: How about the Corner Grill?

Jenny: That's no better. I was thinking of a place with nice salads.

Alice: What about The Attic?

Jenny: It's really not worth all this time deciding. Let's just go to The Tavern and be done with it.

In the first circumstance, we can assume that whatever Alice suggests, Jenny would follow. In the second, it seems likely that whatever Alice suggests, Jenny would disagree.

As dependencies and counterdependencies become a habitual way of relating, they guide, shape, and often overshadow the specific content of conversation. Eventually, at the extreme, the content of what the individuals say comes to have little impact on the dynamics. When person A says "yes," person B agrees. Or, when A says "no," B consistently disagrees.

Progressive and Regressive Spirals

When the actions and reactions of individuals in a relationship are consistent with their goals and needs, the relationship progresses with continual increases in the level of harmony and satisfaction. This circumstance can be described as a *progressive spiral*. In progressive spirals, the reciprocal message processing of the interactants leads to a sense of "positiveness" in their experiences. The satisfaction each person derives builds on itself, and the result is a relationship that is a source of growing pleasure and value for the participants.

The opposite kind of pattern can also develop, in which each exchange contributes to a progressive decrease in satisfaction and harmony. In these circumstances—*regressive spirals*—there is increasing discomfort, distance, frustration, and dissatisfaction for everyone involved. Perhaps the simplest example of a regressive spiral is provided by an argument:

> *Ann:* Will you try to remember to do the dishes tomorrow morning before you go to work?
>
> *Mike:* You know I get really sick of your nagging all the damned time!
>
> *Ann:* If you were a little more reliable and a little less defensive, we might not need to have these same discussions over and over again.
>
> *Mike:* You're hardly the one to lecture me about memory or defensiveness. If you remembered half the things you've promised to do, we would have a lot fewer arguments. It's your defensiveness, not mine, that causes all of our problems. . . .

Like dependencies, spirals often take on a life of their own, fueled by the momentum they themselves create. What begins as a request to do the dishes can easily become still another in a string of provocations in a relationship where regressive spirals are common. And, by contrast, "Hi, how are you?" can initiate a very positive chain of events in a relationship characterized by frequent progressive spirals.

Over time, the spirals that characterize any relationship alternate between progressive and regressive. However, in order for a relationship to maintain strength, momentum, and continuity, the progressive phases must outweigh and/ or outlast the regressive periods.

FACTORS THAT INFLUENCE PATTERNS

We have looked at the role communication plays in the evolution of relationships and the patterns that develop within them. In this section, we will focus on the factors that influence these patterns. A number of elements have an impact on interpersonal communication. Particularly important are stage and context of interaction, interpersonal needs, and style, power, and conflict.

Stage of Relationship and Context

Communication patterns in a relationship vary greatly from one stage to another. Naturally, people meeting each other for the first time interact in a different manner than people who have lived together for several years. The nature of interpersonal patterns also varies depending on the context in which conversation is taking place. People meeting in a grocery store are quite likely to act and react differently to one another than if they are talking in a bar or at a business meeting. Together, these two factors account for much of the variation in the patterns of communication within relationships.

Interpersonal Needs and Styles

Beyond the rather direct and obvious impact of stage and context, the interpersonal needs and styles of the individuals involved represent other influences on communication within relationships.

Often noted as especially important in this way are the interpersonal needs for *affection, inclusion,* and *control.* William Schutz has suggested that our desires relative to giving and receiving affection, being included in the activities of others and including them in ours, and controlling other people and being controlled by them are very basic to our orientations to social relations of all kinds.[27]

We each develop our own specific needs relative to control, affection, and inclusion, as we do in other areas. The particular profile of needs we have, and how these match with those of other people, can be a major determinant of the relational patterns that result. For instance, we could expect that one person with high needs for control and another with similarly strong needs to be controlled would function well together. The former would fall comfortably into a dominant leadership role, while the latter would be very willing to follow. If, on the other hand, two people who work or live together have similarly high (or low) needs for control, one might predict a good deal of conflict (or a lack of decisiveness) within the relationship.

Interpersonal *style* also plays a key role in shaping the communication patterns that emerge in relationships. As discussed earlier, some people are more comfortable operating in an outgoing, highly verbal manner in their dealings with others, while others characteristically adopt a more passive and restrained interpersonal style, due either to preference or apprehension about speaking in social situations. Those who use a more outgoing style deal with their thoughts and feelings in a forthright, assertive manner.[28] If they want something, they ask for it. If they feel angry, they let others know. If they feel taken advantage of, they say so. If they don't want to comply with a request, they have little trouble saying "no!" In contrast to an externalizing style of interpersonal communication, the internalizing style involves "absorbing" the verbal and nonverbal messages of others, giving the outward appearance of acceptance, congeniality, and even encouragement, regardless of one's thoughts or feelings.[29] For any of several reasons, people who are prone to use the internalizing style often "bottle up" thoughts, opinions, and feelings. If they are angry, it is seldom apparent from what is said. If they disagree, they seldom say so. If they feel taken advantage of, they may allow the situation to continue rather than confront it openly.

Though few of us use either style exclusively, we often favor one approach over the other in the majority of our dealings with people; and, depending on the style of the people with whom we are in relationships, this factor alone can become a primary influence in shaping our interactions and our relationships, as is suggested in the following conversation:

> ***Tom:*** Georgia, you wouldn't mind taking me home tonight after work, would you? I know I impose on you a lot, but Mary needed the car again today, and I know you're the kind of person who doesn't mind helping out now and then.

> ***Georgia:*** Well, I was going to stay late tonight, but if you have no other way, I . . .

Tom: Hey thanks, Georgia. I was sure I could count on you. How are things anyway? Really busy, I'll bet. Well, listen, I'd better get back to work. I'll meet you by your car at 5:00. Thanks again.

Tom's externalizing style, in combination with Georgia's internalizing style, will no doubt be critical factors in defining many of the interactions that take place between them.

Power

Interpersonal communication within relationships is also shaped by the distribution of power. Where one individual is employed by the other, for instance, the relationship is *asymmetrical*, or uneven, in terms of the actual power each has in the job situation.[30] The employer can exercise more control over that facet of their relationship—so long as the other person does not quit—simply as a consequence of the uneven control over resources and decision making.

There are many similar situations where asymmetries affect interpersonal communication. The relationship between a therapist and a patient, a teacher and a student, a parent and a child, or a supervisor and supervisee are among the most common examples. In each, one member of the relationship has control over certain facets of the other's life, a circumstance that generally has a substantial impact on the interpersonal communication patterns that develop.

In peer–peer, colleague–colleague, or other relationships of this type, there is the potential for symmetry. Where this possibility exists, interpersonal communication creates rather than perpetuates any dependencies that result.

Conflict

The presence of *conflict*—"an incompatibility of interest between two or more people giving rise to struggles between them"—can have a major impact on communication dynamics.[31] Communication researcher Alan Sillars suggests that when people are involved in conflict situations they develop their own personal theories to explain the situation. These theories, in turn, have a great influence on how interactants deal with one another.

Sillers finds that there are three general communication strategies used in conflict resolution:[32]

- *Passive-indirect methods.* Avoiding the conflict-producing situation and people
- *Distributive methods.* Maximizing one's own gain and the other's losses
- *Integrative methods.* Achieving mutually positive outcomes for both individuals and the relationship

IMPLICATIONS AND APPLICATIONS

- Being competent in interpersonal communication involves applying our understanding of communication and interpersonal relationships to everyday life. The goal is to use our knowledge to increase our interpersonal satisfaction and effectiveness from our own perspective, as well as from the perspective of those with whom we interact.[33]
- Self-awareness in relationships can contribute to interpersonal communication competence. Psychologist Carl Rogers offers the following personal observations on therapeutic relationships, which can be applied in many other types of relationships as well:[34]

In my relationships with persons I have found that it does not help, in the long run, to act as though I were something that I am not.

I find I am more effective when I can listen acceptingly to myself and can be myself.

I have found it of enormous value when I can permit myself to understand another person.

I have found it enriching to open channels whereby others can communicate their feelings, their private perceptual worlds, to me.

I have found it highly rewarding when I can accept another person.

The more I am open to the realities in me and in the other person, the less do I find myself wishing to rush in to "fix things."

Life, at its best, is a flowing, changing process in which nothing is fixed.

- Empathy and respect for others' opinions, knowledge, and perspective generally enhances communication.
- Listening, observing, and interpreting are vital to communication competence in relationships. Every person reacts to a situation in his or her own way; some people are more interpersonally sensitive than others. The following guidelines can be helpful:[35]

Practice your listening, observation, and interpretation skills.

Try not to be distracted by an emotion-arousing word, phrase, or action.

Adapt to the situation.

Listen to and observe the total person. Attend to both the verbal and nonverbal channels.

Strive to interpret messages according to the other person's codes and meanings, not your own.

Be aware of potential gender-based differences in communication.

- One of the benefits of studying communication is its value for analyzing our relationships and the communication behaviors of our acquaintances, friends, family, colleagues, and intimates. This knowledge can sometimes be productively shared with others to help them better understand their own communication in relationships. Sharing interpersonal perspectives effectively requires sensitivity:

Describe rather than criticize.

Be specific and avoid generalizations.

Focus comments on communication behaviors that the other person can change.

Select a time and place for discussions of relationships that is appropriate and meets the needs of all parties.

Strive to make the discussion and suggestions you may have for others constructive, not destructive.[36]

SUMMARY

In this chapter, we have examined the relationship between communication and relationships. We have also discussed a number of ways of thinking about and characterizing relationships, and explored common communication patterns that can occur. Communication plays a central role in the development and evolution of all human relationships. Relationships also provide perhaps the most important context in which we attempt to use our communication abilities to achieve particular goals and meet particular needs.

In the most general sense, a relationship exists whenever there is reciprocal message processing—when two or more individuals are reacting to one another's verbal and nonverbal behavior. It is by means of interpersonal communication that relationships are initiated, develop, grow, or deteriorate.

Intentionally-established relationships can be considered from several perspectives: whether they are dyadic or triadic; whether they are task-oriented or social in purpose; whether they are short- or long-term; whether they are casual or intimate. We also have discussed dating, love, and marital relationships.

Relationships progress through a series of relatively predictable stages, beginning from an initial social encounter, progressing to stages of increasing interaction and joint rule creation. Many relationships involve some formalized acknowledgement of their status, such as marriage or a legal business contract. A relationship may stall in one of these stages, back up and go forward again, or stop and remain in one stage for an extended period of time.

Over time, communication patterns develop in relationships. Often these dynamics take the form of defensiveness or supportiveness, dependencies or counterdependencies, progressive or regressive spirals, or self-fulfilling or self-defeating prophecies. These dynamics can have a far more significant impact on the form and development patterns of relationships than does the content of interaction.

A number of factors, such as stage and context, interpersonal needs and style, distribution of power, and the presence of conflict play a role in facilitating the development of particular patterns.

ENDNOTES

1. The discussion of dyads and triads draws on the excellent summary of work on this topic provided by William Wilmot in *Dyadic Communication*, 3rd ed. (New York: Random House, 1987).

2. Wilmot, 1987, pp. 121–129.

3. William M. Kephart, "A Quantitative Analysis of Intra-Group Relationships," *American Journal of Sociology*, Vol. 55, 1950, pp. 544–549.

4. Julia T. Wood and Christopher C. Inman, "In a Different Mode: Masculine Styles of Communicating Closeness," *Journal of Applied Communication Research*, Vol. 21, 1993, pp. 279–296.

5. Wilmot, 1987, pp. 121–129.

6. Fred Davis, "The Cabdriver and His Fare: Facets of a Fleeting Relationship," in *Interpersonal Dynamics*. Ed. by Warren G. Bennis, David E. Berlew, Edgar H. Schein, and Fred I. Steele (Homewood, IL: Dorsey, 1973), pp. 417–426.

7. See Michael D. Scott and William G. Powers, *Interpersonal Communication: A Question of Needs* (Boston: Houghton Mifflin, 1978), for a useful discussion of the role of needs in interpersonal communication and relational development.

8. See Joseph Luft, *Of Human Interaction* (Palo Alto, CA: National Press Books, 1969); Sidney M. Jourard, *The Transparent Self* (Princeton, NJ: Van Nostrand, 1964); and Stella Ting-Toomey, "Gossip as a Communication Construct." Paper presented at the Annual Conference of the Western Speech Communication Association. Los Angeles, February, 1979.

9. Based on summary provided by Stephen W. Littlejohn, *Theories of Human Communication*, Third ed. (Belmont, CA: Wadsworth, 1989), p. 161, adapted from Shirley J. Gilbert, "Empirical and Theoretical Extensions of Self-Disclosure," in *Explorations in Interpersonal Communication*. Ed. by Gerald R. Miller (Beverly Hills: Sage, 1976), pp. 197–216.

10. James J. Lynch, *The Broken Heart: The Medical Consequences of Loneliness* (New York: Basic Books, 1979).

11. See discussion in E. Friedman, A. H. Kathcher, J. J. Lynch, and A. A. Thomas, "Animal Companions and One-Year Survival of Patients after Discharge from a Coronary Care Unit," *Public Health Reports*, 95, 1980, pp. 307–312; T. F. Garrity, L. Stallones, M. B. Marx, and T. P. Johnson, "Pet Ownership and Attachment as Supportive Factors in the Health of the Elderly," *Anthrozoos*, 3, 1989, pp. 35–44; and J. M. Siegel, "Stressful Live Events and the Use of Physician Services among the Elderly: The Moderating Role of Pet Ownership," *Journal of Personality and Social Psychology*, 58(6), 1990, pp. 1081–1086.

12. Edwin J. Thomas, *Marital Communication and Decision-Making* (New York: Free Press, 1977), p. 1.

13. See extensive discussion of dating and marriage, summarized in this section, in Michael J. Beatty, *Romantic Dialogue: Communication in Dating and Marriage* (Englewood, CO: Morton, 1986).

14. Anita L. Vangelisti, *Handbook of Family Communication* (London: Lawrence Erlbaum, 2004).

15. Ascan F. Koerner and Mary Ann Fitzpatrick, "Communication in Intact Families," in *Handbook of Family Communication*. Ed. by Anita L. Vangelisti (London: Lawrence Erlbaum, 2004), pp. 177–196.

16. Koerner and Fitzpatrick, 2004, pp. 177–196.

17. Koerner and Fitzpatrick, 2004, pp. 177–196.

18. Barbara J. Wilson, "The Mass Media and Family Communication," in *Handbook of Family Communication*. Ed. by Anita L. Vangelisti (London: Erlbaum, 2004), pp. 563–593.

19. William B. Gudykunst and C. M. Lee, "An Agenda for Study Ethnicity and Family Communication," *Journal of Family Communication*, Vol. 1, 2001, pp. 75–85.

20. The discussion of stages of development of relationships draws on the work of Mark L. Knapp and Anita L. Vangelisti in *Interpersonal Communication and Human Relationships* (Boston: Allyn & Bacon, 1992), and Murray S. Davis, *Intimate Relations* (New York: Free Press, 1973).

21. Knapp and Vangelisti, 1992, pp. 37–38.

22. Leslie A. Baxter, "Symbols of Relationship Identity in Relationship Cultures," *Journal of Social and Personal Relationships*, Vol. 4, 1987, pp. 261–280.

23. Based on Steve Duck, "A Topography of Relationship Disagreement and Dissolution," in *Personal Relationships 4: Dissolving Personal Relationships* (New York: Academic Press, 1982).

24. See discussion of spirals and prophecies in Wilmot, 1987, pp. 121–129, and in Paul Watzlawick, Janet H. Beavin, and Don D. Jackson, *Pragmatics of Human Communication* (New York: Norton, 1967), pp. 51–54.

25. Jack R. Gibb, "Defensive Communication," *Journal of Communication*, Vol. 11, Sept. 1961, p. 41. Also see discussion of supportiveness–defensiveness in Steven A. Beebe and John T. Masterson, *Family Talk: Interpersonal Communication in the Family* (New York: Random House), 1986, pp. 145–150.

26. See Robert R. Carkhuff and Bernard G. Berenson, *Beyond Counseling and Therapy* (New York: Holt, 1967).

27. William Schultz, *The Interpersonal Underworld* (Palo Alto, CA: Science and Behavior Books, 1968).

28. See Colleen Kelley, "Assertion Theory," in *The 1976 Annual Handbook for Group Facilitators*. Ed. by J. William Pfeiffer and John E. Jones (La Jolla, CA: University Associates, 1976); Sharon and Gordon Bowers, *Asserting Yourself* (Reading, MA: Addison-Wesley, 1976); and Colleen Kelley, *Assertion Training* (La Jolla, CA: University Associates, 1979).

29. Brent D. Ruben, "The Machine Gun and the Marshmallow: Some Thoughts on the Concept of Communication Effectiveness." Paper presented at the annual conference of the Western Speech Association (Honolulu: November, 1972), and Brent D. Ruben, "Communication, Stress, and Assertiveness: An Interpersonal Problem-Solving Model," in *The 1982 Annual Handbook for Group Facilitators*. Ed. by J. William Pfeiffer and John E. Jones (La Jolla, CA: University Associates, 1982).

30. Watzlawick, et al., 1967, pp. 67–71.

31. Herbert W. Simons, "The Carrot and Stick as Handmaidens of Persuasion in Conflict Situations," in *Perspectives on Communication in Social Conflict*. Ed. by Gerald R. Miller and Herbert W. Simons (Englewood Cliffs, NJ: Prentice Hall, 1974), pp. 177–178. See also review of definitions and approaches to conflict in Brent D. Ruben, "Communication and Conflict: A System-Theoretic Perspective," *The Quarterly Journal of Speech*, Vol. 64, 1978, pp. 202–210.

32. Alan L. Sillars, "Attributions and Communication in Roommate Conflicts," *Communication Monographs,* Vol. 47, 1980, pp. 180–200.

33. See discussion of communication competence in Brian H. Spitzberg and William R. Cupach, *Interpersonal Communication Competence* (Beverly Hills: Sage, 1984). Also see discussion in Littlejohn, p. 182.

34. Carl Rogers, *On Becoming a Person: A Therapist's View of Psychotherapy* (Boston: Houghton Mifflin, 1970), pp. 15–27.

35. Adapted from Beebee and Masterson, 1986, pp. 182–183.

36. Based on Beebee and Masterson, 1986, pp. 217–219; Gibb, 1961.

CHAPTER

8

Relationships in a Digital Age

Sal 9000 knew she was the one for him. Nene was beautiful, she didn't fight with him, and she attended to him as he wished. In fact, Sal referred to Nene as his dream woman. So he knew that he had to marry her. And when the ceremony took place, it was broadcast live to thousands of people online in Japan.

Anything seem strange yet? If not, keep reading.

The most interesting part of this story is not that two people got married. It is not even that the ceremony was broadcast live online (which is a growing phenomenon, as is broadcasting funerals, for reasons we will discuss later in the book). No, what you will likely find to be the strangest part of this story is that one of the "participants" in this wedding is not a person at all. Can you guess which one?

Sal 9000 is a real person, a 27-year-old from Japan. But his beautiful bride? She is a video game character from the Nintendo DS *Love Plus*.

Now does anything seem strange to you? If you are like most of the students we have discussed this with, you will likely think it is incredibly strange and maybe even a little (or a lot) creepy.

But is this creepy? Sal says he does not feel the need for a human girlfriend, even suggesting that Nene is better than a human girlfriend, stating "she doesn't get angry if I'm late in replying to her. Well, she gets angry, but she forgives me quickly." CNN's Kyung Lah has a short interview with Sal 9000—complete with photos and videos of his wedding—available at http://www.cnn.com/2009/WORLD/asiapcf/12/16/japan.virtual.wedding/index.html?iref=allsearch

Creepy or not, we believe this story highlights and illuminates a lot about relationships in the digital age and relationships in general, for that matter. This chapter (and the next) will discuss this phenomenon and will give some reasoning behind how and why we might use CMC for relationships, both close and acquaintance, and even with ourselves. After reading it, come back and ask yourself again: is the story of Sal 9000 creepy? If you are saying yes now, you will likely still be saying yes later. But hopefully, you will also maybe gain a little understanding into what might be going on in Sal's relationship with Nene and maybe will think a little bit differently about your own relationships as well.

KEY WORDS

ARPANet
E-mail
Social interactions
Social network site (SNS)
Goldilocks effect
Context collapse
Dating Web site
Impression management
Social presence
Telepresence

From *Introduction to Computer Mediated Communication: A Functional Approach* by Westermann et al. Copyright © 2014 by Kendall Hunt Publishing Company. Reprinted by permission.

153

When reading this chapter, consider the following:

- Think back to our earlier discussion of Maslow's hierarchy of needs (Chapter 3). Is there a connection between Maslow and our desire to use new media to connect to others?
- Are online relationships "bad" or "good"?
- How have our assumptions regarding online dating changed in recent years?
- Why is presence important when thinking about the ways we connect online?
- What does the "media equation" tell us about our interactions with mediated individuals?

WE ARE A SOCIAL SPECIES

So, why might Sal 9000 choose to "marry" a video game character? First, it is important to consider a general truth about people. We are social animals. On the whole, we desire interaction with other people. In fact, this is something that is necessary for our survival—so goes the old saying "no man is an island, completely unto himself." Psychologists Edward Deci and Richard Ryan suggest that the need for relatedness—that is, our desire to engage in meaningful relationships with others—is one of the primary factors that motivate people to do things. Thus, it should come as no surprise that people use a communication tool such as the Internet in order to connect with other people. Whether it is an alphabet of symbols for spoken language, books and telegraphs so that we can send written communications, a television show so that an organization can broadcast messages to large audiences, or a message posted on a social media profile, technology allows people to communicate in new ways and have a profound impact on the ways humans communicate with each other. But regardless of the technology itself, a main purpose is to communicate with each other—to engage in decidedly interpersonal communication.

Perhaps, surprisingly to some who assume all technology to be a form of mass communication, research has shown that interpersonal communication is a common use of the Internet. People use various Internet-based applications to connect and interact with other people, and this social interaction cuts across types of relationships: romantic partners, family members, friends, and acquaintances among them. Indeed, this is a bit different from the initial functions of the Internet. When the Internet was first created as **ARPAnet** in 1969, it was designed as an interconnected computer mainframe network that would connect researchers who would have a "place" to share research and information more quickly and easily than by doing it face-to-face. Put another way, it was designed to overcome the space and time limitations of face-to-face communication.

Then a funny thing happened. Two years later, in 1971, ARPAnet added an early electronic "mail" system so that individual researchers could contact each other with specific questions, similar to leaving memos in office mailboxes. As has been pointed out by communication scholar John Sherry and one of this book's authors in 2008, this **e-mail** system became the killer application that led to the early (and continued) expansion of what we today know of as the Internet. It turns out those early ARPAnet researchers, like most other humans, wanted to talk to people with whom they shared similarities. Messages about research would include increasingly interpersonal information as the scientists got to know each other over common work interests and shifted their conversations from being task-oriented to being more social-oriented over time.

We have come a long way since that early ARPAnet, and we have opened the Internet (and the many internets that comprise it) to a much greater number of

ARPANet The Advanced Research Projects Agency Network, this system of networked computers was started in 1969 with funding and oversight from the U.S. military. The network was designed to allow researchers to share data quickly and confidentially across large spaces.

E-mail A form of electronic communication in which users can send each other private messages to digital mailboxes, similar to sending a letter through a traditional mail service.

users than ever before. For example, as of 2013, Facebook boasts over one billion individual accounts, representing nearly one in every seven people living on Earth. Although there is some debate as to how many of these accounts belong to "real" people, we can see that having such a large user base is staggering considering the platform was launched in 2004. Even technologies such as video games, which are not primarily designed for social interaction (or at least, were not designed for social interaction initially), contain a great deal of social communication. In general, people like to interact with other people, and they seem to do so even when the channel is not necessarily designed for this. This goes back to the creation of the Internet from the very first time it was turned on: scientists sharing data also wanted to share their thoughts and opinions on their projects, which evolved into the formation of social bonds across the barriers of one lab or one project. It is apparent when looking at communication technology that while the tools might change, the people do not: people want to talk to people, and we do it even when the application or platform has been created primarily for some other purpose.

ONLINE INTERACTION: BOON OR BANE?

Although there seems to be some agreement that the Internet is indeed used to interact with other people, not all agree on the effects that this large amount of online communication has on users. There are scholars who have discussed how a reliance on online interaction will have detrimental effects on society. In his modern classic *Bowling Alone,* Harvard political scientist Robert Putnam argues for the ways in which media serves to reduce **social interactions**. The title of the book comes from his own observations in bowling alleys, in which he noticed that although more people seemed to bowling overall (at least as of 2,000), membership in bowling leagues was way down. In other words, people were coming to the bowling alley but often were alone: they were coming alone, bowling alone, and then leaving alone. Why is this important? Putnam argued that in the preceding decades people had begun to rely more on solitary leisure activities—primarily media such as watching television at home—to occupy their free time instead of engaging other people in social activities such as bowling. Thus, when folks did decide to go to a bowling alley now and then, they found that their lack of social interactions with others resulted in having to bowl alone; in simplest terms, they had no other friends to bowl with.

Social interactions The Conversations between people central to the human communication process.

Although Putnam got us thinking as researchers, many criticisms have been laid against Putnam's arguments in *Bowling Alone*. The most common one can be summed up by Barry Wellman, (e.g., Wellman, Haase, Witte, & Hampton, 2001) a sociologist at the University of Toronto, who has pointed out that communication technologies such as the Internet can in fact be tools that not only allow and encourage communication between people (we can think specifically of social media programs here), but they can also aid in the creation of new communities that are not restricted to the boundaries of space-time (see CMC in Action: Be It Ever so Digital, There's No Place Like HomeNet!) And overall, the research evidence seems to suggest that people can reap positive benefits from interacting with others online.

This is a classic argument in research—the debate between media usage being a social or individual activity—and we wish to make three points about it. First, *nearly every new communication technology that comes along has similar claims made against it.* For example, when the telephone began to spread through American society, there were critics who worried about the breakdown of social order that would come about because people could now talk to their families and friends without physically going to see them. The evidence for

CMC IN ACTION

Be It ever so Digital, There's No Place Like HomeNet!

Our findings show the variety of ways people are domesticating the Internet—turning a technology invented for scientists and elaborated for electronic commerce into a household feature.

~The HomeNet Project, Carnegie Mellon University

The impact of communication technology on social interaction is a common area of debate in the social sciences, with some arguing that technology separates people while others contesting that it brings us closer together. To address some of these concerns from a scientific approach, scientists with Carnegie Mellon University started The HomeNet Project—a unique series of studies in which families were provided with computer equipment and Internet access in exchange for providing CMU researchers with detailed records of how the equipment was used.

Starting in 1995, HomeNet studied families both in the Pittsburgh area (the home of CMU) as well as a nationally representative survey in 2000–2002, and the results from their work have been surprising to many. As varied as Internet usage is for families across the United States, the

"killer applications"—those programs that are used the most—are almost entirely based around interpersonal communication and social interaction. Although the first study seemed to suggest that increased Internet usage was related to increased depression and loneliness, later studies seemed to suggest that this was a matter of how the computer was being used. In particular, it seemed to affect people new to the technology, and so over time people were better able to utilize the technology to accomplish their interpersonal goals (recall the discussion of transparent technologies in Chapter 3). Overall, the Internet seemed to be used primarily for communicating with friends and family as well as meeting new people. In fact, the researchers found that one of the best predictors of continued Internet usage was people who use the technology to communicate with each other, such as sending e-mails back and forth. While the last of these studies was done in 2002, research is still ongoing as we enter a new age of social media—programs seemingly custom-made to encourage social interaction.

You can read more about Carnegie Mellon University's HomeNet Project at: http://homenet.hcii.cs.cmu.edu/

the phone, however, seems to support the opposite overall. Second, oftentimes these types of claims seem to exist because *people only think about how things have been done, rather than how they can be done*. For example, we would not deny that the telephone or the Internet "changes" society, or at least allows for changes in the way we interact. However, this does not necessarily lead to a breakdown in the overall goals of traditional communication (in fact, if you get nothing else from this book, we hope you get that people seem to use technology to accomplish their already existing goals). Third, we would argue that *both of the preceding situations can be possible*. It is possible that spending a lot of time online can lead to feeling lonelier. It is also possible that it leads to feeling less lonely and can build social capital. It is our contention that this outcome is not a quality inherent in the technology itself, but is more about how a person uses that technology. The Internet and CMC is not a magic wand that will serve to alleviate all the problems that exist in communication (and remember, there are many issues with face-to-face communication as well). It is instead a tool that can be used socially, unsocially, and antisocially.

Social network site (SNS) Internet-based computer programs that allow users to create profiles and share information with other users.

SOCIAL NETWORK(ING) SITES

One of the very interesting recent developments for social interaction online are sites like Facebook. Social media researchers danah boyd and Nicole Ellison define **social network sites (SNS)** as "web-based services that allow individuals to (1) construct a public or semi-public profile within a bounded system, (2) articulate a list of other users with whom they share a connection, and (3) view and traverse their list of connections and those made by others within the system."

So, how do they differ from past technology? Social network scholars Nicholas Christakis and James Fowler (2009) suggest several ways. First, we might say that these differ in scope. Social network sites are enormous, and they allow us to stay in touch with far more people that we ever could face-to-face. This enormity allows us to create a sense of communality, because social network sites increase the scale at which we can share information and contribute to collective efforts (think Wikipedia, Chapter 4). We can also find very specific connections with people we normally would not come in contact with, as we can form communities with those we share similarities with regardless of where they live. Finally, using our virtual identities we can alter to some extent how we are perceived—which can help us form more meaningful connections (for better or worse).

Second, and perhaps the biggest qualitative change is the notion that these types of sites allow for "public displays of connection" (Donath & boyd, 2004). The biggest new change is the ability to broadcast your social network to others publicly and to see others' social networks. In the past, how could you get that information? The effects of these public displays of connection are just starting to be examined.

Online social networking is not just for kids, either. A Pew report in 2013 showed that as of December 2012, 67 percent of all online adults in the United States were on at least one SNS. Women were more likely to use SNS than men, with 71 percent of women online saying they use SNS as opposed to 62 percent of men. Not surprisingly, use of SNS is skewed toward younger adults, with 83 percent of 18–29-year-old Internet users saying they are one. However, 32 percent of online adults 65 years and older reported using at least one SNS as well, which might suggest that the social networking "craze" seems to be one that cuts across different age categories. In fact this is unsurprising, as the desire to socially engage others is not conceptually tied to one age group over another.

But why are so many people turning to SNS? Perhaps, even more interesting than sheer percentages of people who use them is how they are used. A group of Pew studies have examined this phenomenon (for a rundown, visit: http://pewinternet.org/Commentary/2012/March/Pew-Internet-Social-Networking-full-detail.aspx and http://pewinternet. org/topics/Social-Networking. aspx?typeFilter=5). It seems that by and large people use SNS to maintain their social networks. Various Pew studies have found that the average user of SNS has more close ties and is about half as likely to be socially isolated as the average American. Futhermore, Internet users get more social support from their ties, with Facebook users specifically getting the most social support (this will be discussed more in Chapter 8). These findings add more evidence to the idea that we use these tools to help accomplish our social goals and that they are not necessarily a hindrance to positive social relationships.

In short, SNSs such as Facebook have become a major channel of interpersonal communication. The average person has 130 friends on Facebook, and there are people with 500, 1,000, and even 1,500 friends. However, can a person have too many friends on Facebook? What do you think of a person who has 1,500 friends on Facebook? How about a person who has 50 friends? Researchers associated with Michigan State University (Tong, Van Der Heide, Langwell, & Walther, 2008) found curvilinear effects for the number of friends on Facebook and popularity. This means having too few friends makes you appear more negative, but so does having too many friends. This has been called this the **"Goldilocks effect"** of social media (Westerman, Spence, & Van Der Heide, 2012) and has been recently found with Twitter and the number of followers a user has as well.

One of the most interesting parts of social networking sites is the public nature of one's social networks. This brings up another question about what

Goldilocks effect
A phenomenon that explains how having too few or too many friends or contacts can result in others making negative judgments about the social attractiveness of a SNS user.

Context collapse A situation, common to social networking sites, in which information created for a specific audience is shared with multiple audiences at the same time.

happens when all of that information is public and can be seen by others. Does what your friends post on your Facebook change how others perceive you? In short, yes. Research has found that your friends' posts have a big impact on how others perceive you. Posts about being "social" made a person seem more likable, but also more credible, although posts about excessive drinking did the opposite. (Walther, et al., 2008). And, if the pictures of your posters were physically attractive, you were seen as more physically attractive. Other studies (e.g. Vitak, 2012) have proposed the notion of **context collapse**, or how information posted on social media networks often intended for one group of people (for example, or roommates) can quickly find its way to other unintended groups (such as our parents or professors). So, be careful of the company you keep, even on Facebook!

DECEIVING OTHERS ONLINE

One issue that is commonly mentioned in popular press coverage of online interaction is deception. Typically, this portrayal suggests that online interactions are full of lies and that lying is more frequent online than offline—particularly in the realm of romance (see CMC in Action: Manti

CMC IN ACTION
Manti and the Catfish Fry

During the 2012 NCAA FBS football season, traditional power Notre Dame returned to their glory days, reaching (although ultimately losing) the BCS national championship game. The team was propelled all season by all-American linebacker Manti Te'o and his inspirational story. During the season, in the week leading up to a game against rival Michigan State, Manti's grandmother and his girlfriend Lennay Kekua—who had been dying of complications with leukemia—both passed away within 24 hours of each other. Heartbroken, Manti decided to play in the game against Michigan State and recorded 12 tackles, one sack, and a fumble recovery, leading his team to a 20-3 victory. Part of the reason Manti played in the game rather than returning home to Hawaii were the inspirational words of Kekua, who told him that no matter what happened to her, he should continue playing football.

After the season ended, details began emerging about Manti's girlfriend. It seems she may not have actually died of leukemia as was reported during the season. It also seemed that she may not have actually existed in the first place. Instead, it came to light that Te'o was part of an elaborate hoax (most likely as the victim of the hoax), which was designed to make him believe that Lennay Kekua actually existed, created by Ronaiah Tuiasopo. Pictures of his girlfriend existed, but the actual person who those pictures were of did not know they were being used. And Manti had never met his girlfriend face-to-face.

Known as a "catfish," this is defined on Urban Dictionary as "someone who pretends to be someone they're not using Facebook or other social media to create false identities, particularly to pursue deceptive online romances." The phrase was coined by documentary filmmaker Ariel Schulman, who showed a similar story in the 2010 movie *Catfish* and has

worked on a MTV series of the same name. As discussed in Chapter 5, this is just the kind of media coverage that could lead people to think that this is a common phenomenon. But is it?

Online, you can be anyone you want to be because of the restriction of the visual information that would tell you that a person is not who they say they are, right? It is hard to ignore the fact that what happened to Manti Te'o would not have happened face-to-face (or at least would have been incredibly difficult). The lack of nonverbal cues in many online platforms does lead to possibilities for deception that would be hard, if not impossible, to pull off face-to-face. However, as Cornell professor Jeff Hancock has pointed out, social media actually seems to lead to less deception overall, compared to face-to-face interaction. In general, Dr. Hancock suggests that the publicness and permanence of online interaction allows people the ability to go back and check on information that would have been ephemeral in the past. Realization of this makes people leery of posting lies, knowing that someone is likely to call you out on a lie, and that people can later check to see what you have said as well.

For video of Dr. Hancock discussing this notion, go to http://www.cnn.com/2013/01/13/opinion/hancock-technology-lying/index.html

and the Catfish Fry). Of course, the first statement could be true without the second one also being true.

Can people lie online? Of course they can, and they have been since the early days of the Internet. Indeed, in what is likely one of the earliest popular accounts of CMC, an article called "The Strange Case of the Electronic Lover" in *Ms. Magazine* detailed a story about a male psychologist who pretended to be a female in an electronic chat group (The original article can be found here: http://lindsyvangelder.com/sites/default/files/Plinkers.org%20-%20 Electronic%20Lover.htm_.pdf). And the affordances and the limitations make some lies possible that would have been at least very difficult in the past. However, other parts of the channel seem to restrict lying on the whole. So, although catfishing happens, it is probably not as widespread as mediated coverage of it might make it seem to be. In fact, some research suggests that lying is less common online than it is face-to-face. Furthermore, it seems that the kinds of lies that happen online, especially in **dating Web sites**, are similar to the ones that occur face-to-face (Ellison, Heino, & Gibbs, 2006; Toma, Ellison, & Hancock, 2008). A few pounds here, a couple years there, a few fewer gray hairs, a few dollars more, these lies seem to be things that we might call **impression management**. We try our best to make ourselves look good. So, we may shave a couple years off of our age, or we may post a picture that only shows us from our good side.

Dating Web sites Web pages that are specifically designed to help users form and sustain romantic connections with other users.

Impression management The act of disclosing and concealing personal information in order to control the impressions that others form of you.

Social presence When using communication technology, a feeling that one is engaging another person in a nonmediated way.

Telepresence When using communication technology, a feeling that one is interacting in a mediated environment without consciously thinking about this mediation.

PRESENCE: AT THE HEART OF CMC?

People use CMC to connect with others. It even seems that at least much of the time, this connection and online interaction lead to very positive outcomes. But how is this possible? We argue that one of the main concepts to understanding this is called **social presence**, which is a specific form of a larger concept known as **telepresence**.

Telepresence is a concept that derives from various fields. Simply put, it is an "illusion of non-mediation" (Lombard & Ditton, 1997). In other words, it is using media without realizing or acknowledging its use. In some ways, you can think back to the idea of transparent technology from Chapter 3. The concept of telepresence has some important characteristics. First, it is generally considered as a *continuum*. This means that the feeling of telepresence is not an all or nothing game; you are not simply present or absent. Instead, you can feel more or less present at different times. Second, it is *a psychological state*. This means it is not an inherent quality of any given channel, but instead it can be experienced through any channel, given the right circumstances. For example, some people find books to be the most highly presence-inducing channel. This has been characterized as "the book problem" by presence scholars, as it is a relatively low tech medium, and yet can be incredibly engrossing to people who like reading. Third, it *varies across time*. During an interaction (or any other mediated experience like watching a movie) your level of presence will go up and down throughout the experience.

Generally speaking, we can think of telepresence as a combination of the user expectations of three things: content, channel, and user (Pettey, Bracken, Rubenking, Buncher, & Gress, 2010). Certain types of content are more likely to increase the feeling of presence. Also, although stated previously that presence is not inherent in a channel, there are certain characteristics that make telepresence more likely, like interactivity. Finally, some users are more likely to experience telepresence than others. Most of the time, telepresence occurs because of the

CMC IN ACTION

The Death of Clippy

Depending on how old you are, you may remember the Office Assistant known as "Clippy," who would pop up at times while you were working in Microsoft Word, for example. Clippy would come on the screen and ask "useful" questions like "It looks like you are writing a letter. Would you like help?" This assistant was pretty much universally panned by users and critics alike. Even Microsoft has come to realize how bad Clippy was, parodying the Death of Clippy in a recent "trailer" for the release of Microsoft 2010, which can be seen here: http://www.youtube.com/watch?feature=player_embedded& v=VUawhjxLS2I#! (For a list of various parodies of Clippy, please see the Wikipedia page on Office Assistant at http://en.wikipedia.org/wiki/Clippy)

What was wrong with Clippy? Microsoft attempted to provide more cues for this Office Assistant, by offering it as a paper clip agent. However, this story might suggest that more cues are not always associated with increased social presence. We might also suggest that the types of questions Clippy asked seemed unnatural and unhelpful, which served as a reminder that Clippy was not a good agent, and thus left users without a connection to this character. In short, Clippy did not act very human, and so we may have been left feeling rather inhumane toward it.

right combination of these three. The right user has the right content through the right channel, and then telepresence increases.

So far, we have only mentioned telepresence as a general category, but scholars suggest there are different types of it (e.g., Lee, 2002b). The one we will focus on in this chapter is social presence, which can simply be thought of as the experience of feeling connected to another person, or feeling like an interaction is "real," while using some sort of communication technology.

Is this feeling of "realness" strange? We argue that not only is the feeling not at all strange but it is in fact quite natural and, under the right circumstances, a fairly common occurrence. In a book called *The Media Equation,* Reeves and Nass (1996) highlighted their research program that can help us understand why this experience may be so natural and easy to feel. They suggest that the media equation is that "media equals real life," and as such, we tend to interact with mediated objects and people (or both) in the same way as we do real ones (see CMC in Action: The Death of Clippy). This does not necessarily mean that the content shown on television, for example, presents an accurate depiction of real life. Instead, it means that we respond to media as we do real life. Reeves and Nass present a program of research showing this. What they do is take an established finding from interpersonal and social psychology research, and replace one of the people with a computer, and consistently find similar results as the study using two people. They find this despite also finding that people suggest that they know this is a ridiculous thing to do.

If you think this is strange, consider watching movies. Have you ever cried or seen a "friend" cry during a movie? Most likely. And yet, why would this happen? You know that the people on the screen are actors, so it seems kind of ridiculous to cry at movies (unless you are crying because you know how much the actor was paid). And of course, if you stop to think about it, it is ridiculous, and people will articulate it. However, much of our human responses occur without thinking about them.

The human species evolved over a long period, and it evolved to rise to meet a variety of specific challenges (Lee, 2002a). One of those challenges was not communication media, which are incredibly new. For tens of thousands of years, if a person saw something that looked like another person and, maybe more importantly, behaved like another person, it was another person,

CMC IN ACTION

Virtual Morality

If it is the case that most individuals respond to media portrayals as if they are real, then how might this influence the way in which we understand our virtual actions. This was the central question of research by media researchers Sven Joeckel and Leyla Dogruel as well as one of the authors of this book (Joeckel, Bowman, & Dogruel, 2012).

In a study on German and U.S. computer users (both children and adults), participants were asked to play a video game that presented them with a variety of different moral dilemmas dealing with issues of harm, fairness, and loyalty among others. Each person's in-game decisions were recorded, and then the researchers examined the relationship between each user's real-world moral orientations and the decisions they made in the game related to each moral dilemma. The researchers found when individuals were confronted with a moral scenario related to an issue of great importance to their real lives (such as a person who does not like violence) that they would avoid committing a moral violation when given the opportunity. However, when individuals were confronted with a moral

scenario that was not so important to them, the chances of them committing a moral violation were no greater than a coin flip! In other words, gamers seem to make gut decisions when faced with issues of importance to their real lives, but made game decisions when faced with issues that are not particularly important. Put another way, it seems that a video game player's moral decisions in the virtual world are very similar to their decisions in the real world—that is, there does not seem to be a separate virtual morality.

Yet, it is important to note that the video game in this study was one that did not reward or punish moral violations (see social learning theory, Chapter 6). What do you think? Have you ever been bothered by the content of a video game? Have you ever done something in a video game that you would not otherwise do in real life? How might a video game that seems to glorify moral violations change the findings of the preceding study?

More about this study can be found at: http://www.tandfonline.com/doi/abs/10.1080/15213269.2012.727218#preview

not a representation of one on a screen and not a robot or video game character. Thus, we likely evolved to respond to these presentations as human, and if something walks, talks, and acts human, we will respond to it as a human (see CMC in Action: Virtual Morality).

This is because technological evolution outpaces biological evolution. For most of human existence, responding humanly to something because it behaved humanly served us well (you can even consider the way we respond to animals). Our brains have not adapted as fast as technology. Thus, it is our default to respond humanly to something that seems human, and social presence (as well as other kinds) is probably both easy and a natural state because of it. It takes something weird (like a bad acting performance) to start you thinking and get you realizing that this is not "real."

WHY SO MUCH INTERACTION?

Based upon these concepts of telepresence, social presence, and the notions set forth in *The Media Equation*, we might suggest two main reasons that so much social interaction occurs online. First, as we have said before, humans are an inherently social species, and as such the creation and maintenance of relationships is one of our main reasons for communicating in general. We strive to interact with one another as social creatures, and we are rewarded with this interaction in the form of meaningful relationships with others. Second, as has also been said at other points in this book, the Internet (and internet technology in general) is a communication tool that provides many affordances for social interaction, including the ability for social presence. So, when we have a goal (relationships) and a tool allows us to accomplish that goal (a vast network of social others wanting to interact and form relationships), we are likely to use the tool for the goal.

Moreover, we suggest that the Internet specifically and CMC technologies in general are neither inherently good nor bad for relationships. Instead, it and they provide us a tool to use for interaction—and a particularly well-suited tool for fostering interaction at that. In the end, it is the quality of the interaction between two people rather than the manner in which that interaction takes place that is the strongest predictor of the quality of a given relationship. Consider the following passage from Christakis and Fowler (2009).

"Yet, new technologies—whether massively multiplayer online games such as World of Warcraft or Second Life; social network websites such as Facebook or MySpace; collective information sites like YouTube, Wikipedia, or eBay; or dating sites like Match.com or eHarmony—just realize our ancient propensity to connect to other humans, albeit with electrons flowing through cyberspace rather than conversation drifting through the air. While the social networks formed online may be abstract, large, complex and supermodern, they also reflect universal and fundamental human tendencies that emerged in our prehistoric past when we told stories to one another around campfires in the African savanna. **Even astonishing advances in communication technology like the printing press, the telephone, and the Internet do not take us away from this past; they draw us closer to it.**" (p. 257, emphasis added)

REFERENCES

1. Boyd, d. m., & Ellison, N. B. (2007). Social network sites: Definition, history, and scholarship. *Journal of Computer-Mediated Communication, 13*(1), article 11. http://jcmc.indiana.edu/vol13/issue1/boyd.ellison.html

2. Christaikis, N. A., & Fowler, J. H. (2009). *Connected: The surprising power of our social networks and how they shape our lives.* New York: Little, Brown and Company.

3. Deci, E. L., & Ryan, R. M. (1985). *Intrinsic motivation and self-determination in human behavior.* New York: Plenum Publishing Co.

4. Donath, J., & boyd, d. (2004). Public displays of connection. *BT Technology Journal, 22,* 71–82.

5. Ellison, N., Heino, R., & Gibbs, J. (2006). Managing impressions online: Self-presentation processes in the online dating environment. *Journal of Computer-Mediated Communication, 11* (2), article 2. http://jcmc.indiana.edu/vol11/issue2/ellison.html

6. Joeckel, S., Bowman, N. D., & Dogruel, L. (2012). Gut or game: The influence of moral intuitions on decisions in virtual environments. *Media Psychology, 15*(4), 460–485.

7. Lee, K. M. (2004a). Why presence occurs: Evolutionary psychology, media equation, and presence. *Presence, 13,* 494–505.

8. Lee, K. M. (2004b). Presence, explicated. *Communication Theory, 14,* 27–50.

9. Lombard, M., & Ditton, T. (1997). At the heart of it all: The concept of presence. *Journal of Computer-Mediated Communication, 3*(2), article 4. http://jcmc.indiana.edu/vol3/issue2/lombard.html

10. Pettey, G., Bracken, C. C., Rubenking, B., Buncher, M., & Gress, E. (2010). Telepresence, soundscapes and technological expectation: Putting the observer into the equation. *Virtual Reality, 14,* 15–25.

11. Putnam, R. (1999). *Bowling alone: The collapse and revival of American community.* New York: Simon & Schuster.

12. Reeves, B., & Nass, C. (1996). *The media equation: How people treat computers, television, and newmedia like real people and places.* Stanford, CA: CSLI Publications.

13. Sherry, J. L., & Bowman, N. D. (2008). History of the Internet. In H. Bidgoli (Ed.), *The handbook of computer networks: Vol. I. Key concepts, data transmission, digital and optical networks.* Hoboken, NJ: John Wiley & Sons.

14. Toma, C., Hancock, J., & Ellison, N. (2008). Separating fact from fiction: An examination of deceptive self-presentation in online dating profiles. *Personality and Social Psychology Bulletin 34*, 1023–1036.

15. Tong, S. T., Van Der Heide, B., Langwell, L., & Walther, J. B. (2008). Too much of a good thing? The relationship between number of friends and interpersonal impressions on Facebook. *Journal of Computer-Mediated Communication, 13*(3), 531–549.

16. Vitak, J. (2012). The impact of context collapse and privacy on social network site disclosures. *Journal of Broadcasting and Electronic Media, 56*, 451–470.

17. Walther, J. B., Van Der Heide, B., Kim, S., Westerman, D., & Tong, S. T. (2008). The role of friends' behavior on evaluations of individuals' Facebook profiles: Are we known by the company we keep? *Human Communication Research, 34*, 28–49.

18. Wellman, B., Haase, A. Q., Witte, J., & Hampton, K. (2001). Does the Internet increase, decrease, or supplement social capital?: Social networks, participation, and community commitment. *American Behavioral Scientist, 45*, 436–455.

19. Westerman, D., Spence, P. R., & Van Der Heide, B. (2012). A social network as information: The effect of system generated reports of connectedness of credibility on Twitter. *Computers in Human Behavior, 28*, 199–206.

CHAPTER 9

Falling in Love (or Like) Online

When we are trying to form a relationship with somebody, which do you think is better: talking to them online or talking with them off-line?

Maybe you think the answer seems obvious: off-line. If you are like many people, you might argue that online relationships are not as good as off-line, face-to-face (FtF), "real" relationships. After all, online communication usually lacks nonverbal cues—especially touch—which seem crucial for delivering emotionally charged interpersonal messages that are so crucial to a relationship. For example, there are times when you just want a hug from your boyfriend or girlfriend, and one is hard-pressed to replicate such an action online.

But perhaps you answered that using various CMC technologies can be better. It might be the case that you like being able to interact more frequently with your partner—such as sending text messages during a quick break between classes or being able to visit your partner's Facebook page and share information with them when they are not available. Both allow you to overcome space-time barriers. Maybe you have even found yourself in a relationship that moved very quickly online, and you felt it would not have moved that quickly FtF.

We will answer the question in a way that might be very unsatisfying to many of you reading this, but in a way that we believe more accurately reflects what we know from research: it depends. It depends on the goals of the communicators individually as well as their goals for the relationship. The rest of this chapter will explain these dimensions and suggest that both are desirable and functional.

Questions to think about while reading this chapter:

- How important is physical touch to a relationship?

- What is meant by the concept of social capital?

- What is the distinction between weak and strong ties, and why is it important when studying communication technology?

KEY WORDS

Haptic communication
Expectancy violation
Homophily
Node
Bucket brigades
Telephone tree
Media richness theory
Equivocality
Social information
  processing theory
Chronemics
Emoticons
Hyperpersonal
  relationships

DO WE WANT TO TOUCH EVERYONE WE SEE?

When we ask students about the lack of nonverbal cues that often exist online and how that impacts relationships, there is often a suggestion that the lack of nonverbal cues impedes relationships. Usually this discussion centers on touch and how the lack of it is problematic. Indeed, touch is likely a very important part of close relationships. A classic study by psychologist Harry Harlow demonstrated the power of touch using rhesus monkeys (see CMC in Action: Monkey Lovin'). He found that when baby monkeys were presented with two monkey "mothers," the babies would choose to spend most of their time with stuffed monkeys that were soft and cuddly, only visiting the wire monkeys that delivered food to eat. This study suggests that **haptic communication** is an important part of how we share information with each other and how we accomplish our goals and that without such haptics we are diminished in our ability to stimulate meaning.

Touch is a very useful and powerful nonverbal cue. But is the lack of touch a death sentence for relationships? We might suggest that this depends on the kind of relationship you are thinking about and what your goals are for that relationship. For example, it is very likely that if your relationship with your professor does not include touch that you are perfectly okay with this. We do not expect to be touched by our supervisors at work, campus administrators, or our favorite barista, and yet we have perfectly good relationships with each of these people. In fact, in some of these situations touch might be considered inappropriate and could even damage the relationship as touch in each case might be an **expectancy violation** (Burgoon, 1978). However, the kind of relationship that comes to mind most quickly as one in which touch is integral is probably a romantic relationship. Indeed, we largely agree that for most long-term romantic relationships a lack of touch is something that likely will be problematic over the long haul. This is because there are some things that cannot likely be replicated in romantic relationships without actual physical touch . . . yet (see CMC in Action: Reach Out and Really(?) Touch Someone). But, going back to the functional approach that this book is founded upon, are there some things that people can do online that lead to similar outcomes as touch does FtF? Might we even be able to do some of them better sometimes?

But again, there are many instances FtF when we do not want nonverbal cues, as they may interfere with accomplishing our goals. For example, if you walk into your local fast-food restaurant to get a quick meal, you probably do not want the person behind the counter to touch you. Rather, you just want them to take your order and give you your cheeseburger as fast as possible. Touch, and likely many other nonverbal cues, will likely just get in the way of accomplishing those goals. For example, the person behind the counter might be in a bad mood (anyone who has ever worked in the food industry can likely empathize and sympathize), and you may be distracted by their negative nonverbal cues. Such a situation is what CMC scholar Joe Walther refers to as an impersonal interaction, one that is more about the task at hand than the people involved in the task. We will not focus on this kind of interaction in this chapter, but bring it up to make an important point: there are different kinds of relationships one might have with another person—both FtF and using CMC—and not all of them

Haptic communication Sending meaning through the use of nonverbal cues associated with touch.

Expectancy violation A situation in which our assumptions about anticipations of another's thoughts, actions, or behavior are not met.

There are some things that cannot likely be replicated in romantic relationships without actual physical touch.
© solominviktor, 2014. Shutterstock, Inc.

CMC IN ACTION

Monkey Lovin

Before you start reading this section, please know that you may find it upsetting. At best, much of the research that Harry Harlow conducted with monkeys was ethically questionable. At worst, there are no questions; it is just wrong.

Harlow conducted many experiments using monkeys. The goal was to study attachment and love. In the classic study, Harlow would put a baby monkey into a room with two surrogate "monkeys." One surrogate was a wire monkey that had a bottle attached to it to provide food. The other surrogate was a cloth monkey with no food. What Harlow noticed was that most monkeys would only spend time with the wire monkey long enough to get nourishment and then would dart over to the comfort of the cloth monkey. Another study would frighten baby monkeys, and Harlow noticed that many of the scared babies would seek refuge with the cloth monkey.

Another group of studies Harlow conducted would isolate baby monkeys from other monkeys. Some would be totally isolated from any contact with other monkeys. Some would be "partially" isolated; they could see, smell, and hear other monkeys, but they were caged so they could not touch other monkeys. Not surprisingly, the totally isolated monkeys, who were kept that way for up to two years, were severely psychologically disturbed and were nearly impossible to reintegrate back with normal monkeys. However, the monkeys who were raised without touch also were very disturbed, with some even going as far as to engage in self-mutilation. Thus, it seems that touch is very powerful indeed.

If you would like to read the original source, it was published in a 1958 issue of American Psychologist (see reference section at the end of this chapter). There are also many videos available on YouTube about these studies. One showing Harry Harlow discussing and showing examples of some of his experiments can be found here: https://www.youtube.com/watch?v=OrNBEhzjg8I

require or even desire a full range of social cues. We will discuss two such relationship types in more depth: weak ties and strong ties.

BUILDING BRIDGES AND CREATING BONDS

Have you ever heard of Lois Weisberg? Chances are that you have not. Lois lives in Chicago, smokes, is a grandmother, and is not particularly charismatic. In all of this she seems like a relatively normal and unremarkable person. But Journalist Malcolm Gladwell suggests that she might run the world (you can read the Gladwell article about Lois Weisberg from *The New Yorker* here: http://www.gladwell.com/1999/1999_01_11_a_weisberg.htm).

Lois has a particular knack for doing something that many people do not seem to do. Consider that most people follow the principle of **homophily** when creating their social circles. That is, we tend to like and talk to people who are similar to us. Thus, our social circles end up looking a lot like us. However, Lois does things a little differently. Throughout her life, she has reached out and made connections across a wide variety of people. In short, "She's the type of person who seems to know everybody, and this type can be found in every walk of life" (from the article).

Homophily The extent to which two people (or two things) are similar to one another.

So, why would someone like Lois be called out for potentially running the world? To answer this question more fully, it will take some more detail about the structure and power of social networks throughout the rest of this chapter. Lois is a type—a relatively uncommon and extraordinary type, but a type nonetheless. In short, it is because Lois is a connector. She seems to know everybody, or at least people know people who know her. She acts as a bridge, connecting people across various, differing groups. Thus, although you may not know Lois yourself, it would not be terribly surprising if you someday come to realize that someone you know knows her. It seems that Lois is a master of social networking, whether she tries to be or not.

CMC IN ACTION

Reach Out and Really(?) Touch Someone

While it can be debated as to whether or not haptics are a necessary part of the communication process, there have been several advances in the early 21st century (and even before) to replicate touch when using communication technologies. For example, many video game controllers such as the Nintendo Wii feature force-feedback systems that vibrate and shake the controller to simulate pushing a button or switch or even the resistance of a bow and arrow.

But can we actually touch another person?

Virtual reality researcher Jeremy Bailenson and his colleagues at Stanford University's Virtual Human Interaction Lab are among a growing group of researchers who believe we can and that it might help us better communicate in virtual environments. His laboratory has conducted research suggesting that a computer joystick clamped to a laboratory table could successfully "communicate" a

variety of feelings such as disgust, anger, sadness, joy, fear, interest, and surprise with a reliability significantly different than chance. While live handshakes were still better overall, the joystick apparatus was still successful at giving people a sense of the emotions of the "person" with whom they were shaking hands.

Of course, we might not always want to shake hands with a joystick, but perhaps improvements in the technology might make it possible for individuals separated for a variety of reasons—such as romantic partners missing the touch of a partner or hiring managers teleinterviewing a graduating college senior and wanting to make a "handshake deal"—to overcome perceived nonverbal barriers in CMC technology.

For more information about Jeremy Bailenson and the Virtual Human Interaction Lab, including other research about haptics in virtual environments (VHIL), visit http://vhil.stanford.edu/

WHAT IS SOCIAL NETWORKING?

Like most of the things discussed in this book, social networking is not something that was created by the Internet. But if you are similar to many of the students we have worked with, you may equate the idea of social networking with the Internet, especially social media—after all, the terms are often discussed synonymously. However, we are quick to remind that the general concept of social networking is a basic human idea and something we have been doing for a very long time. Once again, the Internet has allowed us to step up our social networking, with potentially very positive and negative outcomes.

So if not invented by the Internet, then what is social networking? Christakis and Fowler (2009) suggested that networks are organized sets of people made up of two things: individuals and their connections. The people part is easy; each individual is a **node** in some social network(s). But the connections among these nodes are the truly interesting part of a social network. It is the way in which individuals are intertwined and the ties that exist among people in a group that really make social networks interesting and sometimes difficult to study. These connections are also what give social networks, and people like Lois Weisberg, their power.

Node In social networking, it is the basic unit of analysis—usually any given person in a larger network of people.

Bucket brigades A type of social network in which one person communicates or interacts with only one other person in a linear fashion, passing information from one to one.

SOCIAL NETWORK STRUCTURES

There are many ways that these types of social networks can be structured. Christakis and Fowler (2009) pointed out some such as **bucket brigades**, where each person in a line is connected to two other people except for the person at each end of the line, who is only connected to one person. Imagine a line of people handing sandbags to each other one at a time to build a wall. Each person hands off the heavy bag of sand so that nobody has to carry the heavy bag for a long distance, saving the group's energy. Another type of organizing is the **telephone tree**, which exhibits spreading linearity, where each person would be responsible for contacting two or some other number of people except those at the end of the tree. Such an example of this would be a chain letter in which one person is asked to send the message to ten (or more, or less) people, who are in turn asked to send to ten more. In this system, information is able to spread quickly across many different groups. In both cases, the systems have neat and clean structures.

> **Telephone tree** A type of social network in which one person is responsible for contacting a set number of people who in turn contact a set number of people "below" them.

First, although both of these network structures have their usefulness, they also have issues. For example, with a bucket brigade, if one person in the line drops their bag or moves slowly, it slows the progress of the entire network. Telephone trees have issues with information only flowing in one direction. Furthermore, most naturally occurring social networks are a lot messier. In networks that we see out "in the wild," there will be certain individuals who are more centrally located with many connections. There will also be those individuals who have fewer connections and thus are more fringe members of a particular network. There are also some people who are densely interconnected within a specific group, but some people who have ties into many groups, although they may only be fringe members of each of those groups. Just as the Internet has no written rules for behavior, neither do the social networks that form using the Internet.

RULES OF SOCIAL NETWORKS

Another very interesting way to think about our social networks—and we will argue that each of us exists within one (if not multiple) social networks—is that they seem to follow five general rules of thumb (Christakis & Fowler, 2009).

1. We shape our networks To a large extent, we choose what groups we want to be part of, and we also choose how many connections to have within and between these groups. In this way, we have a great deal of influence over how our social networks end up being shaped. Much of our choice is this matter is governed by the concept of homophily. The Internet makes it even easier to find people with whom we share similarities, as we no longer are as restricted by space constraints in determining who we talk to. We do not only have to interact with the people that are physically located in the same place as us: in our neighborhood, school, etc. We can seek out people who we are similar to from around the world.

2. Our network shapes us Your position in a social network has a big impact on your life. A person with no close contacts has a very different life from those with many. This is likely one you have thought about before. However, a person with few acquaintances also has a very different life from those with many. This is an idea that you may have never given much thought to, as closeness is often considered an inherent good (Parks, 1982), but as will be discussed in more detail, acquaintances provide some interesting and important benefits as well.

3. Our friends affect us This probably is not too surprising, but the people you associate with have a big impact on your life. If you ever heard your parents say that they did not want you hanging out with another kid because that kid was "trouble," they understood this principle in ways that scientists are really just starting to uncover. Your network has impacts on a whole host of things, including your happiness, weight, drinking behaviors, and so on. Things that spread through networks can be positive (social support) or negative (gossip), but this spread impacts us.

4. Our friends' friends' friends affect us This one is more interesting because it suggests that people you may not even know may have some impact on your life. Again, it may not be much of a surprise that your friends influence you. But who influences them? Their friends do, some of whom you might know, but some of whom you might not. And who influences those people? Their friends. So that spread means you may be influenced by people you do not know, which means there is some hidden power lurking within social networks.

5. The network has a life of its own Finally—and as discussed earlier when talking about network structures—it is important to realize that networks have emergent properties; that is, networks tend to shrink, grow and change based on how they are being used not just by one person but by every individual person in the network. This means you cannot understand them simply by looking at each individual part, but also need to look at each network as a whole. This is one of the toughest parts of studying social networks.

CONNECTION VERSUS INFLUENCE

Some of you may be familiar with the game "Six Degrees of Kevin Bacon," or the idea that you can link any actor or actress to Kevin Bacon in six steps or less. The goal is to get to from someone to Bacon by thinking of movies that people have been in together in as few steps as possible. For example, if you want to get from Kevin Bacon to Samuel L. Jackson, you get there through one person: An actor named Don Whatley. Bacon was in *My One and Only* in 2009 with Whatley, and Whatley was in *xXx: State of the Union* in 2005 with Samuel L. Jackson. There are few actors or actresses not connected through Bacon in six connections or less.

Many have heard this idea, but do you realize where it comes from? It was popularized by a classic research study (Travers & Milgrim, 1969). He gave letters to a few hundred people in Nebraska that were addressed to someone in Boston who they did not know. He asked each person to send it to someone they knew who was more likely to know the person in Boston (or at least more likely to know someone else who might). They tracked how many times it took for the letter to get to the person in Boston, and on average, it took six steps.

Now how does this happen? It turns out that about three people were the main people who ended up getting the letter to its final destination in Boston. In other words, almost all of the letters that got to the final person came through one of three people (Gladwell, 1999). These people are interesting because it suggests that they know a lot of other people and specifically they know a lot of different kinds of people. It is the same with the six degrees of separation game with Kevin Bacon. Bacon is an interesting actor for this game because he has been in many different kinds of movies. And the aforementioned Lois Weisberg becomes such a powerful person because she knows a lot of people from various walks of life and can thus bridge across different groups of people.

However, just because we might be connected to people through six degrees, does not mean we influence that far out. What Christakis and Fowler have found in a variety of contexts is that we do have an impact on our friends, our friends' friends, and our friends' friends' friends. Of course, this influence gets smaller at each step but still is a sizable enough one at that third degree to matter. After this, influences tends to shrink as the people four degrees out and beyond often have little in common with each other, or the message might have changed so much from degree to degree that its core content is lost (think about playing the telephone game in elementary school, where one student tells another student a message—for instance, "mountaineers have big beards and no fears," continuing this process until the student at the end of the telephone line hears something like "scary ears go with beards").

What does all of this say for CMC? First, it suggests a major reason why SNSs are so popular. We like to keep up with our acquaintances, which is why we are told to network in the first place. Prior to SNS, this could be difficult to do. Sites like Facebook have made it much easier to maintain a larger number of these types of relationships. Stephanie Tong and Joe Walther have referred to these as "lightweight" tools. Tong and Walther (2011) pointed out that maybe the biggest potential use (and likely a big use) of SNS is for relational mainte-nance—or helping us both form and sustain our relationships with others. After all, they are social "networking" sites, and people likely use them to network and to manage a number of relationships that in the past would have been dif-ficult, if not outright impossible. They seem to be a way to keep track of previ-ously made acquaintances and help it so no one has "long lost" friends anymore. Anecdotally, high school reunions seem to be on the way out. You do not need to get together with people ten years later to see what they have been up to. You never lose touch with them in the first place.

It also suggests that the number, and possibly the power, of weak ties (Granovetter, 1973) can be greatly magnified here. If people have impact on us out to three degrees FtF and you have 100 friends and acquaintances, who each have 100 more friends and acquaintances (who in turn have 100 more friends and acquaintances), then we are talking about potentially one million people who might have some impact on you. If we up that to 300 friends and acquaintances for each "degree" on Facebook, that substantially increases the number of people who can influence you (and in turn, who you might influence) to 27 million people. (See also, the power of numbers, Chapter 2). Some of the changes for CMC involve scope, as mentioned in Chapter 7.

Do the technologies, such as Facebook and other social media, allow for an increased ability to maintain acquaintances and act as a bridge? Work by CMC scholar Nicole Ellison and her colleagues has extensively examined bridging social capital and social network sites like Facebook and suggested that it may be a powerful use of these kinds of technologies. Repeatedly, they find that those who use Facebook report more social capital—in particular, bridging capital.

Bridging social capital, like the kind that Lois Weisberg seems to display, is incredibly important and is sometimes overlooked when we think about rela-tionships online. However, users of social network sites also report greater lev-els of bonding social capital, which is probably what most people tend to think of when they think of relationships. Again, we see that users of social network sites are able to utilize the channels to accomplish their relational goals overall. We now turn to bonding social capital, or what we might call strong ties, and how these occur online.

BUILDING CLOSENESS ONLINE

People use the Internet for communicating with other people. This is not a really controversial statement, as most of you have likely used some technology to interact with people in a very social way. You may even be doing it while reading this section of the book. However, some early theories about online communication suggested that online communication would not be social. Maybe it is because originally computers were only in large organizations and were designed and used primarily for business functions, such as storing and processing data—they were not intended to foster or even facilitate human-to-human interaction. These theories suggest that people would not, or could not, use CMC to form or manage relationships, as this was something seemingly outside the scope of the technology.

One such theory is known as **media** (or information) **richness theory** (MRT). This theory suggests a rather intuitive idea that some channels are better for some messages. Specifically, MRT argues that an optimal match between the channel used for a message and the equivocality of the message exists. When a message has higher **equivocality** (it has more than one potential meaning or interpretation), using a richer channel leads to greater efficiency because a richer channel is thought to provide more communication information. When equivocality is low, a leaner channel is more efficient because the extra information provided in a rich channel is unnecessary (see CMC in Action: It's Not You, It's Me. <Send>).

One issue with MRT is the distinction between lean and rich channels. In general, a channel can be said to have four characteristics: bandwidth, immediacy of feedback, message personalization, and natural language. Overall, a rich channel allows a lot of these (that is, it is "rich" in the number of cues available for communication), and a lean channel allows less (that is, it is "lean" in the number of cues available for communication). In some cases, this dichotomy can be rather straightforward. If we compared a FtF meeting with one's boss to a written letter from the boss's desk sent to the entire organization, we can likely understand the former being far more "rich" than the latter. The FtF conversation utilizes all of our senses and so has high bandwidth, allows for immediate interaction between myself and my boss, is likely a personalized discussion as we are the only two people in the interaction, and uses our natural spoken language to interact with each other. By contrast, the letter has low

Media richness theory A theory in CMC research that suggests that communication channels can be understood in terms of the number of social cues they provide the user, and there is an optimal matching of communication goal and communication channel based on which cues are desired.

Equivocality Information that has more than one potential meaning or interpretation.

CMC IN ACTION

It's Not You, It's Me. <Send>

Breaking off a romantic relationship can be hard to do because of the often-intense emotions involved in the process. Many of us can remember the somber moment when somebody says "it's not you, it's me" as eyes swell with tears, emotions run hot and cold, and couples (at least, some of them) find a private area to break up so as not to have an emotional outburst in front of family, friends, or strangers.

So, why not just send a text?

Sending a text message communicates a lack of desire to interact while allowing both parties to read the same "it's not you, it's me" message without having to read and respond to the other's nonverbal signals. After all, if one has already made up their mind about the dissolution of the relationship, than what can be gained by further interaction?

Of course, many of you (ourselves included) recognize that the preceding suggestion is remarkably cold and impersonal. But we might ask you to think: Is not a breakup in fact cold and impersonal?

What is your reaction to this suggestion? Using notions of relationships and technology, share your feelings with your class.

bandwidth because it lacks nonverbal information, allows for no direct method of response, is written for all members of an organization, and is likely typed out in a very formal language style expected of company memos. However, these distinctions might be much less clear when dealing with many of the technologies popular today (and likely to be popular tomorrow). Although CMC is often thought of as being rather lean—let us consider e-mail as an example (Daft, Lengel, & Trevinio, 1987), is it truly? E-mail might only allow limited bandwidth and is not particularly immediate, but it does allow for natural language and a great deal of message personalization. And when considering a technology such as Facebook, this becomes even murkier. How these four characteristics interplay in terms of "richness" has not been fully articulated.

The evidence for MRT seems to suggest that there may be something to the approach. When people are asked what channels they would use, they tend to answer in accordance with MRT: by suggesting they would use richer channels for more equivocal messages. However, when actual channel choice is examined, the picture is much less clear. People are often able to use very lean channels rather effectively for incredibly interpersonal messages—such as the love e-mails that helped spread the ILOVEYOU computer virus (see Chapter 2). How is this possible? Newer theories have since been proposed to help address this phenomenon.

SOCIAL INFORMATION PROCESSING THEORY

In addressing some of the conceptual issues with MRT, Walther (1992) offered an alternate perspective to understanding some of the issues with MRT. His Social Information Processing Theory seeks to explain interpersonal processes online and suggests that people can form deep and meaningful relationships online, even using the leanest of channels.

Social Information Processing Theory begins with the assumption that people have the same reasons for communicating with each other no matter the channel they use. People seek to reduce and manage uncertainty, form impressions of others, develop affinity, feel social presence, and so on. These are basic human desires of relatedness and ones we come to find ways to address, even through lean channels that lack nonverbal cues. More recent evidence suggests that more skilled communicators might be better able to accomplish their goals online (Walther & Bazarova, 2008).

So, how are people able to overcome limitations such as a lack of nonverbals online to do interpersonal things? First, it is important to note that time plays an important part in this process. CMC takes longer than FtF. Limits on bandwidth mean that less information gets through at any one given time. Second, it takes more time to type and read than to speak and listen (and look). A useful metaphor is that CMC is like sipping from a straw, and FtF is like gulping from a cup. If information is like the water in the cup, a person can get all of that water (information) using either the straw or gulping. It is just that sipping takes longer.

Another thing that people can use while interacting through CMC is circumventions. Although CMC may offer reduced nonverbal cues, they still seem to be able to utilize what is provided through the channel. For example, people utilize **chronemics** online to send e-mails (Walther & Tidwell, 1995) or post a Facebook message when a friend is away from their computer or engage in more or less rapid Twitter conversations much in the same style they would

Social information processing theory
A theory positing that humans use information to reduce uncertainty in order to forge relationships, and that the medium they use can subsequently impact how those relationships form. But they can and do form.

Chronemics Using a sense of time, such as response latency or pausing during a conversation, to communicate nonverbally.

CMC IN ACTION

I <3 U

How do you put emotion into the written/typed word? Of course, one way to do this is by choosing specific words. No doubt, poets have been using emotional language likely since there has been language to use.

More recently, people have begun to use emoticons, short for emotional icons, to help infuse their words with more emotion. How recently? A 2009 *New York Times* article suggests an emoticon may have appeared in the written copy of a speech given by Abraham Lincoln in 1862 (although it may just be a typo). See http://cityroom. blogs.nytimes.com/2009/01/19/hfo-emoticon/

Scott Fahlman is credited as being the first person to send a digital emoticon :-) when he posted a message to the computer science general electronic bulletin board at Carnegie Mellon University in 1982.

(A reproduction of the thread can be found here: http://www.cs.cmu.edu/~sef/Orig-Smiley.htm).

Today, there exist a whole lot of emoticons, way more than "Honest Abe" or Scott Fahlman likely ever dreamed. Some are pretty elaborate, being way more than a simple ;) or :-) from the past. There are many (incomplete) lists of emoticons that can be found online, including one here: http://www.cs.cmu.edu/~sef/Orig-Smiley.htm

---

> **Emoticons** Using combinations of keyboard symbols to represent facial expressions.

FtF (more rapid responses in a conversation could indicate more interest in the conversation, for example). People may also use **emoticons** to show their emotions, such as smiley faces "=)" or sad faces "=(" and any number of other keystroke combinations to represent different emotional states (see CMC in Action: I <3 U). People have been shown in research to ask more and deeper questions and self disclose more and with more depth when they interact with strangers online (Tidwell & Walther, 2002). In addition, online channels allow individuals to lurk online—that is, they can seek out someone by Googling them (Ramirez, Walther, Burgoon, & Sunnafrank, 2002) or by looking at a social media user's profile and read through different conversations and posts without actually interacting without anyone knowing about it (something much more difficult in real-world interactions, when lurking in on a stranger's conversations is not widely accepted).

Taking the time to effectively interact through CMC and navigating the circumventions necessary to do so takes a good deal of effort. People have to be both willing and able to put forth this effort in order to have relationships online, but it can be done. One motivating factor is the anticipation of future interaction. If you think you will be interacting with a person again (or at the very least, if you want to), you are more likely to put in this effort. In and of itself, it is possible that this increased effort leads to more positive outcomes in relationships started/maintained online.

One of the main notions of SIPT is that impressions and relationships can be formed online, but they just take longer than they do FtF. But how many of you know someone who felt like they had known someone forever even after interacting online? This would go against the ideas of SIPT. To help account for these experiences, Walther (1996) suggested the notion of **hyperpersonal relationships**: ones that become more personal through CMC than they would FtF. To account for how this happens, he suggested that the limitations of the channel, rather than leading to less personal relationships, could actually sometimes lead to this "hyper" personalness. To explain how this happens, Walther goes back to the classic communication model and looks at each of four parts.

> **Hyperpersonal relationships** Relationships that develop online more than they would FtF.

1. First, hyperpersonal happens because of sender effects. Sources of messages online can sometimes use the lack of nonverbals in order to better selectively self-present (put their best foot forward) (Walther, 2007).

2. Second, hyperpersonal happens because of receiver effects. When senders are selectively self-presenting themselves and the cues about the sender are limited, receivers may be better able to idealize the sender. This may be especially likely to happen if the receiver is deliberately seeking new relational partners or if they only have selected information on which to judge them (i.e., they both belong to the same Facebook group, so they have something in common).

3. Third, channel effects come into play for hyperpersonal. Channel allows for greater control (in general) over message construction than FtF. For example, you can pause to think and edit before sending a message (although certainly not everybody takes advantage of this). You also do not have to attend to as many distracting cues (one's own physical back channeling, etc.) This disentrainment (freedom from the rules of FtF interactions) frees one up to pay even more attention to selective self-presentation, and so on.

4. Finally, and perhaps most interestingly, feedback effects come into play. As idealizing receivers send selective messages back to the source, it can lead to behavioral confirmation, where the original source starts to behave more like the partner's idealized expectation of them (a sort of other-fulfilling prophecy). For example, if a person sends a message to a receiver and the receiver really likes the source, the receiver may think the source is really outgoing and fun and will respond positively to that person. As this continues to happen, the source gains confidence and actually starts behaving as more outgoing and fun.

Now throw all four of these things together, and you have a recipe for relationships that take off way faster than they might otherwise do. Are such hyperpersonal relationships common? Maybe at some level, but even at their fullest level, probably not. As Joe Walther has said about people falling in love with others whom they have only met online, "It probably doesn't happen to a large percentage of people, but it happens occasionally, and it's very intense." (http://www.livescience.com/26378-teo-scandal-real-online-love.html)

Think back to Sal 9000 . . . is this what he is experiencing at some level? A hyperpersonal "relationship"? And might this hyperpersonal notion also help explain what happened to Manti Te'o as well?

Hyperpersonal relationships tend to carry a negative connotation, at least from talking about them with our students. But can aspects of the process lead to more "positive" outcomes? Going back to the notion of Beyond Being There (Hollan & Stornetta, 1992), it is important to remember that FtF is not inherently the gold standard. Thinking of things as such and building systems to try to replicate FtF forgets that FtF has its own issues. CMC offers affordances that can help overcome the limitations of FtF in some situations (for example, the ability to overcome space and time restrictions). However, do you sometimes even use the limitations of a channel to your advantage in accomplishing your goals? In other words, is the lack of nonverbals always a limitation? Can nonverbals actually get in the way of effective interpersonal communication? Walther (2008) suggested at least one way in which the lack of nonverbals provided online might be the only way for interpersonal communication to take place. He suggests that sometimes seeing the other person may remind you of negative prejudices you hold toward the other person. Using the example of

Arab-Israeli relations, he suggests that just maybe CMC is the only chance for many members across these groups to have true, interpersonal communication. That is quite a thought . . . that CMC may help bridge the gap for peace in a war-torn area.

REFERENCES

Burgoon, J. K. (1978). A communication model of personal space violation: Explication and an initial test. *Human Communication Research, 4,* 129–142.

Christakis, N. A., & Fowler, J. H. (2009). *Connected: The surprising power of our social networks and how they shape our lives.* New York: Little, Brown & Co.

Daft, R. L., Lengel, R. H., & Trevino, L. K. (1987). Message equivocality, media selection, and manager performance: Implications for information systems. *MIS Quarterly, 11,* 355–366.

Ellison, N. B., Steinfield, C., & Lampe, C. (2007). The benefits of Facebook "friends:" Social capital and college students' use of online social network sites. *Journal of Computer-Mediated Communication, 12*(4), article 1. http://jcmc.indiana.edu/vol12/issue4/ellison.html

Granovetter, M. S. (1973). The strength of weak ties. *American Journal of Sociology, 78,* 1360–1380.

Harlow, H. (1958). The nature of love. *American Psychologist, 13,* 673–685.

Hollan, J., & Stornetta, S. (1992). Beyond being there. *Proceedings of the ACM CHI'92 Conference on Computer-Human Interaction,* 119–125.

Parks, M. R. (1982). Ideology in interpersonal communication: Off the couch and into the world. In M. Burgoon (Ed.), *Communication Yearbook 5* (pp. 79–107). New Brunswick, NJ: Transaction Books.

Ramirez, Jr. A., Walther, J. B., Burgoon, J. K., & Sunnafrank, M. (2002). Information seeking strategies, uncertainty, and computer-mediated communication: Toward a conceptual model. *Human Communication Research, 28,* 213–228.

Tidwell, L. C., & Walther, J. B. (2002). Computer-mediated communication effects on disclosure, impressions, and interpersonal evaluations: Getting to know one another a bit at a time. *Human Communication Research, 28,* 317–348.

Tong, S. T., & Walther, J. B. (2011). Relational maintenance and computer-mediated communication. In K. B. Wright & L. M. Webb (Eds.), *Computer-mediated communication in personal relationships* (pp. 98–118). New York: Peter Lang Publishing.

Travers, J., & Milgram, S. (1969). An experimental study of the small world problem. *Sociometry, 32,* 425–443.

Walther, J. B. (1992). Interpersonal effects in computer-mediated interaction: A relational perspective. *Communication Research, 19,* 52–90.

Walther, J. B. (1996). Computer-mediated communication: Impersonal, interpersonal, and hyperpersonal interaction. *Communication Research, 23,* 3–43.

Walther, J. B. (2007). Selective self-presentation in computer-mediated communication: Hyperpersonal dimensions of technology, language, and cognition. *Computers in Human Behavior, 23,* 2538–2557.

Walther, J. B. (2009). Computer-mediated communication and virtual groups: Applications to interethnic conflict. *Journal of Applied Communication Research, 37,* 225–238.

Walther, J. B., & Bazarova, N. (2008). Validation and application of electronic propinquity theory to computer-mediated communication in groups. *Communication Research, 35,* 622–645.

Walther, J. B., & Parks, M. R. (2002). Cues filtered out, cues filtered in: Computer-mediated communication and relationships. In M. L. Knapp & J. A. Daly (Eds.), *Handbook of interpersonal communication* (3rd ed., pp. 529–563). Thousand Oaks, CA: Sage.

Walther, J. B., & Tidwell, L. C. (1995). Nonverbal cues in computer-mediated communication, and the effect of chronemics on relational communication. *Journal of Organizational Computing, 5,* 355–378.8

CHAPTER 10

"When Do I Get a Break?"

Unexpected Emotions for a Stay-at-Home Dad

Caryn E. Medved

Painting and sculpting had always been Nelson's passion, and then after college this passion turned into his career. As an artist, Nelson always worked nontraditional hours and took time off between projects. Sales of his artwork brought in spurts of income, while his wife Denise's salary at the bank provided for their modest but comfortable life. So when they had their first child two years ago, it made sense for him to be Gabby's caregiver in her early years. What Nelson did not expect was how tough life could be as an at-home dad.

"Okay, Denise," he had said on the phone around noon, "You're lucky. Tonight I'm going to make some mushroom risotto, fresh asparagus, and some luscious tiramisu. You've been working too hard!" Denise had already told Nelson she would not be home until late that Friday night. Long meetings had kept her at the office until after 8 P.M. all week, and Nelson was feeling a little lonely spending his days with Gabby while having limited adult contact.

"That sounds wonderful! I'll stop and get a bottle of wine on the way home. Has Gabby had her nap yet today? I'll be home by 8:30. What a week," Denise replied with a weary voice.

"I'm putting her down as soon as I'm done cleaning up the lunch dishes— I'm hoping she'll sleep long enough that she can stay awake until you get home tonight. With all your meetings you've barely seen her, so hopefully we'll *both* see you later!" Nelson closed.

But Nelson's best laid plans began unraveling when he went to the pantry and there was no risotto. "Okay Gabby, let's get in the stroller. We're taking a walk to the grocery store!" As they walked the three blocks to Balducci's Gourmet Market, Nelson saw a group of mothers playing with their children in the park. He often longed for adult contact, but the one time he stopped over to play with Gabby in the park, he got the looks of quizzical admiration, as if people were thinking, "How cute! A father with his daughter in the middle of the day . . . I wonder where her mommy is . . ." He just found it too hard to have to explain to them why he was staying home. He had tried before, but people could not understand that he actually loved his role as primary caregiver.

In Balducci's, he stared at the shelf and then he asked the sales clerk, "Hey, do you have any risotto? I don't see it on the shelf where it usually is."

"Nope—all out," he responded without stopping.

"Ahhh, Gabby, we'll have to go with this flavored rice junk, but it'll do. Let's go." Later that evening, the dinner situation spiraled for the worse. While Gabby sat in her high chair with some apple slices, the phone rang. The local librarian who commissioned a picture for the lobby said she did not like Nelson's painting. Already upset from the phone call, Nelson realized he forgot the asparagus, and when he opened the box of rice, he accidentally spilled it on the floor. "I'm about to give up—when do I get a break?" he shouted to no one in particular.

Just then, Denise walked in the door with a bottle of wine. "Hey, I got off work early. Isn't it great that we get some extra time as a family?"

"Well isn't that just great," he snapped. To his surprise, in that moment he found himself resenting Denise and her time away from home every day (and recently, every night). "I just managed to drop our entire dinner on the dirty floor. This is ridiculous. Do stay-at-home moms have days like this?" Nelson exclaimed. He tried to sound like he was joking, but he really was feeling upset . . . so much that he was actually choking back some tears.

"It's okay, thanks for trying," Denise said as she took off her coat and put down the wine.

"That's easy for you to say, you haven't been shopping and cooking all day while watching the baby, only to have your meal spill all over the floor!" Nelson complained with an apron on and an empty box of rice dinner in his hand. They tensely stared at each other for a minute. Nelson shook his head and thought to himself, "Why am I so upset? I feel silly! I'm not much of an artist, and I can't even make dinner. How can I find a way to balance my time with Gabby and also have regular adult contact so that I am happy in my life and in my marriage?"

11

"You Don't Just *Not* Get Married"

The Normalization of Gender Role Expectations

Karen L. Daas

Kelly stepped out of her car with hesitation. Her friends would want to know what had happened on her date with Mitch last night, and she was not sure she wanted to share the details. She knew this was supposed to be the happiest moment in her life, but it did not quite feel that way. She had certainly been surprised when Mitch proposed over their dessert, but she had been even more surprised when she realized that she was not sure she wanted to accept the proposal. They had been dating for three years and marriage seemed like the next logical step. Still, she wondered why she did not feel like it was a step she was excited to take. She took a deep breath and headed into the coffee shop.

As soon as she reached the table, Maria asked, "So, what happened last night? I tried to call you after class, but you didn't answer. Don't tell me he broke up with you."

"No, he didn't break up with me," Kelly responded. "He asked me to marry him."

"Wow!" Maria squealed. "Congratulations! Did you talk about a date? You should have it at the country club next fall. I had my wedding there. My pictures were so beautiful, with the mountains in the background and the lake. They have that lovely fountain and . . ."

". . . Maria, we know . . . we were there. We'll get to that in a minute," interrupted Jessica. "Kelly, let me see the ring."

"I don't have it," Kelly said.

"Why not? What kind of guy asks you to marry him and doesn't give you a ring?" inquired Jessica. "Jay showed me the ring before he even asked me. Otherwise, there is no way I would have said yes. Come to think of it, I don't remember what he said since I was so busy staring at my ring." Jessica paused for a moment to study her ring and show it once again to the others at the table, even though they had all seen it numerous times in the three weeks since Jessica had become engaged. "I knew as soon as he showed me this ring that he loves me. I can't even imagine how much he spent. I know they're supposed to spend the equivalent of their salary for two months, but I know he spent much more than that. If that doesn't say love, I don't know what does. Sorry, I'm getting off track. Let's get back to you. Where is your ring?"

Kelly hesitated as she planned her response. "Well," she finally offered, "Mitch has it for now."

Jessica looked confused. "Why did he show it to you if he wasn't going to give it to you? That's just mean of him to tease you with it. Or is it really ugly or something and he has to return it?"

"No, it's not ugly," Kelly replied. "But I'm just not sure I want it right now."

"What is wrong with it? Does he need to have it sized or something? What other reason could there be? I'm so confused," Jessica offered as she tried to make sense of the situation.

"Whatever the ring looks like, it's okay," Maria tried to soothe Kelly. "The important thing is that you love him and he loves you. If the ring is small or not what you wanted, you can always upgrade later. When Matt and I got engaged, he only paid about $500 for my ring. It was all he could afford and fine for the time, but then, for our first anniversary, he bought me a really beautiful ring. He had started working at the law firm by then. I still have the original in my jewelry box because it has sentimental value for me, but I *love* this ring."

"It's not about the ring," Kelly finally confessed. "The ring is beautiful and I don't care how much it costs."

"Does it look like the one you have in your book?" Ashley interrupted.

"What book are you talking about?" Maria questioned. "Have I seen the book? Should I know what you're talking about?"

Kelly was quiet for a moment, thinking about Ashley's question. She knew exactly the book Ashley was talking about.

Ashley and Kelly had grown up together. They had been neighbors, classmates, and best friends for as long as she could remember. They used to play wedding with their dolls and sometimes even played dress-up, using curtains for veils as they pretended to walk down the aisle with twin brothers. At that age, Ashley and Kelly planned on marrying twins so that they could become sisters-in-law and guarantee that they really would be friends forever.

When they were in junior high and feeling too old to play with dolls, they each started a bridal book. They would cut pictures out of magazines or write down ideas of what they wanted for their perfect wedding based on what they had seen in movies and on television. They had even taken pictures at Ashley's older sister's wedding and cut out the parts they wanted for their own. They had given up the idea of marrying twins since they did not know any, but Ashley had taken to cutting out pictures of men she thought she could marry and creating entire stories in which she gave the men personalities and planned her life. First there was the big wedding, then the children, and finally, happily ever after.

When Ashley began obsessing about the image of the perfect man, Kelly began to shy away from working on her bridal book. She feared that Ashley had set up unrealistic expectations, and she did not want to find herself in a similar situation. At one time, Ashley had even confided in Kelly that she had the perfect wedding planned and would begin to make formal arrangements once she found a guy to fit into her vision. When Kelly asked how Ashley would know the guy, Ashley responded that it did not really matter who the guy was as long as he went along with Ashley's plans. This confession had caused fear in Kelly as she began to think that Ashley might be alone forever, and she tried to introduce new activities that would keep Ashley's mind off of the bridal book. Kelly's reluctance to fantasize about their weddings had put a strain on her friendship with Ashley, which began to deteriorate more when Kelly started dating and Ashley started spending too much time alone. They had remained friends throughout high school and now college, but Ashley seemed to resent Kelly, especially once she had started dating Mitch seriously.

Despite the fact that Kelly had not pulled out her bridal book in almost five years, she knew exactly where she had stored it and, more importantly, the ring to which Ashley was referring. It had been in an advertisement for a three-stone ring with channel set diamonds. The woman in the picture looked so happy, as if she could never love anyone more and she knew that she would be happy for the rest of her life. Kelly knew a ring could not promise happiness—it certainly had not for her parents, who had divorced when she was eight—but something about the woman's eyes as she stared at that ring and rested on her fiancé's shoulder made Kelly think that an engagement ring was definitely a step in the right direction.

Coming back to the present, Kelly answered Ashley. "No, it doesn't look like that ring . . . it's a bit simpler . . . but that's not why I don't have it." She could not help but wonder if the understated ring had contributed to her decision at some level. She did love Mitch and did not think the ring mattered, but she was a little disappointed with the style he had chosen.

Beyond the ring, though, Kelly was a little disappointed with the proposal as a whole. Not only was she not expecting Mitch to propose, but she was also not anticipating that he would do so in such a cliché manner. Had he never watched any of the proposal reality shows on television? Did he really think there was no better option than during dessert at a fancy restaurant? And why would he propose now, when they were months away from graduation and neither of them could barely afford their own apartments let alone a nice wedding or a house? She had really expected more from him.

"Hello? Kelly," Jessica pulled her out of her thoughts. "I'd still like to know why you're not wearing your ring."

"Because I haven't decided if I'm going to marry him," Kelly stated.

"Why wouldn't you marry him?" Maria asked. "You two have been together almost three years."

"I know. We have been together a long time," Kelly replied. "But I still do not feel like I am ready to marry him. I have been enjoying the relationship that we have. I am not sure I am ready for it to change. What if it is a mistake to marry him now?"

"Do you think there's someone better out there?" Ashley probed.

"It is not that," Kelly responded. "I have not even thought about whether there might be someone else for me. Actually, when I think about the future, I can see Mitch and me together. The thing is that I am just not sure that I want to get married."

"I don't understand you at all," Ashley interjected. "You are so lucky to have someone who wants to marry you. Why would you say no? I don't even have a boyfriend. I would *kill* to be in your shoes."

"I wish you were in my shoes," Kelly said. "It's not that I don't love Mitch or that I think there's someone better out there. I'm just not sure marriage is for me and I'm almost certain that it's definitely not right for me at this time in my life. I want to go to graduate school and maybe join the Peace Corps. I'm not sure I could do all of that if I were married."

"But just think how wonderful it would be if we could plan our weddings together," coaxed Jessica. "You could help me plan mine and once mine is over, we'll start planning yours. I'll be able to give you all sorts of tips. Maybe we could even shop together and get some deals if we both agree to use the same photographer or caterer or . . ."

"Jess, can we talk about whether she is going to get married before we start trying to plan a double wedding," Ashley interrupted.

"For your information, I am not talking about a double wedding," Jessica responded harshly. "As much as I love you, Kelly, I am not sharing my day."

"You need to think about someone other than yourself for a minute," Ashley sighed with frustration. "Kelly, have you thought about what might happen if you say no? Mitch might be really upset or, worse yet, he might break up with you. What if he breaks up with you? You never know if you're going to meet someone new. You could be alone the rest of your life. Doesn't that scare you?"

"Yes. No. I don't know." Kelly began to scan the faces of her friends. She wanted their advice, but she needed to make sure that what she decided was based on *her* needs rather than her friends' opinions. "I appreciate all of your advice, but I need to think about this. And I need to think about what to tell Mitch. I don't want to break up with him, but I'm only 22 and I don't want to get married right now. I still have so much to do with my life."

"Well, you could always have a long engagement," Ashley offered.

"Oh, good idea," Maria said. "Matt and I were engaged for a year before we were married. That gave me plenty of time to plan my wedding and start working on how we would combine our furniture. He had a hideous coffee table."

"You'll have to tell me how you managed to get rid of that," Jessica said. "Jay has this ugly chair that does not match any of my furniture. I do not want him moving that thing into our new apartment."

Kelly, becoming truly frustrated, lashed out, "I don't think you are listening to me. I am not concerned about a long engagement or furniture. I just don't feel like I want to get married . . . definitely not now and maybe not ever."

Ashley gasped. The friends sat silently at the table for a moment before Jessica spoke. "I understand your fears. They are only natural. I was scared to death when Jay showed me the box, but as I thought about how much I love him, I knew that marrying him was the right thing to do. I could not imagine my life without him, so why would I give him the chance to get away?"

"I felt the same way when Matt proposed to me," Maria confirmed. "It is a big change to get married, but it is such an achievement to be able to spend the rest of your life with someone. To hear you say that you do not feel like you want to get married, that is your fear talking, not your heart."

"I appreciate that both of you are happy being married or almost married," Kelly said, "but why are you trying to push me into this? Do you understand that I want something different for myself? I thought you were my friends."

"We are your friends," Maria stated with a touch of hurt in her voice. "We're just trying to keep you from doing something that you might regret. Have you really thought about what it means to turn down a proposal? That could be really bad for your relationship."

"I suppose it could," Kelly conceded, "although I would like to think that Mitch knows me well enough to understand. I don't understand why it is so important to get married. Does it mean that I'm not committed if I'm not married?"

"It's that you don't just *not* get married," Ashley concluded. "You're a woman and that's what you are supposed to do. If you don't want to get married, then what is the point of dating in the first place? It doesn't make sense to run the race if you don't want to win it."

"I agree," Maria said. "So what are you going to tell Mitch?"

Kelly closed her eyes and began to think about all of the things she had been told since she was a young girl. She always thought she would get married and have children someday, but now that the question had been asked, she had no idea how to answer it. She knew she would be running into Mitch later that afternoon . . .

CHAPTER

12

Groups

IN THIS CHAPTER

Why . . .

- Groups often don't measure up to our expectations.
- Group size is important to group effectiveness.
- The "wheel" communication pattern leads to efficiency but low satisfaction.
- Common roles emerge in groups of all kinds.
- It's good to bring a laptop to a meeting.
- Too much cohesiveness can be detrimental to groups.

Groups: Fiction and Fact

Why People Join Groups

Types of Groups

- Task and Social Dimensions: Productivity and Morale
- Contrived and Emergent Groups

Group Development

- Group Communication Networks
- Stages of Development

Group Culture: Symbols, Rules, and Codes

Decision Making

- Consensus
- Compromise
- Majority Vote
- Decision by Leader
- Arbitration

Roles and Responsibilities

- Task-Oriented Roles
- Group-Building and Support Roles
- Individualistic Roles

Leadership

- Functions of Leadership
- Approaches to Leadership
- Follower and Member Issues

Cohesiveness

- Symptoms of Too Little Cohesiveness: Boredom and Indifference
- Symptoms of Too Much Cohesiveness: The Groupthink Syndrome

Conflict in Groups

Mediated Groups

Implications and Applications

Summary

Each of us spends a great deal of time in groups of various kinds. As members of families, peer groups, clubs, work groups or teams, religious groups, and other social groups, we are selectively exposed to the world around us. As we grow from infancy to adulthood, the groups in which we participate generate a wide range of demands and opportunities for us; and, in the process of adjusting to them, we develop, change, and grow.

As with relationships, groups are created and maintained by people engaged in reciprocal message processing. As we shall see, the communication process makes groups possible and is essential to every facet of group functioning.

Groups differ from relationships in terms of the number of people involved, the resources available for decision making, and the complexity of the communication dynamics that result. The presence of additional individuals and more complex communication dynamics is, on the one hand, a very positive characteristic of groups. With increased size comes additional people to address issues, undertake projects, and solve problems. On the other hand, the larger size also leads to problems associated with agreeing on goals, ensuring that information is available to all group members, defining roles and responsibilities, providing appropriate leadership, creating cohesiveness, and avoiding undue pressure on individuals toward conformity. See Table 12.1.

TABLE 12.1   *Characteristics of Groups: Consequences of Size*

Benefits	Costs
Additional Members to Assist with Activities	Effort Needed to Develop Consensus on Goals
	Effort Needed to Keep Members Informed
Additional Members to Participate in Decision Making	Effort Needed to Include Members
	Effort Needed to Counteract Pressures Toward Conformity
Additional Resources for Problem Solving	Effort Needed for Leadership

GROUPS: FICTION AND FACT

A decision about this year's group project has to be made. The board—of which you are a newly-elected member—has proposed a service project to help homeless people in the community. A meeting of the group is scheduled to approve the recommendation and begin the planning process.

This group has a fairly simple and straightforward agenda. A decision has to be made, and a recommendation is on the table. You envision a brief meeting of the group at which members will share information and opinions and begin planning together to achieve the common goal.

The meeting is scheduled at what is supposed to be a good time for everyone. Eleven members of the group are present at the designated starting time. One member arrives fifteen minutes later. Six people are absent, and no one is sure why.

As discussion proceeds, it becomes clear that five of the members present disagree with the proposed project.

Three members in attendance are vocally opposed to the idea. (Two don't like the idea, and the third—an unsuccessful candidate for board membership during the last election—doesn't feel the board sought enough input from members in arriving at its recommendation). Of those not present, two people are reportedly opposed to the idea, but no one seems to know the reasons for their disapproval.

The other three members in attendance haven't spoken; one looks angry, one bored, and a third seems to be working on an unrelated writing assignment of some kind while others are engaged in discussion.

Unfortunately, the realities of group life often do not match our expectations.[1] In the abstract we tend to think of groups as collections of active, supportive, and enthusiastic people, working together rationally and unemotionally to pursue shared goals. In fact, groups are composed of individuals with varying motivations, emotions, attachments, perspectives, and needs who come together to negotiate a framework for communication that permits collective action. While this goal seems to be relatively straightforward, the process by which individuals pursue it may not be.

WHY PEOPLE JOIN GROUPS

People join groups to pursue individual needs in a social context. Groups assist individuals in meeting a number of goals, including: socializing and companionship, support for personal development or change, spiritual growth, and economic gain. A number of factors go into individual decisions as to which groups to join, among them:[2]

- Attractiveness of the group's members—including physical, social, and task attractiveness
- Attractiveness of the group's activities and goals
- Attractiveness of being a member of a particular group—personal, social, symbolic, occupational, or economic benefits

TYPES OF GROUPS

Task and Social Dimensions: Productivity and Morale

Groups are created to serve a number of goals. Often, the primary objective is *productivity*— the completion of a task or job. Examples are organizing a party, building a house, or carrying out community service projects. We can distinguish several types of task-oriented groups:[3]

- *Duplicated activity group.* Each member does the same job. Examples: All members plant trees or prepare letters for mailing.
- *Assembly line group.* Each member works on a different part of the task. Examples: Some members dig holes, others plant trees, and others water and clean up; or some members fold letters, others add the stamps, and others stuff and mail.
- *Judgmental, problem-solving and decision-making group.* Members of the group identify and choose among possible answers, strategies, or options. Examples: A group decides how many and what kind of trees to plant, where to plant them, and plans the planting process.

There are also groups in which the primary goal is to create positive *morale*—and to facilitate members achieving personally- or socially-oriented goals, such as interpersonal support, encouragement, and diversion. Social clubs and discussion groups are examples. See Figure 12.1.

To a greater or lesser extent, most groups serve a combination of task-, personally-, and socially-oriented goals. Even in what might seem to be a rigidly task-oriented group, such as a work group or team on an industrial assembly line where productivity is the primary measure of success, good morale is also important. This is especially the case if members of a task group will

Figure 12.1
Membership in various groups can be an important part of our lives.
© Lee Snider Photo Images, 2014. Shutterstock, Inc.

need to work together for some period of time. In such cases, good morale may enhance productivity; and, conversely, poor morale can undermine it. Within groups whose goals are primarily social, task orientation can also be essential, even in deciding where to meet, what projects to undertake, where to eat, or what movies to attend. Most groups—such as families, service clubs, or religious or professional groups—require a fairly even balance between concern for productivity and morale. Task orientation is necessary to carry out group activities; personal and social orientation are necessary to encourage full participation and to encourage positive feelings by members toward the group and one another.

Contrived and Emergent Groups

Some groups are *emergent.* Such groups form naturally out of the spontaneous activities of individuals. Acquaintances who become friends and begin to go places and do things with one another provide an example of an emergent group.

More often, groups are *contrived*—intentionally formed for specific purposes.[4] Contrived groups typically have specific, stated goals or objectives, such as to serve the community, to share professional interests, to complete a work project, to help members quit smoking, or to support a political candidate. Sometimes, groups that are initially emergent shift to contrived, such as when acquaintances decide to form a club or work group.

GROUP DEVELOPMENT

Group Communication Networks

In a two-person relationship, there is the possibility of only one reciprocal communication linkage. With three interactants, there are six possible message-processing pairs: person 1 with person 2, person 1 with person 3, person 2 with person 3, persons 1 and 2 with person 3, persons 1 and 3 with person 2, and persons 2 and 3 with person 1. When we consider the possible interpersonal linkages in a group of four members, there are twenty-five potential communication relationships! The addition of just one more person creates the potential for nineteen additional communication linkages.[5]

In groups that are emergent, reciprocal message-processing linkages—*networks*—develop naturally, often spontaneously. Networks begin to form as individuals meet and get to know one another. With the passage of time, the network becomes well-developed as all members of the group participate in interaction. Theoretically, as shown in Figure 12.2, the network will evolve to include all group members, at least minimally.[6]

In actual practice, a number of patterns of linkage are possible, as shown in Figure 12.3. In the *circle* network, each group member interacts with two other people. Person A interacts with Person B and Person E, Person B with Person A and Person C, and so on. The *wheel* configuration describes a situation in which all messages flow through one individual—Person A. Person A interacts directly with all members of the group, but none of the others interact directly with one another. In a *chain,* members interact in a serial, straight-line manner. The *all-channel* pattern denotes a network in which each member of a group sends messages to, and receives messages from, every other member. In any group, some linkages in networks are utilized more and others less; some people become central to the network, others peripheral; still others may become isolated from others in the network. And, clearly, patterns change over time.

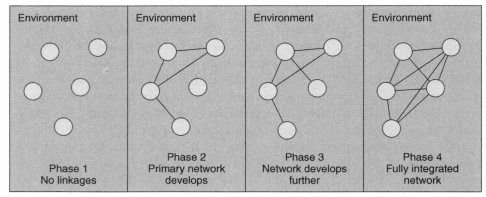

Figure 12.2
The development of linkages in a group is marked by the emergence of networks that connect individuals to one another and define the unit. A group need not progress through all phases but may move from a stage of high integration to stages of lower integration and back again periodically.

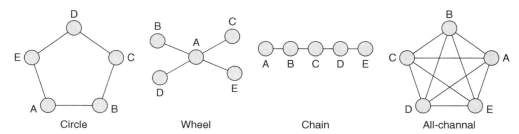

Figure 12.3
In studies of common group communication networks, such as those shown here, centralized networks (like the "wheel") contributed to rapid performance, but the error rate was high. Low centralization (such as provided in the "circle") was found to be associated with a high degree of individual satisfaction. Researchers also noted that being in a key position in a network, one requiring that information be channeled through one individual, led to information "overload."

Source: Harold J. Leavitt, "Some Effects of Certain Communication Patterns on Group Performance," *Journal of Abnormal and Social Psychology, 46,* (1951), pp. 38–50; M. E. Shaw, "Some Effects of Unequal Distribution of Information Upon Group Performance in Various Communication Nets," *Journal of Abnormal and Social Psychology, 49,* (1954), pp. 547–553.

Stages of Development

Groups that are formed to accomplish a specific task (such as writing a report) may follow a predictable pattern. Studies of the development of task-oriented groups suggest that they move through the following phases:[7]

1. Orientation phase
2. Conflict phase
3. Emergence phase
4. Reinforcement phase

The first stage, *orientation*, consists of getting acquainted, expressing initial points of view, and forming linkages relative to the task at hand. In the early stages of a group's work, the discussion tends to focus on "small talk," such as the weather, the setting, circumstances that brought the individuals together, goals of the group, and so on.

As the group proceeds to work on its task, roles and responsibilities are considered. During the *conflict* phase, the expression of differing points of view leads to polarization. Gradually, accommodations are made among members and subgroups with differing view points, as the group begins to take on an identity of its own in the *emergence* phase. As the group's project nears completion, cooperation among individuals in the network increases, as does support for—and *reinforcement* of—the group's solution.[8]

These stages are general descriptions of the development of a group. Not all groups follow these stages in precisely this order. Some research indicates that many groups may not proceed in this orderly fashion at all.[9] Sometimes groups move from one stage to another and then back again. Nevertheless, whether or not a particular group follows this model, this sort of typology helps us to understand the nature of group process.

A number of factors influence the dynamics of groups as they evolve. Among these are: the amount of structure within the group; the time available to the group for completion of the task; the group size; the group members' attitudes and feelings about the task, topic, and one another; and the nature of the task.[10] The following task characteristics are particularly important to a group's progress:[11]

- *Task difficulty*. The amount of effort required to complete the job
- *Solution multiplicity*. The number of reasonable alternatives available to solve the problem
- *Interest and motivation*. Interest generated by the task
- *Cooperation requirements*. The degree to which cooperation by group members is necessary to complete the task
- *Familiarity*. The extent to which the group has had experience with a particular task

GROUP CULTURE: SYMBOLS, RULES, AND CODES

As networks develop, symbols, rules, and codes of various types emerge and become standardized through communication, as shown in Figure 12.4. The process creates the group's *culture*. Some aspects of group culture develop naturally, as with slang phrases among members of a club or social group, or informal "dress codes" in a peer group. In other instances, symbols, rules, and codes result from systematic efforts by members of a group. In such cases, symbols and rules are created to give the group an identity, to differentiate it from others, or to identify or differentiate a particular group from a larger unit of which it is a part. The decorated jackets of street gangs serve this function, as do handshakes, team names and logos, or the "secret words" of fraternities and sororities.

Culture plays a pervasive role in the dynamics of groups. It provides members of a group with a sense of individual and collective identity and contributes to the development of order, structure, and cohesiveness in the overall operation of the system.

Terrence Deal and Allen Kennedy observed major corporations and developed a description of elements of culture that can be applied to small groups as well as to large organizations.[12] They discuss the values, heroes, and rites and rituals characteristic of every culture.

Values are the basic concepts and beliefs of a group. They form the heart of a group's culture and establish the standards of achievement. Core values

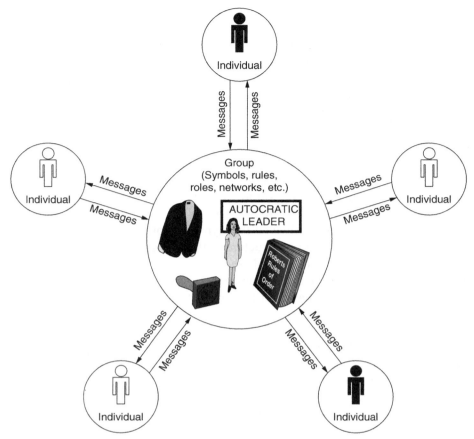

Figure 12.4
Through their verbal and nonverbal behavior individuals collectively create the groups to which they belong and the cultures, symbols, rules, jargon, and other conventions characteristic of each. Once created, the culture of the group "acts back upon" its members. Over time, individuals are greatly influenced by the group, and in turn individuals collectively create the group.

(such as customer service or "people come first") indicate what is important to a group. Group members who support the group's values are more likely to succeed. For example, members of a research and development team in a high technology company may be expected to quickly invent products that are innovative and ahead of the competition. People in this type of group are rewarded for being risk-taking. A person who continually says, "I don't think we can do this," would be unlikely to succeed in this type of group.

Cultures and groups often have *heroes* who personify the group's values. These people (whether real or fictitious) provide role models for group members to follow. Heroes may be people who began a highly successful organization (like Walt Disney) or people who became memorable by overcoming a difficult time in the group's life. For example, a group of students working on a class project may valorize the person who brought a laptop to the group meeting, thereby saving the group from endless hours taking notes and editing the final paper.

Rites and rituals are the routines of everyday life in a group. These activities may consist of nothing more significant than everyone in a group shaking hands and introducing themselves at the beginning of an exercise, or they may be elaborate, formal ceremonies like initiation rituals. These activities communicate and reinforce the values of the group. Although some rites and rituals are traditional and maintained over time, groups must be careful to adapt their rites and rituals as the membership of the group changes and society's attitudes toward various beliefs progresses. For example, hazing is no longer an appropriate way to initiate a person into a campus organization.

DECISION MAKING

One of the major activities of most task-oriented groups is decision making. Decisions range from simple and straightforward questions such as when to hold a meeting, to more complex and entangled questions about group policy and activities. Rules that guide decision making in small informal groups emerge naturally as members spend time with one another. In larger, more structured groups, decision-making sessions are generally convened and given a specific name—*meetings*. During meetings, the behaviors of individuals follow a number of reasonably well-defined rules, some emerging spontaneously, with others following group traditions, formalized bylaws, or parliamentary procedure.

There are a number of methods by which groups can make decisions, among them: consensus, compromise, majority vote, decision by leader, and arbitration.[13]

Consensus

Consensus refers to a process which requires that a group arrive at a collective decision with which all members genuinely agree. For example, through discussion, it becomes apparent that every member of a club likes the idea of doing a service project for senior citizens, and the group decides to undertake this kind of project.

The following rules have been developed to help a group reach consensus:[14]

1. Members should avoid arguing for their "pet" proposals.
2. Groups should avoid "us against them" stalemates in which each side in a dispute must either "win" or "lose."
3. Members should not comply with a group majority if they do so only to avoid conflict.
4. Groups should not use rules for decision-making that allow them to avoid conflict, such as a "majority wins" rule.
5. Groups should view differences of opinion among members as natural and helpful.
6. Members should consider that their early, initial agreements are suspect and premature.

Compromise

Compromise is a process of negotiation and give-and-take to arrive at a position that takes account of—but may not be completely consistent with—the preferences of individual members. For example, some members of a club want to do a service project for senior citizens, while others favor a project for the homeless. Through discussion, the group decides to undertake a project for homeless seniors.

Majority Vote

Majority voting is a method for arriving at group decisions mathematically. A decision is made when it is supported by a majority of members. In very formal groups, there may be a specific definition for majority (for example, 50 percent plus 1 or two-thirds). For example, four members want to do a project for senior citizens; six want to do something for the homeless. The decision is six-to-four in favor of a homeless project.

Decision by Leader

Leader decision making involves the imposition of a resolution by a group's leader. In this instance, it is a decision by proclamation. For example, the group is unable to meet because of bad weather, and a decision is made by the club president that this year the group will do a service project for senior citizens.

Arbitration

Agreement through a process of formal negotiation between parties unable to reach a decision by other means is called *arbitration*. For example, two subgroups exist within the club. One is determined to do a project for seniors, while the other insists that something should be done for homeless people in the community. Members of each group have very strong personal convictions about the matter. Discussion and a trial vote reveals that there is a five to five split, with no one willing to change his or her position. An imposed decision risks permanently alienating members. The head of the local community agency coordinating the organization is invited to the next meeting to help the group reach a decision.

More often than not, arbitration is used in conflicts between, rather than within, groups—for instance, a deadlock between labor and management over terms of a contract. These groups may also have very specific rules for arbitration.

ROLES AND RESPONSIBILITIES

In small informal groups, member roles and responsibilities develop primarily as the result of informal, often unverbalized, agreements. In larger and more formal groups, individual roles and responsibilities may be made explicit. In clubs, for instance, the responsibilities and duties of officers, committee members, and other positions are generally detailed in written bylaws or a constitution. And in workgroups or teams, the mission, goals, time constraints, and resources available may be specified.

In a now classic article on group roles, Benne and Sheats outlined three types of roles that develop in groups over the course of time:[15] (1) roles related to the completion of the task, (2) roles related to building and supporting the group, and (3) individualistic roles. Within each of these broad categories, a number of specific roles are identified.

Task-Oriented Roles

- *Initiator-contributor.* Suggests or proposes new ideas or changed ways of regarding the group problem or goal
- *Information-seeker.* Asks for clarification of suggestions made in terms of their factual adequacy and for authoritative information and facts pertinent to the problem being discussed
- *Opinion-seeker.* Asks for clarification of the values pertinent to what the group is undertaking, of values involved in a suggestion made, or of values in alternative suggestions

- *Information-giver.* Offers facts or generalizations which are "authoritative" or relates his or her own pertinent experience to the group problem
- *Opinion-giver.* States his or her belief or opinion pertinent to a suggestion made or to alternative suggestions
- *Elaborator.* Spells outs suggestions in terms of examples, offers a rationale for suggestions previously made, and tries to understand how an idea or suggestion would work out if adopted by the group
- *Coordinator.* Shows or clarifies the relationships among various ideas and suggestions, tries to pull ideas and suggestions together, or tries to coordinate the activities of various members of subgroups
- *Orienter.* Defines the position of the group with respect to its goals by summarizing what has occurred, points to departures from agreed-on directions or goals, or raises questions about the direction the group discussion is taking
- *Evaluator-critic.* Subjects the accomplishment of the group to some standard or set of standards of group functioning in the context of the group task
- *Energizer.* Prods the group to action or decision, attempts to stimulate or arouse the group to "greater" or "higher quality" activity
- *Procedural-technician.* Expedites group movement by doing things for the group—performing routine tasks such as distributing materials or managing objects for the group (e.g., rearranging the seating)
- *Recorder.* Writes down suggestions, makes a record of group decisions, or writes down the results of the discussion

Group-Building and Support Roles

- *Encourager.* Praises, agrees with, and accepts the contribution of others
- *Harmonizer.* Mediates the differences between other members, attempts to reconcile disagreements, relieves tension in conflict situations through jesting
- *Compromiser.* Operates from within a conflict by offering a compromise, admitting a mistake, or moving toward another position
- *Gatekeeper/expediter.* Attempts to keep communication channels open by encouraging or facilitating the participation of others or by regulating the flow of communication
- *Standard setter.* Expresses standards for the group to attempt to achieve in its functioning or applies standards in evaluating the quality of group processes
- *Group observer.* Keeps records of various aspects of group process and feeds such data with proposed interpretations into the group's evaluation of its own procedures
- *Follower.* Goes along with the movement of the group, more or less passively accepting the ideas of others, serving as an audience in group discussion and decision making

Individualistic Roles

- *Aggressor.* May work in many negative ways, including deflating the status of others, expressing disapproval of the values, acts or feelings of others, attacking the group or the problem it is working on, joking aggressively, or showing envy toward another's contribution by trying to take credit for it
- *Blocker.* Tends to be negative and stubbornly resistant, disagreeing and opposing without or beyond reason, and attempting to maintain or bring back an issue after the group has rejected it

- *Recognition seeker.* Works in various ways to call attention to himself or herself, including boasting, reporting on personal achievements, acting in unusual ways, or struggling to prevent being placed in an "inferior" position
- *Self-confessor.* Uses the audience opportunity the group setting provides to express personal, nongroup-oriented "feeling," "insight," or "ideology."
- *Dominator.* Tries to assert authority or superiority by manipulating the group or certain members of the group
- *Help seeker.* Attempts to call forth "sympathy" responses from other group members or from the whole group
- *Special interest pleader.* Speaks for the "small business owner," "the grass roots" community, the "soccer mom," "labor," and so on, usually cloaking his or her own prejudices or biases in the stereotype which best fits his or her individual need

LEADERSHIP

No doubt the role that receives the most attention in any discussion of groups is that of the leader. The basic role of a leader is to coordinate the activities of individuals so that they contribute to the overall goals and general adaptability of the group.

In groups of two, three, or four individuals, patterns of leadership are almost totally the result of the needs, preferences, and communication styles of the individuals involved. Leadership may well be a subtle, even unnoticeable, aspect of the group's operation. In larger groups, leadership is an essential, formalized, and often highly visible element in the day-to-day and long-term functioning of the group. In either case, the role involves the design, implementation, and/or supervision of procedures, policies, or mechanisms necessary to bring about the desired coordination of the individuals and activities of the group.

Functions of Leadership

Leadership is conducted through communication. But leaders are responsible for accomplishing certain goals. The basic functions of leadership fall into two categories: (1) group maintenance functions, and (2) group achievement functions. A synthesis of these functions is provided by Baird and Weinberg.[16] They list:

Group Maintenance Functions
- Promoting participation
- Regulating interaction
- Promoting need satisfaction
- Promoting cooperation
- Arbitrating conflict
- Protecting individual rights
- Providing exemplary behavior
- Assuming responsibility for group failure
- Promoting group development

Group Achievement Functions
- Informing
- Planning
- Orienting

- Integrating
- Representing
- Coordinating
- Clarifying
- Evaluating
- Stimulating

Approaches to Leadership

Leadership is an interactional process that helps people in organizations manage their environment. Effective leaders plan and select actions that help organizations or groups accomplish their goals. In addition, they may assist individuals to understand the obstacles they face in accomplishing their tasks so that they can be overcome. There are a variety of points of view as to what constitutes good leadership.[17]

Good-Leaders-Are-Born Approach.   The traditional view held that leadership is a *trait*—an ability one inherits. In this perspective, "good leaders are born not made." The assumption is that leadership qualities are inherent within one's personality. Either we possess or do not possess these qualities. According to this approach, the challenge of leadership involves finding people who have "the right stuff." This theory was often used to keep certain groups of people out of leadership positions, and it is not widely followed today.

One-Best-Style Approach.   Another approach views leadership as a matter of style. Decision making can be wholly centralized or can be totally diffused among members of a group. If the decision making is centralized (controlled by the leader), the leadership style may be characterized as *autocratic*. The autocratic leader uses authority to direct group activities. Typically, this type of leader tightly controls information, assigns members to roles and responsibilities, and has formal systems of accountability. When authority is shared, the leadership style is described as *democratic* or *participatory*. This type of leader gets members of the group involved in decision making and has a more open sharing of information. Moreover, roles and responsibilities are determined, at least in part, by the group. A third approach to leadership—*laissez-faire*—is a "hands-off" style, in which no authority is exercised by the leader. From the perspective of the "one-best style" approach, the challenge of leadership is determining whether the autocratic, democratic, or laissez-faire style of leadership is most effective in a given situation.

Based on studies comparing leadership styles and their effects, it was first thought that the democratic style was superior in terms of group productivity and morale. However, further research confirmed that some groups functioned very well with more authoritarian leadership. Examples are military groups, surgical units, and athletic teams. A reasonable conclusion is that there is no ideal leadership style for all groups and circumstances; rather, the appropriateness of a particular style depends on the nature and purpose of the group.[18]

Contextual Approach.   The contextual approach views leadership as the result of individual abilities (inherited plus learned), the purposes of the group, pressures put on the group from outside, and the way members in the group talk, work, or relate to one another.[19]

Bormann and Bormann offer the following description of this approach to leadership:

> The contextual view recognized that some people learn to play the game of being leader and that they tend to have certain opening moves they use in starting the game whenever they join a new work group. To some extent, the way they try to be leader depends upon what they think about the group. They do not approach the squad at basic training in the army with the same expectations they display toward a peer discussion group. . . . Such an explanation provides a more complete view of leadership than does either the trait approach or the one-best-style approach. It includes the idea that leaders are to some extent born, but it also suggests that potential leaders can acquire skills and improve talents.[20]

No matter which leadership style is chosen, it is important to remember that, as communication scholar J. Kevin Barge reminds us:[21]

- Leadership is enacted through communication.
- Leaders refine, develop, and modify the organizing systems of their organizations or groups to maintain viability in a complex, changing environment.
- The key to successful leadership in the future is the ability to coordinate diverse groups of people working on differing tasks in a changing and unstable environment.

Follower and Member Issues

For the individual, leadership is an important element that differentiates the involvement in a group from participation in relationships. In relationships, each individual has a direct hand in creating and controlling the system, its culture, communication patterns, rules, and roles. This is not often the case with groups, since we are usually initiated into—rather than initiating—them.

Becoming a participant in any group involves an initiation into the culture and communication patterns of the unit. Our training for membership in groups begins during our earliest years. As a child in a family, for instance, a good deal of compromise, accommodation, and fitting in is required. The child must learn the family's rules as to what to do, when to do it, what to say, and where to say it.

Later, as the child seeks to attain membership in various other groups, a similar process operates. Entry into certain clubs, fraternal orders, and religious groups makes this process of fitting in a very explicit part of the initiation of a new member into the unit. Even in those social and work groups where there is no formal apprenticeship, internship, or trial period, the individual must come to terms with the group's rules and realities in order to be accepted and to function effectively as a member.

Thus, in those instances in which one's role requires *adjustment* to the situation rather than the *creation* of that situation, the initial function of communication is identifying and fitting oneself to the ongoing rules and structures made by others. This generally means that becoming a member of a group is a less active, less creative, more accommodating—and for some a more frustrating—process than becoming part of a relationship.

COHESIVENESS

Cohesiveness refers to group loyalty.[22] A cohesive group is one in which members have a "team spirit" and are committed to the group's well being. As Ernest and Nancy Bormann note in *Effective Small Group Communication*, the essence of the concept of cohesiveness is aptly reflected in the motto of Alexandre Dumas's *Three Musketeers*: "All for one and one for all."

The relationship between communication, cohesiveness, and performance is important in any group. It is through communication that cohesiveness—or the lack of it—is fostered. Moreover, the presence or absence of cohesiveness influences the patterns and quality of communication within a group. When present, cohesiveness also encourages task and social dimensions of productivity and good morale:[23]

- Cohesive task groups are more productive. They do more work because members work cooperatively, distribute the work load well, and use time efficiently.
- Cohesive groups have higher morale because their members value and feel like they are a part of the group. Members pay attention to, appreciate, spend time and effort with one another, and share success as well as failure.
- Cohesive groups have efficient and effective communication because channels are open. Members are present, receptive, and committed to ensuring the communication necessary to promote productivity and high morale.

Symptoms of Too Little Cohesiveness: Boredom and Indifference

There are a number of symptoms and consequences of low cohesiveness.[24] These include a lack of member involvement, the absence of enthusiasm, and minimal question asking. Meetings are quiet, even boring, with members behaving in a polite but apathetic manner. Even important decisions are handled routinely, and the prevailing sentiment is best expressed as, "Let's get this over with."

Symptoms of Too Much Cohesiveness: The Groupthink Syndrome

Cohesiveness and loyalty to the group can have a down side. In *Groupthink*, Irving L. Janis explains that decision-making groups can actually be *too* cohesive.[25] Within highly cohesive groups, pressure to agree with the group can become very powerful. A *norm*, or accepted standard, of avoiding disagreement may develop. The group can be so cohesive and team-oriented that opinions that contradict the majority view may go unverbalized and/or be inadvertently overlooked. The *groupthink syndrome* occurs because members place great value on loyalty and being a team player. One of the characteristics of groupthink that makes it particularly troublesome is that the process often occurs without the awareness of the participants.

Groupthink Warning Signs.   The presence of certain factors signals the potential for groupthink. These include:[26]

- *Overestimation of the group's power and morality.* Assuming the group is not accountable to others and that it is pursuing the morally correct course of action
- *Closed-mindedness.* Ignoring or distorting alternative viewpoints
- *Pressures toward conformity.* Subtle and not-so-subtle influence toward agreement among group members and lack of willingness to acknowledge or discuss differences of opinion

Consequences of groupthink may include: an incomplete survey of alternatives and options, failure to examine risks of preferred choices, failure to reappraise initially-rejected alternatives, poor information search, selective bias in processing information at hand, and failure to work out contingency plans.[27]

CONFLICT IN GROUPS

At various stages in the development of any group, conflict is inevitable. The conflict may have to do with disagreements over a group's goals, member roles or responsibilities, decision making, resource allocation, group dynamics, relationships among particular individuals, or any of a number of other factors.

Conflict is not inherently a problem. In fact, while the experiencing of conflict is generally unpleasant, we know that without conflict, quality, diversity, growth, and excellence may be diminished for individuals, relationships, or groups. Thus, the goal is not necessarily to eliminate conflict. Rather, the objective in any situation should be to better understand conflict, to be able to identify its origins, to be able to determine its potential for making a positive contribution, and to be able to resolve or manage it productively.

A number of approaches have been developed to analyze and resolve conflict within groups. One interesting approach classifies conflict based on two dimensions:[28]

- *Assertiveness.* Behaviors intended to satisfy our own concerns
- *Cooperativeness.* Behaviors intended to satisfy the concerns of others

Considered in combination, these two dimensions describe five different styles of conflict.[29] See Figure 12.5.

1. *Competitive style.* High in assertiveness and low in cooperativeness. Example: the tough competitor who desires to defeat others—a "fight orientation."
2. *Accommodative style.* Low in assertiveness and high in cooperativeness. Example: the easygoing, undemanding, and supportive follower.
3. *Avoiding style.* Low in assertiveness, low in cooperativeness. Example: the low-profile, indifferent, group isolate—a "flight orientation."

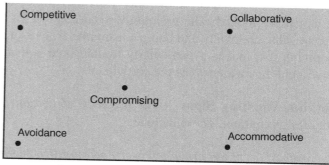

Figure 12.5
Five Conflict-Management Styles and Their Relationships
Source: Reprinted from *Organizational Behavior and Human Performance*, Vol. 16, No. 1, by Thomas L. Ruble and Kenneth W. Thomas, "Support for a Two-Dimensional Model of Conflict Behavior", pp. 143–155, Copyright © 1976, with permission from Elsevier.

4. *Collaborative style.* High in assertiveness, high in cooperativeness. Example: the active, integrative problem solver.
5. *Compromising style.* Moderate in assertiveness, moderate in cooperativeness. Example: the "meet-you-half-way," "give-up-something-to-keep-something" approach.

This framework is useful for understanding origins of conflict within groups. Moreover, it suggests how certain styles and strategies can be helpful in resolving and managing conflict.

MEDIATED GROUPS

As new communication technologies continue to be developed, more and more group interaction is taking place through mediated channels. For example, a group of engineers may "meet" in a video-conference in which each engineer sits alone in a conference room watching a monitor that projects images of the other group members who are sitting in various other locations around the world. Another group may use a computer program to help them analyze a large body of information and come to a decision. Still another group of citizens may log on to their local computer network and exchange messages about a topic of concern to them, such as the new school budget. Some college instructors have set up discussion rooms, listservs, or message boards so that their students can continue class discussion online.

These mediated modes of discussion have the potential to link together people who live and work in very remote locations. The potential for creating a global sense of community is enormous. As this technology becomes available to more people throughout the world, the possibilities for new types of group interaction will continue to expand.

IMPLICATIONS AND APPLICATIONS

- Groups are complex social systems made up of individuals who bring their own unique orientations—perspectives, goals, needs, values, experiences, styles, and motivations—to group membership.
- Groups are successful to the extent that the diverse orientations of members can be coordinated, channeled, and/or focused.
- Success has two dimensions: productivity and morale. From the perspective of productivity, a group is successful when the job is done. In terms of morale, a group is successful when people feel satisfied. Sometimes these two outcomes go together in groups; sometimes they do not. For instance, taking time to focus on members' personal and social needs, which may contribute to good morale, is time taken away from work on completing a task. However, if a group is to work together on more than a single task, effort spent to foster positive morale in the short-run often is rewarded by contributing to increased productivity in the longer term. And, even in the short-run, poor morale can have major consequences in terms of the quality of decision making and on productivity.
- The communication dynamics and networks that emerge within a group often by accident frequently take on a life of their own. Once particular cliques or subgroups form, for instance, they are often self-perpetuating.
- The way in which new members are initiated into groups is a critical aspect of group development. The kind of orientation new members receive, and

the place they initially occupy in group communication networks, may have long-term consequences for the new members' thoughts about, and actions toward, the group.

- Every group has its own culture and its unique symbols, rules, and codes. These serve to contribute to the group's identity and provide a basis for commonness among members.

- Often without the intention of group members, cultures support and encourage some kinds of behavior—for instance, cooperativeness, aggressiveness, service, or racial or gender bias—while discouraging others. By analyzing communication patterns and practices, one can become aware of the implicit values and behaviors that are endorsed and encouraged by particular group cultures. This knowledge can be put to good use by individual members and the group as a whole to evaluate and refine goals and operations.

- Decision making is the central activity of many groups. When we think about quality decision making, we think in terms of *what* decision is made. *How* decisions are made, however, is often as important. Issues related to the "how" of decision making have to do with the *process* a group goes through in deciding. Issues related to the "what" have to do with the *product* of group decision making. Various decision-making methods are available; and each has pluses and minuses in terms of the quality of the process and product. A decision made by a knowledgeable leader for the group may be a better decision than one less informed members would reach through discussion and compromise. However, discussion and compromise are likely to result in better feelings and greater commitment to the decision by members, because they play a more active part in the process. Ideally, decision making should be undertaken in a way that provides the best of both a process- and product-orientation.

- Communication researcher Randy Hirokawa notes that groups need to fulfill a set of critical functions to make successful decisions.[30] His list includes:

  1. The group must come to understand the nature of the dilemma it faces.
  2. Group members must agree on the requirements for an acceptable solution.
  3. The group must identify a range of realistic alternative proposals for solutions.
  4. The group needs to thoroughly and accurately assess the positive consequences of each alternate proposal.
  5. The group must thoroughly and accurately assess the negative consequences of each alternative proposal.[31]

- Cohesiveness is an important element of successful groups in terms of performance, morale, and effective communication. Techniques that foster group cohesiveness include:[32]

  Increasing the amount of communication among members

  Giving a group an identity and emphasizing it: talking about the group as a group

  Building a group tradition by recognizing special dates or occasions

  Emphasizing teamwork and striving to increase the attractiveness of participation in the group

  Encouraging the group to recognize good work

  Setting clear, attainable group goals

Providing rewards for the group

Treating members like people worthy of respect and dignity, not like parts in a machine

- Extreme pressure toward group loyalty and being "team players," can stifle dissent and critique—both of which can play essential parts in creativity and quality decision making. Some techniques that can be used to lessen the likelihood of the group-think syndrome include:[33]

Leaders can encourage members to be critical.

Leaders can avoid stating their own preferences and expectations at the outset.

Members of the group can discuss the group's deliberations with trusted associates outside the group and report back to the group on their reactions.

Experts can be periodically invited to meetings and should be encouraged to challenge the views of group members.

A member who is articulate and knowledgeable can be appointed to the role of devil's advocate, with the task of looking for alternatives, questioning the group's direction, and assuring that possible objections are considered.

Leaders can allocate time during each meeting to review minority, opposing, or alternative points of view.

- Conflict is an inevitable, and not necessarily a negative, aspect of group life. It is important to learn to recognize the potentially positive functions of conflict for the individual and for the group as a whole. Learning to understand and manage conflict, rather than always striving to eliminate or suppress it, can be productive.

SUMMARY

We spend a great deal of time in groups of various kinds—working at our jobs, participating in clubs and associations, attending community or religious functions, and taking part in social activities. The groups in which we participate over the course of our lifetime create a wide range of demands and opportunities for us; and, in the process of adjusting to these, we develop, change, and grow.

As with relationships, groups are created and maintained by people engaged in reciprocal message processing. Groups differ from relationships in terms of the number of people involved, available resources, and complexity. Groups are created to serve a number of goals and purposes. Some groups serve primarily task-oriented functions and emphasize performance. Others stress personally- or socially-oriented functions and morale. Most groups are concerned with both types of goals. Groups may be contrived or emergent. In small social units, group communication networks evolve naturally. In larger and more formalized groups, networks are often purposefully established to regulate the flow of information.

Groups move through a series of stages as they evolve. The dynamics involved depend on a number of factors, including the difficulty of their tasks, the number of alternative solutions, and the interest created by the tasks. Groups develop a culture—their own symbols, rules, and codes.

The major activity of some groups is decision making, and a number of methods are available for doing this. Roles and responsibilities also are central to the functioning of groups. In smaller groups, roles and definitions of responsibility evolve naturally. Some roles are related to task completion. Others have to do with team building and support; still others are individualistic. In larger, more structured groups, roles and responsibilities are often formal rather than informal, created rather than natural, explicit rather than implicit. Leadership accomplished through communication is basic to groups of all kinds.

Cohesiveness is an important factor in group functioning. It is important for productivity, morale, quality decision making, and effective communication. The groupthink syndrome occurs when members—often unknowingly—become preoccupied with maintaining cohesiveness within a group. Conflict is an inevitable, and often productive, aspect of group functioning.

Mediated communication allows us to participate in groups even if the members are not in the same location. Technology such as the Internet allows group members to overcome barriers of time and space.

ENDNOTES

1. See discussion of "realistic" and "unrealistic" views of groups in Ernest G. Bormann and Nancy C. Bormann, *Effective Small Group Communication,* 4th ed. (Edina, MN: Burgess, 1988), pp. 2–4.

2. Gerald L. Wilson and Michael S. Hanna, *Groups in Context: Leadership and Participation in Small Groups* (New York: Random House, 1986), pp. 110–114; and Bormann and Bormann, 1988, pp. 64–72.

3. Based on distinctions suggested in Charles Pavitt and Ellen Curtis, *Small Group Discussion: A Theoretical Approach,* 2nd ed. (Scottsdale, AZ: Gorsuch Scarisbrick, 1994), pp. 26–29.

4. See Lee Thayer, *Communication and Communication Systems* (Homewood, IL: Irwin, 1968), pp. 188–190.

5. A formula for computing the number of such linkages has been provided by William M. Kephart in "A Quantitative Analysis of Intra-Group Relationships," *American Journal of Sociology,* Vol. 55, 1950, pp. 544–549.

$$PR = \frac{3^N + -2^{N+1} + +1}{2}$$

Note: PR is the number of potential relationships, and N is the number of persons involved

6. See Richard W. Budd, "Encounter Groups: An Approach to Human Communication," in *Approaches to Human Communication.* Ed. by Richard W. Budd and Brent D. Ruben (Rochelle Park, NJ: Hayden-Spartan, 1972), especially pp. 83–88; and Gerald Egan, *Encounter: Group Processes for Interpersonal Growth* (Belmont, CA: Brooks/Cole, 1970), pp. 69–71.

7. B. Aubrey Fisher, "Decision Emergence: Phases in Group Decision-Making," *Speech Monographs,* Vol. 37, 1970, pp. 53–66, and *Small Group Decision Making* (New York: McGraw-Hill, 1974); see also B. Aubrey Fisher and Donald G. Ellis, *Small Group Decision Making* (New York: McGraw-Hill, 1990), pp. 153–157.

8. Marshall Scott Poole and Jonelle Roth, "Decision Development in Small Groups (IV): A Typology of Group Decision Paths," *Human Communication Research,* Vol. 15, 1989, pp. 323–356.

9. See Fisher, 1970, and discussion in Stephen W. Littlejohn, *Theories of Human Communication,* 5th ed. (Belmont, CA: Wadsworth, 1996), pp. 292–293.

10. Wilson and Hanna, 1986, pp. 27–30.

11. Marvin E. Shaw, "Scaling Group Tasks: A Method for Dimensional Analysis," *JSAS Catalog of Selected Documents in Psychology,* Vol. 8, 1973, M. S. 294. See discussion in Wilson and Hanna, 1986, pp. 28–29.

12. Terrence E. Deal and Allen A. Kennedy, *Corporate Cultures: The Rites and Rituals of Corporate Life* (Reading, MA: Addison-Wesley, 1982), pp. 21–84.

13. Based on Wilson and Hanna, 1986, pp. 68–71.

14. These rules were developed by J. Hall and W. H. Watson, "The Effects of a Normative Intervention of Group Decision-Making Performance," *Human Relations*, Vol. 23, 1970, pp. 299–317. For a more comprehensive discussion of consensus rules, see Pavitt and Curtis, 1994, pp. 433–436.

15. Kenneth Benne and Paul Sheats, "Functional Roles of Group Members," *Journal of Social Issues*, Vol. 4, 1948, pp. 41–49.

16. John E. Baird, Jr., and Sanford B. Weinberg, *Group Communication*, 2d ed. (Dubuque, IA: Brown, 1981), p. 215.

17. Based on discussion by Bormann and Bormann, 1988, pp. 127–130 and J. Kevin Barge, *Leadership: Communication Skills for Organizations and Groups* (New York: St. Martin's Press, 1994), chap. 1.

18. Bormann and Bormann, 1988, p. 129.

19. Bormann and Bormann, 1988, p. 129.

20. Bormann and Bormann, 1988, p. 129.

21. Barge, 1994, chap. 1.

22. Bormann and Bormann, 1988, p. 55.

23. Based on Bormann and Bormann, 1988, p. 55.

24. Bormann and Bormann, 1988, pp. 56–57.

25. Irving L. Janis, *Groupthink: Psychological Studies of Policy Decisions and Fiascos*, 2nd ed. (Boston: Houghton Mifflin, 1982). See discussion in Littlejohn, 1996, pp. 286–287.

26. Wilson and Hanna, 1986, pp. 197–198; based on Janis, 1967.

27. Wilson and Hanna, 1986, p. 198; based on Janis, 1967.

28. T. L. Ruble and K. W. Thomas, "Support for a Two-Dimensional Model of Conflict Behavior," *Organizational Behavior and Human Performance*, Vol. 16, 1976, pp. 143–155. See discussion in J. P. Folger and M. S. Poole, *Working Through Conflict* (Glenview, IL: Scott, Foresman, 1984), pp. 40–41.

29. Ruble and Thomas, 1976; Folger and Pool, 1984, p. 41.

30. See, for example, Randy Y. Hirokawa, "Group Communication and Decision-Making Performance: A Continued Test of the Functional Perspective," *Human Communication Research*, Vol. 14, 1988, pp. 487–515.

31. Pavitt and Curtis, 1994, p. 283.

32. Bormann and Bormann, 1988, pp. 74–76; see also Pavitt and Curtis, pp. 96–97.

33. Janis, 1982; see discussion in Littlejohn, 1996, pp. 286–287.

13

Organizational Communication

Todd T. Holm, PhD

Director Profession Communication
Expeditionary Warfare School
Marine Corps Base Quantico

LEARNING OBJECTIVES

- After reading this chapter, students should be able to explain the evolution of communication studies that led to organizational communication.
- After reading this chapter, students should be able to justify the use of Theory X and Theory Y management styles based on organizational context.
- After reading this chapter, students should be able to explain how the Industrial Revolution influenced the workplace.
- After reading this chapter, students should be able to list Fayol's *Functions of Management*.
- After reading this chapter, students should be able to explain the "Hawthorne Effect" and discuss how it led to the Human Relations Movement.
- After reading this chapter, students should be able to critique Taylorism showing both its positive and negative aspects.
- After reading this chapter, students should be able to describe various organizational metaphors and explain how they influence how people perceive the organization.
- After reading this chapter, students should be able to recommend an organizational metaphor for use in a given organization based on the goals, purpose, and context of the organization.
- After reading this chapter, students should be able to analyze and ascertain a company's organizational culture by using Deal and Kennedy's components of strong culture.
- After reading this chapter, students should be able to explain how Sonya Sackman's idea of organizational culture as a dynamic construct blended the dominant organizational culture paradigms.

My first real venture into a formal organization, and thus my first experience with organizational communication, started at around 5:00 am in southern Missouri in the summer of 1982. I got off a bus which was part of a convoy of busses containing about 160 "new employees" and was greeted by an angry gentleman who yelled "Follow me and don't stop running!" as he took off sprinting around the corner of a brick building. I was a new recruit for the Army National Guard. I spent the next 13 weeks in Ft. Leonard Wood Missouri in Basic and Advanced Individual Training. I would learn to walk and talk all over again. I would learn some skills that I would take with me and use for a lifetime (leadership, determination, responsibility, and prioritization), other skills that would help put me through college (carpentry and construction), and some skills I was fortunate enough to never need to use.

While it was an experience different than anything I had ever had before, and one I would never want to repeat, it forever changed me in many positive ways. It made me stronger, not just physically but emotionally, and in some ways mentally. It gave me confidence and self-respect. I would not be where I am today if I hadn't had that experience. The first real day of basic training is long; it is physically and emotionally draining. You are yelled at, you cannot do anything right, you can't dress yourself right, you can't shave right, you can't eat fast enough, you take too long tying your boots, and the whole time there is a cadres of drill sergeants yelling at you, berating you, belittling you, pushing you, and breaking down any sense of self-esteem you had when you stepped into their world. Maybe the only things that keep you from sneaking away in the middle of the night after day one are pure exhaustion and the knowledge that doing so would make you a wanted fugitive and your life would be over. Despite all that, I will readily identify it as one of the best things I ever did.

So, how is an organization like the U.S. military able to treat "new employees" like this and still have a loyal following from its membership long after they leave the service? How is it that the smallest, most rigorous branch of the military, the Marine Corps, generates such loyalty that retired Marines will readily correct you if you refer to them as *former Marines?* "Once a Marine, always a Marine." That is part of what inspired my interest in Organizational Communication. Perhaps more importantly, how could I use my experience in the military to teach my students how to be better leaders in their own organizations? If those are questions that resonate with you, perhaps the study of organizational communication is a good fit for you.

PROGRESSION OF DISCOVERY

The field of communication (rather broadly defined) was an integral part of the original canons of education. The *Trivium* (Latin for *the three roads*) formed the foundation of the liberal arts education around a 1000 years ago. The *Trivium* consisted of grammar, logic, and rhetoric (Joseph, 2002). It was through the study of language, reasoning, and rhetoric that you came to understand what motivated people. You came to understand what mattered to people and how to move them to action. Great orators were highly revered because they had mastered these subjects. They received their training from learned professors in churches or in their homes because, at the time, universities were not a physical place but rather a socially constructed environment wherever the students and teachers gathered. Eventually all of that changed and civilizations built buildings dedicated to higher education, but the original canons of educations were maintained. Surprisingly, the study of organizational communication doesn't stray far from these canons.

Leap forward about 900 years and you will notice how the industrial revolution changed education in the United States. In much the same way that business was focused on finding the "one best way" to conduct business through efficiency studies, we looked for more efficient ways to educate our children. We moved from one-room school houses to conglomerated schools in which everyone was divided into classrooms by age, they were taught a standard curriculum, the teacher (much like a factory supervisor) stood at the front of the room on an elevated platform spewing knowledge, and children were rapped on the knuckles with rulers for misbehaving. Grammar, logic, and rhetoric were lumped under the heading of "English" and teachers focused mostly on the mechanics of writing. The understanding of what stirred men to action was swept to the side for the more practical practice of sentence diagramming.

Up until the mid 1950s in the United States, public speaking classes in college curriculums were taught primarily though English Departments. The spoken word, it was reasoned, was not much different than the written word and the English faculty were, therefore, best equipped to teach it. But in the period from the 1950s to the 1970s and the 1980s, we saw an explosion in the field of communication studies. Speech Departments broke off from English and began to study the uniqueness of their own discipline. We understood that not all communication was the same and that the way we address a group of 1,000 was different than the way we addressed a group of 10 and that was different than the way we addressed our family. So context shaped the emerging departments. Classes were offered in interpersonal communication, business and professional speaking, and small group communication. We held true to our roots and taught rhetoric and persuasion. Business strongly influenced the development of new communication departments because they wanted to know how to use communication as a tool to make companies better, stronger, and more profitable. Speech Departments began to teach leadership and team building. We began to see the first real signs of what we now call organizational communication. We continued to develop contextually and have seen the emergence of several other subfields including health communication, family communication, instructional communication, computer-mediated communication, intercultural communication, and more. But I was fascinated by the vast number of variables and challenges found in the study of organizational communication.

IN THE BEGINNING . . .

Most organizational communication textbooks will spend the first chapter trying to define organizational communication. They will provide a variety of definitions, each as good or bad as the next. Some will focus exclusively on businesses while others take a broader perspective and also look at nonprofits, healthcare, academic institutions, religious organizations, clubs, and even social movements. There seems to be some consensus that what we are talking about when we speak of organizational communication is how organizations (not just small groups and not usually family groups) interact to co-create a way of accomplishing their goals.

The interesting thing was that the more I studied organizational communication the more I began to simultaneously realize two things: (1) these theories put into words what I had always seen but could not articulate and (2) there was so much more that I needed to learn. I found some theories in total contradiction and yet both sides rang true for me. Theory X and Theory Y Management (McGregor, 1960) could not be more opposite and yet I saw the

"THE LOWELL GIRLS"

In 1823 in a mill opened in Lowell Massachusetts that was a prime example of how the industrial revolution was changing the way organizations worked. This mill was very different in a number of important ways. First, it moved work out of family homes into a factory setting. In the past textiles like yarn had been created in homes and then brought to a central location for purchase by trading companies. The group of businessmen known as the "Boston Associates" opened this textile factory as one of the very early factories in the United States. So just the fact that workers collected at a place to work to produce goods was different. But this factory was even more unique in that they preferred to hire you women as workers. You must understand the social context of the early 1800s to realize how revolutionary that was. Women rarely worked outside the home. Women had very limited career path opportunities. Women could be a school teacher, possibly a librarian in a big city, maybe a nurse in a hospital, or someone who worked cooking or baking in a family business. But generally, the socially acceptable (and excepted) practice was that a young woman would find a man and start a family and the man would work and she would raise children. So when they opened a factory that was different, they hired young women to work in that factory. You can imagine what the nearby people probably thought. The women who worked there became known as "Lowell Girls."

The factory was run as many factories are today, they even had a handbook that identified the rules of behavior both in and out of the workplace for the women who worked there. You might be surprised at how different some of the rules are from what we would consider acceptable today and you might be equally surprised by the things the handbook covered that are still relevant issues today. For example, employees were not hired or would be terminated if they were habitually absent from public worship on the Sabbath or were known to be immoral. Obviously, a violation of labor laws today. But a lot of the other rules covered issues workers still struggle with today. Healthcare for example, in the Lowell factory, a physician came in once a month to vaccinate all who needed it free of charge. There were issues of job stability then too. So the handbook said that everyone hired was considered engaged for 12 months, and people who left sooner or did not comply with all these regulations would not be entitled to a regular discharge. So essentially they had a one-year contract but they could be fired for cause. If you were going to leave before the end of your contract, you were expected to give notice to your "overseer" two weeks before leaving. Employee theft was an issue and the handbook explained that if you took things from the factory you would be prosecuted. It also explained when and how often employees were to be paid. Some of these things were new and some were just a written record of common practices, but all were part of an employee handbook which itself was a new idea.

validity in each. But I get ahead of myself. My exploration did not begin with Douglas McGregor's managerial theories of the 1960s. I began where most students begin, with the key theorists of the industrial revolution: Fayol, Weber, and Taylor.

THE SCIENCE OF ORGANIZING

Initially, organizational communication scholars borrowed research from other fields and co-opted it as their own. As a discipline we often borrow from sociology, anthropology (especially for qualitative research methodologies), psychology, business, and even biology (General Systems Theory was a product of biologist Ludwig von Bertalanffy). That is by no means a complete listing, but it gives you an idea of from whence we came. During the industrial revolution, no one had ever heard of organizational communication and few had really heard of management. Most businesses were family owned and most products were made by an individual who may or may not have undergone some kind of apprenticeship before striking out on their own. The only notably organizations of size were the church, the government, and the military. Each was service based and very hierarchical. This was only slightly helpful to the production facilities that were rapidly developing.

Industries such as mining hired people to do jobs and if they couldn't do the jobs they were fired, if they did them poorly they were fired, if someone else could do a job better you were fired. Companies did not train employees; there was no operations manual to read to learn how to do a job. You figured it out, or they fired you. But the large companies and standardization that accompanied the Industrial Revolution necessitated a new way of doing business. Not surprisingly, this placed greater emphasis on management, which meant more *Organizing* and more *Communicating* and the foundations of organizational communication were being laid.

French mining engineer Henri Fayol was one of the first to look at the idea of managing workers. He recognized that it was not just a matter of telling people to do things, rather a supervisor's job included organizing, planning, forecasting, and coordinating. Giving commands and directing work was still an important part of the job and it was critical that the supervisor be respected enough that control could be exerted over the masses. But the new ideal for a supervisor was more of a thinker than a boss. The comparison to military equivalents could be drawn. While the supervisor used to be the sergeant who would discipline and motivate troops and lead the charge into battle, the new supervisor was to be more of a logistics officer and military strategist.

Fayol developed his *"Functions of Management,"* which are still defended by professionals today (McLean, 2011). Mclean argues that today's managers still need to fulfill Fayol's five functions of managers:

1. To forecast and plan
2. To organize
3. To command
4. To coordinate
5. To control

If you look at that list and think he is covering some pretty basic stuff, remember, he was the first one to cover it. The wheel is pretty basic now but there was a time when man didn't have the wheel. He is a critical part of business evolution and the development of organizational communication as a field of study. Fayol went on to develop 14 Principles of Management:

1. **Division of labor**: Fayol forwarded the idea of "work specialization," so under this paradigm you would find a group of people who were very good at painting widgets and that, and that alone, would be their job. They didn't build widgets, they just painted them.
2. **Authority**: Giving orders was nothing new to management but Fayol pointed out that with the authority to give orders comes the responsibility for those orders. If a manager gave the wrong orders, it was the manager who was at fault.
3. **Discipline**: Fayol recognized and embraced rules. He believed if there was a clear understanding between management and the workforce about what the rules were, and why they were in place, and if the rules were applied equally to all, then you would have good discipline. To him discipline was not so much a matter of punishment (although good managers did exercise the judicious use of punishment when rules were broken) as it was of controlled order and commitment to conducting business.
4. **Unity of command**: He saw the need to clear supervisor–subordinate relationships and said each employee should get orders from just one superior.
5. **Unity of direction**: He wanted to make sure that there was someone looking at the big picture, so he believed everyone doing the same kind of work should be under the supervision of the same manager. You didn't put one

manager in charge of people rowing on the starboard side of the boat and another in charge of those on the port side. Everyone should be working toward the same objective.

6. **Subordination of individual interests to the general interest**: The needs of the many outweigh the needs of the few or the one. What was best for the organization was more important than what was best for the individuals or a small group.

7. **Remuneration:** He developed a lot of favor with the workers because he said workers must receive a fair wage for their services.

8. **Centralization:** Fayol saw centralization as reducing the importance of the subordinate role. Centralized power puts power and control at the top of the organizational chart. He recognized that lower level workers sometimes needed power but the key was to find a balance that placed the majority of power at the top where the thinkers were.

9. **Scalar chain**: Probably influenced by military protocols, Fayol believed that communications should follow a chain of command he called the Scalar Chain.

10. **Order**: Everything and everyone was to be in their proper place at their appointed times. This was a matter of efficiency.

11. **Equity**: While the previous mindset for supervisors was to try to get as much out of workers for as little pay as possible, Fayol thought that struggle was counterproductive and said managers should be fair and even kind to their subordinates.

12. **Stability of tenure of personnel:** While previous incarnations of managers had been quick to fire employees, Fayol recognized the organizational investment in cultivating a good employee and that employee turnover was inefficient. Good managers made sure there were viable replacements in case people were ill or left the organization.

13. **Initiative**: He saw the value in letting people run with an idea. We now call it organizational buy-in but it started with his idea that employees who were allowed to originate and carry out plans would put more energy into that work because they had a vested interest in seeing it succeed.

14. **Esprit de corps**: Fayol saw that people working together was much better than people working in the same place. He said it was a manager's duty to promote a team spirit and build harmony and unity.

These were the first directions given to managers about how to be managers. While they might seem rudimentary to us today, it is only rudimentary because of Fayol's work. He was revolutionary in his approach and it made the workplace more efficient and standardized. But when it came to standardization, Max Weber (pronounced "vay bore") led the charge.

German sociologist Max Weber could be considered the father of modern bureaucracy. The word bureaucracy comes from French and Latin words. In French, *bureau* means office or desk, in Latin Kratos (the root of *cracy*) means political power or rule. So a bureaucracy could be considered "rule by the desk." Weber preached the importance of standardization, documentation of procedures, and rules that bound managers as well as employees. Weber saw the value of a bureaucracy and identified six major principles of bureaucracy. I found four of them particularly interesting (if you would like to see all six many authors have talked about them and the information is readily available on the Internet):

1. **Hierarchy:** Centralized decision making and top down communication characterize this organizational chart. You answer to the level above you, the level below you answers to you.

2. **Management by formal rules and regulations:** Every rule is documented; every rule is applied equally to all in the organization. This allowed for more control at the top because the top of the hierarchy made rules, changed rules, and did away with rules. Those under the top followed the rules.

3. **Organization by functional specialty:** Weber promoted specialization. We still use this today. Universities group departments by college. Departments group faculty by their specialization. Weber saw the need for specialized skills and specialized training. If you worked security you didn't also work on the production line. You were hired because of special skills and those special skills served the company. Helping you get better at your specialty was good for the company and the company supported it.

4. **An impersonal workplace:** Everyone was to be treated the same. Weber saw *equal* as *fair*. If the work day started at 8:00 am and ended at 5:00 pm, all workers reported at 8:00 am regardless of home-life, transportation availability, or other circumstances. You could not come in at 8:15 and just take 45 minutes for lunch. Managers were not to get to know employees because it might give the appearance of favoritism, family members should not work with, and certainly never work for, each other to prevent nepotism.

Weber's ideas guided the largest of companies and governments. The bureaucratic workplace can be a cumbersome, loathsome giant that is slow to change, bloated, and inefficient. But it has its benefits too. When I recently took a new position at the Marine Corps University's (MCU) Expeditionary Warfare School (EWS) after spending 25 years teaching in traditional colleges and universities I was a bit apprehensive. I didn't really know what was expected of me. But when I arrived I found three very neatly arranged file folders on my desk. The first was a welcome binder with my name on the cover. It contained the MCU mission statement, instructions on how to submit time and attendance records, a list of all training courses I was required to complete, and information about the Quantico Marine Corps Base. The second was a collection of lesson cards and educational objectives for each and every assignment students at EWS received during their 10-month training cycle, and a calendar for the training cycle. The third folder was labeled "Professional Communication Monthly Turnover Binder" and it listed the 12–20 projects I needed to work on in each month of the year. It was very helpful; it gave me a clear insight into what was expected of me in this new position. I was very grateful and thanked my supervisor for having someone go through all the work of putting it together. He explained that it was no problem, there was an SOP (Standard Operating Procedure) for briefing a new Communication Program Coordinator and all they did was collect the documents to go in the folders. While I thanked my supervisor, I really have Max Weber to thank for the folders.

I now work for the Marine Corps which is part of the Department of Defense which is part of the U.S. Federal Government which is arguably the largest bureaucracy in the world. It can be frustrating. While Max Weber's idea of bureaucracy has become almost synonymous with inefficiency, the third classical research, Frederick Taylor was all about efficiency.

American engineer Fredrick Taylor was the epitome of a left-brain thinker. His engineering background no doubt contributed to his linear understanding of the world. But it was his work with efficiency studies that really earned him his notoriety. His exhaustive collection of empirical data from *"time* *and motion studies"* lead to him being labeled the father of "Scientific Management." He was always looking for the "one best way" of doing any task. Taylor was all about working smarter not harder.

Unlike Weber, Taylor thought a positive relationship between manager and worker was important. He believed ". . . each man should daily be taught by and receive the most friendly help from those who are over him, instead of being, at the one extreme, driven or coerced by his bosses, and at the other left to his own unaided devices. This close, intimate, personal cooperation between the management and the men is of the essence of modern scientific management." Taylor saw the relationship between management and worker as more about collaboration than control. Taylor based his four Principles of Scientific Management on this underlying assumption. Here is what Taylor had to say in his 1911 book *The Principles of Scientific Management* (pp. 36–37).

These new duties are grouped under four headings:

First. They develop a science for each element of a man's work, which replaces the old rule-of-thumb method.

Second. They scientifically select and then train, teach, and develop the workman, whereas in the past he chose his own work and trained himself as best he could.

Third. They heartily cooperate with the men so as to insure all of the work is being done in accordance with the principles of the science that have been developed.

Fourth. There is an almost equal division of the work and the responsibility between the management and the workmen. The management take over all work for which they are better fitted than the workmen, while in the past almost all of the work and the greater part of the responsibility were thrown upon the men.

Taylor believed that there was not only "one best way" to do a job, but "one best person" to do the job and "one best compensation package" for doing the job. For example, ore comes in a variety of types and some ore is considerably heavier than other ore. But Taylor saw that workers were using the same shovel for all types of ore. For the heavy ore, the shovel was not even close to full and workers struggled with it, for the lightest of ores, the shovel was as full as possible and was still considered light. Taylor decided that workers needed large shovels for light ore and smaller shovels for heavier ore. This created an optimal use of shovels. He also felt workers should be given periodic breaks so they could be more productive longer. One of his classic stories about worker efficiency involves a worker he called Schmidt who had been hired to load pig iron. At the onset of his experiment, Schmidt loaded and average of 12.5 ton of pig iron a day for a wage of $1.15 a day. But after Taylor developed a scientific system of working, Schmidt was averaging 49 tons of pig iron a day for a wage of $1.85 per day. Over 60% more money and nearly a 400% increase in productivity.

Taylor was very successful at Bethlehem Steel, he double mill production, cut material handling costs in half, and increased wages 60% on average. Despite this success, he was forced to leave Bethlehem Steel because of problems with other managers and some unhappy workers. Other locations went on strike when management tried to impose scientific management techniques and *Taylorism* developed a bad reputation in industry.

EFFICIENCY STORY ABOUT FORD

In 2015, Ford Motors is releasing a new version of their best-selling F-150 pickup truck. Normally when you have the best selling vehicle on the road you wouldn't mess with it too much. You would keep up with technology advancements but not make sweeping changes. But Ford took a different approach. They decided to tackle the biggest problem facing pickups on the road today: fuel efficiency. When you are trying to make a vehicle more fuel efficient, you can either reduce its horsepower (less power means less fuel) or reduce its weight (less mass to move means less power needed). There are other things like aerodynamics and hybrid technologies, even things like gearing and axle ratios can create more efficient vehicles. But when you are selling a work truck, you can't really reduce the power because power is one of the main reasons the consumer is buying the product. Reducing the mass is also difficult because the truck needs to be rugged. Because of changes in metallurgy and computer-aided design, the engineers at Ford were finally able to make a lot more of the truck out of aluminum. While the frame will still be steel, the rest of the truck will be made with a lot more lightweight aluminum, which alone reduced the weight of the vehicle 450 pounds.

But because it was lighter, the springs, frame, and engine could also be lighter. The new truck is 700 pounds lighter than previous models, which has taken the fuel efficiency from the estimated 21–22 MPG of the previous model to an estimated 27–28 MPG for this model according to Slate.com (although Ford.com estimates it will only be a 20% mileage gain). The new more efficient truck has more pulling power and aluminum isn't prone to rust and corrosion like steel. Now think about this in terms of scale. In August of 2014, Ford sold nearly 70,000 F-150 trucks. The F-150 is over 4 percent of all of the cars on the road today. If it is getting 20–30% better gas mileage that means that for every four times the 2014 F-150 fills up at the pump, the 2015 F-150 will only fill up three times. Companies with fleets of trucks can reduce fuel costs considerably. This is an idea that Fayol would have loved as much as consumers.

Gross, Daniel (12 Sept, 2014). Ford's Big Gamble. Slate.com http://www.slate.com/articles/business/the_juice/2014/09/ford_f_150_pickup_truck_the_auto_company_is_gambling_on_aluminum.html

http://www.ford.com/trucks/f150/ (Accessed 2/14/2015)

END OF AN ERA

While these men all had different backgrounds and approached management from very different perspectives, their work did seem to share one flawed premise: Behavior was based on rational thought. They assumed that workers and management acted the way they did "for good reason." But the fact is that people are not inherently logical operators. Organizations were not massive well-oiled machines; they were collections of human beings with unpredictable actions and sometimes befuddling motivation. But it took more research to prove to management that sometimes people are just weird.

THE HUMAN ELEMENT

There was certainly validity to Taylor's methodology and finding the best way to design a work station or workplace environment to maximize productivity is something we still study today. But today we call it ergonomics and it is used to prevent fatigue and injury and give people a more positive outlook. Our office chairs have lumbar support and adjustable arms. Computer monitors are mounted on swing arms that make them adjustable, executives are moving to standing desks, the wall color is chosen to soothe and relax workers, natural lighting is used whenever possible, and some companies are intentionally building parking lots a block from the building so workers at least get some exercise. A healthy, happy employee is a productive employee. Companies will take care of you so that you will be more productive. Because unhappy employees behave irrationally and sabotage equipment, involve themselves in counter-productive office politics, and engage in work slowdowns (intentionally or unintentionally). Mostly, workers want to be recognized for their work and appreciated. An accidental lesson learned from research that led us to the next evolution in organizational communication.

THE HUMAN RELATIONS MOVEMENT

Western Electric was conducting research on optimal work environments to determine the best working conditions and best ways to conduct their business. But the researchers made an interesting discovery: when they made working conditions better, efficiency increased as expected. You don't need a PhD to understand the basics of variable manipulation in empirical research. When you manipulate a variable you expect to see a cause–effect relationship. If you give a car more gas it goes faster: cause and effect. But in this research something unexpected happened. When they returned conditions to normal, efficiency increased again. That would be like stepping down on the accelerator pedal and having the car go faster but then having it go faster still when you took your foot off the pedal. If they did something like increase the heat in the room and productivity went up, when they returned it to normal productivity went up again, but if they then lowered the temperature, productivity went up again (Landsberger, 1958).

You can see how this would baffle researchers. They looked for confounding variables that were somehow impacting the study (time of day, sunlight, weather, phase of the moon, whatever) but could find no external variables that could account for this productivity anomaly. Then one of the researchers did something completely antithetical to the research methodology and virtually unheard of in this kind of research; the researcher asked the subjects what was going on.

It turns out the people on the line were interested in the fact that they were being studied. They liked the idea that someone was paying attention to them and they worked harder because they were getting attention. It didn't matter what the variable being changed was, it mattered that they were being given attention. This has become known as the *"Hawthorne Effect"* (named after the "Hawthorne Works" plant outside of Chicago it the town of Cicero, IL where the research was conducted). Subsequent research brought more attention to the element of human interaction and how teams of people can create synergy.

You could say that this was the first real organizational communication research. It looked at how messages (unintentional though they may be) influenced the effectiveness of the organization. *Elton Mayo* and some colleagues furthered this research by looking at how work groups and group dynamics can both positively and negatively impact productivity. Their study, involving a group of men who assembled telephone switching equipment, showed that workers will bond together and manipulate productivity levels to their own benefit and even band together and tell management the same lies for the betterment of the group members. To make matters even more confusing, Roethlisberger and Dickson (1939) found that when it came to the human element, there was no "one best way" to do things. After conducting thousands of interviews with employees, they found that people who worked under the same circumstances experienced those circumstances differently. A room that was at just the right temperature for one person might be too hot or too cold for another. A supervisor who ascribed to Max Weber's idea of an impersonal relationship with workers may be relished by one worker because he or she doesn't want the boss knowing about their personal life. While the person next to them may feel it is important that the boss understand their home life to understand what is important to them.

These discoveries really placed human beings and human communication at the center of effective management practices. It solidified the importance of a dynamic and fluid model of human interaction in organizations. When it came to people there was no one best way, but perhaps if we backed up a little, we could shape people's perceptions about the work place. Communication is, in my opinion, the art of shaping perceptions. Sometimes we do this through a process of *cognitive restructuring*. For example, the Soviet Union and America were allies during WWII but by the 1950s the Cold War had started and we changed our perception of the Soviets. We were no longer allies who worked together, we were at war ideologically. By the 1960s people were building bomb shelters in their backyards because the Russians were going to nuke the United States any day. We had a completely new mental picture of Russia and the people of Russia. If we create that kind of change in an entire population of people, think how we could change the perceptions of people in the work place. Organizational communication was about to bust out of its little compartment in communication studies like a racehorse out of the chute.

THEORIES WITH CLEVER NAMES

In 1960, a man named Douglas McGregor proposed two theories for managers based on the idea that human behavior and human motivation with critical components of the workplace. He dubbed them Theory X and Theory Y (apparently the first 23 letters of the alphabet had been taken). While the theories are nearly polar opposites you will probably find yourself nodding along with both theories.

Theory X operates from the premise that workers are inherently lazy and will go to great lengths to get out of work including worker sabotage, doing jobs poorly so you don't ask them to do it in the future, arriving a few minutes late, and leaving a few minutes early every day. Workers were treated a lot like prisoners with heavy supervision, discipline in the form of punishment was the order of the day and threats were the managers' best way of gaining compliance. Under this framework employees were seen as being motivated exclusively by money. So docking someone's pay was the most common threat and punishment. It is a hierarchical system where the manager has all the power.

While that sounds harsh, you have to admit there are instances in which it is a reasonable because, after all, there are jobs people really don't want to do; skin diver at a waste water treatment plant for example. Humor aside, this kind of management approach would fit in a situation where employees are undermotivated and the opportunity to underperform is plentiful. Think about the fast food industry. Few people are there to make a career of it (although many people in management have made a career out of working for the major fast food chains). But the line workers usually don't want to be there and don't want to do the work. If you have ever been a student worker for your university you have probably been a part of, or at least heard about, people working hard to not work. I remember a graduate student talking about being on the summer painting crew and how he hoped the boss would leave before his soccer match started so he could watch it. Another student told me they would assign three of them to a job that was a one person job and they would take turns working for 20 minutes and then go on break for 40 minutes and play games on their cell phones.

Sometimes the job itself is so critical that a hard-nose approach must be taken. For example, military, police, and fire fighting personnel sometimes operate under this model. In these circumstances, the physical conditioning alone may need to be forced on the workers and there is little room for latitude in the process these occupations follow. In some cases, it really does come down to "do it the way we say or people die." So there are jobs and people who need this kind of management style for the organization to be successful.

Theory Y operates from assumptions that are nearly opposite to those of Theory X. Theory Y believes that workers are indeed self-motivated and people want to do their jobs and do them well. Managers should focus on making sure workers have all the resources they need to do their jobs well. Managers should make the parameters of the final product or service clear but leave the workers to figure out the best way to accomplish those objectives. The hierarchy is flattened and almost inverted in some cases because the managers become support for the workers. The working environment is much different than Theory X. There is trust and respect between workers and managers. Praise is the motivator rather than threats.

When I first saw this model I liked it but thought the idea that people actually like to work and want to work might be a little unrealistic. I was young and enjoyed the occasional weekend of doing nothing but watching TV or sleeping. But one of my professors pointed out that when I am doing those things I am not doing "nothing." Even sleeping accomplished a purpose and while I might be able to sleep for 12 or 14 hours, I wouldn't spend my whole weekend sleeping no matter how tired I was. To sit in an office (for example) and do nothing all day would be incredibly difficult. To sit and look straight ahead, reading nothing, listening to nothing, and doing nothing (including sleeping) would be very hard on us mentally. By nature our minds are inquisitive, we have an innate desire to do things and create things. Nothingness is a punishment in prison. When prisoners misbehave they are placed in solitary confinement where they can do very little, they are allowed minimal reading materials, no radios, music, or television, no computer access, and they are usually not even allowed paper to write on or art supplies. They are punished with nothingness. Ironically, that is often the same thing we do with gifted children in elementary school. When they finish their in-class assignments faster than everyone else they are told to sit quietly and not disturb other children.

Obviously, there are places where Theory Y management style will thrive. Advertising agencies, college campuses, and engineering firms all depend on smart people achieving their potential unfettered by restrictive or demanding management practices. Obviously deadlines still need to be met and workers still need to comply with established standards, but the management job is more *facilitation* than forced compliance management.

You may notice that the biggest difference between these two theories is *management attitude*. Theory X seems harsh and mean like Ebenezer Scrooge and Theory Y sounds like it came out of the free love movement. Both seek to accomplish the same endgame but with a different attitude. But do not under estimate the importance of attitude. Educational researchers Robert Rosenthal and Lenore Jacobson published a research article demonstrating the impact of teacher (manager) attitude on student learning. This later became known as Pygmalion Effect. The study was simple enough, young students were given an aptitude test designed to determine their IQ. Scores were collected and names were chosen at random and given to the teacher of those students. The teacher was told this was a list of academically gifted students. At the end of the year, the students were retested and the testing showed that the randomly chosen students on the gifted list, now tested significantly higher than their classmates. It would appear that what we (as teachers, managers, even friends) expect people to be is eventually what they become.

Theory Z was developed by Dr. William Ouchi and it was heavily influenced by Japanese management practices. It was more like Theory Y than Theory X and focuses more on people being happy in the work place. Managers had to have confidence in workers, they had to operate from the assumption that workers would be able to get the job done, done well, done on time, and done within the budget. The idea was if you could find good people and give them the resources they needed to do their jobs well (including additional education and training provided or paid for by the organization), you would create loyalty to the organization. If you treated employees well, paid them well and praised their work, they would stay with the company and the investment in those people would be returned many times over.

As we start to see the millennial generation entering the workforce with a different mindset than previous generations, this management philosophy may need to change. Millennial (those born between the 1980s and late 2000s) workers are less likely to have organizational loyalty and far more likely to jump from one company to the next using the training and experience they gain at one company to get a better position at the next. They expect the "rise to leadership to come faster, while boomers believe one should 'pay one's dues'" (Barnes, 2009, p. 60).

FINDING MY PATH

The 1980s were filled with this explosion of organizational communication research. Some of it was rigorous scholarship; some could have been labeled pop culture junk science. Somewhere in the middle I found my path. I wanted to understand how organizations worked, I wanted to figure out what motivated people, and I wanted to know about what made one group of people the poster children for synergy and another similar group the poster children for dysfunction. The search for those answers took me down many paths, none of them wrong, each of them adding to the base of knowledge I would need to answer these questions. Of course, the reality is there are no hard and fast answers, but I was able to develop a much better understanding of this dynamic, multifaceted quagmire we were calling organizational communication.

Like much of communication studies, organizational communication overlaps with sociology, psychology, management, and even anthropology in not just its research methods but also in its theoretical underpinnings. I soon saw the value of focus groups and in-depth interviews as research methodologies. I saw how the study of industrial sociology closely mirrored communication research and how psychology played into everything from leadership to productivity. We were all connected through organizations. *General Systems Theory* (Karl Ludwig von Bertalanffy) talked about super and supra systems and subsystems and permeability of membranes and interdependence and it all made sense to me. Organizations weren't like machines, they were like organisms. That realization led me to study organizations in a new way, through the organization's use of metaphor.

ORGANIZATIONAL METAPHORS

When I realized how that change in metaphor impacted my understanding of organizational communication I became interested in the power of metaphors in organizations. There has been a progress in the metaphors we have used to describe our organizations over the generations. Fayol, Weber, and Taylor were fans of the "machine metaphor." Some organizations still use this metaphor today. It is an impersonal hold-over from the first half of the 20th century. No doubt a result of the industrial revolution where parts and products became standardized and we began training specialists. If an employee quit, died, or was fired, another employee simply took his place. People, like parts, were interchangeable. The best organizations operated like well-oiled machines. Everyone was in synch with everyone else. Materials came in at a regulated rate, production moved along on assembly lines thanks to Henry Ford, and output rates were steady. Money wound the Swiss watch that was the American factory. It was a beautiful thing to behold. But there was a small problem with this metaphor and, again, it was that pesky human element. After all, people are not machines, therefore groups of people are not large machines and while there are situations in which the machine metaphor works, it certainly became less important as we shifted from a production-based economy to a service-based economy. So we looked for a new metaphor and found our answer in the works of a theoretical biologist Karl Ludwig von Bertalanffy. An extrapolation of his General Systems Theory gave us a new understanding of organizations, organizational *life*, and organizational communication.

Organisms—Organizations were living breathing entities, each with its own personality and you could "breathe new life" into a company, you could "resuscitate a dyeing organization" with "new blood." Individuals were the "heart" or "soul" of an organization. You might meet the "brains of the operation" or the "backbone of the company." While the company might be compartmentalized like the cells of a plant or the organs of the body, things like money and power permeated the compartmental barriers and spread throughout the organization like blood, nutrition, and water did in organisms.

We began to look at the idea of wholeness. Each cell, organ, or system of the metaphorical body played its part and contributed to the overall synergistic success of the organism that was the organization. Just like plants, animals, and all things organic, organizations evolved. This factor alone was crucial as the 1970s, 1980s, and 1990s were a period of unprecedented change. Not only was there a technological explosion bigger than the industrial revolution, but our economy itself was changing. No longer were we in a solely production-based economy. Now we were becoming a service-based economy. That meant organizations needed to adapt, they needed to evolve, or they would certainly go the way of the Dodo Bird. Organizations were being pulled in multiple directions; they were producing, selling, and providing customer support after the sale. Few living organisms did this and we needed a new metaphor. But fortunately, there is never a shortage of metaphors.

Team—Now this made sense! When you bring together a group of people to work toward a common goal they were a team. We aren't machines and we aren't plants, we are people and when people work together we are showing teamwork. We were teams! This was no doubt heavily influenced by Japanese business practices and the international mergers of the 1980s. The Japanese placed heavy emphasis on the team metaphor. This was a familiar and readily applicable metaphor. Nearly everyone had been part of some kind of athletic or academic team in high school. Most people had positive memories of those experiences. Teams were inherently competitive and it was a competitive marketplace. We needed teams of people working toward the common goal of the group for the greater good. Winning is a team effort. You would *give the ball* to your *star player* and let them run with it. We tried hard to *put wins on the board*. We had to *score points* with our customers. Staying late at work was going into *extra innings*.

Ideally this metaphor works . . . providing everyone is in it for the greater good. But that's not always the case. Way back in 1972, Insko and Schopler proposed the *Group Locomotion Hypothesis*. Simply put the hypothesis states: Members of the group are motivated to achieve the group's goals. So if you are the member of a group that is trying to get more people to donate blood you probably have an underlying desire to get people to donate blood. Maybe a transfusion saved your life or you learned about the national shortage when a family member underwent surgery. You want to solve the blood shortage problem. That's great and a powerful motivator. Unfortunately, not everyone is intrinsically motivated by their jobs. A fast food worker only has so many ways to flip burgers. Sure, trying to have the fastest drive-through service in your region is a great goal, but you can only get that award so many times before it fails to motivate. Commissioned-based sales programs like the ones found at car dealerships do not facilitate teamwork. They inherently create competition between salesmen. Not everyone works for the greater good. And we found ourselves moving on to the next great metaphor that brought everything into focus, and this time it was the family metaphor.

Family—Someone said, gee this group is like my "family" and the heavens opened and the light shown down on managers from above. YES! We Are Family! It was not just a touchy feely metaphor, it was a way of thinking about your world. From a management perspective, it was fantastic because nobody quits their family. Families look out for each other. Family members put the family first. When the family hit hard times, everyone pulled together to get through it. Everyone still answered to a mother/father (founder or CEO). But there was no need to rush out the door at 5:00 to be with your family, you were already with family. The family cared about its children (notice the ability to cast leaders in a dominant role that is often unquestioned). Families are warm and accepting and caring (obviously not true of all families). Families make us feel safe and we have loyalty to our family because after all blood is thicker than water (a phrase that is as meaningless as it is true). American business latched onto this metaphor with great resolve. It was not because they wanted so desperately to care for their workers and this metaphor finally allowed for that. No, if you think about it, it is quite the opposite. No group can abuse you more, talk to you more poorly, offend you more deeply, and still expect you to sit down at a dinner table with them or help them out when they need help.

These were the major metaphors but it is not an inclusive list. Some organizations used a military metaphor, some nurturing metaphors like farming, others, like Disney, used a theatre metaphor (over a period of time they shifted to a family metaphor). There is a seemingly endless supply of metaphors from which to draw: Some are more controlling, others more creative, some service oriented, and others production oriented. No one metaphor is going to fit every organization, as a founder or partner in an organization you would want to devote a significant amount of energy and thought to your organizational metaphor because metaphors, like stories and parables, help us fill in gaps when there is no directive for appropriate action.

ORGANIZATIONAL CULTURE

Once I realized how powerful metaphors were in shaping organizational culture I became very interested in organizational culture. Some companies seem to have "strong" organizational culture (Apple, 3-M, Del Computers, even Disney), while others were labeled as having "weak" organizational culture (usually floundering companies like Chrysler before Lee Iacocca took over). I wanted to learn more about culture and how culture influenced organizations and how the people influenced the culture and the seemingly symbiotic relationship between people, culture, and success.

Researchers seemed to be divided between one of two paradigmatic camps (Smircich, 1983): *Culture was something an organization had* or *organizations don't have cultures, they are cultures* (Weick, 1983). The first seemed very applied and the second very theoretical. They both agreed that culture was a driving force behind organizational action. They agree it is critical and yet they see it very differently.

THE CULTURE AS *VARIABLE* APPROACH

Those who saw culture as ***"something an organization had"*** saw culture as a tangible component of the organization; it was as tangible as a rule or a person. It was something we studied so we could understand it, because if we could understand it we could predict it, if we could predict it we could manipulate it, if we could manipulate it we could manipulate everyone and everything about the company. Researchers like Deal and Kennedy (1982), Trice and Beyer (1984), Shein (1992), and to some extent Smircich (1983) saw the power of organizational culture and they looked for ways to help managers harness that power and make organizations more effective.

Deal and Kennedy identified components of "strong cultures" as a way of identifying an organization's culture, and at the same time it was a way of creating (or changing) an organization's culture. For example, one of the components they identified was organizational heroes. If you saw that your organization had heroes that were less than model employees you could see where people were getting the wrong idea. If you can identify that you can change that, if you change that, you change the culture. Let's say you worked for a law firm and one of the heroes of the law firm was the dearly departed founder who, or so the story goes, would regularly drink his way through depositions in the afternoon. You have identified one reason there is a heavy drinking culture in the firm and why afternoons seem far less productive than they could be. Deal and Kennedy saw the value of identifying what communicated organizational culture because they believed if you could identify what was sending the message, and you changed the message, you could change the culture. Culture was linked to success; changing culture could change your organization's success. They identified four components of strong cultures:

> **Values:** The values, beliefs, and visions of an organization should be easy to identify. More importantly, any organization that has been around for more than just the briefest amount of time will have values. If they are not identified by the organizational leadership, they will develop organically. Sometimes organic development works out for the organization, especially if the group is intrinsically motivated. But careful planning on the part of management can lead to a more focused and productive value system. For example, while some organizations promote stability, 3M's promotes the value of innovation, which led to the development of the post-it note.

> **Heroes:** Most organizations have stories about organizational heroes. These tend to be people who epitomize what the organization stands for. It might be a record setting salesperson or someone who worked their way up from the proverbial mailroom. But those heroes represent what the ideal organizational member is like.

Rites and Rituals: The number of possible rites and rituals is almost endless. Most schools have some kind of honor roll or dean's list that recognizes students with outstanding academic records. I worked at a community college that gave out a "bulldog award" annually for the person who overcame the most adversity while completing a degree. Sports teams are filled with superstitions and rituals. These serve as a bonding opportunity (participating in the ritual is the proverbial "drinking the Kool-Aid" step) but they also focus on what is important to the group.

Cultural Networks: What this comes down to is the manner in which the organizational culture is transmitted. It can be through formal or informal training and communication such as new member orientation, newsletters, or training manuals; or it can be through informal discussions. When I joined the Marine Corps University Expeditionary Warfare School as a civilian employee, they signed me up for MCAP (Marine Corps Acculturation Program) to teach me what I needed to know to work within the Marine Corps culture.

THE CULTURE AS *WAY OF BEING* APPROACH

While those researchers thought of culture as a variable in an organization, the other paradigm was that organizational culture was something an organization *was*, not something it had. It was the personality of the organization; we could not manipulate it because it was bigger and deeper than that. It was a result of every member and every policy and every condition inside and outside the organization. It was far too complex to be manipulated. The best we could hope to do was learn to ride the wave of organizational culture. Culture was not produced from one given source (or even from Deal and Kennedy's four sources). Culture was a big stew of heroes, traditions, rituals, people, leadership styles, awards, mission and vision statements, technology, physical space, organizational size, the economy, the geo-political situation, and possibly hundreds or thousands of other influences. Trying to change culture would be like trying to nail Jell-O to the wall. The nail would go in easily and have no real effect.

While culture could not be changed or manipulated by managers, it was constantly changing. It was like a river; while you never step in the exact same river twice, the river is always familiar (and wet). Organizations were entities that not only produced goods and/or services but also, as a byproduct, produced culture. Studying organizational culture was a way of "sense making" for members of the organization. But the polarity of the camps was troubling to me.

UNNECESSARY BIFURCATION

I was torn. I saw the value of each perspective. I read and read and read some more. I needed an answer. Then I found Sonya Sackmann 1990 article in *Communication Yearbook* where she described culture as a "dynamic construct." Now it made sense. It wasn't a matter of culture was one or the other: Culture was both. Every person who entered the organization changed its culture; every action by organizational members changed the culture but in the way creamer changed coffee. People influenced culture and culture influenced people. It wasn't one way and static, it was omnidirectional, ongoing, and fluid. It was a *dynamic construct*.

About the same time I came to this realization I found a unique subset of groups that was not addressed in organizational communication research; it was what I liked to call short-term organizations. These were groups like disaster relief organizations, event planning groups, and even groups with high, planned turnover rates like student organizations and college sports teams. When culture is based on deep-seated value systems that are developed over years I wondered how those values were passed to new members in these unique organizations. I wondered how some organizations seem to be able to develop and maintain positive and "strong" cultures that resulted in organizational success while others rode the rollercoaster of success.

LEE IACOCCA STORY

In the late 1970s, the Chrysler Corporation was struggling. That is actually an understatement: they were on the verge of bankruptcy. They were losing millions of dollars and had been forced to recall a couple of their cars. In 1979, they posted the largest corporate loss in U.S. history: $1.2 billion. Chrysler owed over $4 billion dollars. That is when Chrysler hired the now legendary Lee Iacocca as their president, Iacocca had risen to prominence when he ushered in the now iconic Ford Mustang.

It was clear that the only way Chrysler was going to stay afloat was with a federal bailout. The problem was Lee Iacocca himself had been very outspoken about his belief that the government should not bailout big business and specifically the automotive industry. But with a huge debt, unpaid suppliers, an unsellable inventory, and tens of thousands of workers' jobs on the line he went, hat in hand, to congress and asked for a bail out. The politicians didn't go easy on him but in early 1980 President Jimmy Carter did sign a loan guarantee act that provided Chrysler with $1.5 billion in loans and required them to find an additional $1.4 billion from other sources.

The turnaround was quick and stunning. Iacocca instituted a number of changes designed to change the direction of the company and the attitudes of the people. He started by taking a salary of one dollar for the first two years and making it known that he had also cut the salaries of top executive. While those cuts were relatively small (between 2% and 10%) given the nature of the financial crisis, it sent a message that everyone was in this together and Iacocca was going to lead by example. That was probably instrumental in getting labor unions to accept wage cuts. He also redirected what the company was doing. In the years leading up to this point, Chrysler had repeatedly cut research and development. The Chrysler cars of the 1970s were only cosmetically different. Parts were literally interchangeable across years and in some cases across models. Iacocca dumped millions into R&D. Then he did something the American people hadn't seen before, he went on TV and told us about what he was doing. He showed us the world's largest research and development facility that Chrysler was building. He introduced the first 5/50 warranty. For five years or 50,000 miles, your car was under warranty (a strategy that is standard now and has been greatly expanded). He also went on TV and sold cars himself and he created a rebate program that was unheard of at the time. He touted the "Chrysler Advantage" and told the American consumer "If you can find a better car, buy it."

But this wasn't just a change in marketing. He changed the culture of the organization. Chrysler's safety reputation went from being one of the worst to one of the best. Their tired old same-old-same-old car lines were halted and a new line rolled out and it was just what America wanted. The new cars were fuel efficient, safe, and stylish. The Chrysler K-Car Series was basic, reliable, affordable transportation and it took a huge portion of the market (my mother had one). They also introduced the Dodge Caravan, the world's first mini-van, it is still one of the best selling vehicles on the market today. Chrysler was a success again. They paid back their government loans seven years ahead of schedule. People were proud to make Chrysler vehicles and Americans were proud to drive them. In 1981, two years after Chrysler was on the verge of bankruptcy, Chrysler posted profit of over $11 million in the second quarter. A small profit by industry standards but a huge turnaround for the company.

Lee Iacocca knew that turning the company around wasn't about changing policies or setting new goals. He knew he had to change everything about the failing organization and that meant changing the way employees felt about the organization. It also meant changing the way the consumer felt about the company and its product. He addressed the challenges of changing the company's reputation from people both inside and outside directly. His commercials directly confront the company's new standards in safety, fuel efficiency, and design. He compared Chryslers to luxury autos by name and told people if they could find a better car they should buy it, showing his faith in the product.

ORGANIZATIONAL CHANGE

I will admit I have a personal bias for applied communication research. I wanted to know what I could to influence organizations. I wanted to know how managers could use the information provided by communication scholars to make organizations work better. I found that what I was really interested in doing was creating organizational change. I had read about people like Lee Iacocca who had turned the Chrysler Corporation around in the 1980s but when he left the corporation devalued, diminished, and eventually became lost in a series of corporate transactions and mergers with Daimler and is now Chrysler LLC. Clearly, this huge corporation was subject to change, but the question remains how does organizational change take place and more importantly, how can we create positive organizational change? These were questions I needed to be able to answer for my own career. For 25 years, I served as a Director of Forensics (that is speech and debate for those of you who were thinking about crime scene investigators). In that capacity, I had the opportunity to work with four different college and university teams who went from being teams who "attended national tournaments" to being schools who were nationally recognized and took home team sweepstakes trophies from national tournaments. I have no delusions of grandeur that allow me to think I am solely responsible for those turnarounds. Those were the result of some very talented students, the hard work of all of the coaches on staff, and the development of positive team cultures. However, I do credit the research into organizational culture and organizational change I had done as part of my doctoral program at Ohio University with a good deal of the transformation of the team cultures.

Because of the rapid membership turnover in college activities (in theory, you have an entirely new student body every four years), maintaining a team culture may prove to be more difficult than manipulating a team culture. When I started working with a new team I looked for and at those things researchers examined to determine organizational culture. If those things were in line with our mission I promoted them, if they ran in opposition to what I wanted to see from the team culture I set about to eliminate or change them. Sometimes it was a matter of co-opting the language of the position and other times it was a matter of arguing for a substitution of goals or values. I found that changing culture in short-term organizations was something an organizational leader could do. Let me offer just a few examples of how I used what I learned from organizational communication research to influence the teams with which I worked.

CHANGING VALUES

Intercollegiate speech and debate is very competitive. That is inherent in the activity. However, one of the teams I worked with had developed a team value that said competition should be about having fun, not winning. Rather than try to change the value from fun to win, I decided to co-opt the idea. My argument, which became a team mantra, was "I've won and I've lost, winning is more fun. Let's have more fun." You have to admit, it is hard to argue with that. If fun is the value, more fun should be even better.

CHANGING HEROES

When I started at one program, there was a belief that winning was the result of some innate talent and you either had that or didn't. Hard work and dedication could only get you so far and then you would be beaten by people who were just better than you because they were born with a gift you lacked. To some extent that is probably true in many fields. Some people are athletically inclined and excel in all sports. Some people seem to have a gift for music or art and it comes easily. But everyone who achieved greatness in their fields from Mozart to Tiger Woods will attest to the criticalness of practice and dedication to the craft. As I tried to understand how this perception developed I noticed that our best varsity members did not work in the team room. Because of issues with previous coaches, they also did not come in for coaching sessions often. But because they were talented and dedicated to their own craft they were competitively successful. But younger members of the team didn't see the process they only saw the end product. To the rookies, it looked like magic or divine intervention. Because the varsity members were successful, they were team heroes. So I asked the varsity members to do more of their preparation where younger members could see them working. During our long trips to tournaments, I would initiate discussions about the process people went through in writing speeches and talked about revisions and not only did I find that younger members let go of the idea that success was not correlated with effort but I found that varsity members actually signed up for more coaching appointments and consequently were more competitively successful.

CHANGING RITUALS

At one of the schools, the team was not so much a team as it was a group of individuals who traveled to tournaments together. I remembered Fayols idea of Esprit de Corps and tried to find a way to bring the group together more as a group. To that end, I invited the team to my house for team dinners on Tuesday nights. The first couple of weeks I cooked for them. Then we started a tradition of team members taking turns making their favorite dish for the team. We had some wonderful meals and great times and the unplanned (but not unexpected if I had thought about it) result was that the team started to adopt a family metaphor. The ritual of meeting at a home (not a restaurant or dorm) to break bread and talk created a familial environment. They were separated from their biological families and this group now seemed like a good surrogate.

CHANGING CULTURAL NETWORKS

I noticed that maintaining a team culture was an ongoing process. Just because I had all the ducks swimming in the same direction one year didn't mean we were going to pick up from where we left off the next year. I looked for ways to make our values and goals readily evident to new members. We did this through everything from team shirts to charts on the wall for all to see (and ceremonial updating of charts) to debriefings after major events to see what the team learned. We put more things in writing, we brought back successful alumni to talk to the team, and we made a conscious effort to formalize elements of our team culture. We made sure new members knew our mantras and sayings.

I found that focusing on inculcating new members into the team was critical in maintaining a positive team culture. So I started looking at organizational socialization research. You can read Connie Bullis's article in Communication Monographs (1993) if you are interested in organizational socialization. I found organizational assimilation and organizational identification to be very helpful to me as I tried to create intrinsically motivated teams with "strong" cultures. Some researchers found that organizational identification (how much of a person's identity was associated with being part of an organization) was an indicator of how committed to the organization they were (Cheney, 1983; Cheney & Tompkins, 1987; Sass & Canary, 1991). For example, I have a brother who works for the 3M company and will refer to himself as a "3Mer," many people will affiliate with a political party, or even a sports team (maybe you have a friend who is a Husker or a Cheese-head).

I was interested in increasing commitment to the programs I was directing by increasing the participant's sense of organizational identification. While the bulk of the literature on organizational identification focused on businesses and, to a lesser extent, nonprofit organizations, I found transferable concepts. To create a sense of ownership I promoted peer coaching programs that made students responsible for the success of their teammates. This also created organizational buy-in because students felt they were responsible for team success more than before.

A MOMENT OF REFLECTION

As I look back over a 25- year career in coaching and directing forensics programs, I don't think it is coincidence that my most competitively successful teams were the four that followed my doctoral study of organizational communication. So many of the things I learned as part of that research influenced how I subsequently ran programs. I think one of the hardest things for many managers, administrators, and other people of power in organizations to do is to turn the theoretical concepts they study into practice. Researchers like Fayol, Weber, and Taylor wrote for practitioners, they were very pragmatic so managers could read what they wrote and put it into action the next day. In many regards, they were prescriptive. They told managers what to do. But scholars in the 21st century are less likely to prescribe and more likely to offer observations (even about empirical research). But both types of research can inform you as you move through your career.

Taylor proposed the idea of *scientifically selecting* the right person for the job rather than just grabbing people almost at random to fill positions. As I thought about that it influenced the way I recruited students to the teams I ran. I realized that setting up a recruiting booth at the school's fall activity fair was essentially a "catch as catch can" approach. So we began to specifically target groups we thought would be most likely to excel at competitive speech and debate. If I were setting up an intermural rugby team I would recruit from the existing athletic groups and hang fliers in the recreation center, because that's where "jocks" hung out. But I was looking for nerds (and I say that with the utmost affection and respect) and that meant recruiting from nerd nirvana—The Honors Program. I began by getting 10 minutes in the first week of classes to talk to each of the Honors Program's basic course.

When I reflected on the *General Systems Theory* I realized that if my program were a part of the human body it would be a tooth. Our national success was attractive, we were on the school's web pages as a crown jewel, but we were essentially self-contained. A tooth can easily be extracted and while it would be missed, it would not have ripple effects. With higher education hitting the hardest economic times in history, everyone was looking for a way to reduce expenses and I didn't want that to be my program. So I reached out to other programs and developed partnerships by offering a special program that took over 50 Honors Program students to the Forensics National Novice Tournament. The program offered public debate forums and forensics showcases three times each semester that students attended as a requirement of their basic communication course. These were attended by over 1,800 students annually. I sent forensics students to work phone-a-thons and give tours for the Admissions Office, and we held summer institutes for high school students. Each one of those things engrained us a little more into the larger university system. We moved from being a tooth to being more like the jaw (you have to love the organic metaphors).

I worked hard to develop and maintain a strong *organizational culture* in the programs. Some of my students from as much as 15 years ago recently had a brief Facebook discussion about the different sayings and mantras that I had engrained in them. As I watched that discussion unfold I was proud to see that the *core values* I had tried to instill were still with them and that many of them have taken those ideas and sayings (or a variation) into their own workplaces. They were the sayings that promoted dedication, preparation, and excellence. I was elated to see that some of those ideas were taken with them after they graduated.

As I look back at that part of my career and reflect on the things I did to generate *organizational change* I am very satisfied with what I was able to accomplish. As I look ahead at the next phase of my career with the Marine Corps University, I realize making changes will be simultaneously easier because of a culture of constant revision and more difficult because of the depth of the Marine Corps culture. But I am confident that my understanding of organizational communication will once again help me as I move to the next phase of my career. I have already seen changes in our faculty professionalism that has left me playing catch-up.

I hope that you have enjoyed my little trip down memory lane and that some of the subject matter was intriguing to you. This is by no means a comprehensive coverage of what is entailed in organizational communication. I didn't touch on organizational storytelling, recognition-based reward systems, anticipatory socialization, and a plethora of other issues. Many of the great names of organizational communication research like Charles Redding, Frank Jablin, Dennis Mumby, Linda Putnam, Gary Kreps, and Mary Helen Brown (one of my personal favorites for her work with organizational narratives) were not even mentioned. There is so much more to study and learn. I hope you find the study of the way people come together and use communication to socially construct the companies for which they work and the organizations to which they belong fascinating. I would be delighted if you had an interest in organizational culture and organizational change. But above all I hope you see how important the communication (intentional or otherwise) of organizational members is to the success of the organization.

BIBLIOGRAPHY

Barnes, G. (2009). Guess who's coming to work: Generation Y. Are you ready for them? *Public Library Quarterly*, *28*(1), 58–63. doi:10.1080/01616840802675457

Bullis, C. (1993). Organizational socialization research: Enabling, constraining, and shifting perspectives. *Communication Monographs*, *60*(1), 10–17.

Buzzanell, P. M. & Stohl, C. (1999). The Redding tradition of organizational communication scholarship: W. Charles Redding and his legacy. *Communication Studies, 50*, 324–336.

Cheney, G. (1983). On the various and changing meanings of organizational membership: A field study of organizational identification. *Communication Monographs. 50* (4), 342–362.

Cheney, G. & Tompkins, P. K. (1987). Coming to terms with organizational identification and commitment. *Central States Speech Journal, 38*, 1–15.

Deal, T. E. & Kennedy, A. A. (1982). *Corporate cultures: The rites and rituals of corporate life*. Reading, MA: Addison-Wesley.

Insko C. A. & Schopler, J. (1972). *Experimental social psychology*. New York, NY: Academic Press.

Joseph, S. M. (2002). *The Trivium: The liberal arts of logic, grammar, and rhetorical*. Philadelphia, PA: Paul Dry Books, Inc.

Landsberger, H. A. (1958). Hawthorne Revisited, Ithaca.

McLean, J. (2011). Fayol—standing the test of time. *Manager: British Journal of Administrative Management, 74*, 32–33.

McGregor, D. (1960). *The human side of enterprise*. New York, NY: McGraw Hill.

Ouchi, W. G. (1981). *Theory Z: How American business can meet the Japanese challenge*. New York, NY: Avon Books.

Roethlisberger, F. L. & Dickson, W. (1939). *Management and the worker*. New York, NY: John Wiley & Sons.

Rosenthal, R. & Jacobson, L. (1968). *Pygmalion in the classroom*. New York, NY: Holt, Rinehart & Winston.

Sass, J. S. & Canary, D. J. (1991). Organizational commitment and identification: An examination of conceptual and operational convergence. *Western Journal of Speech Communication, 55*(3), 275–293.

Shein, E. (1992). *Organizational culture and leadership: A dynamic view*. San Francisco, CA: Jossey-Bass.

Smircich, L. (1983). Concepts of culture and organizational analysis, *Administrative Science Quarterly, 28*(3), 339–358.

Trice, H. M. & Beyer, J. M. (1984). Studying organizational cultures through rites and ceremonies. *Academy of Management Review, 9*(4), 653–669.

Von Bertalanffy, L. (1968). *General systems theory*. New York, NY: Braziller.

Weick, k. (1983). Organizational communication: Toward a research agenda. In L. Putnam & M. Pacanowsky (Eds.), *Communication and organizations: An interpretive approach* (pp. 13–29). Beverly Hills, CA: Sage.

14

Intercultural Communication

Samantha Kay Smith & Yea-Wen Chen

LEARNING OBJECTIVES

After reading this chapter, you should be able to:

- Develop a general understanding of intercultural communication as an area of inquiry
- Understand how cultural identities impact intercultural communication interactions
- Identify challenges and opportunities of engaging in intercultural communication in everyday interactions
- Appreciate the relevance of intercultural communication in an increasingly globalized world
- Appreciate the importance of becoming a sensible, competent, and culturally sensitive communicator in intercultural encounters

BACKGROUND ON THE STUDY OF INTERCULTURAL COMMUNICATION

Opening Personal Narrative from Sammy Kay

The room was crowded with people, a jumble of languages "assaulting" my ears, making me increasingly aware that I knew no other language but English and was at the mercy of those around me. It was my first time out representing the Association for Cultural Exchange (ACE) as the new President for the upcoming year, and I was keenly aware of the need to win over the international community if I wanted my organization to succeed. So, I did what I always do: smile, be as friendly as possible, and try to start out on a positive note. Show them I'm here not just to work and create a successful environment for us all, but to also show that I'm here to listen, to be their friend and an ally, and a resource when navigating a culture that they weren't raised in.

"They think you're the stereotypical, stupid American." I can always trust my friend, and Vice President to be brutally honest about whatever is on her mind. However, this is not what I had been expecting. Yes, I know that I can come off a little strong at times, especially if I'm still figuring out my place in a new situation. I'm unintentionally loud, smile all the time, especially if I'm nervous or uncomfortable, stay close to people I feel at least a little connection with, and have come by the nickname "Chatty Kathy" quite honestly. But "stereotypical, stupid American" was not the identity I had been trying to convey. What about "friendly peer, ally, hard worker, and possibly friend?" Guess not. I had to realize that, when working with a large group of international students from vastly different countries, I couldn't work within all of their cultural understandings and be true to myself at the same time. Now was the time to be pulling out all my resources, from those who had walked the same path before me.

It's impossible for me to learn all of the cultural norms for every culture represented here in the over 100 countries that send students to Ohio University. I have enough trouble interacting with students from the same state, let alone from other countries. But, I was lucky. No matter what my first impression had been, these students were stuck working with me for two years. I had time to prove myself to them and attempted to change the minds of those who had taken my first impression as the "stupid American."

Over the past two years, I have made great strides with members of the international community. Being able to push my nerves aside, I could tone down my exuberance and start strategizing how I needed to portray myself as culturally sensitive as possible. I learned which cultural group members might appreciate my loud, chatty, bubbly-ness, and with which cultural groups I need to tone myself down. In addition, I've learned to look at myself through an intercultural lens—considering both my own and others' cultural references. Intercultural communication has managed to influence the way I act around others, and open my eyes to the different ways of being, acting, and behaving across cultures to which I am exposed every day.

The opening narrative from Sammy Kay, the first author and a senior at Ohio University at the time of writing this chapter, illustrates some of the tensions, challenges, and opportunities that we will explore in this chapter. The purpose of this chapter is to introduce the topic of intercultural communication. For our purpose here, **intercultural communication** is understood broadly as communication between individuals and groups who are perceived or experienced as "unalike culturally" in terms of group memberships such as nationality, race and ethnicity, and regionality (Rogers & Steinfatt, 1999, p. 267). Intercultural communication is also referred to as communication between and/or across cultures, or the study of culture and communication. We will define the quintessential term *culture* later in this chapter. This chapter begins with brief contextualization of intercultural communication as an area of study. Then, we consider different definitions of "culture," the importance of negotiating cultural identities, and intercultural communication in everyday contexts. Finally, we end the chapter with a discussion of what it means to become a competent communicator in intercultural encounters in this increasingly globalized world.

Brief Historical Background

"Our loyalties must transcend our race, our tribe, our class, and our nation; and this means we must develop a world perspective. No individual can live alone; no nation can live alone, and as long as we try, the more we are going to have war in this world."

Martin Luther King, Jr. (1967)

Since Martin Luther King's famous quote in 1967, the world we inhabit has become a more interdependent and interconnected "global village." The phenomenon of people from different cultural backgrounds interacting, however, is not a new or recent one. For instance, if we define culture in terms of race, people from different racial groups have been interacting for centuries. However, intercultural communication in our current times is different from other periods in history in some important ways (Sorrells, 2013). First, intercultural communication today is much more frequent and intense. Towns in northeast Ohio, such as the one Sammy Kay came from, were predominantly one cultural group only 50 years ago. Now they are attracting immigrants from other countries, and people from other states all over the United States, bringing people from many cultures together. Second, as the term "global village" suggests, people around the globe are becoming much more interdependent today. For example, look at the labels on your clothing or your class supplies. There is a good chance that some of these will be made in a different country. Third, individuals and families are moving across all kinds of cultural borders and boundaries at an unprecedented rate. Think about your family and families you know. Most likely, you know someone born in another culture, or whose parents were. Knowing this means that each and every one of us have an obligation to learn more about how to better communicate and interact with people from different cultural backgrounds.

One way to grasp intercultural communication is to first understand how the study of intercultural communication has emerged. The subject of intercultural communication has intrigued and interested scholars and practitioners across disciplines such as anthropology, sociology, linguistics, international relations, and global studies, to name a few. Undoubtedly, there are multiple stories, or multiple versions of different stories, of how the study of intercultural communication began within and across these disciplines. For our purpose here, we will focus on the study of intercultural communication within the discipline of communication in the United States. When understanding **history** as stories that we tell to make sense of what happened in the past, collectively intercultural communication scholars have offered several stories about its historical past. Among them, one more commonly shared history centers on the work of anthropologist Edward T. Hall, known as Ned to family and close friends. Hall first wrote this groundbreaking idea in his 1959 book, *The Silent Language*, arguing that: "Culture is communication and communication is culture" (Hall, 1959, p. 186).

In this version of history, the root of intercultural communication can be traced back to the work of Edward T. Hall and colleagues at the Foreign Service Institute (FSI) of the U.S. Department of State in the early 1950s (Leeds-Hurwitz, 1990). To this date, the FSI remains the Federal Government's primary training institution that prepares and supports U.S. diplomats, foreign affairs community, and related professionals to advance U.S. interests overseas and at home. Hall's involvement with FSI was driven by a problem that many recognized in the 1940s: "many American diplomats were not fully effective abroad, since they did not speak the language and usually knew little of the host culture" (Leeds-Hurwitz, 1990, p. 264). *Culture* in this context was often treated synonymously as nation-states or national cultures such as Chinese, French, and U.S. American cultures. To address this problem, Hall and colleagues developed training programs that stressed, instead of a single culture at a time, interactions between members of different cultures and broadened the concept of culture to include the study of communication, especially nonverbal communication. It is commonly accepted that Hall's work at the FSI during that time led to the "birth" of intercultural communication as a field of study in the late 1960s and early 1970s (Hart, 2005). If you were Edward T. Hall, what would you have done to train, prepare, and support U.S. diplomats and workers before they embark on their foreign journeys? What would you emphasize in your trainings with regard to communication and culture? On the other hand, if you were in the position of the foreign diplomats and workers, what you would like to know, learn, or experience in such pre-departure trainings? In a way, those are the kinds of questions and issues that continue to drive a number of studies of intercultural communication today.

While intercultural communication grew out of efforts to train U.S. diplomats and technical assistance workers, intercultural communication since then has grown, expanded, and diversified. One way to think about intercultural communication as an area of inquiry is to understand other labels that are sometimes used interchangeably with intercultural communication. Some of these labels include cross-cultural communication, international communication, development communication, and critical intercultural communication. ***Cross-cultural communication*** tends to focus on comparing and contrasting communication processes across two or more different national cultures such as Japan and the United States (Oetzel, 2008). The goal of cross-cultural communication is to understand the influence of cultural differences on communication choices and behaviors without examining interactions between members of these cultural groups. ***International communication*** is the study of mass-mediated communication between entities (such as governmental, nongovernmental, or transnational agencies and corporations) from two or more countries (Rogers & Hart, 2002). ***Communication and development*** (a.k.a. developmental communication or communication development) concerns with the study of social change brought about by the application of communication research and technologies from one culture to another (Rogers & Hart, 2002). ***Critical intercultural communication*** is a power-based approach to study culture and communication by paying close attention to how macro conditions and structures (e.g., economic institutions and market conditions) play into micro processes of communication between members of different cultural groups (Nakayama & Halualani, 2010). In this chapter, we, in the spirit of inclusivity, put forth this view that the "field" of intercultural communication encompasses all these specialized areas while recognizing important distinctions between and among the terms. After all, as all kinds of cultural crossings become increasingly common, the distinctions between and among the terms can become messy and blurry.

John Condon and Fathi Yousef published one of the first textbooks of intercultural communication in 1975, titled *An Introduction to Intercultural Communication*. It was indeed an "introduction" as it was one of the first attempts to name and chart a relatively new area of study at the time. In 1965, the subject of intercultural communication was introduced as "interpersonal communication across cultures" (p. v) and Condon and Yousef framed it through the lens of encountering differences. Since then, there have been many more textbooks on intercultural communication that differ in approaches, focuses, and scopes. For example, John Oetzel (2008), who was a junior colleague to John (Jack) Condon at the University of New Mexico, publishes an intercultural communication text from a layered approach. Oetzel treats, considers, and examines culture at individual, interpersonal, organizational, and societal layers. Another text by Kathryn Sorrells (2013), who was a student of Condon's at the University New Mexico, (re)orients intercultural communication through globalization and social justice. The different approaches indicate that intercultural communication remains an enticing, exciting, and complex subject.

Intercultural Comunication in the Context of Globalization Today

Broadly speaking, globalization can be understood as "the compression of the world and the intensification of consciousness of the world as a whole" (Robertson, 1992, p. 8). As the continued compression of the world has resulted in widening the gaps between the haves and the have-nots, Kathryn Sorrells, refers to globalization as "the *contested processes* that contribute to and the vastly *inequitable conditions* of living in our contemporary world" (2010, p. 171, emphasis in original). On one hand, processes of globalization promote the study of intercultural communication. On the other hand, conditions of globalization also shape our understanding intercultural communication.

Martin Luther King, Jr. urges each of us to "develop a world perspective." His call is more important than ever today as the world we inhibit becomes increasingly interconnected across economics, politics, social issues, and so forth. Then, what does "a world perspective" mean for our current time? What will it take for each of us to develop such a perspective appropriately and effectively? What conditions and factors encourage or discourage such a perspective? When taking a world perspective, what social, ethical, or moral obligations do we have toward one another as fellow citizens? In a way, those are the kinds of the questions that become the undercurrents driving the study of intercultural communication. At its core, the study of intercultural communication can be understood as systematic explorations of how individuals, groups, and entities from different cultural backgrounds can better communicate, understand, relate, work together, and live with and among one another.

While the study of intercultural communication might sound straightforward, the processes of actually studying it have proven to be much messier, complicated, and, at times, contested. We will explain here using the idea of "the stranger" that has captivated a number of intercultural communication scholars, researchers, and practitioners. The notion of the stranger provides a useful lens to think about someone who is perceived as from different cultural backgrounds. The stranger, defined by German sociology, Georg Simmel, is "someone who is a member of a system but who is not strongly attached to the system" (as cited in Rogers, 1999, p. 458). The idea opens doors for exploring (a) views, experiences, and behaviors of the stranger, (b) how the stranger relates to the system in which she/he finds herself/himself, and (c) relationships and interactions among the stranger and those who consider her/him the stranger, to name a few. However, in interactions, it is not always clear who the stranger is to whom, is it? How *strange* does one need to be to be labeled as the stranger? Once the stranger learns more about the system or becomes more attached to the system with time, is this person still the stranger? And who decides or can decide? In other words, studying relationships and interactions between people from different cultural backgrounds is not as clear-cut as it sounds.

One of the pioneering women of intercultural communication, LaRay M. Barna, has written about what she calls six stumbling blocks in intercultural communication. They are (a) assumptions of similarities, (b) language differences, (c) nonverbal misinterpretations, (d) preconceptions and stereotypes, (e) tendency to evaluate, and (f) high anxiety. As much as we, as individuals and societies, have become more sophisticated in our thinking about cultures and others, many of the stumbling blocks that LaRay Barna (1998) initially wrote remain relevant today. We have organized and developed this chapter to provide some ideas that we think are useful to better understand and help address these stumbling blocks.

Why Study Intercultural Communication?

Intercultural communication is becoming increasingly important in the globalizing world due to at least five reasons: social media, migrations, changing demographics (especially in the United States), reducing conflicts, and engaging with difference. First, as a generation that is surrounded by technology, it is not hard to use social media to speak with someone from around the world, or around the block. Our world is becoming more and more connected, with our ability to telephone, email, instant message, tweet, Facebook, and video chat with those a world away from us. We can talk to anyone, anywhere, at any time. Additionally, we now have Internet access at all times with laptops, tablets, and smart phones; there is not a time of day where we cannot be connected to the rest of the world and people of different cultures. While our ability to speak with anyone at any time is a blessing, especially for organizations with contacts overseas, there remains a problem. Although we are capable of looking into just about any culture without leaving our own home, how often do we actually envelop ourselves into another culture? Unfortunately, most of us rarely do so. Further, speaking with someone in another country via video chat is not the same as going into that country and experiencing their culture. In past generations, to meet someone of another nationality, you would have to travel to experience the culture. Now, we can be in contact with them instantly. But, are we really in contact with them? Do we see the cultural similarities and differences clearly through a computer screen? For example, Sammy Kay has made friends in England, Brazil, and Holland. Though she has never been to these countries, Sammy Kay is able to maintain these friendships through social media sites such as Facebook and emails. However, it does not necessarily mean that she understands and can work within these cultures.

Second, the global village, the world viewed as a community, is truly the world we are living in today. And this should compel us to regard ourselves as *global citizens*. Simply look around your classroom, residential hall, dining hall, or any other place you frequent around campus and you will find students and professors who are from different parts of the world. With our world becoming so interconnected, we are all more than citizens of a town, state, country, race, ethnicity, and any of the other categories the world places us in. We are truly global citizens. We will be encountering people from different cultures every day of our lives, starting for some in college, but continuing through our relationships with friends and family, in the workplace, and through how we view others, either through the media or in person. This takes us to a need to understand global citizenship. Globalization is inevitable. Today, there is a global repositioning of people that includes legal and undocumented immigrants, temporary workers, refugees, retirees, and visitors. According to reporting by the International Organization for Migration (IOM) in 2013, the United States is the top migrant destination in the world, hosting 20 percent of all migrants (about 42.8 million). With these kinds of numbers, it is impossible for us to function in our daily lives without having at least a chance of encountering someone from a different culture. Intercultural communication also provides a window into communicating with other cultures, and how members of different cultural groups interact with one another. This field affords us core foundations of what it means to communicate successfully with individuals and groups from different cultural backgrounds. Further, knowledge of intercultural communication can help us not only to better speak with people from other cultures but also to better communicate within our own society.

Third, changing demographics around the world demands understanding how these changes impact communication and culture. Intercultural communication does not just end at the international level. Different cultures are also seen between different races, genders, classes, religions, rural or urban, and even families. This means that you will encounter different cultures in your individual life, within the same town as you. At a personal level, effective intercultural communication can create stronger personal relationships and ties (Adler, 1975; Oetzel, 2008). Look around your classroom. Each person most likely comes from a different city than you, or at least a different cultural background. Take Sammy Kay and one of her cousins, Danielle, for example. Sammy Kay was raised in a different culture in her hometown, a place where high school football is the big event of every year. Danielle was raised in a small town where the McDonalds' has chandeliers and little attention is paid to the high school football team. For only living an hour's drive apart from each other, these cultures are incredibly different.

Fourth, intercultural communication can help us better handle conflicts that arise between different cultures. Diversity in our world offers many opportunities, from being able to bring many different experiences together when in teams to gaining a new outlook on life. Intercultural communication has the power to create both peace and conflict. With the many different cultural backgrounds, the possibility for having conflict increases than when everyone is from the same background. Some of these conflicts can arise simply from ignorance of another's culture, as the problems that arose for Sammy Kay within the international community. Other parts of these conflicts are created from deep-seated, long-standing historical hatreds, such as the Israeli-Palestinian Conflict, or the hate between the Greeks and Turks. These conflicts can escalate into full wars, affecting thousands.

Lastly, this field can assist us in engaging with difference more meaningfully. While possibly creating conflict, diversity can also create peace and harmony within groups when dealt with properly. A number of communication scholars have examined the conditions and communication techniques needed to bring people together after years of conflict and hatred (e.g., Brown & Levinson, 1987; Chen & Ma, 2001; Oetzel, 2008; Oetzel & Ting-Toomey, 2003; Pondy, 1967). With tools and perspectives such as empathy, we can use diversity to bridge conflicts, from the small problems we face in organizations on campus, in large companies, and spanning the global conflicts that now have the ability to touch and affect each of us. When joining as one, we can solve the largest conflicts of the world using the tools of intercultural communication and the diversity in our world.

CULTURE, IDENTITY, AND COMMUNICATION

While LaRay Barna (1998) considers the stumbling blocks in intercultural communication, Martin, Nakayama, and Flores (2002) identify four building blocks to think about the dynamic nature of intercultural communication—culture, communication, context, and power. How one conducts oneself in intercultural interactions is informed, affected, and shaped not only by one's cultural backgrounds and communication behaviors but also by any relevant contextual factors and power relations at play. For example, as a second-generation Japanese-American businessman, Koji needs to conduct himself both similarly and differently to be effective when doing businesses in Japan as opposed to in the United States due to a myriad of factors that are cultural, individual, contextual, and historical. In some instances, Koji's Japanese counterparts might expect him to understand and speak the Japanese language whereas his U.S. counterparts might be surprised that he speaks English fluently even though English is his native tongue, not Japanese. In other instances such as when doing businesses in less-wealthy countries, Koji might enjoy greater economic power and higher social status than in his home country. Influences of culture, communication, context, and power might not always be clear to the intercultural interactants, which does not mean they do not matter. Part of the challenge is to learn to become aware of how they might matter or affect intercultural communication practices.

ACTIVITY POP-OUT BOX 1

"How you perceive you" versus "How others perceive you"

Instruction: On a piece of paper, draw *two identity pie charts* that describe your multiple identities. Consider your "selves" that are important or meaningful to you and focus on groups that you are a member of or belong to. One identity pie chart represents how you view your selves. In this pie chart, draw your self-avowed identities (i.e., how *you* view yourself): "*I am* _____." The other identity pie chart represents how you think others view you. Draw your other-labeled identities: "*You are* _____."

After you have finished your two identity pie charts, find a classmate whom you have not interacted with and introduce yourself using the two identity pie charts. It is okay to share only to the extent that you are comfortable. Please note both similarities and differences.

Discussion Questions

1. How would you compare and contrast your two identity pie charts?
2. What does this activity illustrate about the nature of identity?

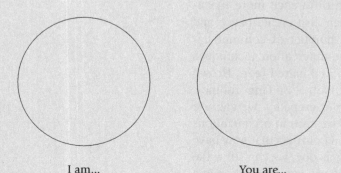

I am...   You are...

Besides the four building blocks for thinking about intercultural communication dynamics, we, the authors, believe that another important block is **identity**, broadly defined as a person's sense or conception of self. How people understand, experience, or become aware of their identity, or identities, largely depends on culture, communication, context, and power. People have multiple identities such as nationality, race, ethnicity, gender, sexuality, age, religion, spirituality, socioeconomic status, political affiliation, and occupation. To us, identity is an especially important issue for intercultural communication because intercultural encounters often invokes, challenges, or redefines our identity or identities. For example, Yen, a native of Taiwan, moved to the United States to pursue her master's degree. Before coming to the United States, Yen had never considered herself "Asian" because Asia was just an arbitrary geographical term that meant little to her at the time. However, after being repeatedly confused as Japanese, Thai, or Korean by people with whom she came into contact, she was challenged to reconsider her sense of selfhood and the idea of "being Asian" started to mean more than it did before. In a way, we could say that the meaningfulness of race relations in the United States influence Yen's experiences here. Now try out the exercise in pop-out Box 1 that illustrates the interactive nature of identity.

DEFINING CULTURE

What does "culture" mean to you? One quintessential challenge of the study of intercultural communication is to define culture—a familiar yet extremely complex term—in ways that allow scholars and practitioners to understand and capture it without reducing or oversimplifying its complexities. Though culture is often thought of in terms of foods, customs, and costumes, especially in popular media, culture is much more than that. Anthropologists Clyde Kluckhohn and Arthur Kroeber (1952) identified over 150 concepts and definitions of culture. The bottom line is that culture is central to how each of us view, experience, engage with our lives, one another, and the world around us. In the field of intercultural communication, scholars have approached culture in at least three fundamentally different ways based on their research goals and interests.

Culture as a Speech Code   One group of scholars approach culture as a **speech code**—"a system of socially-constructed symbols and meaning, premises, and rulers, pertaining to communication conduct" (Philipsen, Coutu, & Covarrubias, 2005, p. 57). Influenced by anthropological work, this group of scholars are interested in understanding how members make sense of their worlds and figure out what to pay attention to, ignore, or guide their behaviors. To this group of scholars, what distinguish and differentiate cultural communities are their distinct speech codes, and speech codes constitute the meanings of communicative acts. That is, a culture is a community of people who share similar ways of communicating and decoding communicative acts. For example, Carbaugh (2002) found that, for members of the Blackfeet Indian Nation located in a reservation in Montana, USA, their primary mode of communication is "a deeply communicative silence" that centers on a listener active form of nonverbal copresence and nonlinguistic togetherness.

Culture as a Comparable Pattern   Another group of scholars approach culture as a **comparable pattern** that is learned, shared, modified, and passed down among members of a community. In other words, culture is understood as "a complex frame of reference that consists of patterns of traditions, beliefs, values, norms, symbols, and meanings that are shared to varying degrees by interacting members of a community (Ting-Toomey, 1999, p. 10). Some of the most researched and widely cited cultural patterns come from the work of Dutch social psychologist Geert Hofstede (e.g., 1991). Professor Hofstede conducted comprehensive studies analyzing employee values collected within IBM between 1967 and 1973 in more than 70 countries. Based on this body of work, Professor Hofstede has identified value patterns that distinguish national cultures from one another. He has termed these comparable patterns: Individualism versus Collectivism, Masculinity versus Femininity, Power Distance, and Uncertainty Avoidance. We will discuss these comparable cultural patterns in greater details later.

These categories inform many intercultural interactions. These categories are easy to see once your eye is trained to them. One example is the cultural differences between U.S. American and Chinese students across college campuses in the United States. In most U.S. American families, the individual student and their parents are the ones paying for a college education. Beyond that, the student is expected to secure as many scholarships as possible, maybe grants, and then rely on student loans to pay for the rest. In quite a few of the Chinese students at Ohio University, their entire family, including grandparents, aunts, and uncles, bring their money together to send the best and brightest in their family to attend college in the United States. These students are expected to come home once they finish their education and help support their entire family financially. One way of explaining this cultural difference is using the idea of individualism-collectivism. We can argue that the United States has an individualistic culture, with the individual having to take care of himself or herself. Meanwhile, China has more of a collectivistic culture, with the group coming together to ensure the best for everyone.

Culture as a Site of Struggle and Contestation   Still another group of scholars approach culture as **sites of struggles and contested meanings**. Martin and Nakayama (1999) define culture as "a site of struggle where various communication meanings are contested" (p. 8), taking into account the important roles that contexts and power relations play in intercultural communication. In considering this definition of culture, Sammy Kay recalled and reflected on a recent incident that happened during the International Street Fair. This fair is put on once a year by the International Community at Ohio University to share their cultures with one another, including food, performances, and a parade celebrating our global diversity. Many students and community members come to learn about and celebrate other countries. While setting up national flags for the fair, Doli, a female student from India, contested about featuring flags from Western countries. Doli asserted that any country that had colonized others should not be represented. As a U.S. citizen, this is not something that I would hear on an everyday basis. Also, it is a difficult idea to process that I and many Western citizens might still hold power over many groups our ancestors once colonized. However, Doli was confident to make her claim because of the 15 people present, only 2 were from Western countries. This unique group composition allowed the power balance to shift. Further, the meaning of the word "colonizer" was contested, as some students questioned whether India was a colonizer with its struggles with Pakistan and others, Doli included, asserted that it was not. This incident illustrates the importance of context and shifting power relation in how individuals and groups struggle and contest making meanings out of intercultural encounters.

Defining Cultural Identity

Identity has remained an important area of inquiry for the study of intercultural communication. At its core, scholars of culture and communication are concerned with how we come to know, understand, and experience a sense of the self in interactions with cultural others. This is particularly important because our identities influence the way we communicate, relate to, and engage with one another.

Following Cultural Identity Theory, **cultural identity** is the enactment and negotiation of social identification by group members in a particular interactional context that demonstrates their affiliation and understanding of the premises and practices required to be a group member (Collier, 1998; Collier & Thomas, 1988). Each of us identifies with, or belongs to, multiple groups based on gender, class, race, nationality, age, professional or political affiliation, and so on. Thus, it is important to bear in mind that each of us has *multiple* *cultural identities* that we experience, enact, and negotiate on a daily basis. There are times when some of our cultural identities conflict with each other (such as "a gay Republican"). Mixed identities, such as biracial people, gender fluid individuals, or dual citizens can also conflict with one another as we travel through our daily lives.

In essence, cultural identity theory posits different properties and processes associated with cultural identity enactment, including scope, salience, intensity, avowal, and ascription (Collier, 1998; Collier & Thomas, 1988). First, cultural identities differ in **scope**, or the breadth in terms of the number of people or frequency with which a certain identity, such as nationality, applies. Second, cultural identities vary in **salience**, or importance of particular identities relative to other identities across contexts, time, and interaction. For example, a working-class Asian woman in the presence of a group of working-class Asian men might be more acutely aware of her identity as a woman than her other identities. Third, cultural identities differ in the levels of **intensity** with which they are communicated. For example, Gust Yep (2002) discusses how he is often labeled the identity of an Asian American because he "looks Asian American." However, Professor Yep prefers the label "Asianlatinoamerican" to highlight his claim to multicultural identities in the United States. Fourth, **avowals** are cultural identities that an individual enacts to represent oneself as group members to others. That is, avowals are identities that you see, label, and make meaning about yourself. Fifth, **ascriptions** are identities that are attributed, assigned, or labeled by others to one's groups. That is, ascriptions are identities that others view, name, and describe you and your group. There are often tensions and contradictions in the cultural identities that are avowed and ascribed since they involve different experiences, levels of agency, histories, perspectives, and power relations. For example, one of Yea-Wen's neighbors in New Mexico proudly avows as "Spanish American" because her family can trace their root back to Spain. However, she is often mistakenly ascribed as "Mexican American" because of her darker complexion, which upsets her. Overall, besides recognizing multiple cultural identities, it is also important to understand that the nature of cultural identity is simultaneously personal and social, fluid and stable, and individual and group-based (Yep, 2004).

Negotiating Cultural Identities

Identity categories require constant negotiations of who we are and who others are in relation to us. The concept of **negotiation** can be understood as "a transactional interaction process whereby individuals in an intercultural situation attempt to assert, define, modify, challenge, and/or support their own and others' desired self-images" (Ting-Toomey, 2005, p. 217). Have you ever noticed that, when you are with different people, different parts of your "self" come forward? When around family, you might be fighting against their views of you as a student, trying to prove your adulthood. Around professionals in your field, you might be clinging to your student identity, aware that you do not know as much as they do. Your gender or racial identity might surface when around others who are speaking badly about your gender or race. Or your political views might be quieted when the rest of your family starts condemning them.

As social constructions, different identity categories are created and recreated to serve different social functions as we interact with others. These categories divide us into different groups and cause us to react and be treated differently, depending on the situation. Some identities are more privileged than others, allowing them to be expressed openly, freely, and without conflict. These identities are often part of the dominant culture. Other identities are marginalized, with the person being more careful about who knows about this identity. For instance, heterosexuals as the dominant group can assume that others they meet are also heterosexual. In contrast, members of the LGBT (Lesbian, Gay, Bisexual, Transgender/Transsexual) community have to inform others of their sexuality and "come out of the closet" so people do not assume. Further, certain identities allow people to pass as members of the dominant group. LGBT community members can often pass as heterosexual, or there are biracial or Latinos that can pass as Caucasian. Of course, people can out these identities, showing them to people around you, such as when a gay teenager is out-ed to his or her parents, or at school. These identities have to be negotiated and decided upon as we continue through our everyday life.

Negotiating identities can be a tricky and complicated process. Although each person has multiple identities, we often forget that and only think about and focus on one or two of their identities. This idea is known as **identity freezing** and results in ignoring many of a person's other identities (Ting-Toomey, 2005). With such attitudes, it is no surprise that we have to negotiate our identities with others. A great example of negotiating cultural identities comes from a friend of Sammy Kay's. This college student, Hassan, was originally born in the Middle East before his family came to the United States so his parents could pursue their education. This has resulted in Hassan growing up with two cultural identities: one from the Middle East and one from the United States. Hassan grows very upset with those who point out that he is Americanized, despite his deep understanding of the U.S. culture. Through my years of knowing him, I have seen him choosing between (a) being perfectly fine with recognizing his understanding of the U.S. culture and (b) refusing to recognize that he was raised most of his life in the United States. He is Middle Eastern and deciding between whether he is against and for his U.S. American identity across contexts, situations, and people whom he is interacting with.

CHALLENGES AND OPPORTUNITIES OF INTERCULTURAL COMMUNICATION ACROSS EVERYDAY CONTEXTS

Many students of communication often hear "intercultural communication" and believe that if they have never traveled abroad, it does not apply to them. However, you do not need to be a world traveler to experience intercultural communication. Cultures differ within our country or even within our home state. Sammy Kay has a roommate from Boston, and their different cultural ideals often clash. Or think about how different Athens, home of Ohio University, is from Cleveland, Columbus, or Cincinnati. While all are from the United States, or even Ohio, cultures differ, even from family to family.

Often we are stuck with the idea that someone has to look or sound differently from us to have a different culture. As an illustration, in an Asian history class, the professor asked everyone to introduce themselves. "Michael" introduces himself, and being Asian, the professor asks him: "What's your real name?" Considering that many of the Asian International students at Ohio University often take on American names to make it easier for others to say, the professor assumes that Michael has done the same. Instead, the student informs the professor that Michael is his real name, and that he is from Cleveland. The professor has made a common mistake, pre-supposing that because Michael looked differently, he must be from a different country, and therefore a different culture.

There are also many opportunities to experience intercultural communication and hone your skills. One particular opportunity exists with the many international students enrolled in U.S. colleges and universities. Interacting, working, or befriending international students can be an amazing intercultural opportunity. Many international student organizations put on events to share their cultures and want to learn about U.S. culture also. At Ohio University alone, there are approximately 100 countries represented by international students each year. Many colleges want to celebrate their cultural diversity, so international events such as Chinese New Year, the Indian celebration of Diwali, the Japanese Cherry Blossom Festival, or holidays pertaining to the countries represented are celebrated. This gives students a chance to experience other cultures and also reflect on their own.

You can also experience intercultural communication through other avenues. As mentioned earlier, there are cultural differences between different states and within them. Examining one's cultural heritages is another avenue. Sammy Kay's heritage is mostly from the United Kingdom and Germany, and that family culture and traditions would be very different from her friend who has mostly French and Scandinavian heritage. Not only that, but different religions have different cultures. Christians are different from Muslims, who are different from Buddhists, who are different from Hindus. Even within a religion, people from different sects or denominations will have different cultures. Sammy Kay's Catholic roommates are quite different from her Presbyterian family. Through our interpersonal interactions with everyone, we are communicating interculturally. Understanding intercultural communication can help us in our everyday lives, even when communicating with people who we believe to be from the same culture as ourselves.

Intercultural Relationships

Despite popular beliefs, "*intercultural relationships*" are not necessarily more conflicted or problematic than "*intracultural relationships*." It is important to remember that intercultural relationships deal with both cultural similarities and differences. Also, intercultural relationships can be safer spaces for building intimate understandings about other cultures and thus can serve as critical sites for challenging stereotypes.

Take intercultural friendships for example. What the term "*friend*" means and what characterizes friendship differ across cultures. Gareis (2000) examined friendships between German students and their U.S. host families, and found that the differing categorizations of the word "friend" in German and U.S. cultures caused confusion and misunderstanding in their friendships. While cultural differences do affect intercultural relationships, it is equally important for intercultural friends and partners to recognize similarities between them and coconstruct their own relational identities (Lee, 2006). Think about what being a friend means to you. Now what does being a friend mean to some people you are close to?

Due to changing demographics and attitudes, intercultural romantic relationships, such as interracial marriages, are on the rise. The number of interracial heterosexual couples in the United States has increased dramatically in the past decades, growing from 1% in 1970 to 9.5% in 2010. The percentage of interracial unmarried households was as high as 18% in 2010 (U.S. Census Bureau, 2012). On the surface, interracial romantic relationships seem to have become "normal" or "less unusual" over the past 50 years. Discourses such as "race does not matter anymore" or "we do not see color anymore" might further facilitate interracial couplehood. However, this does not mean that interracial romantic partners no longer have to deal with racial and cultural differences. Childs (2005) suggests that interracial relationships, especially Black-White couples, represent "racial transgressions" (p. 4) and expose racial borders, which can reveal problems of race that are otherwise hidden especially to Whites. Interracial relationships often show just how different cultures can be between races, despite being raised in the same geographical location.

Besides friendships and romantic relationships, another important type of intercultural relationships especially for bridging cultural divides is—intercultural alliance. Collier (2002, 2003a) argues that intercultural allies recognize

---

RESEARCH POP-OUT BOX 2

What matters in the development of intercultural friendship?

A colleague and Yea-Wen (Chen & Nakazawa, 2009) are interested in better understanding what factors affect the development of intercultural and interracial friendships. In particular, we wanted to examine how culture might affect self-disclosure patterns in the process of developing intercultural and interracial friendships. We focused on self-disclosure because it has been identified as a key feature of friendship formation and maintenance both in intercultural and intracultural friendships. We understood self-disclosure as the multi-dimensional process of revealing personal information about oneself to another. Thus, we conceptualized and conducted a survey study with 252 participants measuring their (a) cultural orientation (i.e., individualism-collectivism), (b) six topics and five dimensions of self-disclosure patterns (e.g., attitudes and opinions, tastes and interests, positive/negative disclosure, and honesty and accuracy of disclosure), and (c) levels of relational intimacy. Overall, we found that, as relational intimacy increased, all six topics and four of five dimensions of self-disclosure also increased. In other words, closer intercultural and interracial friends self-disclosed more to

each other both in terms of topics and dimensions. We also found that reciprocity in self-disclosure was important in developing intercultural and interracial friendships in that friends tended to mirror each other's self-disclosure patterns. Last but not least, we found that relational intimacy had a greater impact on close intercultural and interracial friendships than cultural orientation (i.e., individualism-collectivism). That is, in close and more intimate intercultural and interracial friendships, cultural differences had less impact or mattered less. One implication from our study is to recognize the important role that developing personal relationships plays in overcoming potential challenges posed by cultural differences in intercultural communication.

Citation: Chen, Y.-W., & Nakazawa, M. (2009). Influences of culture on self-disclosure as relationally situated in intercultural and interracial friendships from a social penetration perspective. *Journal of Intercultural Communication Research, 38*(2), 77–98. doi:10.1080/17475750903395408

their cultural differences and interdependence and emerge when parties (a) recognize power differences and unearned privilege, (b) acknowledge the impact and relevance of history, and (c) use orientations of affirmation. Collier (2003a) states that "there are more ideological forces, institutional policies and practices, and social norms that reinforce hierarchy and elites keeping their privileges in place than there are ideologies, polices, practices and norms encouraging and rewarding intercultural alliances" (p. 14). The collection of essays in *Intercultural Alliances: Critical Transformation* (Collier, 2003b) demonstrates specifically how forces like histories, whiteness ideology, academic institutions, and political policies act to constrain alliance relationships. Hence, it is important to consider not just individual factors but also structural factors in forming intercultural alliance.

Global Workplace

Driving down Main Street and you'll see a McDonalds, Wendy's, Walmart, Kentucky Fried Chicken, and an Apple Store. What city is this? New York? Los Angelos? Tokyo? Berlin? Vienna? Cairo? Today, so many of the corporate businesses are not able to be local or simply to work in one country. Many businesses work between numerous countries and tons of cultures, requiring a need for even the most common employee to be able to work in multicultural settings. Workplaces are moving away from a *monolithic organization*, or one that is predominantly composed of members of the majority group (Cox, 1991; Oetzel, 2008). An example of this would be an organization made up of only White men from rural Ohio, thus resulting in a workplace where the culture of each man is already the same as the others. While there are still many organizations and companies with local cultures like this, on the worldwide scale, many are *plural organizations*, which has a population of employees that is representative of the larger population (Cox, 1991; Oetzel, 2008).

Oetzel (2008) explains that there are four types of organizations in our current world (adapted from Stohl, 2001).

- *Domestic:* Identify with one country and dominant culture
- *Multinational:* Identify with one country while doing business in several countries
- *International:* Identify with two or more countries, each with distinct cultures
- *Global:* Identify with the global system; transcends national boarders

These four types of organizations are seen all over the world, from your hometown, local bakery, to the United Nations. Let us look at one specific well-known corporation: McDonalds. While originally starting in the United States, McDonalds is known worldwide, with restaurants and offices in tons of countries around the world. While continuing to stick with their original menu, with Big Macs and fries, McDonalds is also adopting to the local cultures. With menu items like the McArabia in the Middle East, McCurrywurst in Germany, and Bubur Ayam McD (a type of chicken porridge) in Malaysia, what kind of organization do you believe that McDonalds is?

Dutch psychologist Geert Hofstede (1980) laid out five dimensions that could impact workplace culture, especially in international workplaces with many cultures represented.

1. *Individualism versus Collectivism:* Individualistic cultures tend to value individual identity, personal autonomy, individual rights, and responsibility, while collectivistic cultures tend to focus on the needs, interests, and goals of the group. The dominant culture of the United States as a whole can be understood to embody an individualistic tendency, focusing on what you can do for yourself, and expecting each person to "pick themselves up by the bootstraps." In comparison, cultures such as Asian and Latin American are more concerned with the group as a whole, instead of the individual.

2. *Power Distance:* Different cultures and organizations have different power structures. Ones with larger power distance tend to value a hierarchy with authority and status difference demanded to receive more respect. On the other hand, cultures with lower power distance tend to focus more on equality, and allowing both the authoritative figures and the subordinates to communicate openly and freely with one another. Think about organizations you are involved in. What kind of power distance is there between you and your boss, advisor, or executive board? Do you call your boss, advisor, or executive board by their first or last names? Do you like it that way, or another way?

3. *Uncertainty Avoidance:* Most people fear facing the unknown, and tend to avoid it. Cultural groups differ in their tendencies to avoid, accept, or embrace levels of uncertainty. Simply look at your group of friends. A majority of us have lots of friends that are similar to ourselves: the same race, religion, values, and culture. How often do you approach someone from a different culture to just talk with them? How about to make friends with them? Or work with them?

4. *Masculinity versus Femininity*: Hofstede (2001) compares the ideas of masculine and feminine cultures. According to Hofstede, masculine cultures are ones that tend to emphasize distinct differences in gender roles between men and women, more work-focused, and emphasize results. In contrast, feminine cultures allow gender roles and characteristics to overlap and stress the importance of balancing work/life, community, and environmental issues more than work results.

5. *Confucian Dynamism:* This specific dimension focuses on cultural characteristics of East Asian countries. These characteristics include persistence and long-term orientation to time, the importance of status, thriftiness, and collective face-negotiation strategies.

Along with these five dimensions, these organizations can have stationary locations where employees travel to work, or the newer idea of a virtual workplace. According to Ahuja and Carley (1999), a virtual organization is "a geographically distributed organization whose members are bound by a long term common interest or goal, and who communicate and coordinate their work through information technology"(p. 743). The virtual workplace allows co-workers to live a world away from each other and still work on the same projects. However, as stated before, this can end up polarizing our work organization, hurting the work culture and not allowing workers to get together and truly have these intercultural experiences that help us learn from one another.

With the virtual workplace, we can find numerous organizations teaming up from all over the world to come together to promote social justice causes. Looking specifically at the organization, Kiva, an online organization that brings together people from all over the world to provide loans for others together, a virtual organization is clearly at work here. With six communities that the loan applicants fit into (rural communities, start-ups, green, youth, housing, and transportation), and applicants, and lenders from all over the world, this is truly a global workplace. Kiva brings together people from other cultures to work through cultural differences, and allowing for them to help one another. This trend is becoming more popular, with social justice moving from the local level and further to create global movements with people from all over the world involved. These alliances between people of different cultures helps increase the awareness of what people in other countries need but also how we, as human beings, can work together to help one another. Kiva provides places for exactly this to happen, people from around the world to contribute just a little to help one another. (For more information on Kiva, 2013, visit www.kiva.org.)

While there is a coming together in virtual, online spaces, there are also many places for people to come together in the same geographic location. For students at Ohio University, there is the Global Leadership Center that provides a two-year undergraduate certificate. This provides students with the skills to "serve as internationally-minded, skilled, attuned, professional and experienced leaders in all walks of life" (http://www.ohio.edu/glc/). In a rapidly changing and globalizing world, students are now being prepared even more to work with other cultures in professional settings. This is an amazing opportunity for Ohio University students as they work toward finishing their undergraduate's degrees. These types of skills are applicable with any degree a student gaining the skills to push them over the top for employers. The Global Leadership Center also gives students a chance to learn and hone their skills before they are sent out to test them. Learning the basics in this chapter and from other intercultural classes, students are better prepared to work interculturally than when they first arrived.

Media Messages about Cultural "Strangers"

So much of what we know about other cultures comes from the media. As stated earlier, the media gives us a chance to go from our own living room to another country and culture. For many students before college, we are not given many chances to get to know people from other cultures. Unless you were given the chance to study abroad, host a study abroad student, travel extensively, or live in an incredibly diverse community, few of us have been given the chance to truly connect with another culture. Looking at an international context, we are not always given the chance to travel as extensively as we would like, thus, we rely on the media. We rely on how the news portrays certain countries, how television shows and movies show specific ethnicities, nationalities, and cultures. To show exactly how much the media affects us, we are going to look at a case study with the 2012 Movie of the Year, and three Oscar winning film, *Argo*.

Argo is based on the true story of a rescue mission during the 1979 Iranian Hostage Crisis. Directed by Ben Afflect, who also stars in the film as the lead, Antonio "Tony" Mendez, *Argo* is a secret mission to get into postrevolution Iran to rescue six U.S. Americans who escaped the U.S. embassy and hid with the Canadian Ambassador before they could be taken hostage by Iranian revolutionaries. Mendez hatches a plan to put together a fake movie and go into Iran, claiming to be scouting for film locations, and leave with the six as his film crew. A quick-paced film, full of suspense and thrills as the viewers wonder if they will ever get out alive, while the Iranian revolutionaries quickly begin to close in. After a very dramatic hold up in the airport, and then the revolutionaries driving after the plane that is already started down the runway, the group gets away, returning home to the United States. Ending with mixed emotions, the Canadian Ambassador getting the credit for the six employees' safe return, Mendez forgotten since the mission was classified.

Shortly after the release of *Argo*, the film was praised as a cinematic masterpiece. However, it was also greatly criticized by two specific groups: Latino groups, and the Iranian people and government. Since the film was released, Latino communities criticized Ben Affleck, its director, for casting himself with the lead role, Antonio "Tony" Mendez. The real Mendez is of Mexican ancestry, and many Latino communities, both in and out of Hollywood grew angry at the fact that Affleck did not even audition any Latino actors for the part. Second, the Iranian government and many of its people are upset with the crude and glossed over reality of postrevolution Iran. This goes not only into how the people were portrayed, as villains, but into the simplest parts of the culture, including greetings. Critics state that the film could have fixed these inaccuracies and yet, it did not. With this overview of the issues with *Argo*, we will now start looking more into how this can change our ideas and actions in intercultural communication.

Hollywood and the media as a whole realize that they are providing windows into other worlds that not everyone has a chance to look into. With each part that is filmed, recorded, and sent out to the awaiting public, an agenda is formed, whether consciously or unconsciously. The media does not tell us what to think, but they do tell us what to think about it (Oetzel, 2008). Going back to the film *Argo*, Affleck had a chance to change how Latinos are portrayed in Hollywood. One of the main grievances many Latino critics have is that this was the perfect opportunity to place a Latino actor in a lead role, one that does not make him a gang leader or drug dealer, a gardener or farm worker (Jr, 2013). These are roles that few Latinos get to break out of in Hollywood, and whether Affleck intended to keep *Argo* in that stereotype or not, he did. This simply reassures those who have never met someone of Latino ancestry that they fit the cultural stereotypes of being subservient, lazy, or violent.

Argo also had a chance to portray the reality of the Iranian Hostage Crisis. At the beginning of the film, there is a short animated piece that attempts to explain the backdrop for the Crisis and the Iranian revolution. The explanation is simplistic at best, portraying the United States as an innocent bystander, who simply did what any good country would do: allow another national leader into its boarders to receive cancer treatments. This is a typical Hollywood story of good versus evil. However, this is far from the truth. In the midst of the Cold War, the United States worked to put Iran into the hands of a young king, Resa Shah Pahlavi, instead of letting Iran, and its oil, fall into the hands of the Soviet Union. While Iran flourished under the Shah, there was a large discrepancy with how the wealth was distributed, causing unrest among the young and poor. Along with this, the Shah's personal police cracked down on a traditionalist movement, a group of Muslims who did not want to adopt Western ways, as the Shah was. Eventually, the Shah was forced to flee to Egypt by the protests against him. United States President Jimmy Carter did not allow the Shah into the United States right away, unable to decide whether to help the Shah suppress the revolution, or work with the opposition to ensure a smooth transition. Carter was also distinctly worried about what the revolutionaries would do to the people at the U.S. embassy, something he was right to worry about. Carter allowed the Shah to enter the U.S. when information came of how severe the cancer was, claiming it to be a humanitarian choice (The Iranian Hostage Crisis). This part of history is definitely much more complex than *Argo* leads viewers to believe.

These faux pas go further than simply placing a certain ethnicity into specific jobs but also can define an entire culture and completely misrepresent it.

If we were to believe that Iranians were how *Argo* portrays them, we would believe that all are similar to the revolutionaries. This means that they would all be large, kind of scary looking bearded men who run around everywhere they go, and shout in Farsi at everything. They are a bit trigger happy with the guns that every single one man carries, and if you so much as look at them the wrong way, you are going to end up hanging from a crane with a rope around your neck for everyone to see, or laying on the cement with your brains blown out. Iranians would completely hate the United States. Period. They would be impossible to hold a civilized conversation with, and the only way to work with them is to trick them into getting what you want. This is how *Argo* portrays Iranians. One thing that it does forget is that those who stormed the U.S. Embassy, while in the film it appears to be every single Iranian in the city, was actually a group of students. Not every Iranian hated the United States, and not all of them thought that they American citizens should be killed, or even held hostage. This is inaccurate, but paints a powerful picture. So why is Iran and its people portrayed this way? It is unknown specifically; the reasons could be cognitive, or simply done for more cinematic action. But, it does happen. Why? These portrayals could be blamed on ethnocentrism, which is a belief that one culture is superior to another (discussed later in the chapter) (Bennett, 1993; Oetzel, 2008, p. 98). The fact that it appears that little attention was given to correct portrayal of the Iranians shows exactly how important representing that culture was to the producers and director.

The media is another way we globalize the world. Consider the fact that popular culture is the largest U.S. export and that more than 50% of the revenue for U.S. films is generated from international sales (Sorrells, 2013; Thussu, 2006). This not only means that we are determining how our own culture views these minorities but also how other cultures view each other, and themselves. How would someone who has never met an Iranian believe they acted if their only understanding of the culture and people came from *Argo*? What about someone from outside of the United States? These portrayals formed a distorted view of how an Iranian acts. This is a form of *cultural homogenization*, or the convergence toward common cultural values and practices as a result of *global integration*, and cultural imperialism, the domination of one culture over others through cultural forms such as popular culture, media, and cultural products (Sorrell, 2013). This not only eradicates other cultures but also allows the dominant culture to decide how people should view other cultures. The United States is currently exporting its culture as a commodity, and with it, destroying other cultures.

Of course, not all portrayals of the Stranger have been negative. As Kathryn Sorrells notes in her chapter on media, these others can lead to discussions coming out into the open. When Ellen Degeneres, star of the popular sitcom *Ellen* and current talk show host, came out as a lesbian (both in person and the character she played) in 1997, an international discussion of lesbians and gay men on prime-time TV and the social acceptability of lifestyles that differ from the heterosexual norm ensued (Sorrells, 2013). This continues to happen today. With *Argo* gaining so much criticism, it is opening the field for conversation about how minorities are represented in the media. News programs from CNN to ABC to NBC talked about the disappointment and disapproval of the film from both communities and those who disagree with the way the Cultural Strangers are being portrayed. And, as stated earlier, the media can provide windows into cultures we would have now ability to see into otherwise. Most of us do not have the financial resources or time to travel all over the world and experience each culture to make our own decisions on it. Instead, we

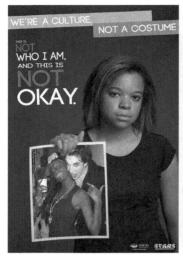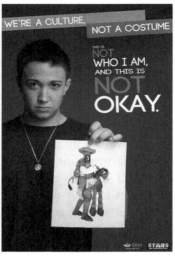

Two examples from the S*T*A*R*S original poster campaign from 2011. From S*T*A*R*S*. Copyright © 2011 by Ohio University. Reprinted by permission.

have to depend on the media to provide those glimpses into those worlds and explain to us what is happening. With the media often taking a U.S. American point of view, it is hard for us to have a truly intercultural experience through these mediated windows.

The media has also become a tool to fight against these stereotypes and half open windows into other cultures. An amazing project that has become nationally recognized was created by Ohio University's S*T*A*R*S (Students Teaching Against Racism in Society). Wanting to bring recognition to problematic Halloween costumes hits home with the Athens community, who hosts a large block party every year for the holiday. College students and Athens citizens come together for fun, but S*T*A*R*S wanted to point out the culturally insensitive costumes, such as geishas, Arabian terrorists, and Native Americans with the huge headdresses. Starting fall of 2011, S*T*A*R*S released their "We're a Culture, not a Costume" campaign. Posters showed Ohio University students of various races and ethnicities holding pictures of insulting costumes. Each poster had the phrase "This is NOT who I am, and this is NOT okay" alongside the photos. S*T*A*R*S has continued to point out stereotypes that plague our society in the following years, putting out new posters every year. This campaign has gone beyond the Athens community and has started a national conversation about how we view others and what is culturally insensitive.

ENGAGING WITH INTERCULTURAL COMMUNICATION

As the world becomes increasing interconnected, learning how to engage with cultural others becomes more and more unavoidable, important, and necessary. To embrace the challenges of opportunities of everyday intercultural communication, we would like to offer some practical concepts and skills in the space below.

Move from Ethnocentrism to Ethnorelativism

One of the first ways to embrace other cultures is to change our perceptions of our own cultures and others. This is often quite difficult, since most of us automatically believe that our culture is the best culture. This is not unusual, with few of us seeing little besides our own culture, and finding it uncomfortable to be a Stranger in another culture. However, this is a very ethnocentric view. **Ethnocentrism** is the view that your group's way of thinking, being, and acting in the world is superior to others (Sumner, 1906). This is a view that was very popular throughout history, often resulting in colonization and the decimation of other cultures. However, in our increasingly globalized world, this is a very dangerous point of view. It is these views that result in dehumanization, legitimization of prejudices, discrimination, conflict, and violence. If we combine these views with power, we can destroy other cultures through imperialism, colonization, oppression, war, and ethnic cleansings (Sorrells, 2013).

According to Milton Bennett (1993), there are three stages of ethnocentrism: denial, defense, and minimization. In the first stage, denial, other cultures are simply not considered in a person's everyday life. Instead, other cultures occur in other places, even if a different cultural display appears right before the person. People in this stage often are isolated from others, or purposely separate themselves from people different from themselves. The second stage, defense, is when a person finds other cultures threatening. This threat makes other cultures more tangible and creates a defense against them. People in this stage view other cultures negatively and their own culture as superior. The last stage of ethnocentrism, minimization, is when people find the similarities between cultures and trivialize the differences. The basic parts of any culture are believed to be the same, such as eating, procreating, and dying, which is not always true. The other part of minimization is when people believe that every human being is the product of an overarching principal, law, or imperative. An example of this is the statement "We are all God's children" (Bennett, 1993).

Ethnocentrism often blinds individuals and groups, resulting in a very narrow view of the world. It results in negative terms and nicknames given to different races, nations, genders, sexualities, and cultures. The narrow views of the world, and the actions and attitudes that come from these ideas, can put a quick end to any attempt for successful intercultural communication (Sorrells, 2013). With how globalized and interconnected our world is, this requires us to have more humble attitudes and an open mind. Instead of being ethnocentric, intercultural communication scholars want to embrace **ethnorelativism**, or using other culture's frame of reference to interpret their behaviors and recognizing they are valid (Ting-Toomey, 1999). "Cultural difference is neither good nor bad, it is just different …. One's own culture is not any more central to reality than any other culture, although it may be preferable to a particular individual or group" (Bennett, 1993, p. 46).

It is difficult to move away from an ethnocentric view, but once done can be maintained frequently. The United States is an often quoted example of ethnocentrism but also ethnorelativism. Citizens of other countries know much more about U.S. politics than U.S. citizens know about other countries. The U.S. rhetoric proclaims the country as the greatest and most powerful nation on Earth (Sorrells, 2013). Without looking critically at these ideas, it is easy for U.S. citizens to become ethnocentric. At the same time, the amount of cultural diversity in the United States can result in an amazing view of ethnorelativism from its citizens.

Making this shift is not something that can be done with the flip of the coin. Instead, the best thing to do is be patient and consistently work toward an ethnorelative frame of mind. Bennett (1993) offers six stages to move away from ethnocentrism and to ethnorelativism.

1. *Acceptance*: This is the first stage to become more ethnorelative. To cross this threshold, one must do two things.

    a. *Respect for Behavior Differences:* This is often easier to understand as verbal and nonverbal cues vary from culture to culture. Language barriers are easier to notice, while our nonverbal cues are subtler. Some people sit very close and like to be in constant contact with one another, while others keep a good distance between themselves while talking. This phase is really stressing recognition of others and not judging others.

    b. *Respect for Value Difference:* What we value is quite different depending on different cultures. Recognizing what other people value and enjoy, along with respecting that makes people more real to us. The best way to learn about values is to talk about them. No matter how much we try, we will not always understand the values other people hold, but we can respect them.

2. *Adaption:* In this phase, new skills are acquired to gain a different worldview, adding onto our other abilities.

    a. *Empathy:* Empathy is "the ability to experience some aspect of reality differently from what is 'given' by one's own culture" (Bennett, 1993). This requires a shift in our frame of reference. Instead of looking at a culture from our own perspective, we look at it from those people's frame of reference.

    b. *Pluralism:* Adopting a pluralistic point of view helps grasp more than just one culture. Pluralism and empathy go hand in hand, to experience and then adopting the view, at least when interacting with people of the same viewpoint. Shifting from your cultural frame to another one is a great way to hone your ethnorelativism.

3. *Integration:* The last phase gives us the ability to move from culture to culture, adapting and integrating into each with flexibility.

    a. *Context Evaluation:* This skill brings about the ability to shift from one context to another. People of different cultures often gather in one place. Flexibility when interacting with different people often helps navigate these areas. Grasping the context to their actions and words will make you much more aware of how to communicate with others.

    b. *Constructive Marginality:* This is the point of ethnorelativism that brings people out of all cultural identities. This is not to say they do not have a cultural identity, but that they can easily and seamlessly go between intercultural situations.

These phases of ethnorelativism are not the end for all for moving away from ethnocentrism. Some people only get to certain points because of their access to other cultures. However, being aware of the steps will help you become a better intercultural communicator and global citizen.

Navigating Culture Shock

If you have ever studied abroad or lived unfamiliar cultural contexts, you will be able to relate to the term **culture shock**. Culture shock is the psychological and emotional reaction people experience when they encounter a culture that is very different from their own (Furnham & Bochner, 1986). This boils down to the new experiences, unfamiliar symbols and actions, and social discourses that are unfamiliar to the traveler, and now surrounding them. This can be very disorienting, especially when in a culture that is completely different from one's own. One thing must be made very clear; however, this is not a negative reaction to traveling abroad for long periods of time. Culture shock is a normal part of traveling abroad, and by being informed, you can combat it.

    Lysggard (1955) breaks down the different stages of culture shock: honeymoon, crisis, recovery, and adjustment. In a quick breakdown, the honeymoon phase is usually when the travelers have first arrived, and are excited and fascinated by the things going on around them. They have positive expectations of their time in that culture, and are able to overlook some of the different parts of the culture. In the second stage, crisis, the fascination begins to wear off and problems between the traveler and the culture begin to arise. This is when the traveler begins to feel alienated, especially with the natives of the culture expecting the traveler to have picked up on their cultural nuances. During this stage is when many travelers get homesick and want to return home. The recovery stage is when the traveler starts to adjust and realize that there are positive parts of the culture and its people again. This is when the traveler can start to laugh at his or her mistakes, and not take criticism to heart, along with starting to really understand the culture. The last stage is adjustment, where the traveler as fully adjusted to the culture, and can mostly pass for a member of the culture. This is where they are truly enjoying the culture they are now a part of.

Gullahorn and Gullahorn (1963) added on two more stages to Lysggard's original five. This goes into the idea of **reverse culture shock**. This is when a member reenters his or her own culture after being in another culture for an extended amount of time. The traveler is first excited to return home, to friends and favorite foods, but once home, begins to see flaws in the native culture. They begin to see how narrow-minded some old friends are, and in return, these friends think that the traveler is "stuck up." The traveler begins to miss the culture he or she has just returned from. Lastly, the traveler is resocialized into his or her home cultures. They begin to remember the positives of their culture, and recognize they were being quick to judge their old friends. There is a recognition that there is no right or wrong in culture, and they simply just function differently. This often means that the traveler is excited to travel abroad again, but is currently content to stay with his or her home culture.

The amount of culture shock experienced by a traveler depends a lot on his or her home culture, the host culture, and the attitude the traveler has. If the home and host culture are similar, it will be easier for the people to adjust. For example, if Charlie, from England, were to travel here, to the United States, or to New Zealand or Australia, he would experience less culture shock since the cultures are similar, in comparison to if he were to travel to Japan, or Saudi Arabia. Traveling to a culture similar to your own means that it will be much easier to assimilate and understand the culture. This will lessen the culture shock that will be felt, although this is not a suggestion to only travel to cultures similar to your own. The level of culture shock also depends on how accepting of outsiders the host culture is. If the people are willing to help newcomers adjust to the culture, and are kinder when correcting and helping with mistakes made by the traveler, the impact of culture shock will be lessened. Culture shock also depends on the attitude of the traveler, if they are willing to acknowledge that they do not know everything, and can accept the criticisms of those from the host culture.

If you Google tips for surviving culture shock, you will find tons of posts from eHow.com, different study abroad blogs, university's international office websites, and travel websites set up to document study abroad trips. "The American Resident" is a website specifically for U.S. citizens who are living overseas, and provides a list of 13 tips to help survive culture shock (13 Tips to Cope with Culture Shock, 2011). Many of these seem rather straightforward, including remembering that everyone gets some sort of culture shock and addressing your basic needs, such as housing, food, specific places, phone numbers, and other key information you need to know. This information includes local laws and traditional business hours (13 Tips to Cope with Culture Shock, 2011). One suggestion they give is to take a tour or two of your new home. This may seem like a very tourist-like action, which many long-term travelers want to avoid. However, tours are a great way for newcomers to acclimate themselves with the city, it is also a good way to learn about some of the history, important places, and a little of the culture. A few other tips are to

- Stay organized
- Find a routine
- Find new favorite hang outs, restaurants, grocery stores, and so on.
- Exercise
- Make your home a safe place to avoid the culture when you need it
- Boost your self-esteem and set goals to meet

The last two tips shared go hand-in-hand, whether moving to a new country, or simply a different part of the United States, share your feelings with others. If you are with other exchange students, or people who are not from the host culture, share with them. These are the people who will understand best what you are feeling through the culture shock. "Try not to talk to people back home because they will worry, and try not to complain to locals because they may not understand" (13 Tips to Cope with Culture Shock, 2011). While you should share with other expats, avoid negative people! If you are around negative people about this new place, they will ruin your experiences and make you miserable. Ashley, a college student, is just starting to understand the positive experiences of Ohio after spending more time with native Ohioans, who actually know the nooks and crannies. Instead of getting to know the people who were natives when she moved here in middle school, she spent all her time with other kids whose parents moved the family to Ohio against their child's desires. This fostered an environment of negativity, and now, 10 years later, she has just recently admitted that there are interesting things to do, the people are not as weird as she first assumed, and that where she has been living is not as bad as she originally thought.

Just remember, be open and remember the wise words from Clifton Fadiman: "When you travel, remember that a foreign country is not designed to make you comfortable. It is designed to make its own people comfortable."

Developing Intercultural Communication Competence

Developing intercultural communication competence is a lifelong process. In essence, we can understand **intercultural communication competence** as "the ability to *effectively* and *appropriately* execute communication behaviors to elicit a desired response in a specific environment" (Chen, 1990, p. 247). This is something that can be started in college and continue throughout your life. The best way to become competent with intercultural communication is to practice. Universities are meccas of culture, with people from all around the world gathering to share ideas and experiences. This is an amazing place to start interacting with people from other cultures.

As stated at the beginning of the chapter, Sammy Kay got involved in the international community at Ohio University during her second year there. As we all do, she stumbled and bumbled around, attempting to create good relationships and work with the other students who have different values, skills, and opinions than her. However, the best way to learn is to try. After three years working with the international community, Sammy Kay is not going to say that she knows how to interact with every culture perfectly every time. She has learned quite a bit about how to listen to people from other cultures and interact with them. She knows she has to be patient, and have an open mind. She has to recognize her friends' cultures, but does not use that as their sole defining feature. She is respectful, and asks questions if she does not understand why they do not like something she did, or if they do something she is not familiar with. Most of all, she treats each one as a human and a friend. In three years, she has learned that it is often the best way to have successful communication practices. Recognizing our differences and similarities, and going beyond them to get to know the person inside, just like we do with any other friend. Sometimes it just takes more time than with friends of the same culture.

Some of the best ways to develop your competence for intercultural communication include listening, respect, and being mindful of power balance. First, being open minded and really hearing what people have to say is important to create a strong connection. Listening can help bring people together and is the best way to learn about another person's culture. Second, respecting one another is incredibly important. These are the same ideas we were taught as children, and it translates easily up into our adulthood. Just because a culture is different does not mean they are wrong. Respecting the culture and the differences between them, even if you do not quite understand them, is very important. Lastly, the power balance, as mentioned earlier, is very important when speaking with someone from a different cultural background. It is important to remember that some cultural groups afford authorities respect and accept the status quo more readily than others. How might such differing value tendencies affect intercultural interactions?

To round off this chapter, Sammy Kay and Yea-Wen have asked some of the Ohio University students who work with different cultural groups to share their advice. What tips and tricks do they have to share with you as budding intercultural communicators? And what do you think about their advice?

- "Respect is the absolute biggest thing to keep in mind when communicating with people from other cultures. Be open-minded, and recognize that even when there are differences in opinion, they do not necessarily have to be a hindering factor in maintaining valuable cross-cultural contact. Even little things, like saying 'That's so weird!' can be construed as disrespectful, so watch how you word things!"—Jessany Middleton, Ohio University Class Freshmen, Undecided Major, from Dayton, Ohio

- "When interacting with a person of another culture, the first barrier I come across is anxiety. This anxiety stems from the realization that this person comes from a culture that is so vastly different that it is quite likely I will embarrass myself by my lack of cultural knowledge. But, when I focus on the first encounter not the fact that this person and I have fundamental differences, but that we have fundamental similarities, the anxiety becomes much more manageable. After the similarities have been established, confronting the differences leads to a much deeper and connected understanding of the individual and the cultural components they bring with him or her."—Elizabeth Forbes, Ohio University Senior, Global Studies Major, from Marietta, Ohio

- "I think the most important thing when talking with someone who has grown up in a different culture is to remember that: things that seem obvious to you will not be obvious to them, and vice-versa. Cultural differences at their most basic form are differences in how people think (or are taught to think) about the world around them. Before judging the behavior of someone from a different culture, you should try to consider the cultural barrier between you. Snap judgments only lead to more misunderstandings. Also, remember that the way you act in intercultural communication will change depending on whether you are in your own country or not. If you are the foreigner, you

CAREER POP-OUT BOX 3

Spotlight on Janet Bennett, PhD, Director of Intercultural Communication Institute (http://www.intercultural.org/) So, what can you do with a degree and expertise in intercultural communication? Dr. Janet Bennett's career offers some answers. Dr. Bennett is not just an academic scholar with a PhD degree specializing in intercultural communication and anthropology but also a trainer, coach, practitioner, consultant, and a public speaker with international reputation and reach. As a scholar, Dr. Bennett has published many journal articles and book chapters on the subjects of developmental "layered" intercultural training and adjustment processes. As a trainer and consultant, Dr. Bennett designs and conducts intercultural competence and diversity training for colleges and universities,

corporations, NGOs, and government and social service agencies. As the Executive Director of the Intercultural Communication Institute that offers professional development opportunities for people working in education, training, business, and consulting, Dr. Bennett offers her visions, insights, and leadership in translating intercultural communication theories and research to inform everyday intercultural practices. Not surprisingly, one of the perks that come with being an interculturalist are opportunities to travel in and experience different cultures. Dr. Bennett often receives invitations to offer workshops and/or serve as keynote speakers for various occasions and conferences on cultural diversity and international training and education both in the United States and around the world.

should do your best to follow the general rules of the host culture (while still maintaining your own personality, of course). If YOU are the host, you have the advantage of your norms being the ones that get used. But be respectful and understanding, because some rules seem so obvious to us and they are never explained to outsiders."—Amanda Tragert, Ohio University Senior, Global Studies and German Major, from Athens, Ohio

- "Do not talk to them like they are dumb. Speak slowly but not so slow to act in a way that is degrading to their intelligence. Once spoken and they do not understand, then maybe it is appropriate to slow it down more. Be concise and to the point. Do not use too many hand gestures. Using them [hand gestures] every other word is insulting. Smile and have patience with language barriers."—Aaron Comstock, Ohio University Graduate Student, Music Education, from Baltimore, Ohio

REFERENCES

13 Tips to Cope with Culture Shock. (2011, October 6). Retrieved from The American Resident: http://www.theamericanresident.com/2011/10/13-tips-to-cope-with-culture-shock/

About Us. (2014). Retrieved from Kiva: http://www.kiva.org/about

Adler, P.S. (1975). The transition experience: An alternative view of culture shock. *Journal of Humanistic Psychology, 15,* 13–23.

Ahuja, M.K. & Carley, K.M. (1999). Network structure in virtual organizations. *Journal of Computer-Mediate Communication, 3,* 1–35.

Barna, L. M. (1998). Stumbling blocks in intercultural communication. In M. J. Bennett (Eds.), *Basic concepts of intercultural communication* (pp. 173–189). Yarmouth, ME: Intercultural Press.

Bennett, M. J. (1993). Towards ethnorelativism: A developmental model of intercultural sensitivity. In R. M. Paige (Eds.), *Education for the intercultural experience* (2nd ed., pp. 21–71). Yarmouth, ME: Intercultural Press.

Brown, P. & Levinson, S. (1987). *Politeness: Some universals in language use.* Cambridge, MA: Cambridge University Press.

Carbaugh, D. (2002). "I can't do that" but "I can actually see around corners": American In dain students and the study of public "communication." In J. N. Martin, T. K. Nakayama, & L. A. Flores (Eds.), *Readings in intercultural communication: Experiences and contexts* (2nd ed., pp. 138–149). Boston, MA: McGraw-Hill.

Chen, G.-M. (1990). Intercultural communication competence: Some perspectives of research. *The Howard Journal of Communication, 2*(3), 243–261.

Chen, G.-M. & Ma, R. (2001). *Chinese conflict management and resolution.* Stamford, CT: Ablex.

Childs, E. C. (2005). *Navigating interracial borders: Black-White couples and their social worlds.* New Brunswick, NJ: Rutgers University Press.

Collier, M. J. (1998). Researching cultural identity: Reconciling interpretive and post-colonial perspectives. In D. V. Tanno & A. Gonzales (Eds.), *Communication and identity across cultures, International and Intercultural Communication Annual, XXI* (pp. 122–147). Thousand Oaks, CA: Sage.

Collier, M. J. (2002). Intercultural friendships as interpersonal alliances. In J. N. Martin, T. K. Nakayama & L. A. Flores (Eds.), *Readings in intercultural communication: Experiences and contexts* (2nd ed., pp. 301–310). Boston, MA: McGraw Hill.

Collier, M. J. (2003a). Negotiating intercultural alliance relationships: Toward Transformation. In M. J. Collier (Ed.), *Intercultural alliances: Critical transformation* (Vol. 25, pp. 1–16). Thousand Oaks, CA: Sage.

Collier, M. J. (2003b). *Intercultural alliances : Critical transformation.* Thousand Oaks, CA: Sage.

Collier, M. J. & Thomas, M. (1988). Identity in intercultural communication: An interpretive perspective. In Y. Y. Kim & W. B. Gudykunst (Eds.), *Theories of intercultural communication, International and Intercultural Communication Annual, XII* (pp. 99–120). Newbury Park, CA: Sage.

Condon, J. C. & Yousef, F. (1975). *An introduction to intercultural communication.* New York, NY: Macmillan.

Cox, T.H. (1991). The multicultural organization. *The Executive, 5,* 34–47.

Furnham, A. & Bochner, S. (1986). *Culture shock: Psychological reactions to unfamiliar environments.* New York, NY: Methuen.

Gareis, E. (2000). Intercultural friendship: Five cases studies of German students in the USA. *Journal of Intercultural Studies, 21,* 67–91.

Global Leadership Center. (n.d.). Retrieved from Ohio University: http://www.ohio.edu/glc/

Hall, E. T. (1959). *The silent language.* New York, NY: Doubleday.

Hart, (2005). Franz Boas and the roots of intercultural communication research. In W. J. Starosta & G.-M. Chen (Eds.), *Taking stock in intercultural communication: Where to now?* (pp. 176–193). Washington, DC: National Communication Association.

Hofstede, G. (1980). *Culture's consequences: International differences in work-related values.* Beverly Hills, CA: Sage.

Hofstede, G. (1991). *Cultures and organizations: Software of the mind.* Maidenhead, UK: McGraw-Hill.

Hofstede, G. (2001). *Culture's consequences: Comparing values, behaviors, institutions, and organizations across nations* (2nd ed.). Thousand Oaks, CA: Sage.

Jr, R. N. (2013, January 10). Latino should have played lead in 'Argo'. *CNN.* http://www.cnn.com/2013/01/09/opinion/navarrette-argo-affleck-latino/.

Kiva. (2013). Retrieved from Kiva: www.kiva.org

Kluckhohn, C. & Kroeber, A. (1952). *Culture: A critical review of concepts and definitions.* Cambridge, MA: Harvard University Peabody Museum of American Archeology and Ethnology Papers 47.

Lee, P.-W. (2006). Bridging cultures: Understanding the construction of relational identity in intercultural friendship. *Journal of Intercultural Communication Research, 35,* 3–22.

Leeds-Hurwitz, W. (1990). Notes in the history of intercultural communication: The Foreign Service Institute and the mandate for intercultural training. *Quarterly Journal of Speech, 76,* 262–281.

Lysgaard, S. (1995). Adjustment in a foreign society: Norwegian Fulbright grantees visiting the United States. *International Social Science Bulletin, 7,* 45–51.

Martin, J. N., Nakayama, T. K., & Flores, L. A. (2002). A dialectical approach to intercultural communication. In J. N. Martin, T. Nakayama & L. A. Flores (Eds.), *Readings in intercultural communication: Experiences and contexts* (2nd ed., pp. 3–13). Boston, MA: McGraw Hill.

Nakayama, T. K. & Halualani, R. T. (Eds.), *The handbook of critical intercultural communication*. New York, NY: Blackwell.

Oetzel, J. G. (2008). *Intercultural communication: A layered approach*. New York, NY: Pearson Education/ VangoBooks.

Oetzel, J. G. & Ting-Toomey, S. (2003). Face concerns in interpersonal conflict: A cross-cultural empirical test of the face-negotiation theory. *Communication Research, 30*, 599–624.

Philipsen, G., Coutu, L. M., & Covarrubias, P. (2005). Speech codes theory: Restatement, revisions, and response to criticisms. In W. Gudykunst (Ed.), *Theorizing about intercultural communication* (pp. 55–68). Thousand Oaks, CA: Sage.

Pondy, L. R. (1967). Organizational conflict: Concepts and models. *Administrative Science Quarterly, 12*, 296–320.

Poster Campaign. (2013). Retrieved from S*T*A*R*S: http://www.ohio.edu/orgs/stars/Poster_Campaign.html

Robertson, R. (1992). *Globalization: Social theory and global culture*. London: Sage.

Rogers, E. M. (1999). Georg Simmel's concept of the stranger and intercultural communication research. *Communication Theory, 9*(1), 58–74.

Rogers, E. M. & Hart, W. B. (2002). The histories of intercultural, international, and development communication. In W. B. Gudykunst & B. Mody (Eds.), *The handbook of international and intercultural communication* (2nd ed., pp. 1–23). Thousand Oaks, CA: Sage.

Rogers, E. M. & Steinfatt, T. M. (1999). *Intercultural communication*. Prospect Heights, IL: Waveland Press.

Sorrells, K. (2010). Re-imagining intercultural communication in the context of globalization. In T.K. Nakayama & R.T. Halualani (Eds.), *The handbook of critical intercultural communication* (pp. 171–189). New York, NY: Blackwell.

Sorrells, K. (2013). *Intercultural communication: Globalization and social justice*. Los Angeles, CA: Sage.

Sumner, W. G. (1906). *Folkways: A study of the sociological importance of usages, manners, customs, mores, and morals* (p. 12). Boston, MA: Gin and Company, 1906.

The Iranian Hostage Crisis. (n.d.). Retrieved from PBS: American Experience: http://www.pbs.org/wgbh/ americanexperience/features/general-article/carter-hostage-crisis/

Thussu, D.K. (2006). *International communication* (3rd ed.). London, England: Hodder Arnold.

Ting-Toomey, S. (1999). *Communicating across cultures*. New York, NY: Guilford.

Ting-Toomey, S. (2005). Identity negotiation theory: Crossing cultural boundaries In W. B. Gudykunst (Ed.), *Theorizing about intercultural communication* (pp. 211–233). Thousand Oaks, CA: Sage.

Yep, G. A. (2002). My three cultures: Navigating the multicultural identity landscape. In J. N. Martin, T. Nakayama & L. A. Flores (Eds.), *Readings in intercultural communication: Experiences and contexts* (2nd ed., pp. 60–66). Boston, MA: McGraw Hill.

Yep, G. A. (2004). Approaches to cultural identity: Personal notes from an autoethnographical journey. In M. Fong & R. Chuang (Eds.), *Communicating ethnic and cultural identity* (pp. 69–81). Lanham, MD: Rowman & Littlefield Publishers.

15

Health Communication

*Tomeka Robinson, Cody Clemens, Danny Valdez,
& Vincent Hendershot*

KEY WORDS

Health
Health communication
Health belief model
Biomedical model
Biopsychosocial model
Patient empowerment
Managed care
Health Maintenance
  Organizations (HMOs)
Preferred Provider
  Organizations (PPOs)
Health Savings Account
Public health
Health promotion
Health promoters

LEARNING OBJECTIVES

After reading this chapter, you should be able to:

- Develop a general understanding of health communication as an area of inquiry
- Identify the general health communication theories
- Understand the nature of health communication and current issues within the field
- Appreciate the importance of health communication within public health contexts
- Identify some challenges and opportunities within the field

BACKGROUND ON THE STUDY OF HEALTH COMMUNICATION

Defining Health Communication

You are sitting in a waiting room patiently waiting for your turn with your new physician. You are anxious wondering what questions you should ask, how much will the visit cost, can you appropriately describe your issue, what will the perception be of you? When the nurse calls your name, you take a deep breath, go in and hope for the best.

Narratives like this are not uncommon in health care settings. You may have experienced similar feelings when visiting your local physician. The doctor–patient interaction falls within the domain of health communication. But health communication does not start and end with the doctor's office. Health communication is a part of everyday life. Everything from viewing our favorite television medical dramas to the family remedies espoused by our grandparents, our ideas and perceptions about health and wellness are shaped by many factors. These factors include, but are not limited to, health care professionals, family members, friends, and advertisements. We also influence the people around us with our own health beliefs and behaviors.

Health communication is a two-way interdependent process. The sharing of information and the construction of meaning flows from both the sender and the receiver. While most believe that health communication only involves health professionals like doctors and nurses, patients are actively involved in the interaction. Patients bring their own ideas, experiences, and biases into the health care setting and thus contribute to the message construction.

Another reason that health communication is interdependent is that health itself is interdependent. According to the World Health Organization (WHO), **health** is defined as "a state of complete physical, mental, and social well-being, and not merely the absence of disease or infirmity" (WHO, 1948). This definition highlights that health involves more than just a physical condition. Health involves emotions, interpersonal relationships, and physical ability. Moreover, the Centers for Disease Control (CDC) define **health communication** as "the study and use of communication strategies to inform and influence individual decisions that enhance health" (CDC, 2013). The field of health communication began through the work of social science scholars that started to examine communication variables in health care settings (Bandura, 1969; Feldman, 1966; Zola, 1966). This prompted communication scholars to delve deeper into this phenomenon and develop a field that has a rich and varied literature (Kreps, Bonaguro, & Query, 1998).

Health a state of complete physical, mental, and social well-being and not merely the absence of disease or infirmity.

Health communication the study and use of communication strategies to inform and influence individual decisions that enhance health.

WHY STUDY HEALTH COMMUNICATION?

Now that we understand that basic meaning of health communication, it is important to ask ourselves why we study this topic as a component of broader and more comprehensive communication studies. Health communication is a fascinating subject that is both dynamic and complex. It is one of the fastest growing areas of communication research and the demand for health communication scholars extends beyond academic settings. Given the many different components of health communication, it is not surprising to see the relevancy of the subject in areas such as interpersonal, organizational, and societal communication arenas.

Interpersonal Factors

First, one of the most basic human rights is access to good healthcare. The underlying logic is that we will inevitably fall ill one day and require the professional expertise of someone within a healthcare system. Unfortunately, not everyone in the world has access to a good healthcare system; but everyone in the world should have access to the information needed to promote and uphold a good doctor–patient relationship. Simply put, one of the reasons we study health communication is to advocate the development of interpersonal relationships between health professionals and the lay public. For example, we have an elderly woman who is beginning to exhibit symptoms of an undi-agnosed illness. She can either: (1) choose to go and see a doctor or (2) refuse a doctor and instead rely on self-medicating until her symptoms subside. Though the wiser decision seems more obvious. More often than not, a man or woman will opt to self-medicate over seeing a doctor because they do not understand their rights as patients within a broader healthcare system. If we study these interpersonal relationships, then we can better understand patterns or trends that can lead toward the development of strategies, or even policies, that better explain or educate the public about their rights and access to good healthcare.

Organizational Factors

Back to our patient example—the woman is finally convinced that she needs to see a doctor. Having understood her rights as a patient and having full faith in the healthcare staff, she books an appointment for the following day. Not long after she arrives at the doctor's office, however, she is faced with another roadblock. When asked about her insurance policy, she doesn't know what to answer. More often than not, many do not understand or know the deeper orga-nizational technicalities that exist in health systems, which harms both access to healthcare and good relationships between the healthcare structure and patients. The organizational development within health systems is another area of health communication research and one that we will go deeper into later.

Societal Factors

The fascinating thing about health communication is that it is not limited to our patient example. Everyone in the world, at one point, will require the services of the doctor. One thing that is completely universal in our society is our interdependence on health. Our society in the United States is dynamic and changing. Everyday new trends emerge, new marketing strategies are formulated, health campaigns are shaped, and so on. While health is univer-sal, what is different are the cultural dynamics we use to seek those health systems. Societies around the world are just as dynamic as the United States and have their own unique sets of cultural dispositions to attain health. The problem, however, is that we oftentimes do not understand them because of our own barriers. As communication scholars it is our job to keep abreast of those trends and help overcome societal barriers. Though health is universal, an overwhelming disparity exists regarding access.

HEALTH COMMUNICATION THEORIES

Regardless of where you are from, you are inevitably going to get sick. The spread of disease is something that medical professionals in the field do their best to treat and prevent. Health communication researchers and theorists have been studying the ways that medical professionals communicate through examining, diagnosing, and treating all types of disease. In doing so, several theories and models to explain the ways medical professionals communicate with patients to handle diseases have been developed. It has also been their mission to educate and promote their observed practices to medical profes-sionals and patients across the globe.

You may not realize it yet, but influencing and persuading someone to believe that an unhealthy action they are participating in is unhealthy is a very powerful concept; this model is known as the *health belief model*. If you look at medicine and health with the approach of, I have a disease, this is what caused it, now as my medical doctor I need you to fix me, believe it or not; you are following the *biomedical model*. Finally, if you are a person that believes one must acknowledge and respect a variety of factors, such as physical and mental health, as well as, social interaction and emotion, in order to get better from a disease or to stay healthy; you are more in line with the *biopsychosocial model*. Health communication professionals want medical professionals and patients to understand that the holistic concept of health and the way in which we communicate are not mutually exclusive. In the following paragraphs, the health belief model, the biomedical model, and the biopsychosocial model are discussed.

The Health Belief Model

Health belief model a theory that proposes five primary considerations based on people's behavioral choices and the likelihood they will be motivated to change their behaviors.

The **health belief model** is utilized to communicate, educate, and promote healthy behavior to audiences through organized health campaigns (Kohler, Grimly, & Reynolds, 1999). The health belief model proposes five primary considerations based on people's behavioral choices and the likelihood they will be motivated to change their behaviors (Rosenstock, 1960; Stretcher & Rosenstock, 1997). The five primary considerations are: (1) if people do not change their unhealthy behaviors, they will be negatively affected, (2) the unfavorable effects will be substantial, (3) in order to prevent an unwanted outcome, one must participate in an effective behavior change, (4) investing in prevention behavior, with both time and money, is in fact valuable, and (5) people are motivated to act through an inspirational or awakening experience; such as a motivational speaker, a form of incentive, or a tragic accident (Rosenstock, 1960; Stretcher & Rosenstock, 1997). Thus, in order for a person to believe they need to change an unhealthy behavior, they must be motivated by a life-changing moment, unfavorable experience, or they must be able to see that the benefits outweigh the costs.

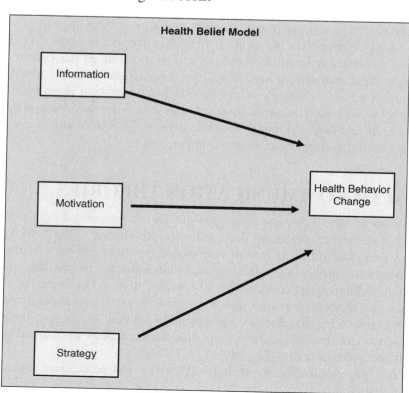

When developing an effective health campaign, it is essential that facts and statistics that will appeal to the target audience be provided. The health belief model enforces that people are motivated and persuaded to act through action cues. Researching the wants and needs of target audiences and catering to those wants and needs are how effective health communication occurs. People are not just going to change unhealthy habits just because a health professional tells them their behaviors are unhealthy. The campaign message needs to be effective and it must have a purpose in order to get the message across to the target audiences. When appropriate facts and statistics can be coupled with an inspirational story to motivate the target audience, people participating in unhealthy behaviors will be more likely to change their unhealthy behaviors to healthy ones. Educating and encouraging a person to believe in how beneficial participating in healthy behaviors can be, is a very powerful cure for disease.

Biomedical Model

The **biomedical model** is adopted when a person thinks of health and disease as something that is grounded solely in biochemistry and something that can only be cured through modern medicine and technology (Kleinman, 1980; Roter & Hall, 1993). This model is based on Western medicine and it is often criticized for being exclusively pathology oriented instead of being preventative oriented (Schreiber, 2005). Biomedicine has also been critiqued as being an inadequate tool when it comes to the doctor understanding the whole patient; meaning past patient experiences, patient medical history, and the questions they may have about their own health are ignored (Kolb, 1979). The biomedical model does not see the interpersonal relationship as being vital to care. Instead, the curing of the disease is the number one priority (Schreiber, 2005). Fixing the disease is not a bad thing, but when it comes to doctor–patient relationships; the biomedical model is often utilized to describe doctor-powerful or authoritarian relationships (Schreiber, 2005).

> **Biomedical model** a theory that focuses on health and disease as something that is grounded solely in biochemistry and something that can only be cured through modern medicine and technology.

The biomedical model can be an effective model in most cases when it comes to fixing disease and understanding what is wrong with the human body. In some cases though, the doctor looks at fixing the patient in a very step-by-step procedure instead of taking the time to understand the "whole patient" and develop a solid relationship with their patient. For example, if a patient has flu-like symptoms, the doctor may ask simple questions like: "When did the symptoms start to occur?" "Where does it hurt the most?" "Has it gotten better or worse since you first started to feel sick?" With this model, doctors ask questions that merely require a short answer response (i.e., "Yesterday." "My Head." "Worse.") Doctors do not always give patients the ability to have an open conversation with them in order to get to the bottom of the problem at hand, instead they only tend to worry about fixing the obvious problem in the moment, when in turn it could potentially be something much more serious (Roter, Stewart, et al., 1997). Health communication researchers are attempting to shift from this model to a more holistic approach.

Biopychosocial Model

The **biopsychosocial model** is a theory that involves a variety of aspects when looking at health wellness. With this model, not only are biological factors examined but also psychological, cognitive, and social aspects of a person are all taken into consideration (Engel, 1977). This model encourages doctors to take the time to appreciate and understand all aspects of a

> **Biopsychosocial model** a theory that involves a biological, psychological, cognitive, and social aspects when looking at health wellness.

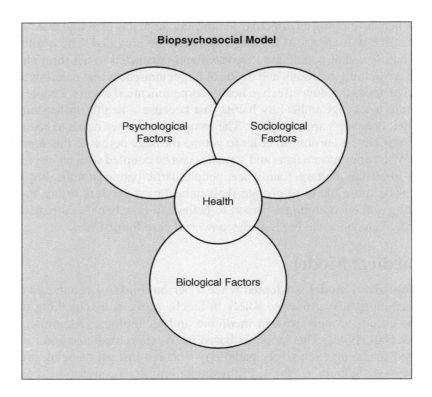

patient's life. The biomedical model, while effective in some ways, is lacking in a few crucial areas. The biopsychosocial model attempts to fill those gaps (Hewa & Hetherington, 1995). According to Tyreman (2006), health is not an isolated phenomenon, but it takes into consideration a person's emotions, relationships, and environment. The popularity of the biopsychosocial model in the world of health communication and medicine has been growing because it encourages doctors to develop relationships with their patients and to ask about and examine their social and psychological interactions.

CURRENT ISSUES IN HEALTH COMMUNICATION

There are two primary areas of inquiry within the field of health communication: health delivery and health promotion (Kreps, Bonaguro, & Query, 1998). The first area, health delivery, focuses on the influence of communication on the delivery of health care. Within this area, scholars address issues of doctor–patient interactions, health care decision-making, and health care teams. The second area, health promotion, centers on the development, implementation, and evaluation of health campaigns to promote public health and safety.

The following sections highlight some of the current areas of inquiry within the field.

Doctor–Patient Relationships

Within our modern society, our growing need for effective and efficient healthcare is clear. One way that scholars within the field attempt to contribute to fulfilling these needs is by analyzing the doctor–patient interaction. You may ask why is it beneficial to research these interactions and how is health communication-based research beneficial to me? Health communication scholars have utilized observant and participant observation to support how patient autonomy influences the delivery, diagnosis, and treatment within healthcare. In order to increase patient autonomy and make this interaction valuable, it's essential for patients to have an understanding of the dynamics between the health-care professional and their role in health care. In this section, we will discuss how power relationships, patient empowerment, common perceptions, and how treating the disease rather than the patient shape how we perceive our own health and how patient–doctor dialogue affects the delivery and function of healthcare.

According to Hassan, McCabe, and Priebe (2007), patients are less likely to have symptom burdens if there is a healthy doctor–patient relationship. The healthier the communication relationship is with the doctor and patient, the better the chance the doctor has on making a confident and concise decision on a treatment plan. When the doctors and patients do not have a healthy communication channel, there is a possibility that the patients will feel uncomfortable and not be completely honest with their doctor. Therefore, developing effective doctor–patient communication is essential.

Power Relationships   From our busy schedules at work to our quick trips to the grocery store, we are accustomed to a lifestyle that focuses on the duration of our tasks, rather than the effectiveness. With this fast pace mentality, the 15 minutes interacting with your doctor can define the balance of power with all health decisions. In the doctor's office, who has the power to define our health, which is right or wrong, and who really decides whether a treatment is appropriate? When we have a health issue we tend to seek a professional and this resource provides us with an abundance of knowledge. The amount of knowledge the patient has can affect the likelihood of adopting healing modes of action. Ultimately, you have the choice whether to follow the doctor's instructions, therefore, you have the ability as a patient to pose questions, research prescribed medicine, and request additional information to ensure the best possible healing method is utilized.

Patient Empowerment   **Patient empowerment** means that patients have considerable influence in medical matters (Hardey, 2008). Patients have the ability to decide whether to adopt the requested behaviors and the doctor has a responsibility to explain them. The health professional has the obligation to target the problem, define the issue, and provide a solution. Typically, the patient abides by the doctor's request without seeking additional information about the issue and the provided solution. With this imbalance of power and imbalance of personal responsibility, it is often difficult to distinguish who exactly has control over your health. In order to ensure that you are receiving the best possible health outcome and that it's tailored to your personal beliefs and traditions, being an active patient will be beneficial for both parties. Active patients pose questions about holistic and modern healing methods, more affordable medicines, insurance plans, general information about their doctor, and so on. Asking questions allows for increased patient autonomy. Although this may require a significant amount of research and patience, this relationship will thrive based on the increase of trust, knowledge, and empowerment from both the patient and the doctor.

It may seem that finding a doctor that values your socioeconomic status, spiritual beliefs, demographics, and so on is time consuming and requires a lot of effort, and you are right. When choosing a health professional that meets your needs and your requests, it is essential to research and consider the doctor

> **Patient empowerment**
> the ability for patients to
> be more active in health
> encounters.

and the influential role they have in our society. A doctor should be educated and be aware of not only the biological aspect of the patient but also know the traditions, values, and beliefs of the patient. The short interactions doctors have with their patients are crucial and being an active patient will ensure your health professional is aware of your desires. With the combination of doctors healing the patient rather than the disease and the patient being knowledgeable about the demand for doctors, this should permit better doctor–patient communication.

Culture and Health Communication

In recent years, due to the progression and expansion of medical schools, focus on eliminating health disparities, and improving the quality of health care, the study of culture has been a prevalent topic in resolving and improving our health. The concept of culture in regards to health communication can be defined as the structure of the communicative framework in which individuals define their values, beliefs, and modes of action (Dutta, 2006). Due to the increase of health coverage and increase of transnational trade, the demand for culturally sensitive education and understanding within hospitals and health promotion campaigns is necessary. In a society that is so diverse being able to successfully communicate health messages through a culturally centered approach will increase the awareness of how health, disease, and illness are perceived. One way to deal with these changes is the culture-centered approach. The culture-centered approach is an emerging approach to health communication questions the social constructs of culture in traditional health communication theories and applications (Dutta, 2006) You may ask, how would approaching health through a culturally sensitive lens increase my understanding of my health? It actually makes a big difference.

With the increase of diversity within businesses, health organizations, and society in general, identifying how we develop our opinions and share health information will increase patient satisfaction and increase patient autonomy. In order to increase patient autonomy and patient empowerment, being conscious of the levels of acculturation and assimilation of multicultural populations can help doctors adjust to various cultural values. As our melting pot continues to grow within the United States, being culturally competent will enable health promoters to provide effective health communication efforts that can eliminate cultural barriers and promote healthy and informative messages. Think about a time you went to the doctor, have you ever observed how culture influenced your ability to ask questions/clarification based on access and structure? Did your cultural background come up at all? Frequently, patients tend to frame their perceptions of illness based on the context in which they feel included rather than excluded. The study of culture, however, can help to element these cultural barriers (Dutta, 2006).

The focus to eliminate health disparities and eliminate marginalized communities in recent years was launched to ensure we have not only a happy nation but also a healthy one. Health communication scholars have shifted their focus from healing the patient rather than just healing the disease. With a strong focus on culture, doctors have the ability to appeal to the patient's personality style, their perceived susceptibility, perceived threat, and the context in which they are in will determine the type of supporting mechanism for the patient (Du Pré, 2010). At this point, you may be feeling that culture embodies a large magnitude of principles and seems challenging to appeal to each party, and you're right. The influence of culture on health is undeniable and health communication scholars are seeking to understand this relationship more.

Health Organizations

Health care in today's society is a growing field for a variety of reasons, but one of the major ones is that managing the health care system is becoming more and more complex; not only in the United States but also across the globe. **Managed care** can be defined as, an arrangement where insurance companies accept the risk for providing a defined set of health services through using a specific set of providers for a defined population, as well as, for a fixed or regular per capita payment (Davidson, Sofaer, & Gertler, 1992). Managed care organizations are what organizes the way that the health care system operates, all of the expenses that come with health care, and the culture of the organization (Du Pré, 2010). Within the managed care organization umbrella, there are a variety of options that the consumer can choose from when deciding to manage their care. The following paragraphs will go more in depth at some of those options and the frequently used terms within health organizations.

Managed care
an arrangement where insurance companies accept the risk for providing a defined set of health services through using a specific set of providers for a defined population, as well as, for a fixed or regular per capita payment.

Health Maintenance Organizations   A **Health Maintenance Organizations** or **HMOs** are extremely popular in today's society because they are known to be a "one-stop shop" when it comes to managing health care organizations (Du Pré, 2010). According to the Henry J. Kaiser Family Foundation and Health Research and Educational Trust (2011), there are approximately 70,239,338 people enrolled in HMOs in United States currently. The way a HMO works is the organization hires physicians and other medical care providers to work directly for the HMO and those worker's salaries are covered specifically by premiums the HMO members pay monthly (Du Pré, 2010). Premiums are paid by HMO members in order to offset the costs of managed care plans. Premiums are often taken out of a subscriber's paycheck from the organization for which they work (Du Pré, 2010). Along with the premium taken out of the subscriber's paycheck every month, there is also a copay required by the subscriber every time they go to the doctor (Du Pré, 2010). A copay can range anywhere from $0 to $50 and must be paid at every visit. Having a health maintenance organization is an effective way to manage care, but as with every system it has its positives and negatives depending on the person and family.

Health Maintenance Organizations (HMOs)
organization hires physicians and other medical care providers to work directly for the HMO and those worker's salaries are covered specifically by premiums the HMO members pay monthly.

Preferred Provider Organizations   **Preferred Provider Organizations** or **PPOs** are still under the managed care organization umbrella, but they operate a little differently than the HMOs. PPOs like HMOs still have a monthly premium that the subscriber has to pay every month, but unlike the HMO, the subscriber may also have a deductible (Du Pré, 2010). What this means is that instead of a copay every time they visit the doctor, they have to pay a

Preferred Provider Organizations (PPOs)
organizations that have a monthly premium that the subscriber has to pay every month and subscriber may have a deductible.

QUICK GUIDE TO HEALTH ORGANIZATIONS

Health Maintenance Organizations or **HMO's** the organization hires physicians and other medical care providers to work directly for the HMO and those worker's salaries are covered specifically by premiums the HMO members pay monthly

Preferred Provider Organizations or **PPOs** PPOs like HMOs still have a monthly premium that the subscriber

has to pay every month, but unlike the HMO, subscriber may have a **deductible**

Health Savings Account or **HAS** tax-exempt savings plans that people have the opportunity to set aside money specifically for health care purposes

percentage of the medical bill (Du Pré, 2010). PPOs unlike HMOs give the subscriber the option to contract with independent care providers (Du Pré, 2010). HMOs rely heavily on the doctors and medical organizations that they hire directly and their subscribers are only able to use those specific hired doctors and organizations (Du Pré, 2010). Whereas PPOs have the opportunity to pick and choose who they would like to receive their care from, as well as, take advantage of all of the discounted rates provided for PPO subscribers (Du Pré, 2010). Another thing that is unique with PPOs is that the subscriber has a discounted rate, which means that they pay a different amount depending on what type of services provided. PPOs and HMOs are the two most popular options for managing health care; each one has their pros and cons. If you are unsatisfied with the two most popular options, you do have other options when trying to manage health care.

Health Savings Account
tax-exempt savings plans that people have the opportunity to set aside money specifically for health care purposes.

Health Savings Accounts   A popular option to manage care for younger people with few health problems is a **Health Savings Account** or **HSA.** HSAs are tax-exempt savings plans that people have the opportunity to set aside money specifically for health care purposes (Du Pré, 2010). These savings accounts are very similar to an IRA, but they are solely designed for health care. In the United States, as long as you are a tax-payer and a part of a high deductible health plan, you qualify to set up and utilize a HSA (Du Pré, 2010). You are able to utilize the funds in a HSA for several years, as they do not expire annually. Regardless of which managed health care plan you choose, as an individual, you have to pick which one is best for you and your family.

Public Health

Public health the science of protecting and improving the health of families and communities through promotion of healthy lifestyles, research for disease and injury prevention, and detection and control of infectious diseases.

Another area that health communicators are focused on is that of public health. According to the Center for Disease Control (CDC), **public health** "the science of protecting and improving the health of families and communities through promotion of healthy lifestyles, research for disease and injury prevention and detection and control of infectious diseases" (CDC Foundation, 2013). The scope of public health is very broad and attempts to encompass everyone through continuous interactions from health promoters, health educators, healthcare workers, and any others with vested interest in community wellness. But to get a better understanding of public health, let's examine each component of the definition in context.

Health promotion the process of enabling people to increase control over and to improve their health.

Health promoters people who are actively involved in the process of creating and distributing health promotion messages.

Promotion of Healthy Lifestyles   Over the course of several years, the perspective of public health has changed greatly. As recent as 2001, the concept of public health was viewed almost solely as a prevention science that was concerned with researching first, then treating chronic and communicable diseases through intense preventative education measures. As trends and ideologies changed, so did the perception of what good public health should be. Today, public health is not viewed as a prevention science, but as a holistic science, which refers to the "maximizing of human potential through positive life choices" (Myers, 2011). The holistic model of public health is of great importance to communication scholars because it takes into account the complexities of human interaction. Public health and holistic wellness examine trends within the social sphere to find likes and interests of the population. From the information that is gathered, it becomes easier to create health campaigns and health programs that directly relate to the individual; which, in theory, makes the program easier to adhere to.

Research of Diseases and Injury Prevention   In order to promote public health and create the health-specific directives and programs, it is important to know the science of what we are trying to promote. The second component of public health is the continuous and ongoing anatomical and biological research about specific health conditions. Behind the flashy curtain of public health promotion, scientists are working around the clock to understand, prevent and treat new and emerging diseases and other health related conditions. Without this very crucial research, there is no basis for ANY health program to exist. For example, if it weren't for the preexisting hard evidence that tobacco causes cancer, then it is likely that tobacco consumption would be much higher because (1) no one said tobacco is bad, and (2) without the hard evidence there is no basis for health promotion or a health promotion campaigns. In fact, every disease or condition that health communication scholars study, or health promoters try to circumvent is possible because of the science that preceded it. It was research-based science that explained how we could prevent and treat diabetes. It was also research-based science that downgraded the severity of HIV from a death sentence to a chronic condition (Scandlyn, 2000). In short, the continuous and evolving hard-science research paves the way for the strategies and methods promoted by health educators and health communication scholars. Without this crucial component of public health, the social science aspect of our studies would not exist.

Detection and Control of Infectious Diseases   The final component of public health is concerned with understanding where the needs for public health are best met through mathematical statistics. Epidemiology is "a relatively new discipline [that] uses quantitative methods to study diseases in human populations to inform prevention and control efforts" (Bonita, Beaglehole, & Kjellström, 2006). Like the research science before it, epidemiology is another behind-the-curtain science that helps health programmers determine (1) what type of program is needed and (2) where the program is best utilized. Epidemiology became popular for several reasons, but perhaps the biggest of them all is that disease researchers and health programmers did not want to do their own work blindly. Having understood what programs work, and the science behind diseases and human conditions in the public health sphere, epidemiology helps look at the concentration of these phenomena all around the world. More importantly, epidemiological data is crucial in helping us determine whether or not existing methods are improving public health through constant reconfiguration of statistics and prepost experimental designs. As the data changes, we get a better understanding if the current policy measures and programs in place are improving public health, or making the problem worse.

   In sum, the three components of public health work interchangeably in our dynamic society to improve the health-related quality of life for people around the world. All of these components are inextricably linked, and removing just one component would have disastrous implications on public health. In the future, as trends continue to change, it will be interesting to note if new components emerge within public health. Given that public health has changed greatly within the decade, the likelihood is incredibly high.

Health Promotion

The last area of inquiry that we will discuss is that of health promotion. According to the World Health Organization (2013), **health promotion** is "the process of enabling people to increase control over and to improve their health. It moves beyond a focus on individual behavior toward a wide range of social and environmental interventions." These efforts may involve the use of many communication channels and are carried out by health promoters. **Health promoters** are people who are actively involved in the process of creating and distributing health promotion messages (Du Pré, 2010). In order to accomplish their missions, health promoters go through a series of steps in the designing of a health promotion campaign. The CDC (2013) recommends the following steps for conducting successful health promotion campaigns:

Step 1: Describe the problem
Step 2: Perform market research
Step 3: Define market strategy
Step 4: Develop interventions
Step 5: Evaluate your plan
Step 6: Implement your plan

Describing the Problem   Being able to clearly articulate the problem should be the main goal of any health promotion campaign. Within this step, the health promoter will define the public health problem (what is occurring, what should be occurring), who is affected and to what degree, and what could happen if the problem is not addressed. Additionally, the health promoter should outline the potential audiences and group them into segments. This will allow the promoter to design efficient and effective strategies for reaching each audience. The CDC (2013) also recommends that a SWOT (strengths, weaknesses, opportunities, and threats) analysis be conducted within this step.

Perform Market Research   During this step, the goal is to understand the target audience better. Special attention will be paid to the audience's characteristics, attitudes, beliefs, values, behaviors, and the perceived benefits and barriers to behavior change. This information will be vital to the creation of the health promotion campaign.

Define Market Strategy   The market strategy is the plan of action for the health promotion campaign. During this stage, the promoter selects each of its target market segments and defines their current behaviors versus the desired behaviors. By identifying the behaviors that each audience segment is currently doing and analyzing whether they can change, the health promoter is able to prioritize their audiences and focus more on the audiences that are ready for change. After identifying the audience focus, the last part of this strategy is to describe the benefits that your campaign will offer. In other words, you want to make sure that your campaign maximizes any benefits that the audience will get for adopting the new behavior and in turn, you minimize any barriers that might prevent behavioral change.

Develop Interventions   **Interventions** are the "methods used to influence, facilitate, or promote behavior change" (CDC, 2013). The health promoter's responsibility in this step is to provide a detailed plan of what the campaign will entail. The first step is to assemble the team that will work on the campaign and assign very clear roles. Then specific, measurable objectives for each intervention activity must be outlined. After this, the program plan with the timeline and budget can be developed. Special attention should still be paid to the benefits that your campaign will offer. Timelines must include key deadlines and milestones. Creating graphics of the timeline help to keep the team motivated and on track. Budgets will include both direct (expenses directly related to your project or activity) and indirect (expenses that don't directly relate to your project or activity) costs.

Evaluate Your Plan   Planning how you wish to evaluate the program while you are developing the plan is essential. A clear understanding of whether the campaign was implemented how you intended (process measures) and whether the appropriate changes took place (outcome measures) must be thought through in the planning stages. There are a few areas for evaluation that the CDC (2013) point to: identifying program elements to monitor, selecting the key evaluation question, determining how the information will be gathered, and developing a data analysis timetable and budget. Campaigns that do not plan for evaluation in the beginning are not as successful.

Implement Your Plan   Implementation is when all the hard work between planning and preparation comes together. There are several activities that must take place during this stage. The first is to prepare for the launch of the campaign. This is when the program materials are produced, staff are hired and trained, and the program launch is planned. Second, the execution and management of intervention components must be conducted. During this stage, special attention is paid to the coordination of efforts of all personnel, making sure that policies and procedures are followed, and planning and directing modifications in program activities when there is a need for change. The third step is to execute and manage the monitoring and evaluation plans. Documentation of all intervention activities should begin in this stage. The last step is the modification of intervention activities according to feedback. By using audience feedback based on the evaluation procedures you selected earlier, tweaking activities to better serve your target audience becomes easier.

SUMMARY

Health communication is an exciting and growing field. The development of effective communication patterns and strategies between patients and physicians helps to build trust and can lead to better health outcomes. Additionally, the understanding of culture, health care organizations, and public health allows steps to be taken to move toward disease prevention, patient empowerment, and treatment for a diverse population. Finally, media messages have the potential to promote or discourage healthy behaviors. By developing health promotion campaigns that are clear and appropriate, health outcomes can improve. Health communication is especially important in our country and globally right now and the role of well-trained health communicators will continue to increase for decades to come.

WORKS CITED

Bandura, A. (1969). Principles of behavior modification. New York, NY: Hold, Rinehart, & Winston.

Bonita, R., Beaglehole, R., & Kjellström, T. (2006). *Basic epidemiology* (2nd ed.). New York, NY: World Health Organization.

Center for Disease Control and Prevention Foundation. (2013). Retrieved from http://www.cdcfoundation.org/

Davidson, B. N., Sofaer, S., & Gertler, P. (1992). Consumer information and biased selection in the demand for coverage supplementing Medicare. *Social Science and Medicine, 34,* 1023–1034.

Du Pré, A. (2010). *Communicating about health: Current issues and perspectives.* New York, NY: Oxford University Press.

Dutta, M. J. (2006). Theoretical approaches to entertainment education campaigns: A subaltern critique. *Health Communication, 20*(3), 221–231.

Engel, G. L. (1977). The need for a new medical model: A challenge for biomedicine. *Science, 196,* 129–196.

Feldman, J. (1966). *The dissemination of health information.* Chicago, IL: Aldine.

Hardey, M. (2008). Public health and web 2.0. *Perspectives in Public Health, 128*(4), 181–189.

Hassan, I., McCabe, R., & Priebe, S. (2007). Professional-patient communication in the treatment of mental illness: A review. *Communication & Medicine, 4,* 141–152.

Henry J. Kaiser Family Foundation and Health Research and Educational Trust. (2011). Total HMO enrollment: 2011 summary of findings. Retrieved May 29, 2013, from http://kff.org/other/state-indicator/total-hmo-enrollment/#table

Hewa, S. & Hetherington, R.W. (1995). Specialist without spirit: Limitations of the mechanistic biomedical model. *Theoretical Medicine and Bioethics, 16,* 129–139.

Kleinman, A. (1980). *Patients and healers in the context of culture* (Vol. 3). Berkeley: University of California Press.

Kohler, C. L., Grimley, D., & Reynolds, K. (1999). Theoretical approaches guiding the development and implementation of health promotion programs. In J. M. Raczynski & R. J. DiClemente (Eds.), *Handbook of health promotion and disease prevention* (pp. 23–49). New York, NY: Kluwer Academic/Plenum.

Kolb, L. C. (1979). Commentary. The biomedical model. *Man and Medicine, 4,* 286–292.

Kreps, G. L., Bonaguro, E. W., & Query, J. L. (1998). The history and development of the field of health communication. In L. D. Jackson & B. K. Duffy (Eds.) *Health communication research: Guide to developments and directions* (pp. 1–15), Westport, CT: Greenwood Press.

Myers, J. (2011). Wellness as the paradigm for counseling and development: the possible future. *Counselor Education and Supervision, 30*(3), 183–193.

National Institute of Health. (2013). Retrieved from http://nih.gov/

Rosenstock, I.M. (1960). What research in motivation suggests for public health. *American Journal of Public Health, 50,* 295–301.

Roter, D. L. & Hall, J. A. (1993). *Doctors talking with patients/patients talking with doctors.* Westport, CT: Auburn House.

Scandlyn, J. (2000 February). When AIDS became a chronic disease. *Western Journal of Medicine, 172*(2): 130–133.

Schreiber, L. (2005). The importance of precision in language: Communication research and (so-called) alternative medicine. *Health Communication, 17,* 173–190.

Stretcher, V. J. & Rosenstock, I. M. (1997). The health belief model. In K. Glanz, F. M. Lewis, & B. K. Rimer (Eds.), *Health behavior and health education* (pp. 41–59). San Francisco, CA: Jossey-Bass.

Tyreman, S. (2006). Causes of illness in clinical practice: A conceptual exploration. *Medicine, Health Care and Philosophy, 9,* 285–291.

Zola, I.K. (1966). Culture and symptoms: An analysis of patients presenting complaints. *American Sociological Review, 3,* 615–630.

AUTHOR BIOGRAPHIES

Tomeka M. Robinson, PhD is an Assistant Professor of Communication Studies and the Director of Forensics at Marietta College. Her interests lie at the intersections of health communication, policy, and culture. Dr. Robinson primarily teaches courses in public speaking, health communication, and group communication. She received her BS from McNeese State University in Biology and Speech Communication, MA from Texas A&M University in Health Communication, and PhD from Texas A&M University in Health Education.

Cody M. Clemens is a graduate of Marietta College where he earned his BA in Organizational Communication & Public Relations; he received a minor in Health Communication, as well as, a certificate in Leadership Studies. Clemens' academic interests are in the fields of health communication, organizational communication, health and culture, and training and development. Currently, Clemens is working as an Executive Team Leader for Target in Pittsburgh, PA while he is pursuing a MA in Communication Studies with an emphasis in Corporate Communication. Long term, Clemens would like to earn his PhD to become a professor and teach health and organizational communication at the collegiate level.

Danny Valdez is a MS student in Health Education at Texas A&M University. His interests are minority health, minority health disparities, and health/fitness culture. He aims to pursue a PhD and attain a job in academia working mostly with disadvantaged families in the lower Rio Grande valley.

Vincent Hendershot is a graduate of Marietta College where he earned his BA in Spanish; he received a minor in Health Communication. Hendershot's academic interests are in global public health and health disparities. Currently, Hendershot is pursuing a MS in public health at Kent State University with an emphasis on global public health. Long term, Hendershot would like to work in public health in Latin America.

CPSIA information can be obtained at www.ICGtesting.com
Printed in the USA
LVOW01s1612110815

449591LV00002B/3/P